OPTIMAL RESPONSIVENESS: HOW THERAPISTS HEAL THEIR PATIENTS

SELF
PSYCHOLOGY
AND
INTERSUBJECTIVITY

A Series of Books Edited By
Peter Lessem, Ph.D.

Self psychology and intersubjectivity share a commitment to the centrality of the empathic-introspective stance in psychoanalysis and psychoanalytically informed psychotherapy. The series provides authors working from both perspectives a forum to articulate their unique contributions to the larger psychoanalytic community.

Using Self Psychology in Child Psychotherapy:
The Restoration of the Child
Jule Miller III

**Optimal Responsiveness: How Therapists
Heal Their Patients**
Howard A. Bacal, Editor

OPTIMAL RESPONSIVENESS: HOW THERAPISTS HEAL THEIR PATIENTS

Edited by
Howard A. Bacal, M.D.

JASON ARONSON INC.
Northvale, New Jersey
London

This book was set in 11 pt. Adobe Caslon by Alabama Book Composition of Deatsville, Alabama and printed and bound by Book-mart Press, Inc. of North Bergen, New Jersey.

Library of Congress Cataloging-in-Publication Data

Optimal responsiveness : how therapists heal their patients / edited
    by Howard A. Bacal.
        p.   cm. — (Self psychology and intersubjectivity)
    Includes bibliographical references and index.
    ISBN 0-7657-0114-6 (alk. paper)
    1. Psychotherapist and patient.   I. Bacal, Howard A.   II. Series.
RC480.8.068   1998
616.89′14—dc21   97-24483

Printed in the United States of America on acid-free paper. Jason Aronson Inc. offers books and cassettes. For information and catalog write to Jason Aronson Inc., 230 Livingston Street, Northvale, New Jersey 07647-1731. Or visit our website: http://www.aronson.com

This book is dedicated to Jacqueline, Shana, Liane, and Benji, to whom I will always be grateful for an invaluable kind of responsiveness—ongoing love—when my focus on what is good for my writing has distracted me from responding to what was optimal for them. And to Toffy, who is always with me.

Contents

PART II:
OPTIMAL RESPONSIVENESS IN CLINICAL PRACTICE

Preface

HOWARD A. BACAL

A new generation of therapists is starting to take a fresh look at what actually heals the patient. Psychoanalysts and psychotherapists of every theoretical persuasion have been constrained and pressured by the spurious ideal of providing interpretive intervention in an ambience of "optimal frustration" as the only legitimate and ultimately effective responsivity to the patient. In addition, there is a growing awareness among psychoanalytic practitioners of what patients have always known but have never had validated—that therapeutic experience derives not only and probably not primarily from the insight derived from interpretation of psychopathological motivation but rather from the experience of a relationship with a therapist who is prepared to respond in a variety of ways that are therapeutically specific both to their particular suffering and to their struggle to reach their particular goals in life. I have introduced the term *optimal responsiveness* to conceptualize this experience from the perspective of relational self psychology and to describe how good therapists actually work.

In contrast to the Freudian vision, which regards interpretation as the essential contribution of the psychoanalyst, and insight as its therapeutic effect on the patient, the work of Ferenczi, Alexander, and others whom we have come to call object relations therapists, such as Balint and Winnicott, as well as, more recently, Kohut, anticipated the idea of optimal responsiveness in their emphasis on the variegated responsivity of the psychoanalyst and the psychotherapist that may contribute to a therapeutic experience for the patient, an experience that may or may not be evoked by interpretation or mediated by insight.

I define optimal responsiveness as the responsivity of the psychoanalyst or psychotherapist that is psychologically most relevant, useful, and appropriate for a particular patient and his illness. The concept of optimal responsiveness rests upon a theory of therapeutic specificity: that it is the specificity of interaction between a particular patient and a particular therapist that will be helpful. Optimal responsiveness does not essentially entail frustration, gratification, or so-called neutrality, which have variously been regarded by psychoanalysts and psychotherapists as essential to therapeutic work. Conceptually, optimal responsiveness may effectively replace them, although it may include any of them in any particular instance. Therapeutic functioning often constitutes responses that are very different from, and that may comprise much more—and sometimes much less— than, what our theories or our teachers have told us it does. The concept of optimal responsiveness thus accords legitimacy to the varying emphases on verbal and nonverbal activity, interpretive intervention—transferential or reconstructive—or other kinds of behaviors, including empathic attunement, confrontation, support, recognition, sharing of affects and subjective experience (self-disclosure), restraint, validation or invalidation, and enactment—all of which variously play a part in the effective conduct of all psychoanalyses and dynamic psychotherapies.

In practice, optimal responsiveness serves as a general indicator of the therapist's job insofar as it corresponds to the patient's experience of the analyst's therapeutic functioning. As a therapeutic principle, optimal responsiveness implies that there should be no interdiction against any responses that may be optimal for the patient unless they interfere with the therapist's professional functioning or his or her personal tolerance. There should also be no categorical imperatives for any particular form of intervention. Optimal responsiveness comprises the analyst's acts of communicating to his patient in ways that that particular patient experiences as therapeutically usable.

The concept of optimal responsiveness also includes the recognition that the therapeutic process comprises the operation of a complex, more-or-less unique, reciprocal therapeutic system for each therapist–patient couple. Thus, the optimal responsiveness concept implies a reconceptualization of what we have called countertransference. The ongoing responsivity of the patient to specific psychological needs of the therapist is ubiquitously a precondition for the therapist to respond optimally to the patient, and the withdrawal of this responsivity is likely the most frequent determinant of countertransference reactions—reactions that would more accurately be described as *relatedness reactions*. Yet, we must distinguish between the negative effect on the analyst of the patient's unresponsiveness and the effect of the analyst's spontaneous reactive affectivity to the patient that may constitute an optimal response (Gil Spielberg, personal communication).

The chapters in this book ubiquitously affirm what is becoming generally regarded as a psychoanalytic truism yet has rarely been explicitly acknowledged: that empathy, as described by Kohut, is not only the fundamental method of analytic data-gathering; it is, in the form of empathic attunement, also one of the most potent therapeutic responses that the psychoanalyst can offer the patient. Yet, it is demonstrable that self psychology's tacit—and sometimes explicit—promotion of empathic attunement as the only response that is therapeutically effective is untenable.

This book includes chapters by seventeen colleagues who share my enthusiasm for pushing forward the frontiers of our knowledge about the therapeutic process. These chapters, which are preeminently informed by the burgeoning new understandings that are emerging from self psychology and intersubjective relational perspectives, advance and deepen our knowledge of the concept of optimal responsiveness in theory, and enhance its usefulness as a principle that guides our work in treatment and training. My colleagues' contributions have added an abundance of original thinking to the psychoanalytic literature.

Each chapter discusses and illustrates how the principle of optimal responsiveness provides a practical indicator for effective therapeutic work in psychoanalysis and psychotherapy, and its application in the supervisory process. One of the chapters reports a study that validates many of the ideas described in this book as well as suggests directions for further research.

Rather than present a summary of the contents of this book, I offer a brief commentary at the beginning of each chapter.

Howard A. Bacal, M.D.
Los Angeles, California, 1998

Acknowledgments

I am preeminently indebted to my patients, as they have taught me and continue to teach me every day what my limitations and capabilities are with respect to optimal responsiveness.

I want to thank my colleagues who have written chapters for this book. Their thoughtful, scholarly contributions to its theme and their patience with a prolonged editing process are responses that have been truly optimal.

Contributors

Howard A. Bacal, M.D., F.R.C.P.(C). Training and Supervising Analyst, Institute of Contemporary Psychoanalysis, Los Angeles; Training and Supervising Analyst, Southern California Institute of Psychoanalysis, Los Angeles; Training and Supervising Analyst, Toronto Institute of Psychoanalysis; Supervising Analyst, Institute for the Psychoanalytic Study of Subjectivity, New York; private practice, Los Angeles.

Beatrice Beebe, Ph.D. Core Faculty, Institute for the Psychoanalytic Study of Subjectivity, New York; Clinical Associate Professor, New York University Postdoctoral Program in Psychotherapy and Psychoanalysis.

Francis Broucek, M.D. Teaching Faculty, Topeka Institute for Psychoanalysis; Teaching Faculty, Kansas City Institute for Psychoanalysis.

Carmely Estrella, Ph.D. Dissertation, California Institute for Clinical Social Work; member, Society for Clinical Social Work; Board Certified Diplomate in Clinical Social Work; Clinical Consulting Faculty, California Institute for Clinical Social Work.

James L. Fosshage, Ph.D. Cofounder, Board Director, and Faculty, National Institute for the Psychotherapies, New York; Core Faculty member, Institute for the Psychoanalytic Study of Subjectivity, New York; Clinical Professor of Psychology, New York University Postdoctoral Program in Psychotherapy and Psychoanalysis.

Bruce Herzog, M.D. Senior candidate, Toronto Institute of Psychoanalysis; psychiatrist in private practice.

Lynne Jacobs, Ph.D., Psy. D. Supervising and Training Analyst, Institute of Contemporary Psychoanalysis, Los Angeles.

Alan R. Kindler, M.B.B.S., F.R.C.P.(C). Assistant Professor of Psychiatry, Faculty of Medicine, University of Toronto; Training and Supervising Analyst, Toronto Institute of Psychoanalysis; Faculty, Toronto Institute for Contemporary Psychoanalysis; Faculty, Institute for the Advancement of Self Psychology, Toronto.

Frank M. Lachmann, Ph.D. Core Faculty, Institute for the Psychoanalytic Study of Subjectivity, New York; Training and Supervising Analyst, Postgraduate Center for Mental Health.

Susan G. Lazar, M.D. Training and Supervising Analyst, Washington Psychoanalytic Institute; Founding Member, Institute for Contemporary Psychotherapy, Washington, D.C.; Clinical Professor of Psychiatry, Georgetown University School of Medicine, Uniformed Services University of the Health Sciences, George Washington University School of Medicine.

Kenneth M. Newman, M.D. Training and Supervising Analyst, Chicago Institute for Psychoanalysis; Attending Psychiatrist, Michael Reese Hospital and Medical Center.

Walter Ricci, M.D. Training and Supervising Analyst, Topeka Institute for Psychoanalysis; Training and Supervising Analyst, Kansas City Institute for Psychoanalysis.

Estelle Shane, Ph.D. Training and Supervising Analyst, Institute of Contemporary Psychoanalysis, Los Angeles; Training and Supervising Analyst, Los Angeles Psychoanalytic Society and Institute.

Morton Shane, M.D. Training and Supervising Analyst, Institute of Contemporary Psychoanalysis, Los Angeles; Training and Supervising Analyst, Los Angeles Psychoanalytic Society and Institute.

Maxwell S. Sucharov, M.D. Board Member, Western Canada Psychoanalytic Psychotherapy Association; Clinical Assistant Professor, Department of Psychiatry, University of British Columbia.

David M. Terman, M.D. Training and Supervising Analyst, Chicago Institute for Psychoanalysis.

Peter G. Thomson, M.B.B.S. Training and Supervising Analyst and former Director, Toronto Institute of Psychoanalysis.

Ernest S. Wolf, M.D. Supervising and Training Analyst, Chicago Institute for Psychoanalysis.

Part I

Reconceptualizing the Therapist's Job

Optimal Responsiveness and the Therapeutic Process[1]

HOWARD A. BACAL

EDITOR'S COMMENT

This chapter is the paper in which I first introduced the term *optimal responsiveness* into psychoanalysis (Bacal 1985). The use of the concept was motivated by a dual purpose: (1) to dispute the contention that the treatment process inherently includes frustration, and (2) to elaborate a principle that would both conceptualize and guide the analyst's contribution to the therapeutic experience of the patient.

"Optimal" does not mean "perfect." Objections that are occasionally expressed to the use of the word *optimal*, because it places an unrealistic burden on the therapist by implying an expectation of perfect performance, reflect both unawareness of the meaning of the word and an incomplete understanding of the concept of optimal responsiveness. "Optimal" de-

---

1. This chapter is an edited version of "Optimal Responsiveness and the Therapeutic Process" (Bacal 1985) in *Progress in Self Psychology*, volume 1, edited by A. Goldberg.

notes the "most favourable (natural) conditions (for growth . . .)" (*Oxford Dictionary*); and "a condition, degree, amount or compromise that produces the best possible result" (*Collins English Dictionary*). These definitions indicate the appropriateness of the term *optimal responsiveness* as I employ it in psychoanalytic treatment to connote the facilitation[2] of the patient's therapeutic experience. A thoroughgoing appreciation of the meaning of the optimal responsiveness concept must also include an understanding of what determines its limitations, which I discuss in Chapter 7. While it is always our aim to do the best we can for our patients, we sometimes discover what is most therapeutic for them through their reactions to our responses that feel anything but optimal. At these times, the intersubjective analysis of what went wrong constitutes another experience of optimal responsivity, one that can be equally as therapeutic for the patient. Yet, the recognition that the analysis of such disruption is therapeutic is significantly different from the view that therapeutic effect must entail an "optimal frustration." In Chapter 2, Walter Ricci and Francis Broucek explicate how the latter precept came to occupy such a central place in psychoanalytic theory and technique.

References

Bacal, H. A. (1985) Optimal responsiveness and the therapeutic process. In *Progress in Self Psychology*, ed. Arnold Goldberg, vol. 1, pp. 202–227. New York: Guilford.

Winnicott, D. W. (1965). *The Maturational Processes and the Facilitating Environment.* London: Hogarth.

❖

---

2. I am grateful to James Fosshage for drawing attention to "facilitation" as a pivotal function of the analyst that is implied by the concept of optimal responsiveness. Its connotation, for me, is Winnicott's notion of the therapeutic effect of a "facilitating environment" (Winnicott 1965).

Although tacitly accepted as an important element in the therapeutic practice of psychoanalysis, the concept of *optimal frustration* has received little theoretical clarification. The publication of Heinz Kohut's (1977) landmark work *The Restoration of the Self* established optimal frustration as a central aspect of the curative process viewed from the perspective of self psychology. With one of his critics, Kohut (personal communication, 1977) recognized the problematic nature of the question "What is optimal?," yet he never arrived at a satisfactory answer.

I intend to reexamine this question in light of the related issue of "optimal gratification." My purpose is, in part, to demonstrate the significance of the latter, which has until recently been regarded with some suspicion as a form of countertransference acting-in, evoked perhaps by the patient's acting-in in the transference, or, at most, as a useful but temporary parameter to be discarded at the first possible opportunity.

I will suggest that any discussion of the concepts of optimal frustration and optimal gratification becomes inevitably entangled in insurmountable theoretical difficulties and endless debate when separated from the more useful and encompassing idea of *optimal responsiveness*, defined as the responsivity of the analyst that is therapeutically most relevant at any particular moment in the context of a particular patient and his illness. Empathy or vicarious introspection is the process by which the therapist comes to understand the patient by turning in to his inner world. Optimal responsiveness, on the other hand, refers to the therapist's acts of communicating his understanding to his patient.

OPTIMAL FRUSTRATION

The origin of the term *optimal frustration* is not clear. Although he credits Bernfeld (1928) with its first mention, Kohut (1972) appears to have first applied it to the psychoanalytic process. The idea of optimal frustration, however, has always been a cornerstone of psychoanalytic treatment. As early as 1946, Anna Freud wrote:

> [As analysts,] we have to play a double game with the patient's instinctual impulses, on the one hand encouraging them to express themselves and, on the other, steadily refusing them gratification—a procedure

which incidentally gives rise to one of the numerous difficulties in the handling of analytic technique. [p. 13]

. . . The ego [of the patient] is victorious when its defensive measures effect their purpose . . . and so transform the instincts that, even in difficult circumstances, some measures of gratification is secured. [p. 193]

However, the "measure of gratification" to which Anna Freud referred was not regarded as an aspect of the analytic process, but as one of its results.

While still working within the classical psychoanalytic perspective, Kohut and Seitz (1963) defined optimal frustration as an experience that is intrinsically related to that of gratification in the therapeutic process:

Optimal frustrations involve sufficient delay in satisfaction to induce tension-increase and disappointment in the attempt to obtain wish-fulfillment through fantasies; the real satisfaction occurs quickly enough, however, to prevent a despairing and disillusioned turning away from reality. [p. 356]

Kohut indicates that the infantile impulses that have encountered optimal frustration are transformed into neutralizing psychological structure by the internalization of innumerable experiences of optimal frustration, but that "[t]he barrier of defences, on the other hand, which walls off an unmodified residue of infantile strivings, is the result of the internalization of frustrating experiences and prohibitions of traumatic intensity" (Kohut and Seitz 1963, p. 369).

In other words, *optimal* frustration of instinctual impulses promotes the development of internal structure comprised of transformed, or sublimated, instinctual drives; whereas *traumatic* frustration causes a protective barrier to be built up around these impulses, which are left unchanged. Gratification, or "real satisfaction" must be an inherent element of the therapeutic process at some point and in some measure, or else "optimal" frustration will be anything but optimal. Yet, Kohut and Seitz do not satisfactorily define what optimal frustration and its associated optimal gratification amount to in the psychoanalytic process. Nor, to my knowledge, has this theoretical lacuna been redressed elsewhere.

In *The Analysis of the Self*, Kohut (1971) reiterates his position, still within a classical framework, but focuses now upon the importance of optimal frustration for narcissistic equilibrium rather than for drive modulation:

> As continues to hold true for the analogous later milieu of the child, the most important aspect of the earliest mother–infant relationship is the principle of optimal frustration. Tolerable disappointments in the pre-existing (and externally sustained) primary narcissistic equilibrium lead to the establishment of internal structures which provide the ability for self-soothing and the acquisition of basic tension tolerance in the narcissistic realm. [p. 64]
> . . . The skillful analyst will assist the patient in keeping the patient's discomfort [vis-á-vis the necessary, i.e., therapeutic, frustration of the narcissistic transferences] within tolerable limits; i.e., he will conduct the analysis according to the principle of optimal frustration. [p. 199][3]

Further, Kohut (1972) stated that omnipotent objects "become internalized every time the child discovers a flaw in them, providing the discovery is not of traumatic degree but optimally frustrating" (p. 869)

Kohut thus saw optimal frustration as central to the process of transmuting internalization, which he regarded as the essence of the process of analytic cure. As he wrote five years later,

> Little by little as a result of innumerable processes of microinternalization, the anxiety-assuaging, delay-tolerating, and other realistic aspects of the analyst's image become part of the analysand's psychological equipment, *pari-passu* with the micro-*frustration* [my italics] of the analysand's need for the analyst's permanent presence and perfect functioning in this respect. In brief, through the process of transmuting internalization [via optimal frustration] new psychological structure is built. [Kohut 1977, p. 32]

Kohut (1977), however, also questions the validity of the view that some individuals with severe psychopathology have had caring mothers

---

3. In a letter dated a year later Kohut (1972, September 23) also makes the point that "the *drive*-curbing behaviour of the selfobject is in essence experienced by the child as a *narcissistic* injury [and therefore] . . . structure formation is always due to a loss of the prestructual selfobject, not of the drive-curbing true object."

who, in attempting to gratify their children's wishes, have deprived them of the optimal frustration that would have enabled them to develop a mature ego. While acknowledging the possibility that these individuals might not have been sufficiently frustrated as children, he suggests that the determinants of their illness appeared to be more complex when viewed from the perspective of an analysis conducted on the basis of self psychology. By way of illustration, he suggests, in effect, that these mothers simultaneously disregarded their children's needs for parental confirming-admiring responses and approval of their own capacities. That is, their illnesses (his illustration was that of a fetish) were not due to overgratification but rather to a "specific traumatic absence of maternal empathy for the healthy grandiosity and the healthy exhibitionism of . . . [the child's] forming independent self" (p. 74).

Although Kohut recognizes that insufficient frustration or "excessive gratification" may contribute to psychopathology, he suggests that the pathogenic factor is not the "overgratification" of some instinct, but the accompanying traumatic insufficiency of recognition and "gratification" of a selfobject need. In this context, it is instructive to recall an aphorism that Kohut (1977) introduced in a now-famous passage in *The Restoration of the Self*:

> Man can no more survive psychologically in a psychological milieu that does not respond empathically to him than he can survive physically in an atmosphere that contains no oxygen. . . . The analyst's behaviour vis-à-vis his patient should be the expected average one—i.e., the behaviour of a psychologically perceptive person vis-à-vis someone who is suffering and has entrusted himself to him for help. [p. 253]

There is an apparent contradiction between this view and the recognition of the therapeutically beneficial effects of frustration. In order to explore this contradiction intelligibly, it is necessary to consider the difference between "optimal" frustration and "traumatic" frustration, and their relationship to so-called empathic failure.

Optimal Frustration and Traumatic Frustration

Let me say at once that the notion of empathic failure by parental selfobjects cannot by itself answer the question of what is traumatic, since it is likely that not all empathic failures lead to long-range deleterious effects on the psyche of the child. Indeed, since optimal frustration by selfobjects is regarded as essential to the growth and development of the self, empathic failure by selfobjects in childhood, as well as by the analyst as selfobject at a later stage, should according to this theory be welcomed. The central issue, both developmentally and in analysis, is what will lead to structural deficit or defect and what will be "optimal," in the sense of curative, leading to transmuting internalization of experience that its structure-building or fault-reparative?

However, the question still remains, What is "traumatic"? The earliest conception of trauma focused on isolated events, in particular on sexual seductions. The idea of trauma as the product of ongoing processes and relationships was not recognized before the contributions of such object-relations theorists as Balint, Winnicott, and Khan (1963) with his notion of cumulative trauma. All would agree, however, that trauma involves a degree of intensity that is too great for the ego to master and has far-reaching effects on psychic organization. For example, Kris (1956) distinguished between "shock trauma," the effect of a single powerful experience imping-ing on the child, and "strain trauma," the accumulation of frustrating tensions. Kris, however, did not emphasize the quality of the relationship, but conceived these events as occurring within a drive–tension–discharge model (Kligman 1983). Kohut and Seitz (1963) also regarded the quantita-tive factor as a distinguishing element of trauma, but they also suggested that the qualitative factor was significant.

> The differences between experience of traumatic and optimal frustra-tion are differences in degree. It is the difference between one mother's harsh "N-o!" and another mother's kindly "No." It is the difference between a frightening kind of prohibition on the one hand, and an educational experience, on the other. It is the difference between one father's handling a child's temper tantrum by an equally hostile counter-tantrum and another father's picking up the child and calming him— firm but non-aggressive, and loving but not seductive. It is the difference between an uncompromising prohibition, which stresses only what the child must not have or cannot do, and the offering of acceptable substitutes for the forbidden object or activity. [pp. 369–370]

According to Balint (1969), there are three conditions or phases associated with the occurrence of trauma. In the first stage of the traumatic process, the relationship between the child and the potentially traumatogenic object must be characterized by a certain intensity and be a mainly trusting and loving one. Trauma occurs, in this situation, when the adult does something highly exciting, frightening, or painful, either once and quite suddenly, or repeatedly. This action may involve an excess of tenderness or cruelty, whether or not sexuality is involved, and may result in severe overstimulation of the child or, if the child's approaches are ignored, in rejection and deep disappointment. The first two phases outlined by Balint are necessary but not sufficient to produce trauma. In order for trauma to occur the adult must act with indifference toward the child's experience, whether excitement or rejection.

Balint's thesis goes beyond merely quantitative considerations pertaining to the degree or intensity of traumatic experience (i.e., the field of one-person psychology) to the study of the quality of object-relationship (i.e., the field of two-person or multiperson psychology). In this way, Balint extends the work of Ferenczi (1933), who suggested that the real shock to the psychic organization of the child who is interfered with sexually is the adult's betrayal of the child's trust. The trauma derives from the fact that the child's tender or playful love is mistaken for passion and either responded to or rejected and is not primarily due to the stimulation or frustration of the child's innate sexual drives.

Classical analysis, however, fails to make a meaningful distinction between the pathogenic and the pathogenic that is also traumatic—a distinction, I would suggest, that is of great clinical importance. This failure on the part of classical analysts and current object-relations theorists stems from their attempt to understand the effects of the environment in the context of a theoretical position that is essentially a one-person psychology, where excessive or pathological drives are regarded as the determinants of the psychopathology. From the self-psychological perspective, this is not an issue, as the theory presupposes that psychopathology results from a failure of environmental response to the needs of the child's developing self. Although Winnicott adopted this position quite early, he did not systematically explore its clinical significance. Self psychologists, on the other hand, have only recently adopted the insight of early object-relations theorists such as Balint regarding the specific quality of the relationship between a particular child and a particular parent as the context of pathogenesis, and that between a particular therapist and a particular patient as the context in which pathology is potentially resolvable. In both cases, the relationship is a product of the interaction of two vulnerabilities and two capacities, those of the parent and those of the child and, later, those of the analyst and those of his patient (Stolorow et al. 1983).

It has never been our intention, as analysts, to either traumatize or frustrate our patients, however optimally, but to understand them. Consequently the notion of optimal frustration is not tenable as a working clinical concept; however, the idea of optimal gratification conceivably could be. For to be understood can be deeply gratifying and is, perhaps the most important function performed for us by our selfobjects. It is possible that the gratification of being understood by one's selfobject is of central importance in the curative process. If internal structure could not be built and defect repaired through the experience of being understood, the analyst would be wasting much of his time doing good work instead of making calculated errors thought to lead to manageable disruptions between himself and the patient and, thus, to transmuting internalization through the associated optimal frustration and its understanding. This confusion can be resolved if we reflect that no one comes for understanding unless they feel they have not been understood. As analysts, we are constantly confronted with a complex spectrum of varying degrees and kinds of frustrated need for understanding, sometimes of a traumatic order. Our responses must satisfy (a better word, perhaps, than gratify) the frustrated need for understanding of a particular patient or they will not be helpful. We will, as therapists, make mistakes, if only as a result of the analytic inertia that is inherent in our technique and, thus, inadvertently trigger or intensify the patient's frustration. The patient, moreover, will inevitably reenact his frustration with us in an attempt to right the original wrong. In many, perhaps in the majority of, instances, if we understand, as and when our patients need us to, frustration will not be a factor in the therapeutic process. We are not analytic machines, however, and upon the not infrequent occasions when we fail, when we are in a state of empathic lapse, or when our responsive understanding is not accurate, we will encounter a patient who is frustrated with us.

The word *optimal* means "a condition, degree or compromise that produces the best possible result" (*Collins English Dictionary* 1979, p. 1032). Since our approach to psychoanalytic therapy is to do the best we can and we do not, indeed we cannot, set out optimally to frustrate our patients, I suggest that the idea of optimal frustration is really an after-the-fact metapsychological explanation of what happens when the analytic relationship breaks down, retrievably. From the patient's point of view, it breaks down when his selfobject needs are greater than the analyst's capacity to understand and respond at a particular moment. (Stolorow and his colleagues [1983] have discussed this issue in terms of dissonant intersubjective states between patient and analyst.) Furthermore, the patient's apparent stubborn resistance and "negative therapeutic reaction" may not represent an intention to defeat the analyst, but are caused, at that moment, by the breakdown of the analyst's empathy and the patient's incapacity for reciprocal empathic resonance (Bacal 1979, Brandchaft 1983, Wolf 1981, see also Chapter 12). When, however, the "intersubjective disjunction" cannot be resolved, even by an honest scrutiny of countertransference, and a "decentered" (Stolorow et al. 1983) perspective on the part of the analyst, it may be useful to consider whether the patient's feeling that he is not optimally responded to may be attributable to a traumatic injury or frustration that has caused a defect or deficit in the self, that is, whether he has been seriously hurt in a state of extreme vulnerability (Balint 1968, 1969). I propose that an experience is traumatic to the psyche of the child if it has apparently caused a degree of defect or significant enfeeblement of the self, in our patients, that is not responsive to ordinary interpretative work. This operational definition of traumatic experience can be crucially important as a guide in our treatment of those patients for whom the resumption of selfobject relatedness, after disruption, is especially difficult to achieve, and sometimes impossible to restore by ordinary analytic work—even in instances where both patient and analyst agree they are grappling with the relevant issues.

Freud's counsel to frustrate the patient's wish for libidinal gratification has, unfortunately, often been taken as a directive to block all satisfaction within the analytic situation. As Wolf (1976) noted, "a misreading of this rule of abstinence creates a cold and critical ambience and will result in transference artifacts that are easily mistaken for derivatives of aggressive drives (p. 113). . . . Ideally the psychoanalytic situation . . . [should] yield the optimally facilitating ambience for the ongoing psychoanalytic process" (p. 111).

I would agree with Wolf's (1976) assertion that "contemporary psychoanalysts need rather less constraint and more freedom to engage the analysand in the analytic process" (p. 104), because of the increasing numbers of patients whose pathology is the result of serious disorders of the self. The real "danger" inherent in the analytic situation is not the possibility that the analyst might respond sexually to his patient, as such behavior is governed by moral and ethical principles and cannot seriously be regarded as a valid part of the therapeutic process. The danger is rather that the analyst, by assiduously or rigidly avoiding any interaction with his patient except that of verbal exchange, may inadvertently deprive the patient of the experience of therapeutic relatedness.

Interpretation and Therapeutic Relationship

Balint (1969) argued that we have "two major therapeutic methods, one of which is interpretation and the other the creation of a therapeutic relationship between the patient and ourselves. Compared with the first, the techniques for the second method have been much less well studied and it is important that we should start investigating them" (p. 435).

The self-psychological understanding of the therapeutic process and its associated analytic technique more closely represents a synthesis of these two facets of therapy, "interpretation and relationship," than the traditional psychoanalytic model. There are, however, contradictions and inconsistencies still to be resolved.

For some time, Kohut was undecided as to whether interpretation or relationship is the fundamental therapeutic component in psychoanalysis. In *The Restoration of the Self*, Kohut (1977, p. 31) held that interpretation and insight are not in themselves what cure the patient, but are the means by which the essential curative factor, the beneficial structural transformation of the self, is effected. For example, Kohut described his work with Mr. M as follows:

> In Mr. M's case, the essential psychological fact (the reactivation of the decisive genetic determinant . . .) was that he experienced his mother, and in the transference the analyst, as traumatically unempathic vis-à-vis his emotional demands and as unresponsive to them. True enough, the analyst might occasionally wish to point out (in order to retain a realistic framework—if, for example, because of the intensity of the frustrations he experiences in the transferences, the patient might seriously consider quitting the analysis) that the patient's expectations and demands belong to his childhood and are unrealistic in the present. And he might at the appropriate moment also wish to explain to the

patient that the intensity of his childhood needs may have led to a distortion of his perceptions of the past (in Mr. M's case, to a falsification of his perception of his adoptive mother's personality). The essential structural transformations produced by working through do not take place, however, in consequence of such supportive intellectual insights, but in consequence of the gradual internalizations that are brought about by the fact that the old experiences are repeatedly relived by the more mature psyche. [pp. 29–30]

By reliving these early experiences *with the analyst* the patient transmutes (i.e., converts and assimilates) into his self structure the "anxiety-assuaging, delay-tolerating, and other realistic aspects of the analyst's image" (p. 32)—that is, the function of the analyst as a selfobject. Regardless of whether it is "optimal frustration" or "optimal gratification" that produces this curative process of transmuting internalization, Kohut emphasizes the curative effect of *relationship*.

Although Kohut never explicitly addressed the issue of interpretation and relationship as complementary aspects of therapeutic work, the clinical process in psychoanalytic self psychology illuminates their interacting functions. Let us consider, for example, from the self-psychological perspective, a therapeutic situation in which frustration is not a significant factor in the relationship between the analyst and the patient. In what he judges to be a facilitative ambience (Wolf 1976), the analyst communicates through interpretation his empathically determined understanding of the patient's inner world. The patient's response, although perhaps a negative one, nevertheless indicates that the intervention has been successful, that is, accurate and useful. If the analyst's intervention takes the form of a transference interpretation, it would also be considered mutative (Strachey 1934). While some would argue that all interpretation frustrates or irritates in that it causes a degree of narcissistic injury by revealing to the patient something he does not know about himself, at least consciously, I believe that the feeling of being deeply understood is more frequently a rich and gratifying one that relieves frustration and tension.

Since optimal frustration has not occurred here, but understanding and explanation instead, must we conclude that transmuting internalization and related structure building have not taken place and that the apparent therapeutic gain will be shown during the termination phase to be illusory? As I have already indicated, the patient brings *to* the analyst his frustration at not being understood so that any additional frustration caused by the analyst's lack of understanding cannot be regarded as optimal. In this situation, the interaction between the analyst and patient did not generate frustration; rather, the analyst recognized the frustration that the patient brought to him and the patient felt understood by this response. In Wolf's (1981) terms, harmonious or reciprocal empathic resonance took place between analyst and patient: "At the moment that I really understand what is going on in the analysand, I also know that he really understands what I am doing" (p. 7). The accuracy of the analyst's empathic insights is confirmed by the patient's expression of his own empahthic grasp of the analyst's psychological activity at that moment. A process of transmutation of the analyst's functions into the patient has begun. The interaction has been optimal from both the analyst's and the patient's point of view and neither need question the appropriateness of the gratification he receives in this way.

As this suggests that frustration is not a necessary condition for transmuting internalization and real structure building to occur, what, if any, is the therapeutic element in the working through of "optimal" frustration? According to the clinical model emphasizing optimal frustration, the patient's reaction to the therapist's supposedly empathically derived communication (or silence) tells the analyst that he has not been attuned to his patient's psychological state. The patient's frustration is manifested in resistance[4] until, under favorable circumstances, the analyst is able to overcome his empathic lag (Bacal 1979) and perhaps, in addition, achieve an increased awareness of some aspects of his countertransference. Finally, the process of mutative interpretation is completed by a careful analysis of the events that precipitated the disruption and, concomitantly, of the analogous childhood experiences.

In this situation, the analyst believes that his interpretation is empathically correct until the patient's response makes him reconsider its accuracy. Simultaneous with the correction and clarification of the disruption, the analyst is able to restore the previous harmonious selfobject relationship with the patient and, in the process, a transmuting internalization occurs.

---

4. I understand resistance here as a variety of blockages of communication that are defenses not against drives, but against the anxiety of retraumatization (Wolf 1981).

If both the foregoing processes are therapeutic, what is the common curative element? It is, I believe, the patient's experience of the analyst's *optimal responsiveness*; and the quality of the therapeutic relationship at that moment confirms, for the analyst, that his response is usable by the patient. In the second example, the resumption of the harmonious selfobject relationship is therapeutic, not because the understanding of disruption is therapeutic, but because *understanding* is therapeutic.

Although interpretation is often the way in which analysts are optimally responsive to their patients, it is not a sufficient or appropriate expression of responsiveness in every case. The continuing controversy among psychoanalysts as to what constitutes a valid addition or alternative to interpretation is due to our failure to evolve a framework for the systematic consideration of the *psychoanalytic* nature of the therapeutic relationship and how it relates to the interpretive process. (Gill [1982] and Lichtenberg [1982a, b] address this issue.) Acceptance of the importance of *relationship* for the analytic process has until recently been limited to the recognition of the part it plays in the so-called working or therapeutic alliance. Although Wolf's (1976) recognition of an analytic ambience that is therapeutic represents an important advance, many analysts consider the therapeutic aspects of relationship in treatment as a necessary evil, or at best, as a temporary parameter making possible the resumption of "real" analysis. As analysts, we evade this issue because it raises the specter of transference and countertransference acting-in. Those of us who have extended the scope of psychoanalytic treatment to include the more serious disorders of severely traumatized people, however, have found an in-depth understanding of the analytically legitimate therapeutic aspects of our relationship with our patients increasingly important.

OPTIMAL RESPONSIVENESS AND THE DEVELOPMENTAL LINE OF EMPATHY

In the final address to the fourth annual self psychology conference, Kohut (1981) stated that the most important insight contained in *How Does Analysis Cure?* is that "analysis [ultimately] cures by giving explanations, i.e., interpretations." He maintained that the analyst must proceed from understanding to explanation, from showing that he is attuned to his patient's inner life, his feelings, thoughts, and fantasies, to the next step, interpretation. Kohut (1981) defined the advance from understanding to interpretation as a progression "from a lower form of empathy to a higher form of empathy," and described the analogous development within the individual with the following example:

> A child and the mother are in the park. The child was a young child who clung to the mother. The sun was shining, pigeons were walking around there. All of a sudden, the child felt a new buoyancy and daring and it moved away from the mother toward the pigeons. He goes three or four steps and then he looks back. The general interpretation of that is that he is anxious, he wants to be sure he can come back, to be encased in her arms, cradled, et cetera. That is true, but something more important is true. He wants to see the mother's proud smile; he wants to see her pride [looking] at him walking out now, on his own — isn't that wonderful — and at this moment, something extremely important had happened: a low form of empathy, a body-close form of empathy expressed in holding and touching . . . is now expressed only in facial expression and perhaps later in words: I am proud of you, my boy.

Kohut (1981) believed that interpretation in psychoanalysis performs a parallel function for the patient as these events in the development of the child. In this process, the "bodily holding" or "merger" phase is superseded by a much higher form of empathy, verbal interpretation, which is a psychological message on a more evolved level of understanding. In the case of the severely damaged patient, this process may be a very prolonged one.

As we have already noted, Kohut was for some time undecided as to whether interpretation or relationship is the therapeutic component in psychoanalysis. Although he maintained at different times that it was not interpretation but the relationship that essentially cured, he still firmly believed in the healing capacity of insight. Kohut's (1981) recent view that progress in the therapeutic process from understanding to interpretation represents a parallel advance on the part of the patient from a lower to a higher level of what he called the developmental line of empathy, integrates the two major methods of psychoanalysis and confirms the intuitive conviction of many analysts that interpretation and relationship are both curative. This is not merely an academic or semantic issue, but has practical implications for the way we respond as psychoanalysts and as psychoanalytic psychotherapists to our patients. Kohut (1981) felt that future research in self psychology should concentrate on the continuum of empathic stages, "the developmental line of empathy,[5] from its early archaic beginnings to such high levels as barely touching, as barely still having any trace of the original holding that communicates the empathic understanding."

This issue, I believe, can be addressed most effectively in terms of the concept of optimal responsiveness. The analytic attitude that is implied by "optimal responsiveness" is described by Wolf (1976) as follows:

> The decision about a proper response to a patient's demand, be it experienced ever so subtly or directly, must depend upon a proper dynamic understanding of the current analytic situation, its transference implications, and the genetic background. It is thus no different from any other analytic understanding or intervention. Whether to comply enthusiastically or reluctantly, whether to refuse firmly or hesitatingly, or not to respond at all, these decisions belong to the armamentarium of alternative action to be used in accordance with one's total understanding of the analytic process. [p. 107]

Earlier, Winnicott (personal communication, 1967) expressed a similar concern when he stated that the analyst's true function is not to provide the correct interpretation, but to be available to respond with understanding that is appropriate and useful to his patient. In self-psychological terms, the analyst's response must be commensurate with the patient's level of self–selfobject organization or the degree of intactness, defect or deficit within the self.

In many instances this response is communicated through verbal interpretation. Changes in the patient population, however, require corresponding changes in the analyst's vocabulary of response. Kohut (1981) recognized the need on the part of analysts for greater freedom to respond to their understanding of their patients in a passage that, because of its controversial nature, has had insufficient attention from self psychologists who are understandably reluctant to adopt a position that might expose them to accusations of engaging in the "corrective emotional experience" advocated by Alexander (1956):

---

5. After preparing this chapter, I had the opportunity to read an interesting clinical paper by Charles Coverdale (1983), which deals specifically with this topic.

The more one knows, the less one needs to stick to some ritual anxiously, because one *knows* [my italics] what is appropriate and inappropriate. The question [relates] to treating patients with very severe self disorders who cannot possibly benefit from interpretations for [a very long time, perhaps even] many years. They do need an empathic understanding on the closest level we can muster. It does not mean we cannot naturally move slowly and gradually into higher forms of empathy[6] [the form of optimal responsiveness that we call explaining or interpreting to the patient] much later on.

Kohut (1981) supports this controversial view with a clinical example drawn from the lengthy analysis of an extremely vulnerable woman patient:

She lay down on the couch the first time she came, having interrupted a previous analysis abruptly and she said she felt like she was lying in a coffin and that now the top of the coffin would be closed with a sharp click. . . . She was deeply depressed and at times I thought I would lose her, and that she would finally find a way out of the suffering and kill herself. . . . At one time at the very worst moment of her analysis during . . . perhaps a year and a half, she was so badly off I suddenly had the feeling—you know, how would you feel if I let you hold my fingers for awhile now while you are talking, maybe that would help. A doubtful maneuver. I am not recommending it but I was desperate. I was deeply worried. So I . . . moved up a little bit in my chair and

---

6. I am indebted to Dr. Bonnie Wolfe (personal communication, 1983), who responded to my initial presentation of this material with the following comments: "It seems to me that the important issue is whether and how the analyst's empathy can be conveyed to the patient in a way that the patient can experience *as being responsive to him* [my italics]. Sometimes, the patient can discern the analyst's responsiveness only through gestures, tone of voice, or facial expression . . . [and] attempts at verbal communication are experienced as unempathic and non-responsive to the patient's state. . . . I am [here] also reminded of Dr. Basch's nice example of the parent lifting the baby and saying, 'U-u-up we go.' At a more developed state or stage, the patient may be able to utilize (and tolerate) responses that are more predominantly verbal; although this verbal responsiveness may need to be at a primitive level ("you feel that," "it hurts"). At a more advanced level, you may find responsivity in the reciprocal communications [cf. Wolf's (1981) notion of reciprocal empathic resonance] of abstract ideas about psychological functioning."

gave her two fingers. And now I'll tell you what is so nice about that story. Because an analyst always remains an analyst. I gave her my two fingers, she took hold of them and I immediately made a genetic interpretation—to myself. It was the toothless gums of a very young child clamping down on an empty nipple. That is the way it felt. I didn't say anything . . . but I reacted to it even there as an analyst to myself. It was never necessary anymore. I wouldn't say that it turned the tide, but it overcame a very, very difficult impasse at a given dangerous moment and, gaining time that way, we went on for many years with a reasonably substantial success.

Kohut is not alone in responding to his patient in this way. Although few analysts have admitted to similar experiences (Freud apparently did the same for Marie Bonaparte [Bertin 1983]), Winnicott (1947) recognized the appropriateness in certain situations of this kind of intervention:

There is a vast difference between those patients who have had satisfactory early experiences which can be discovered in the transference, and those whose very early experiences have been so deficient or distorted that the analyst has to be the first in the patient's life to supply certain environmental essentials. In the treatment of a patient of the latter kind all sorts of things in analytic technique become vitally important, things that can be taken for granted in the treatment of patients of the former type. [p. 198]

The important clinical issue raised by Winnicott concerns what response on the part of the analyst can be considered optimal in relation to the patient's level of organization of his self–selfobject relationships. This level, as one would expect, corresponds to the position the patient has achieved on the developmental line of empathy (compare Wolf's [1980] idea of the "developmental line of selfobject relations").

The empty nipple for Kohut's patient was the antithesis of a selfobject that would satisfy her selfobject need (not only drive need) to suck. Other selfobject needs may require a responsiveness for which verbal interpretation will not do and we need to study the significance of these optimal responses for the patient, for example, the warmth provided by the analyst's blanket, or the thirst or faintness that elicits a drink,[7] as well as other needs that may be related to the "psychological survival of the self."

In my opinion, there is no such thing as a "parameter," an extraanalytic, or unanalytic, measure we adopt for a time in order ultimately to return to doing proper analysis in the traditional way. We must respond in ways that enable us to communicate understanding to the particular patient with whom we are working. That is analysis.

OPTIMAL RESPONSIVENESS AND THE REPETITIVE AND CREATIVE ASPECTS OF TRANSFERENCE

The concept of transference can be usefully reexamined in light of the idea of optimal responsiveness. As no one simply repeats pathological patterns and distortions, selfobject transferences are better understood as *creative aspects of transference*, since their aim is to forge a link with a selfobject that will be a better version of the old one. This is true of virtually every patient, but particularly significant with respect to severely traumatized individuals in whom the development of the self has been seriously impeded. These patients sometimes create what I have called a *fantasy selfobject* (Bacal 1981) around a nuclear figure whose archaic idealization or mirroring function has virtually no counterpart in the patient's antecedent experiences.

The creative aspect of transference has to do with the area of illusion, the area of play, and what Winnicott (1951) called "the transitional object" and "transitional phenomena." The experience of this kind of illusion is necessary in order for dis-illusion to not become disillusionment and traumatic frustration in analysis. Then and only then will the inevitable dis-illusion with a new version of the old selfobject, now recognizable as "good-enough" in Winnicott's terms, become associated with the ability to tolerate the fact that one's fantasy may or may not always elicit the response for which one hoped. This, in my opinion, is the only frustration that can be considered "optimal," a nontraumatic frustration that alternates and is interwoven with the building of developmentally essential illusion associ-

---

7. Eva Rosenfeld (1966) reported that Melanie Klein gave her a glass of sherry under similar circumstances during an analytic session.

ated with experience of a new responsive selfobject. In this way, confidence in the possibility of a "good-enough" selfobject can begin to develop. In this way, an optimal therapeutic experience with the analyst can occur in which self defect or faulty self structure is repaired and new self structure can be built. Both analyst and patient should feel that progress is resulting from this process. The patient should feel stronger and be able to deal more effectively with the stresses specific to his particular vulnerability. Similarly, disruptions of such an inordinately painful degree that the patient recurrently feels that he cannot go on with the analysis, should not occur.

These ideas assume that there is a basic tendency toward growth and development in every individual that requires the optimal responsiveness of the selfobject in order to be realized. This is, I believe, the implicit assumption that underlies all psychotherapeutic efforts, whether psychoanalytic or not. The concept of "optimal frustration" mainly serves to give analysis respectability. It "proves" we don't think of ourselves as gratifying our patients when we treat them. Related to this image of the hard path that the patient must travel toward cure is that of fixation points of the libido and the idea that patients will adhere to these positions to which they have regressed unless confronted with reality or with the deleterious effects of their continuing to function in their archaic ways with objects. According to this perspective, unless patients are optimally frustrated and exhorted to progress they will simply be gratified by the understanding, demand more and more, and remain where they are. An even less fortunate outcome of "gratification" is said to be the so-called "malignant regression" (Balint 1968) in which the analyst's accession to the patient's demands is thought to produce a spiral of negative, resistive, clinging, and increasingly demanding attitudes. In a previous paper (Bacal 1981), I attempted to distinguish therapeutic regression from malignant regression on the basis of their genesis: therapeutic regression occurs as a result of accurate empathic responsiveness, while malignant regression occurs as a result of catastrophic selfobject failure in patients with particularly vulnerable selves. The latter tend to be those whose selfobjects have been predominantly fantasy selfobjects and who, as children, have been pervasively related to by their significant nuclear figures *as* selfobjects.

An optimal synthesis between the experience of the creative selfobject transference, and the working through of the repetitive transference is necessary. Before he can usefully allow himself to experience the old unempathic selfobject in the new selfobject constituted by the analyst, the patient's self must become stronger as a result of a good deal of positive interaction with this new version of the old selfobject. Sometimes, even where the good selfobject is not of the order of a fantasy selfobject, the analyst may have to be experienced by the patient as a good selfobject separately from the old selfobject and it is countertherapeutic to interpret this self-reparative move as "pathological splitting." Rather, it must be accepted as creative transference relatedness perhaps for some time. (Contrast this to the Kleinian notion of splitting as a way of protecting the good primordial part-object from one's inclination to attack and destroy it.) However, the split-off good selfobject in these cases is often the good *fantasy selfobject*, and, in this situation, when the experience of the split-off bad selfobject occurs in the transference, the patient may fragment dangerously. At these moments, the analyst virtually becomes for the patient the original traumatically unempathic or unavailable archaic selfobject (Bacal 1981), and situations of this sort may be just barely retrievable. I believe that Kohut (1977) may have had something like this in mind when he suggested that defensive structures may sometimes usefully be left intact and that analytic working through in these cases will be carried out predominantly in the area of compensatory structures. The criticism that this would be merely supportive psychotherapy is undermined by the recognition that working through in the area of compensatory structures is related to the creative aspect of transference.

RESISTANCE AND COUNTERTRANSFERENCE

A reexamination of resistance and countertransference throws further light on the relevance of the clinical usefulness of the concept of optimal responsiveness. Resistance in classical analysis refers to the patient's inability or reluctance to participate in the analytic process cooperatively, that is, to free associate. The patient's silence, controlling, acting-in, or acting-out is attributed to his fear of the consequences of expressing his instinctual drives in relation to the analyst. From the perspective of self psychology, resistance to the analytic process is seen as reflecting a fear of re-traumatization through repetition in the analytic relationship of traumatic childhood experiences. This fear is sometimes justified by the analyst's countertransference, of which the patient is usually aware, and which the analyst should not only analyze in himself but judiciously acknowledge to the patient. In some instances, in order for the inevitable frustrations of the patient by the analyst to be nontraumatic and even potentially useful by enhancing the patient's trust in the analyst and contributing to the working through process, the analyst will not only acknowledge this countertransference, but respond to the distress it occasioned with an explanation that his patient can manage and assimilate. Of course, the analyst must not burden the patient with his own problems.

The analyst works within the inevitable limits of his understanding and his countertransference. His personality will determine, to some extent, his capacity to provide an optimal therapeutic experience for his patient. An analyst who is committed to providing an ambience of replenishing deficits will not provide a patient who needs to engage in recurrent disruptions with his analyst (in order to repeat his pathological nuclear situations for the purpose of healing his self defects) with the analysis he requires. On the other hand, an analyst who is committed to the working through of optimal frustration (that is, transference disruptions) will provide the patient who needs developmental experience with a new selfobject and an understanding of this experience with an analysis that may be worse than useless. Often, of course, both are necessary for analytic progress. It is important for us to consider what I would regard as the clinical counterpart of Winnicott's (1952) assertion that "there is no such thing as a baby, . . . [there is rather] a nursing couple" (p. 99), the idea that there is no such thing as a patient, there is only an analytic couple. A good match between the analyst and the patient does not have to be present at the outset. It may evolve as a result of the analyst's willingness to scrutinize the intersubjective context in which his interactions with his patient occur (Stolorow et al. 1983), and from his capacity to respond in a relevant way.

The following clinical example may help to illustrate and integrate the central concepts and issues we have been discussing.

> In her first analytic session, Dr. M., a psychologist in her late twenties, reported a dream that she had not long after her initial interview with her analyst, which took place a few weeks prior to the beginning of the analysis. She prefaced her account of the dream by what was, in effect, an association to it: she said how much she appreciated the generous gesture of the analyst friend who called the prospective analyst to prepare the way for her referral. In the dream the friend appeared as a taxi driver and drove her to a bridge where he said that he had

forgotten the analyst's phone number and address. As she searched in her purse for the directions, the contents, her money, and things she had on her mind, fell out. Her son called "Mommy" to her and, as at home, everything was once again pulling at her.

Although the analyst recognized even then that the dream would have significance for the whole analysis, its meaning was only partially apparent at that time. The interpretation reached, although tentative and incomplete, was that, despite her hope that her relationship with the analyst (whom she associated with her analyst friend) would enable her to enter a world in which she might receive the generosity of which she felt deprived by her parents, she feared she would again be caught up in a relationship in which she would be traumatized by being exposed to and emptied by another's limitless needs and demands.

A few months after the analysis started, she began to convey to her analyst her increasing anxiety about her financial situation. Although she earned a very good salary compared to a number of her colleagues, she was having serious trouble maintaining her standard of living largely because of the meanness and vindictiveness of her estranged husband with regard to child support for her three children.

Proud of her ability to manage independently, it was with great difficulty, embarrassment, and hesitation that she asked the analyst for a small decrease in her fee. He agreed, and there soon followed a second request for a substantial decrease, a request that was associated with continuing anxiety about her ability to cope financially. The analyst was initially reluctant to comply with this second request and the situation was discussed over a number of weeks. Dr. M. reacted to her analyst's reluctance with a complex mixture of desperate insistence, anger, increasing tension, and anxiety, as well as with a continuing sense of shame at having to make the request. Attempts to analyze the issue led only to a heightening of the tension and the analysis showed signs of breaking down. Finally, the analyst acquiesced, and told his patient that he was acceding to her implied request to pay nothing more than the amount that the national health insurance would reimburse her, until such time as she felt she could pay. He also explained that, while he knew that she was aware only of the economic determinants of her need and he was not denying the importance of these factors, he felt the psychological one to be paramount, although at the moment he was not completely cognizant of its significance.

After this, the impasse disappeared, and analytic work resumed. The unfolding of the significant issues and events of her childhood revealed that when she was 3 years old, her father, with whom she apparently had a close, idealized relationship, left the family and moved to a distant city. Her parents were divorced and she was left with her mother, whom she experienced as deceiving and exploiting her throughout her childhood and young adulthood by repeatedly failing to fulfill implicit and explicit promises to meet her emotional and financial needs. Following the departure of her father, she saw him on only two occasions until her late teens, as he did not visit and would not send her a ticket to come to him. Their total contact was restricted to letters, which they exchanged about every 2 months. She maintained her idealization of him, however, and throughout her childhood, never stopped longing for him to come to her. He remained extremely important to her as a sustaining figure. Except for his answers to her letters, she alone sustained this sense of relatedness to him through her capacity to create for herself, where only the barest basis for such a creation ever existed, what I have called a *fantasy selfobject* (Bacal 1981).

Within a few weeks of the analyst's accession to the patient's request, the analysis of its meaning also began. This analysis had not been previously possible while the analyst was committed to a method (which might be described as optimal frustration) of not complying but trying just to understand and interpret. It is not possible to fully elaborate here the analysis of this incident of the fees, which extended over months and continued from time to time over years—as, indeed, one may have guessed from the account of the initial preanalytic dream. The most significant meanings, which were focused in the transference, were her need to create a new selfobject relationship with her analyst as both the mother and the father who would respond with demonstrable generosity; her need to have tangible proof of being protected from becoming entangled in a trusting relationship with someone who would only take from her and drain her of all her resources; her need for the analyst to respond by demonstrating to her beyond a doubt that he would share her burden and that she could in this sense exercise some control over him (money had always been a symbol of control in her family). Deeper than her need to know that she would not have to bear all of the burden herself lay the need of the child within her not to have to feel she had anyone to care for, specifically, the analyst–mother–child. As the analysis proceeded, a lifelong, sometimes suicidal, depression lifted. Her shaky self-esteem and self-assertiveness strengthened impressively, her career moved forward, and she was able to show her talented and very creative work to others, including the analyst, for the first time in her life.

Ultimately, the analysis of the patient's request and of the analyst's eventual responsiveness to that request revealed what were perhaps their deepest meanings. The analyst, by responding to her request, provided her with the first incontestable experience in her life of someone considering her interests before their own. More than anything else, it meant that someone believed in her, that she was worthwhile investing in. Dr. M. needed to effect a shift or change in her analyst in order to create a selfobject response that was significantly different from anything that she had previously experienced. While there was what could be called a gratification of a selfobject need, I would suggest that it was the *responsiveness that was optimal* for the patient at the level of organization of her self–selfobject relationships, in other words, at the level of development of her capacity to experience empathic responsiveness in relation to nuclear selfobjects.

Implicit in this understanding of analytic work is the recognition of the therapeutic significance of what I have called the *creative aspect of transference*, and its associated archaic selfobject, which can, I believe, legitimately be regarded as a "fantasy selfobject" or as a "transitional selfobject." Winnicott (1951) described the transitional object as the "first not-me possession," that is, something that is experienced as part of the world and yet as belonging to me, something about which it is not to be asked, who created it, me or mother? The transitional selfobject can be viewed as a prestage of the transitional object, in effect, a selfobject created by the patient, partly out of himself (in fantasy) and partly out of a sense of pliable surroundings. It constitutes a necessary intrapsychic stage as a precondition for the apprehending of the concrete transitional object, such as a blanket or a teddy bear. (In a sense, it represents, "I know that I can create that inside me.") The fantasy selfobject is created by the patient when the environment provides almost nothing around which he can elaborate a need for the responsiveness he requires. Dr. M.'s demand for a response to a fantasy selfobject need was responded to optimally, which meant, at this level, that it was "gratified." Far from producing a malignant regression, this enabled the analysis to resume and to deepen.

Although the analyst did not subsequently raise the question of the fees, Dr. M. herself brought it up from time to time. She wanted to pay a fee but continued to struggle with her anxiety about paying anything. At the same time, it was evident that she was testing the analyst to see whether he would require her to do so. One day, three years after the analysis began, she reported a "new fantasy" that she felt completed the dream that she had shortly before entering analysis. The fantasy concerned the part of the dream where all her money fell out of her purse and her analyst friend picked it up and returned it to her. She reflected at this moment that she had never paid the cab fare. Apparently, no one paid for the cab ride, which she thought symbolized her need for it not to cost her any more than it had already. She felt that no one took care of her, and remarked, "you can't fall apart when there is no one to take care of you." At that moment, the analyst learned that her disintegration anxiety, with which she was struggling when she needed him to reduce the fees, could not have occurred unless she felt there was a potential selfobject who might respond. She was afraid at that time that she would cease to exist personally, professionally, or in some other sense. She reminded the analyst of the enormous difficulty that she experienced in asking to see him during the recent summer break as she was convinced that he would tell her that he had given her enough, that she was selfish, and that she shouldn't ask for such a thing. On another occasion she referred once again to the part of the dream where all her money spilled out of her purse and her subsequent anxiety about the fee arrangement. The original fantasy underlying the dream seemed to be that if she paid her analyst, he would get all her money and she would starve, and if she didn't pay him, she would survive and he would have nothing. The new fantasy was that she could pay him something at some point and the amount would vary according to what she could afford. She experienced this fantasy as hopeful and accepted the analyst's interpretation that it expressed her feeling that the amount that he would have and that she would have could be regulated. Less than 3 months later, she offered, without anxiety and with a quiet pride, to pay a fee commensurate with her economic situation at that moment.

Kohut has indicated that some patients require a gesture of what he called "preliminary enactment" without which no further analysis can take place. While I would essentially agree that certain patients may need this in a preliminary phase (in this sense, the notion of a "transitional selfobject relatedness" is useful), I suggest that it should not be thought of as a stage to be overcome so that the real analytic work can begin. Rather, it should be regarded as central to analytic work with these patients at the level of the development of their experience of empathy.

Sometimes, for some patients, this need arises as a result of progress, as, to some extent, in the case of Dr. M. She told the analyst that the experience of having both her requests granted, particularly having her wish for an extra session during the holiday break gratified, enabled her to think about his limitations. The knowledge that she was in an atmosphere in which she could make requests combined with the fact that she had grown stronger, enabled her to consider not only what she might ask for but also what she might or might not receive. She felt it was important for her to deal with the analyst's limitations and believed that his tolerance helped her to do so. She estimated his tolerance as falling somewhere between saying yes to one extra session, and refusing altogether. Her initial fantasy was to ask for all of them since the analyst was in town for the holiday, but she decided that he would probably refuse this.

I do not believe that the analyst's accession to his patient's request should be regarded as a parameter. This seems to me to constitute an unnecessary apology on the part of analysts who struggle within the limits of their countertransference and their hard-won theories toward an intelligible flexibility in analytic work. Rather, I would suggest that we reexamine the so-called parameter as a necessary aspect of the analyst's optimal responsiveness for his patient.[8] In order to answer the question of what is

---

8. I am grateful to Dr. Michael Basch (personal communication, 1983) for a number of helpful comments on reading the draft of this chapter. He suggests that a differentiation should be made between "transference of need" and the "transference of solution." "When there is a transference of need, a deficit, then the transitional selfobject relationship is called for; when, however, the patient dem-

optimal responsiveness for a particular patient at a particular time, I believe that we need to consider carefully the creative aspect of the selfobject transference. We need to remind ourselves that the selfobject transference is not predominantly a repetition, but rather is mainly an attempt at the creation of a new kind of relatedness with the frustrating nuclear object. *Fantasy selfobjects, fantasy selfobject relatedness*, and the specific examples of this that I think deserve to be called *transitional selfobjects* and *transitional selfobject relatedness*, are instances of the transformation of traumatic (often quite early) selfobject failures into *creative aspects of selfobject transference* by seriously injured patients. While the analyst need not intentionally enact a part different than the significant parent (what Franz Alexander was accused of), he does have to consider what response will be optimal in relation to the current level of his patient's specific developmental capacity to utilize empathic understanding of his selfobject needs for human relatedness. This will be therapeutic. If, however, the analyst does not wish to or feels he cannot respond to the archaic selfobject demand, no shame should attach to his refusal. Indeed, he may feel that to refuse will constitute an optimal response for that patient's growth. I would suggest, however, that there is less danger in responding to a regressed patient's suggestion as to how he needs to be treated than in refusing on the basis of the unproven thesis that the patient will develop if he is frustrated to the optimal degree.

While frustration is an inevitable part of life, I question whether the analyst can usefully regard it as "optimal" when he is working with his patients. This applies to gratification as well. Neither, per se, are appropriate considerations as part of a therapeutic process. They are legacies of a psychoanalytic morality, an intrusion into the clinical situation of a psycho-

---

onstrates that he is bringing now inappropriate attempts of problem solving into the analysis, then these, I think, must be interpreted genetically, contrasting the analytic to the past situation, rather than taking it for axiomatic that the analyst has made a mistake in his relation to the patient. To use your terms, optimal responsiveness on the part of the analyst is not limited to one or another position. Optimal responsiveness can involve the analyst's functioning as a transitional selfobject at one time, as an interpreter of the patient's past reality at another, and as an interpreter of the analytic or external situation at still another time. This, I think, is in complete agreement with your statement . . . to the effect that there is no such thing as a 'parameter.'"

analytic ethic that regards the patient's "real" unconscious and conscious intent to be the discharge and satisfaction of instinctual drives. Responsiveness, rarely perfect, almost always flawed in some way, can be optimal and comprises the legitimate efforts of our analytic work.

What does the analyst do with those patients for whom his kind of responsiveness does not work? As I have suggested, it is important to recognize that some forms of responsiveness that are crucially therapeutic may entail responses that an analyst cannot or will not, for ideological reasons, provide. For example, the necessary response to patient X may be withheld by analyst Y either because he simply does not respond to "acting-in" or because the patient's need gives him countertransference difficulties. From this perspective, what is designated as optimal frustration may sometimes be a rationalization of countertransference inflexibility on the part of the analyst. While the therapist must be himself, he also needs to be flexible to a degree or he will be correspondingly limited in treating certain patients. Kohut (personal communication, 1978) understood his concept of an average expectable environment as the "normal human responsiveness" promoting the patient's analysis and growth. I would like to stress that this will be different for each person.

CONCLUSION AND SUMMARY

My thesis is that if our analytic responsiveness is optimal (and I would define optimal as relative and specific to the particular patient, not simply a matter of degree as Kohut and Seitz viewed it) then our efforts will be growth producing. Selfobject relationships will mature and the self will become stronger and more free, flexible, and more resilient. An "optimal" frustration can only be optimal when it is optimal for something to be frustrated. It would be interesting to know what this might be. The view that optimal frustration alone produces internal structures is a hypothesis that needs to be challenged. As I believe I have shown, we cannot assume that all internalizing processes occur through frustration. In a good-enough situation, for example, identification and assimilation occur. Similarly the prior internalization of the parent/analyst as a responsive selfobject allows the child/patient to tolerate the former's inevitable unempathic responsiveness when it occurs, and to accept with less disturbance the limitations of the selfobject. This is particularly true in the case of patients whose relations with selfobjects in childhood have been traumatic.

It may well be that transmuting internalizations that occur without engaging transference frustrations are those where deficit (versus defect) is predominantly present, both self deficit and defect being ordinarily encountered together. This would be interesting to research in the psychoanalytic situation.

It is my belief that the notions of optimal frustration, optimal gratification, and the parameter, can usefully be replaced by the concept of optimal responsiveness. The optimal responsiveness of the analyst is determined by the position of the patient on the developmental line of his self–selfobject relations, and on his position on the developmental line of internalization of, and capacity for, empathy. It is not simply part of the ambience (Wolf 1976) or of the "frame" (Pines 1981). Nor is it just an expression of the therapeutic or working alliance. Rather, it is the analyst's job; and interpretation and relationship are its component aspects in psychoanalytic treatment.

References

Alexander, F. (1956). *Psychoanalysis and Psychotherapy: Developments in Theory, Technique and Training.* New York: Norton.

Bacal, H. (1979). *Empathic lag in the analyst and its relation to "negative therapeutic reaction."* Unpublished manuscript.

——— (1981). Notes on some therapeutic challenges in the analysis of severely regressed patients. *Psychoanalytic Inquiry* 1:29–56.

Balint, M. (1968). *The Basic Fault.* London: Tavistock.

——— (1969). Trauma and object relationship. *International Journal of Psycho-Analysis* 50:429–435.

Bernfeld, S. (1928). *Sisyphos, oder veber die Grenzen der Erziehung.* Vienna: Internationale Vereinigung fuer Psychoanalysis.

Bertin, C. (1982). *Marie Bonaparte: A Life.* New York: Harcourt, Brace, Jovanovich.

Brandchaft, B. (1983). The negativism of the negative therapeutic reaction and the psychology of the self. In *The Future of Psychoanalysis*, ed. A. Goldberg, pp. 327–359. New York: International Universities Press.

Collins English Dictionary. (1979). London & Glasgow: William Collins.

Coverdale, C. (1983). Developmental lines in self psychology: selfobject empathy and interpretation. In *Listening Perspectives in Psychotherapy*, ed. L. Hedges, pp. 93–99. New York: Jason Aronson.

Ferenczi, S. (1933). Confusion of tongues between the child and the adults. *International Journal of Psycho-Analysis* 30:225–230.

Freud, A. (1946). *The Ego and the Mechanisms of Defense*. New York: International Universities Press.

Gill, M. (1982). *Transference in the divergent analytic schools*. Paper presented at the annual scientific meeting of The Canadian Psychoanalytic Society, June.

Khan, M. (1963). The concept of cumulative trauma. In *The Privacy of the Self*, pp. 42–58. New York: International Universities Press, 1974.

Kligman, D. (1983). *Psychic trauma revisited*. Paper presented to the psychoanalytic extension program, Toronto Psychoanalytic Society and Institute of Psychoanalysis.

Kohut, H. (1971). *The Analysis of the Self*. New York: International Universities Press.

——— (1972). Letters of September 12th and September 23rd, 1972. In *The Search for the Self*, vol. 2, pp. 867–870. New York: International Universities Press.

——— (1977). *The Restoration of the Self*. New York: International Universities Press.

——— (1981). From the transcription of remarks presented by Heinz Kohut at the Conference on Self Psychology, Berkeley, California, October.

Kohut, H., and Seitz, P. (1963). Concepts and theories of psychoanalysis. In *The Search for the Self*, vol.1, ed. H. Kohut, pp. 337–374. New York: International Universities Press, 1978.

Kris, E. (1956). The recovery of childhood memories in psychoanalysis. *Psychoanalytic Study of the Child* 11:54–88. New York: International Universities Press.

Lichtenberg, J. (1978). *Transmuting internalization and developmental change*. Paper presented at the 1st Annual Self Psychology Conference, Chicago.

——— (1983). An experiential conception of what is curative in psychoanalysis. In *Psychoanalysis and Infant Research*, pp. 214–240. Hillsdale, NJ: Analytic Press.

Pines, M. (1981). The frame of reference of group psychotherapy. *International Journal of Group Psychotherapy* 31:275–285.

Rosenfeld, E. (1966). Unpublished address to the British Psycho-Analytical Society.

Stolorow, R., Brandchaft, B., and Atwood, G. (1983). Intersubjectivity in psychoanalytic treatment, with special reference to archaic states. *Bulletin of the Menninger Clinic* 47:117–128.

Strachey, J. (1934). The nature of the therapeutic action of psycho-analysis. *International Journal of Psycho-Analysis* 15:127–159.

Winnicott, D. W. (1947). Hate in the countertransference. In *Collected Papers*, pp. 194–203. London: Tavistock, 1958.

———— (1951). Transitional objects and transitional phenomena. In *Collected Papers*, pp. 229–242. London: Tavistock, 1958.

———— (1952). Anxiety associated with insecurity. In *Collected Papers*, pp. 97–100. London: Tavistock, 1958.

Wolf, E. (1976). Ambience and abstinence. *The Annual of Psychoanalysis* 4:101–115.

———— (1980). On the developmental line of selfobject relations. In *Advances in Self Psychology*, ed. A. Goldberg, pp. 117–130. New York: International Universities Press.

———— (1981). *Empathic resonance*. Panel discussion at the Conference on Self Psychology, Berkeley, California, October 4.

2

Optimal Responsiveness and Neutrality, Abstinence, and Anonymity

WALTER RICCI AND FRANCIS BROUCEK

EDITOR'S COMMENT

Perhaps the most prominent issue fueling the Freud-Ferenczi controversy about the centrality of insight versus the centrality of experience and relationship in the therapeutic process was whether it was better to frustrate or to gratify the patient (see Hoffer 1991). As Ricci and Broucek point out, Freud, for various reasons, emphasized the importance of frustration, that is, he advocated "abstinence" of transference gratification as a basic therapeutic principle: "the patient's need and longing should be allowed to persist in her, in order that they may serve as forces impelling her to do work and to make changes" (Ricci and Broucek, this volume, p. 45). Ferenczi, faced with an increasing number of difficult patients for whom abstinence appeared to be ineffective, experimented with the usefulness at times of gratifying the patient's needs. Although censured, with probable justification, for some of this experimentation, Ferenczi deserves recognition for his courage in exploring new ways of providing therapeutic responsivity for these intractable cases.

Kohut remarked to me once that he thought that "Ferenczi had the right idea" (Kohut, personal communication, 1977); We may parenthetically observe here that it was remarkable that Kohut was even *familiar* with Ferenczi's work, since Ferenczi's writings were often quite literally on the "banned" list of literature for students in classical psychoanalytic institutes in the United States (John Nemiah, personal communication), and before Kohut developed his theory of self psychology, he was widely acknowledged as one of the most prominent classical psychoanalytic educators. In effect, Kohut made such a striking shift away from classical psychoanalysis with his self psychological perspectives that he drew a reaction from certain of his colleagues that was not dissimilar to what Ferenczi drew from his contemporaries some fifty years previously. It was not only Kohut's new ideas that were vilified by the psychoanalytic establishment; he was himself shunned by a number of his prominent psychoanalytic friends and colleagues, by whom he was formerly regarded as "Mr. Classical Psychoanalysis."

Yet Kohut never conceptualized what Ferenczi was striving for. In effect, Kohut, in theory, leaned toward Freud and asserted that "optimal *frustration*" was the key to psychoanalytic cure. His view was that the firming up or accretion of psychological structure results from what he called the transmuting internalization—the taking over, by the patient, of the analyst's functions when the patient experiences manageable microfrustrations of his or her selfobject needs. That is, despite his recognition that "it was not the interpretation that cured the patient" (Kohut 1977, p. 31) and his emphasis on the centrality of the selfobject relationship in the therapeutic process (that is, his clinical sense of how analysis "worked"), Kohut's final theoretical statement about the frustration/gratification controversy and the experience versus insight issue was that the essence of cure constitutes "the accretion of psychic structure via an optimal frustration of the analysand's needs or wishes that is provided for the analysand in the form of correct interpretation" (Kohut 1984, p. 108). My own experience (Bacal 1997; see also Miller 1985) suggests that Kohut's theory of optimal frustration did not constitute an accurate reflection of his views on the therapeutic process; and one may wonder whether his retention of it rather reflects an attempt to reconcile to some extent with the classical psychoanalytic establishment whose reactions to his ideas were always a source of surprise and pain to him.

Ricci and Broucek imply that the concept of neutrality may also be effectively subsumed under the idea of optimal responsiveness. In addition to introducing the concept of *optimal responsiveness* as a replacement for the notions of *frustration/abstinence* and *gratification* in theory and practice (see Chapter 1; also see Bacal 1992), I also suggested (1992) that, as a principle of therapeutic action, optimal responsiveness may effectively replace the idea of neutrality in the treatment process. What is analytic neutrality? In structural terms, neutrality entails taking a position equidistant between the demands of id, ego, and superego (Moore and Fine 1990). Operationally, however, the idea of neutrality has defied simple exposition—indeed, even general agreement as to its meaning. Moore and Fine describe it as comprising a series of attitudes and activities that includes "keeping the countertransference in check, avoiding the imposition of one's own values upon the patient, and taking the patient's capacities rather than one's own desires as a guide" (p. 127). The concept also defines "the recommended emotional attitude of the analyst [as] one of professional commitment or helpful benign understanding that avoids extremes of detachment and overinvolvement." One of the problems about these notions of neutrality, so defined, is that while they all sound quite reasonable, they don't always facilitate analytic progress—as others, in addition to Ferenczi, have discovered. Another problem is that, from the point of view of the patient, they may be experienced as a noxious frustration and therefore indistinguishable from so-called abstinence. Lindon (1994) has recently advocated eloquently for the elimination of the rule of abstinence and its substitution by *optimal provision*. Lindon's views are entirely consonant with my own.

Attempting to steer a careful course between Freud and Ferenczi, Ernest Wolf has stressed that it is important to avoid equating neutrality with abstinence, since he too regards abstinence as constituting an atmosphere of artificial and harmful deprivation. On the other hand, he recommends that we also avoid creating a need-fulfilling environment, because an ambience of gratification precludes an analytic process in which selfobject transferences—the revival of archaic needs in relation to the analyst—may be mobilized, disrupted, and restored (Wolf 1983). Wolf proposes that an "ideal neutrality" constitutes "a neutrality of affirmation for the whole person that is experienced subjectively as an affirmation of the self" (p. 683). When I suggested to Wolf that this description of "neutrality" is not neutral, he concurred and acknowledged that he was in effect expressing a view that "being on the patient's side" is the most therapeutic stance (Wolf, personal communication, 1992). This is a stance that many of us would regard as therapeutically useful. Insofar as it might be so in any *particular* instance, its adoption would be consistent with the idea of optimal responsiveness.

Overall, the question is not whether we should gratify or frustrate our patients or in some way remain neutral or anonymous with them, or position ourselves as therapeutic analyzers or managers of selfobject disruptions. In this connection, Ricci and Broucek demonstrate their understanding of one of the central aspects of optimal responsiveness—its specificity—when they state that "At a given moment, neutrality, properly understood, might be 'the optimal response' of the analyst. The same is true of abstinence and anonymity." The effective analyst considers whether any of these, or some other kind of response (several of which they describe that were unknown and even unthinkable in an earlier psychoanalytic age) may constitute optimal responsivity, that is, the provision of responses that would facilitate his patient's use of him for therapeutic experience. In Chapter 7, I describe in some detail what I believe to be the nature of this experience.

References

Bacal, H. A. (1992). *Optimal responsiveness: the patient's experience of the analyst's therapeutic function.* Maurice Levine Memorial Lecture. Department of Psychiatry, University of Cincinnati, May.

———— (1997). Optimal responsiveness and analytic listening: discussion of James L. Fosshage's "Listening/experiencing perspectives and the quest for a facilitating responsiveness." In *Progress in Self Psychology*, vol. 13, ed. A. Goldberg, pp. 57–68. Hillsdale, NJ: Analytic Press.

Hoffer, A. (1991). The Freud–Ferenczi controversy—a living legend. *International Review of Psycho-Analysis* 18(4):465–472.

Kohut, H. (1977). *The Restoration of the Self.* New York: International Universities Press.

———— (1984). *How Does Analysis Cure?*, ed. A. Goldberg and P. Stepansky. Chicago: University of Chicago Press.

Lindon, J. (1994). Gratification and provision in psychoanalysis: Should we get rid of the rule of abstinence? *Psychoanalytic Dialogues* 4:549–582.

Miller, J. (1985). How Kohut actually worked. In *Progress in Self Psychology*, vol. 1, ed. A. Goldberg, pp. 57–68. New York: Guilford.

Moore, B., and Fine, B., eds. (1990). *Psychoanalytic Terms and Concepts.* New Haven, CT: Yale University Press.

Wolf, E. (1983). Aspects of neutrality. *Psychoanalytic Inquiry* 3:675–689.

Bacal's seminal paper on optimal responsiveness (Chapter 1) challenged psychoanalysts to reexamine some of their most revered ideas about psychoanalytic technique. Bacal's challenge was an impetus to our own efforts to understand the development of Freud's ideas about technique, particularly those technical recommendations that have encouraged the frustration of patient needs and restrained analysts from exploring alternative ways of responding that might be more optimal.

An appreciation of the centrality of affect and defenses against affect in psychic life is crucial not only to the understanding of the patient in analysis but also to the understanding of the evolution of psychoanalytic theory and technique. In this chapter we attempt to show that psychoanalytic technique owes much to Freud's attempt to "manage" the affectively turbulent psychoanalytic situation by means of the principles of abstinence, neutrality, and anonymity. We believe that when Freud moved away from his earlier views (as advanced in *Studies on Hysteria*) about the centrality of affect dynamics in pathogenesis to an emphasis on sexuality and aggression as the prime movers of psychic life, he also moved away from an analysis of shame as a primary regulating principle in the analytic encounter. Instead of being analyzed, these unexamined shame dynamics were instead unconsciously institutionalized in the principles of neutrality, abstinence, and anonymity. The importance of shame and defenses against shame in the formulation of these technical principles is highlighted here.

The formulation of the principles of neutrality, abstinence, and anonymity occurred under the pressure of three important considerations with which Freud had to deal. First, it was of paramount importance to Freud that psychoanalysis be accepted as part of science, and therefore he felt a need to adopt and display in his writings the proper scientific stance and attitude toward his subject. This concern bears particularly on the concept of neutrality. Freud's second, more practical, concern was a moral and ethical one involving the proper handling of the female patient's highly charged erotic interest in her male analyst and vice versa. The principle of abstinence owed much to this concern. Freud's third concern had to do with his intense investment in maintaining personal secrecy, which strongly influenced his recommendations about anonymity. We discuss how these concerns converged in the formation of the principles of neutrality, abstinence, and anonymity. In pursuing this analysis, we are following Freud in our effort to uncover and identify the sources, conscious and unconscious, of his ideas about technique, regardless of the guise under which they were introduced.

THE SCIENTIFIC ATTITUDE

In approaching the influence of the scientific mindset on Freud's technical recommendations, we briefly review the developmental history of that mindset. Romanyshyn (1989) finds the roots of the scientific Weltanshauung in the development of linear perspective by the fifteenth century Florentine artists Brunelleschi and Alberti. Romanyshyn traces what the art historian William Ivins (1964) described as "the development of perspective from its discovery or invention as a quasi-mechanical procedure to a logical scheme or grammar of thought" (p. 69). What began as an artistic device became a style of thought, a culturally adopted way of perceiving and imagining the world. Although it is not possible within the limits of this chapter to give an adequate summary of Romanyshyn's extensive development of this argument, we will select one theme that he explores, that of Alberti's window. Romanyshyn says:

> In the space of linear perspective the viewer is imagined to be looking at the world as if through a window. This window has become our habit of mind and through it we have become a self which has learned to keep its eye upon the world. Behind the window we have become distant and detached, a self separated and isolated from the world, a neutral observer and recorder of the world's events. [p. 67]

Alberti's window has become, says Romanyshyn, not only a boundary between ourselves and the world but a boundary between two different worlds. On this side of the window is the world of sound and color, a world of sensuous qualities, beauty, and charm. On the other side is the world of measurable quantities and objective events. We will see how Galileo elaborates this theme a little later. Alberti's window (as described by him in his treatise on perspective) is also a veiled one. A grid-like veil divided by thick threads into many parallel sections is stretched on a frame and set between the eye of the painter and the scene to be represented. The veil organizes the world into a geometric composition, but this geometrization of the world is at the same time a fragmentation of the world. This geometrization and fragmentation of the visual scene produced by the grid-like veil becomes the prototype of scientific analytic vision, which breaks the whole into parts, isolates, and decontextualizes. Romanyshyn goes on to say that

> insofar as the way one looks reflects who one is, the geometrization of vision means not only the fragmentation of the world into its parts but also the fragmentation of the self. With the window as grid we have also the genesis of the fragmented self, the self of analyzable parts, the self which is capable of dissecting its attitudes, emotions, and beliefs. Psychoanalysis is born on this side of the window. With the window as grid the spectator has gone into analysis. [pp. 77–78]

Romanyshyn's analysis would seem to explain why the development of self psychology was perhaps inevitable. Self psychology's focus on issues of fragmentation and cohesion of the self speaks to an unconscious awareness of the fragmenting nature of the analytic world view derived from the assimilation of the principles of linear perspective into the scientific mind-set and from there into the cultural unconscious.

We clearly see Alberti's window separating Galileo's world into the two worlds referred to above. This is evident in Galileo's distinction between what were later called primary and secondary qualities.

> Whenever I conceive any material or corporeal substance, I immediately feel the need to think of it as bounded, and as having this or that shape; as being large or small in relation to other things, and in some specific place at any given time; as being in motion or at rest; as touching or not touching some other body; and as being one in number, or few, or many. From these conditions I cannot separate such a substance by any stretch of my imagination. But that it must be white or red, bitter or sweet, noisy or silent, and of sweet or foul odor, my mind does not feel compelled to bring in as necessary accompaniments. Without the senses as our guides, reason or imagination would prob-

ably never arrive at qualities like these. Hence I think that tastes, odors, colors, and so on are no more than mere names so far as the object in which we place them is concerned, and that they reside only in consciousness. . . . If the living creature were removed, all these qualities would be wiped away and annihilated. [1957, p. 274]

So, according to Galileo, we are left with form, extension, motion, location, and number as primary qualities residing in the external objective world and all other qualities seemingly residing "only in consciousness." One would think that more careful consideration would have made Galileo realize, as did later thinkers, that "without the senses as our guides" his primary qualities could be no better apprehended than tastes, odors, and colors. So why would he place only the latter set of qualities on the side of the subject? It is of interest to note that the qualities that Galileo wishes to subtract from the objective world, such as taste, odor, color, and sound, are those qualities that are most affect-arousing. In other words, Galileo's agenda was to bring about an affective cleansing of the world that science investigated by stripping the world of its affect arousing qualities, moving them back into the subject on this side of the window, leaving only matter in motion on the other side that could be clearly dealt with by mathematical reasoning. This anti-emotional bias later came to characterize science in general. The physical sciences were the first to adopt this dichotomy between primary and secondary qualities in going about their daily business regardless of the fact that the distinction was logically untenable. Whitehead (1925) sardonically commented on this affectively sanitized world created by seventeenth century scientists:

Thus nature gets credit which should in truth be reserved for ourselves: the rose for its scent; the nightingale for his song; and the sun for its radiance. The poets are entirely mistaken. They should address their lyrics to themselves, and should turn them into odes of self-congratulation on the excellency of the human mind. Nature is a dull affair, soundless, scentless, colorless; merely the hurrying of material, endlessly, meaninglessly. [p. 54]

To study this "objective" world of science and to deal with it objectively came to mean, after Galileo, Descartes, and Newton, to approach the world dispassionately, to not allow affect to color (or color to affect) one's observations and conclusions. The world was to be understood through reason, observation, and experiment. The attitude of the scientist was to be affectively noninvolved, appropriately distant, and disinterestedly observant—in other words, neutral. Freud's concern with positioning psychoanalysis within the domain of science led him to import this general attitude of the physical scientist into his theorizing and into psychoanalytic technique. Thus, in his *Project For A Scientific Psychology* (1950) his opening statement reads: "The intention is to furnish a psychology that shall be a natural science: that is, to represent psychical processes as quantitatively determinate states of specifiable material particles, thus making those processes perspicuous and free from contradiction" (p. 295). Shades of Galileo and Newton! First-person, subjective experiences were to be reduced to third-person, objective processes. Although Freud abandoned and later disavowed the Project, nevertheless, as Strachey (1966) observed, "The *project*, or rather its invisible ghost, haunts the whole series of Freud's theoretical writings to the very end" (p. 290). While this attitude toward the world adopted by the physical sciences was enormously successful in the furtherance of the aims of physical science, this same attitude when imported into psychoanalysis produced problems. Freud's efforts to place psychoanalysis within the world view of mechanistic science had a significant effect on his recommendations concerning psychoanalytic technique. For Freud as scientist the ideal of neutrality was a priori and therefore conditioned the development of psychoanalytic theory and technique from the outset. We are suggesting that the concept of neutrality did not simply develop empirically out of Freud's experience in the psychoanalytic situation but was *imported* into the psychoanalytic situation as part of Freud's commitment to the scientific Weltanschauung. The proper attitude of the scientist behind Alberti's window (behind the couch?) was to be affectively uninvolved, appropriately distant, and properly positioned for disinterested observation. This was the model of neutrality Freud brought to the psychoanalytic situation; hence, Freud's originally negative view of countertransference as an impediment to the analytic task. Of course, the concept of neutrality has evolved over the years and has been modified in various ways by later analytic theorists but its origin in Freud's commitment to the scientific Weltanschauung seems clear.

By bringing this scientific setup to the analytic situation, Freud allowed for an objectification of the patient that impeded the eventual development of an intersubjective model of the analytic relationship. This objectification carried with it a rich potential for shame experience for the patient while protecting the analyst from similar experiences. The experience of being objectified by the other when one wishes to relate to the other in an intersubjective mode is a potent stimulus for shame, involving as it does an experience of an absence of reciprocity and complementarity in affective responsiveness. (For an extended analysis of the relation between objectification and shame see Broucek [1991].)

In his 1912 paper "Recommendations to Physicians Practicing Psychoanalysis," the anti-emotional bias of the scientific Weltanschauung is quite evident as Freud calls on his colleagues to "model themselves during psychoanalytic treatment on the surgeon, who puts aside all his feelings, even his human sympathy, and concentrates his mental forces on the single aim of performing the operation as skillfully as possible." He goes on to say, "The justification for requiring this emotional coldness in the analyst is that it creates the most advantageous conditions for both parties: for the doctor a desirable protection for his own emotional life and for the patient the largest amount of help that we can give him today" (p. 115). Why does the doctor need protection for his own emotional life? What is it that needs protecting? What potentially disturbing affect or affects are being warded off by this protective attitude? If these questions had been vigorously pursued by Freud, we might have had a theory of the analytic encounter based on an understanding of shame dynamics, instead of drives and defenses against drives.

Freud's surgeon metaphor seemed to encapsulate the correct scientific attitude toward one's subject and left an indelible mark on classical psychoanalytic technique. The discipline required of the analyst to maintain this emotionally detached, anonymous, abstinent, neutral stance was often a source of pride to those who embraced what came to be called the "classical model" of technique. The austerity of the model had a deep-seated appeal to many practitioners partly, we believe, because of the implicit "scientific heroism" embedded in the metaphor of the surgeon's relentless determination to complete the operation undeterred by sentiment and partly also because of what Suttie (1935) referred to as a "taboo on tenderness" (which we will discuss later).

THE CONTRIBUTION OF UNACKNOWLEDGED ETHICAL, MORAL, AND QUASI-RELIGIOUS CONSIDERATIONS TO THE FORMULATION OF THE PRINCIPLE OF ABSTINENCE

Freud introduced the concept of abstinence in his 1915 paper "Observations on Transference Love":

> I have already let it be understood that analytic technique requires of the physician that he should deny to the patient who is craving for love the satisfaction she demands. The treatment must be carried out in abstinence. By this I do not mean physical abstinence alone, nor yet the deprivation of everything the patient desires, for perhaps no sick person could tolerate this. Instead I shall state it as a fundamental principle that the patient's need and longing should be allowed to persist in her, in order that they may serve as forces impelling her to do work and to make changes, and that we must beware of appeasing these forces by means of surrogates. And what we could offer would never be anything else than a surrogate, for the patient's condition is such that, until her repressions are removed, she is incapable of getting real satisfaction. [p. 165]

Freud again discussed abstinence in his 1919 paper "Lines of Advance in Psychoanalytic Therapy":

> You will remember that it was a frustration that made the patient ill, and that his symptoms serve him as substitutive satisfactions. It is possible to observe during the treatment that every improvement in his condition reduces the rate at which he recovers and diminishes the instinctual force impelling him towards recovery. But this instinctual force is indispensable; reduction of it endangers our aim—the patient's restoration to health. What then is the conclusion that forces itself inevitably upon us? Cruel though it may sound, we must see to it that the patient's suffering, to a degree that is in some way or other effective, does not come to an end prematurely. If, owing to the symptoms having been taken apart and having lost their value, his suffering becomes mitigated, we must re-instate it elsewhere in the form of some appreciable privation; otherwise we run the danger of never achieving any improvements except quite insignificant and transitory ones. [pp. 162–163]

In this curious statement Freud seems to be espousing a paradox. Frustration made the patient ill; therefore, in order to cure him/her we must impose more frustration. Is this some form of homeopathy in which like cures like? It is clear in this passage that Freud is basing his recommendations of abstinence on his energy theories. In Freud's way of thinking, work of any kind, including analytic work, is fueled by instinctual energy and therefore the direct discharge of these energies in pleasurable, gratifying activities would rob the analytic work of its needed energy supply. Few analysts today still place much confidence in Freud's ideas about energy dynamics, but they often fail to recognize that if one rejects such energy theories, one of the basic theoretical pillars supporting the principle of abstinence is removed.

Let us take a closer look at Freud's statement: "It is possible to observe during the treatment that every improvement in his condition reduces the rate at which he recovers and diminishes the instinctual force impelling him towards recovery." First, it is not possible to *observe* that every improvement in his condition diminishes the instinctual force impelling him toward recovery, simply because instinctual energy is a *theoretical construct* and not an observable phenomenon. Is the first half of the statement any more valid? We think not. We believe that clinical observation leads to the opposite conclusion that any improvement in the patient's condition is more apt to increase the rate at which he/she recovers rather than decrease it. Freud's theoretical model based on instinctual energy dynamics led him to make "observations" that are not consistent with observations of clinicians not bound by these same theoretical commitments.

Freud's views on abstinence were supposedly derived from the theoretical view that psychoanalysis was primarily concerned with those psychic products that were the result of repressed instinctual drive derivatives and that gratification would interfere with the task of bringing into consciousness these repressed instinctual wishes for the purpose of tracing their genetic origins and thereby making possible their renunciation or sublimation. There is good reason to believe, however, that Freud's promotion of the principle of abstinence was not simply the result of theoretical considerations alone.

It is of considerable historical and psychological importance that Freud introduced the principle of abstinence in the context of the vexing problem of the female patient's romantic and sexual longings for her male analyst (Cremerius 1984); any consideration of gratifying such longings posed obvious ethical and moral problems for Freud. A few years earlier, in 1909, Freud had to deal with the situation in which his heir apparent, Jung, stepped over the line with his patient Sabina Spielrein. Haynal and Falzeder (1993) write:

> It is only a few months later that Jung confesses to Freud that he "devoted a large measure of friendship to her" not daring to write that this meant in reality that he had become her lover, no doubt in the wake of feelings mobilized in the treatment. The whole problem of love is experienced and developed in a very dramatic manner in this trio of Spielrein, an embarrassed Jung trying to justify himself, and Freud who wants to understand and at the same time exert a sort of control. He writes to Jung: "Such experiences, though painful, are necessary and hard to avoid. . . . I myself have never been taken in quite so badly, but I have come very close to it a number of times and had a *narrow escape* [in English in the original]. [p. 362]

In later correspondence, Freud added, "In view of the kind of matter we work with it will never be possible to avoid little laboratory explosions." So Jung's involvement with Sabina Spielrein is reduced to the status of a minor laboratory explosion at one level but at another level is very likely experienced by Freud as not quite so minor in contemplating the future of psychoanalysis, especially when, two years later, Freud had to deal with Ferenczi's troubles.

In July 1911 Ferenczi wrote to Freud about a difficult situation in which he found himself. He had undertaken the analysis of Elma Palos, the daughter of his mistress, and had fallen in love with Elma. Caught in a triangle between his mistress and her young daughter Ferenczi prevailed on Freud to take over the analysis of this young woman who had by then become his fiancée. Here is Haynal and Falzeder's (1993) account:

> There was, in the Freud/Ferenczi correspondence at this time, an exchange of the utmost intimacy between them, with Freud revealing quite openly the most personal details of what he had learned from his analysand Elma. Ferenczi gradually tried to distance himself from what he called his "mishap" in a letter to Freud. Elma, having completed "a piece of analysis" with Freud between the New Year and Easter, 1912, returned to Ferenczi to finish her analysis. In understandably very difficult circumstances, Ferenczi had to admit that he had made a mistake. In a painful to and fro he separated from Elma, encouraged to do so by Freud. There remained within him a sadness to which he was

not easily resigned and to which he perhaps never fully adjusted. [p. 365]

We believe it very likely that these "mishaps," "laboratory explosions," and "narrow escapes" posed a significant threat to Freud's efforts to win acceptance and respect for his fledgling science of psychoanalysis. Rather than acknowledge that ethical and moral considerations dictated the principle of abstinence in the case of "transference love," Freud denied that his recommendations were based on moral or ethical principles or fears about the future of psychoanalysis, but instead were based on the technical considerations growing out of his theory of the neuroses. He (1915) proudly comments, "I am able to trace the moral prescription back to its source, namely to expediency. I am on this occasion in the happy position of being able to replace the moral embargo by considerations of analytic technique, without any alteration in the outcome" (p. 164). Freud's fateful move here is his effort to convert a moral and ethical dilemma into a problem of technique. His solution was the principle of abstinence, which required the frustration of the patient's erotic longings (and the analyst's as well) on purely technical grounds.

Another related consideration that influenced the formulation of the principle of abstinence was the importance that Freud placed on sexuality in his writings. Wolf (1976) comments, "In the social matrix of his time Freud felt constrained to publicly overemphasize restraint and austerity in analytic practice in order to mute criticism engendered by having placed sexuality, and particularly infantile sexuality, at the center of his scientific investigations" (p. 104). We believe that he also felt the need to reign in the activities of his colleagues and set strict limits on what was permissible in the way of gratifying either the patient's or analyst's desires. We would agree with Wolf (1993) that "Freud's emphasis on intrapsychic dynamics and associated emphasis on abstinence, neutrality, and denial of gratification in treatment may well have been motivated by an anxiety driven need to keep his passions and those of his followers in check" (p. 16). By denying that the principle of abstinence was based on expedient concern for bourgeois morality (a denial quite unconvincing to us), Freud denied the role played by anticipated shame and guilt in the formation of the abstinence principle, shame and guilt not simply over gratifying the patient's longings but over gratifying the analyst's own longings as well. Freud instead must offer technical reasons for his principle of abstinence, such as the reasons cited above.

We consider it a matter of the greatest importance that the principle of abstinence made its first appearance in the Freudian corpus as a technical recommendation for dealing with the female patient's strongly charged erotic desires for the male analyst, which included her desire that he should desire her also. It did not arise in a general direction about all types of patients or all types of difficult emotional situations that may arise during treatment, although its elevation to a fundamental principle of technique ("rule") had the effect of thereafter extending the principle to the total psychoanalytic situation.

Quasi-Religious Undertones

In Freud's understanding of analytic work there is a latent assumption that such work is grim and cannot be pleasurable, that it is not real work if it is enjoyable. Real work, according to Freud, cannot proceed in the presence of that analytic enemy, gratification. There is an asceticism involved here, not unlike early Christian asceticism, which dictates the renunciation of pleasure and the embracing of suffering as essential to spiritual salvation.

Under the banner of science, Freud introduced certain moral, ethical, and quasi-religious principles into psychoanalytic technique. The notion of sinning is latently present and unconsciously evoked by words such as *gratifying* and *indulging*. A sense of sinfulness is particularly likely to be evoked whenever analysts are tempted to modify technique in the pursuit of optimal responsiveness rather than optimal frustration because the former term suggests that the analyst is engaged in some form of illicit gratification. Gratification has always been suspect in psychoanalytic thinking; as a violation of the principle of abstinence it has been viewed as something vaguely unethical or suspiciously close to being unethical. The concepts of frustration, abstinence, neutrality, and anonymity coalesced into an ascetic ideal of technical purity that formed the core of the analytic superego. (It was interesting for us to note that *The Random House Dictionary* gives as a definition of the word *ascetic* "[adj]: rigorously abstinent; austere.") Suggested modifications or alterations of psychoanalytic technique (such as those of Ferenczi and Alexander) had to pass the purity test and invariably failed. Psychoanalytic orthodoxy allowed, somewhat magnanimously, some variations in technique under the pejorative term *parameter*. Although permissible under certain conditions, parameters were relegated to an analytic purgatory lying somewhere between the heaven of pure technique and the hell of wild analysis.

As we said earlier, the asceticism of the analytic ego ideal and analytic practice, classically conceived, was not unlike the traditional asceticism embraced by candidates seeking religious or spiritual enlightenment. Although Freud was quite disdainful of things religious and spiritual, he nevertheless incorporated into his analytic ego ideal an asceticism of practice similar to that which characterized various monastic groups. The distinctions between science and religion that Freud was at pains to draw in "The Future of an Illusion" became blurred in this area we have been discussing.

Did Freud always follow his own recommendations? Those acquainted with Freud's handling of his own cases are aware that Freud was not quite so austere and abstinent as he urged others to be. He fed the Rat Man, helped the Wolf Man in many ways, including collecting money for him, and when Rene Spitz forgot his cigarettes, Freud provided them (Spitz even reproached him for this gratification). These were but a few of many instances in which his behavior fell outside the bounds of his own technical recommendations. We don't fault him for that nor do we view it as necessarily an enactment of unanalyzed countertransference. We are more inclined to see these apparent contradictions as reflecting the tension between Freud the human being, who could at times be quite responsive and, yes, gratifying in his dealings with patients; Freud the scientist, trying to view his patient through Alberti's window; Freud the clinical theorist, stuck with a model of neurosogenesis based on a drive theory that seemed to logically demand frustration; and Freud the practical moralist, trying to protect psychoanalysis from scandal that might destroy it.

Further evidence that Freud felt free to disregard his own recommendations is that he undertook the analysis of his daughter Anna, in which case abstinence, neutrality, and anonymity were clearly out of the question. Freud apparently did not think that this precluded successful analysis.

The fact that Freud at times violated some of his own recommendations doesn't mean to us, as some maintain, that he didn't intend for others to take them seriously and that classical technique was therefore largely the invention of later analysts. We think it means he was conflicted about his recommendations perhaps because of some marginal awareness on his part of the defensively motivated nature of these recommendations.

SECRECY, CONCEALMENT, AND FREUD'S PERSONALITY

Roustang (1986) noted that a biologist could understand Watson and Crick's proposed model of DNA without knowing anything about them as persons but a psychoanalyst needs to take Freud's personality into account if he is to understand anything of psychoanalytic theory. As Jones was inclined to say to inquirers about psychoanalysis, "Psychoanalysis is Freud." We believe that it is especially necessary to take certain aspects of Freud's personality into account in order to understand his technical recommendations.

Barron and colleagues (1991) hypothesize that Freud's creation of psychoanalysis as a scientific discipline was related to his decision as a 17-year-old to eavesdrop on the secrets of nature as a natural scientist. They document the ever recurrent references to uncovering secrets in Freud's correspondence and publications and they see this as a leitmotif running through his life. Although he steadfastly devoted his energies to uncovering nature's secrets and the personal secrets of his patients, Freud was very guarded when it came to revealing secrets about his private life. In support of this point, Barron and colleagues cite a passage from Jones's (1955) biography:

> Freud always held very strongly that only he had the right to decide how much of his personality he would reveal to others and how much not: in a general way a quite understandable position. But there were features about his attitude that would seem to pass beyond that and to justify the word privacy being replaced by secrecy. For it would obtain when there were no particular reasons for the privacy or concealment; and then, again, its strength was really remarkable. . . . Somehow he managed to convey the impression that only what he vouchsafed about his personality was a permissible topic and that he would resent any intimate questioning. He never spoke to his children about his youth and early years. . . . Above all as we noticed earlier, there was a striking contrast between the rather unflattering picture he revealed to the world concerning his inner life, notably in the analysis of his dreams, and the quite complete reticence on the matter of his love life. The sacredness undoubtedly centered there, and we have remarked on the quite extraordinary precautions he took to conceal a most innocent and momentary emotion of love in his adolescence. [pp. 408–409]

Barron and colleagues quote a report of Hanns Sachs: "We were standing in front of Goethe's works which filled three bookshelves. Freud said pointing toward it, 'All this was used by him as a means of self concealment'" (Sachs 1944, quoted in Kohut 1978). Barron and colleagues suggest that, given Freud's identification with Goethe, his insight carried with it an autobiographical implication.

Freud went to great lengths to conceal his personal life. In 1885, in a letter to Martha Bernays, he reported having destroyed all his diaries of the previous fourteen years, along with letters, scientific notes, and manuscripts. He did this in anticipation of becoming famous with an eye to frustrating his imagined biographers. In 1907 Freud again destroyed all his notes, diaries, correspondence, and manuscripts, according to Jones.

Barron and colleagues also note how Freud's concern for secrecy affected his relationships with his followers and led to the formation of the committee of five trusted colleagues and himself. This committee, on Freud's instruction, would have to be "strictly secret in its existence and actions" (Jones 1955, p. 153).

Thus, one could make the case that Freud's concern for personal secrecy and concealment was sufficiently ongoing, intense, and pervasive to warrant the term *obsession*. Barron and colleagues speculate about what it was that Freud took such pains to conceal. Our interest is not in trying to uncover the content of what Freud might have wanted to conceal, but rather in the question of what affect motivated Freud's powerful need to conceal. Surprisingly there is no mention of shame in the Barron paper, even though any discussion of Freud's great concern with secrecy would seem to cry out for some consideration of the role of shame in his obsession with concealment. The feeling of painful exposure before the gaze of others is characteristic of shame experiences, and any excessive need for concealment should make one suspect a special vulnerability to shame. There is no good reason to exempt Freud from this general rule. If Freud had a special vulnerability to shame and consequent need for personal concealment and secrecy, would it be surprising if such a concern strongly influenced the evolution of psychoanalytic technique? Freud frankly admitted that the practice of having the patient lie on the couch rather than sit face to face with him sprang from his personal intolerance of being looked at by his patients all day. If Freud's need to reduce personal exposure led to institutionalizing the use of the couch, it would seem likely that it influenced his other technical recommendations as well. In this light, his recommendations concerning analytic anonymity, abstinence, and neutrality could be understood as efforts to conceal and protect the personal life of the analyst from unwanted or feared exposure.

In the same 1912 paper on psychoanalytic technique cited earlier, Freud introduced his well-known mirror simile: "The doctor should be opaque to his patients and, like a mirror, should show them nothing but what is shown to him" (p. 118). In reading Freud's defense of this recommendation, one wonders how much the recommendation owes to Freud's personal need for concealment rather than to the reasons he offered. Freud rejected the idea that it might be helpful to the patient in analysis for the doctor "to afford him a glimpse of his own mental defects and conflicts and, by giving him intimate information about his own life, enable him to put himself on an equal footing. . . . Experience does not speak in favor of an affective technique of this kind" (p. 117). Whose experience? Surely not Freud's (in fact he does not say "*my* experience"). Can one really imagine someone like Freud with his obsession with secrecy and the concealment of his personal life, experimenting with disclosing "his own mental defects and conflicts" to his patients? We tend to think that the recommendation was based not on Freud's personal experience but on the defensive needs of his personality. In a very real sense, it could be said of Freud's technical recommendations concerning abstinence, neutrality, and anonymity, what he said of Goethe's works: "All this was used by him as a means of self concealment."

SUMMARY AND CONCLUSIONS

We have attempted to trace the origins of several basic psychoanalytic principles of technique, laid down by Freud, to certain potentially shame-evoking personal and cultural considerations with which he had to deal. He felt he had to position psychoanalysis within the mainstream of science, which carried with it a need to place the analyst in an affectively detached, disinterested position behind Alberti's window. He also felt he had to defuse certain bourgeois suspicions that psychoanalysis was some kind of licentious enterprise, particularly because of its emphasis on the importance of sexuality in psychic development, but also because he had to deal with the laboratory explosions endemic among his close collaborators. Concerns about personal privacy also strongly influenced Freud's technical recommendations. We contend that Freud formulated the principles of neutrality, abstinence, and anonymity partially in response to these concerns and to make the psychoanalytic situation more affectively manageable.

If Freud's recommendations concerning neutrality, abstinence, and anonymity had their origin in the personal and cultural considerations we have addressed, why were they so readily embraced and given such reverential acceptance by the mainstream of psychoanalysis for so long? We suspect that part of the explanation for the high esteem in which these principles were held was that they provided a loincloth of technique that served to cover the analyst's potential shame over his or her inadequate responsiveness as a human being vis-à-vis another human being. Suttie (1935) referred to "a taboo on tenderness" that became institutionalized in psychoanalysis based on a reluctance to accept the importance of the analyst's "love" in bringing about clinical improvement. Suttie defined love as "feeling-interest responsiveness," which Bacal (1985) reintroduced in the form of his conceptualization of the analyst's task as "optimal responsiveness" (for an overview of Suttie's work, see Bacal and Newman [1990]).

An important caveat is in order at this point, lest we be misunderstood. In focusing on the defensive functions involved in Freud's formulation of these technical principles we are not suggesting that an attitude of neutrality, abstinence, or anonymity is therefore, in itself, unempathic or defensive in nature. At a given moment, neutrality, properly understood, might be the optimal response of the analyst. The same is true of abstinence and anonymity. The problem is that in the historical development of psychoanalytic technique these principles became shibboleths that were relentlessly pursued for their own sake. When pursued for their own sake their influence on the course of the analysis was often destructive, as most contemporary psychoanalysts now understand. Stolorow (1990) makes the point: "Relentless abstinence on the part of the analyst decisively skews the therapeutic dialogue, provoking hostility and tempestuous conflicts that are more an artifact of the therapist's stance than a genuine manifestation of the patient's primary psychopathology" (p. 120).

Another reason for the acceptance of neutrality, abstinence, and anonymity as cornerstones of classical technique was that, when Freud formulated these principles, psychoanalytic theory failed to differentiate between needs for affiliation, attachment, tenderness, affection, affective attunement, mirroring, nurturance, efficacy, and competence on the one hand, and libidinal impulses originating in zonal insistencies (oral, anal, and phallic) on the other. Motivational systems other than the sensual-sexual one were not understood and selfobject needs were subsumed under the concept of sexuality and hence subject to sanctioned frustration under the principle of abstinence. This failure to differentiate between different motivational systems (Lichtenberg 1989, Lichtenberg et al. 1992) has also been responsible for the difficulties analysts have had in achieving optimal responsiveness in the classical psychoanalytic setting, because optimal responsiveness depends on making such differentiations. In throwing out the bathwater of zonally based libidinal gratification, classical analysis also threw out the baby, the legitimate selfobject needs.

In the effort to protect patient and analyst from the danger of unruly libidinal strivings that might undo their therapeutic enterprise, the rule of abstinence was set in place. The rule at the same time embodied a curious obliviousness to the vast number of patients who could also be damaged by the lack of optimal responsiveness. Typically, however, sins of commission are judged more harshly than sins of omission and are more easily detectable. Because sins of omission usually elude the analyst's own self-critique, they are often more destructive than sins of commission. However subtle and unnoticed by the analyst, it is more often his or her sins of omission that give rise to feelings of neglect, deprivation, rejection, shame, rage, and despair in the patient. Such sins constitute poor care of the patient that often resembles earlier poor care, but, sadly, these sins now take place in a "therapeutic" setting and may be obscured or justified by the principle of abstinence.

The emphasis on frustration rather than responsiveness in the analytic situation has been sustained over the years partly by theoretical considerations concerning the role of frustration in the formation of psychic structure. Basch (1991) cited a paper by Beebe and Lachmann (then unpublished, later published in 1994), which outlined four roads to structure formation. "The fundamental process is that of ongoing mutual and self regulation; that is mother and infant form a system in which the responses to one another regulate and maintain the relationship while at the same time the infant is also regulating his own self" (p. 8). Auxiliary forms of structure formation that are particular variants of the basic process include Freud's frustration and gratification (eliminated in the published version of the Beebe and Lachmann paper), rupture and repair (Kohut's optimal frustration), and the structure forming effects of heightened affective moments (Pine). We would add optimal responsiveness (see Chapter 1) to this list.

In Chapter 3 Terman maintains that internalization and structure formation have little to do with frustration. Following Vygotsky (1975) and Kaye (1982), Terman suggests the term *dialogue of construction* to characterize this process of structure formation. "The doing is the making. The dialogue is the structure. The repetition—not the absence or interruption—creates the enduring pattern" (p. 74). This newer understanding of structure formation makes it no longer persuasive to defend technical principles that impose high levels of frustration on the patient on the grounds that this is necessary to bring about structural change.

References

Bacal, H., and Newman, K. (1990). *Theories of Object Relations: Bridges to Self Psychology*. New York: Columbia University Press.

Barron, J., Beaumont, R., Goldsmith, G., et al. (1991). Sigmund Freud: the secrets of nature and the nature of secrets. *International Review of Psycho-Analysis* 18:143–163.

Basch, M. (1991). Are selfobjects the only objects? In *Progress in Self Psychology*, 7, ed. A. Goldberg. New York: Guilford.

Beebe, B., and Lachmann, F. (1994). Representation and internalization in infancy: three principles of salience. *Psychoanalytic Psychology* 11(2):127–165.

Broucek, F. (1991). *Shame and the Self*. New York: Guilford.

Cremerius, J. (1984). Die Psychoanalytische Abstinenzregal. *Psyche-Zeitschrift-fur-Psychoanalyse-und-ihre Andwendungen* 38(9):769–800.

Freud, S. (1912). Recommendations to physicians practicing psychoanalysis. *Standard Edition* 12:111–120.

——— (1915). Observations on transference love. *Standard Edition* 12:159–171.

——— (1919). Lines of advance in psychoanalytic therapy. *Standard Edition* 17:159–168.

——— (1950). Project for a scientific psychology. *Standard Edition* 1:295–397.

Galileo. (1957). *Discoveries and Opinions*, ed. S. Drake. Garden City, NY: Anchor.

Haynal, A., and Falzeder, E. (1993). Slaying the dragons of the past or cooking the hare in the present: a historical view on affects in the psychoanalytic encounter. *Psychoanalytic Inquiry* 13(4):357–371.

Ivins, W. (1964). *Art and Geometry*. New York: Dover.

Jones, E. (1955). *The Life and Work of Sigmund Freud*, vol. 2. New York: Basic Books.

Kaye, K. (1982). *The Mental and Social Life of Babies*. Chicago: University of Chicago Press.

Kohut, H. (1978). Beyond the bounds of the basic rule. In *The Search for the Self*, vol. 1, ed. P. H. Ornstein, pp. 275–303. New York: International Universities Press.

Lichtenberg, J. (1989). *Psychoanalysis and Motivation*. Hillsdale, NJ: Analytic Press.

Lichtenberg, J., Lachmann, F., and Fosshage, J. (1992). *Self and Motivational Systems*. Hillsdale, NJ: Analytic Press.

Romanyshyn, R. (1989). *Technology as Symptom and Dream*. London: Routledge.

Roustang, F. (1986). *Dire Mastery*. Washington, DC: American Psychiatric Press.

Sachs, H. (1944). *Freud, Master and Friend*. Cambridge, MA: Harvard University Press.

Stolorow, R. (1990). Converting psychotherapy to psychoanalysis: a critique of the underlying assumptions. *Psychoanalytic Inquiry* 10:119–130.

Strachey, J. (1966). Editor's introduction to "Project for a Scientific Psychology." *Standard Edition* 1:295–397.

Suttie, I. (1935). *The Origins of Love and Hate*. New York: Julian Press.

Vygotsky, L. (1975). *Mind in Society*. Cambridge, MA: Harvard University Press.

Whitehead, A. (1925). *Science and the Modern World*. Toronto: Collier Macmillan.

Wolf, E. (1976). Ambience and abstinence. *Annual of Psychoanalysis* 4:101–115.

—— (1993). The role of interpretation in therapeutic change. In *Progress in Self Psychology*, vol. 9, ed. A. Goldberg. Hillsdale, NJ: Analytic Press.

3

Optimal Responsiveness and a New View of Structuralization*

DAVID M. TERMAN

EDITOR'S COMMENT

Terman amply confirms my view that the concept of optimal frustration is not relevant to a psychoanalytic perspective on theory or therapy. Terman's clinical experience is that—"changes in . . . patients [occur] because of an understanding of the old and a creation of the new that [arises] from the experience in . . . analysis that [has] nothing to do with frustration" (p. 61). In support of this clinical experience, Terman draws particular attention to the developmental studies of Vygotsky and Kaye that demonstrate that it is not frustration or absence of responsiveness but rather the repeated participation by significant adult figures in constructive cognitive activity and affective attunement with the child that is central to the development of psychic structure.

---

*This chapter originally appeared in *Learning from Kohut: Progress in Self Psychology*, volume 4, edited by A. Goldberg.

On the basis of these studies, Terman also questions the classical view of internalization, as well as Kohut's theory of transmuting internalization via optimal frustration for the laying down of structure for psychological growth. For Terman, it is the experience of the significant transaction itself that results in patterning, which constitutes structure. As Terman puts it, "It is not something which happens and then is separately transposed inside. Rather, the participation changes the child's inner construction" (p. 67). For Terman, the term *optimal responsiveness*, which "emphasize[s] the appropriate ways the analyst can respond in accordance with the patient's phase-appropriate and individually specific requirements for growth and repair . . . emphasizes the necessity for [the analyst's] participation and response in the formation of pattern" (p. 73). This, together with Terman's recognition that "it is the intactness of the selfobject tie that permits the resumption of growth [in cases of early selfobject failure]" (p. 73) affirms my contention that it is the experience of optimal responsiveness to the selfobject needs of the child and the analysand that will determine healthy self-development.

Terman suggests we employ the term *dialogue of construction* to denote the process by which structure is formed. I welcome this term, as it underscores the relational, or interactional, aspect of optimal responsiveness, which I address extensively in Chapter 7 (see also Bacal 1988). Perhaps we might usefully bring both terms together in recognition that the patient's experience of the analyst's optimal responsiveness is an indication that a dialogue of construction is taking place.

Reference

Bacal, H. A. (1988). Reflections on "Optimal Frustration." In *Learning from Kohut: Progress in Self Psychology*, vol. 4, ed. A. Goldberg, pp. 127–131. Hillsdale, NJ: Analytic Press.

---------------- ❖ ----------------

This chapter reconsiders the psychoanalytic theory of structuralization—especially the centrality of frustration. I shall argue that the theoretical emphasis on frustration has neglected the importance and variety of pattern that is generated in transaction, in which a variety of responses and fulfillments play central roles in the construction of self experience, meaning, and expectation.

In his last work, *How Does Analysis Cure?* (1984), Kohut again enshrined the concept of optimal frustration as central to the process of transmuting internalization. He asked the question, "Can abiding functions be acquired by the self without a preceding frustration, however tiny and/or fractionated from the side of the selfobject?" (p. 100). And he answered no. He detailed a three-step sequence: "1) need-activation and optimal frustration via 2) nonfulfillment of the need (abstinence) and 3) substitution of direct need fulfillment with the establishment of a bond of empathy between self and selfobject" (p. 103). With the emphasis on frustration, Kohut put his concepts directly in line with classical theory and carefully divorced his theories and techniques from the onus of providing gratification.

I do not think I need to review the long and weighty reasons for the opprobrium in which the idea of gratification has been held. But since all impulses from which structure evolved were originally conceived by Freud to be sexual, gratification has meant something ranging from the regressive, antitherapeutic, or addictive to—in its most concrete and primitive form— the grossly unethical. So, the concept of frustration, in addition to its theoretical centrality, has acquired the quality of moral purity, if not righteousness.

Because of this, the exploration of these aspects of the therapeutic experience that are satisfying has been hampered. Further, our whole theory of structure formation—the acquisition of pattern and meaning—has been seriously skewed. The clearest exception to this has been the excellent recent work of Bacal, whose contribution I discuss later. In our exploration of the therapeutic process and structure formation, not only will we find other ways to conceptualize structure formation, but we shall also change or discard the concept of gratification insofar as it has connoted the satisfaction of erotic or erotically derived needs.

We are led to this reconsideration by two sources. The first, and more important, is that practice has not conformed well to theory. Reluctantly and increasingly, I have felt that changes in my patients occurred because of an understanding of the old and a creation of the new that arose from the experience in the analysis that had nothing to do with frustration. Often, but not always, interpretation or understandings or aspects of the analytic relationship itself answered—that is, satisfied—deeply held needs. It was the satisfaction of the needs that opened new paths and remade old ones. Some of the case reports in our literature have led me to the same conclusion.

The second source is the data from developmental studies. As investigators have become more sophisticated, their data appear more and more relevant to our own questions. Although we must always be careful about our use of their data—especially since some of the most systematic such studies concern the infant—we cannot help being struck by the complexity and variety of transactions they describe in which the child acquires its enduring regulatory, organizing, and affective patterns. It would indeed stretch our belief in the concept of frustrations as central to the acquisition of pattern, to see these structures arising and developing as the consequence of the absence or interruption of these transactions.

I consider both of these classes of data—the clinical and the developmental—in my discussion of structuralization, and I shall begin with the second, the developmental.

Lev Vygotsky, the Russian psychologist, was the first of the developmentalists to systematically explore the importance of environment in the creation of the child's conceptual world. His ideas about the acquisition of language stressed its interpersonal genesis. More generally, he saw all higher cognitive functions as originating in actual relations between people; for Vygotsky (1978), "an interpersonal process is transformed into an intrapersonal one" (p. 57). For him, language and conceptual development grew out of the nature and process of communication. The structuralization of the mind grew out of human relationships and could not be understood apart from them.

Kenneth Kaye (1982), a modern developmentalist, takes this position yet further. He discusses the difference between Vygotsky's understanding of development and Piaget's. Whereas Piaget's theories, like Freud's, stress development as "inside-out" (as the unfolding of innate, internally determined patterns), to use Kaye's distinction, Vygotsky's is "outside-in." Kaye, to his own surprise, finds that Vygotsky's ideas apply not only to childhood, during and after language acquisition, but to infancy as well. Kaye is even more emphatic about the importance of the parental role in creating and structuring the infant's mind. He sees the infant as an apprentice who is induced into a societal system by the goals and techniques of the parent. He finds "a great deal of asymmetry in the relations between parent and infant, so that the temporal structure that eventually becomes a true societal system will at first only have been created by the parent, making use of built-in regularities in infant behavior rather than actual cooperation or communication" (p. 53). Those structures that appeared to Piaget to evolve autonomously seem, for Kaye, to arise from the matrix *parental* goals and expectations. Speaking of the development of shared intentions, for example, a period beginning at 2 months, Kaye notes that the sharing begins as a "unilateral responsibility [of the parent]. . . . Adults guess at the intentions underlying infant's activity. . . . Parents have many ways of speaking for the child. . . . What the parents are doing is integrating the new child into their already existing social system" (p. 66).

Kaye goes on: "By 8 months or so, the sharing of intentions has become a two-way process. The infant's schemes, differentiated *through experience in certain behavioral frames imposed by adult behavior,* allow him to anticipate the most likely direction of that behavior" (p. 67, italics added). The infant goes on to a phase that Kaye calls shared memory and then to one of shared language. In all of these, Kaye notes, "the parents are constantly drawing the child forward into a more challenging apprenticeship, eventually a full partnership" (p. 68).

The parents "frame" the child's behavior; that is, they provide essential functions and regulations for the child. Kaye describes seven such frames: nurturant; protective; instrumental—the adult carries out what appears to be the child's intention, such as helping him get a toy beyond his reach; feedback, when the adult provides consequences of an action like prohibition or praise; modeling, in which the adult performs an action the child will imitate (often in the context of something the child is attempting himself); discourse, with the parent doing things to the child that have a predictable effect, for example, tickling, getting a response, and repeating, hence creating a kind of dialogue; and, finally, the memory frame, in which the parent remembers what the child likes and does not like and arranges important aspects of the child's world accordingly.

It is within these frames that the child begins to "take turns" and a dialogue evolves. Kaye's contention, again, is that this dialogue is virtually induced by the parent. The parent has the memory, expectations, and skills and by virtue of these moves the child into transactions that eventually create a shared symbolic system and a structure of goals and intentions. Kaye's analysis and description of a dialogue with a 2-year-old illustrates the process. In a situation in which a mother and child are looking at a picture book, the "conversation" is recorded and analyzed. It goes like this (p. 100):

Mother	Child
1. (Points to picture)	
What is that one? (M)	2. Kitty cat. (R)
3. Well, what is it? (RM)	4. Kitty cat. (R)
5. Well, I know there's a	6. Huh? (RM)
kitty in it; what's he	
in? (RM)	
7. What's he riding in? (RM)	8. Airplane (R)
9. Right. (R)	
10. (Turns page) (U)	

Most of the mother's participation involves what Kaye calls "mands" (M). A mand is an act that demands a response (R): a question or a request or pointing. It is by virtue of the mands that the child responds and a sequence develops. The existence and nature of the sequences depend on the mother's framing of the situation. She creates the structure of a dialogue. Kaye notes:

> So the child does not have the problem, as was once thought, of constructing a knowledge of his parents' language from a corpus of overheard speech. Instead he is plunged into ongoing discourse on topics very largely selected by his own interests. His meanings are interpreted, expressed and expiated upon almost before he really means anything at all. . . . The social structure, the discourse itself, is not mastered by children before they go on to the specifics of their parents' syntax and semantics. Adults will create and maintain the discourse structure for them, thus teaching them how to participate in that structure and *eventually take it over as their own*. [p. 103]

The active creation of context results in the child's assimilating and then accommodating—taking in and, as a result, changing—the schemas, the patterns, with which he or she organizes the world. The changing and growth of patterns occur in the context of intense interaction. The *interaction*, not the spaces between the interactions, changes and structures. It is not the *loss* of the transaction, but rather its *presence* that structures.

The structure that emerges—the capacity to understand the labels attached to things and the capacity to take turns (among the many capacities generated in this dialogue)—would be inconceivable without the presence of these transactions. One could argue that it is only by giving the child space/time to absorb such experiences that permanent alteration in the child's mental organization is possible. But it stretches credulity to maintain that the *withholding*, or *delay*, of such transactions is *the* essential step in development of the structures that accrue from them. Further, to concentrate on a hypothetical delay to the neglect of the transaction misses the central areas of experience without which there can be nothing.

Daniel Stern, a psychoanalytic developmentalist, underlies the importance of the parent in helping to create what he calls self. Stern (1985) describes four phases of development of the self that take place during the first two years of life. These are the sense of emerging self, the sense of core self, the sense of subjective self, and the sense of a verbal self. Central to the construction of pattern is the concept of RIG—Representation of Interactions that have been Generalized. Stern finds evidence that self and other are distinguished very early (a finding that, I believe, will necessitate the revision of some of our notions of the nature of early self development) but that the "other" does, indeed, play a crucial role in the function of the self. Indeed, the essential regulatory role of the experience of the selfobject is confirmed and amplied by Stern's (1985) work.

For example, the parent plays a central part in the establishment and maintenance of the core self. This is defined as a sense of agency, coherence, affectivity, and history. It is an experiential, not a cognitive, construct. In that construction, the contouring of excitation is an important dimension, and the vignette of Eric is illustrative.

> Eric is a somewhat bland infant compared with his more affectively intense mother, but both are perfectly normal. His mother constantly likes to see him more excited, more expressive and demonstrative about feelings, and more avidly curious about the world. When Eric does show some excitement about something, his mother adroitly joins in and encourages, even intensifies, the experience a little—usually successfully—so that Eric experiences a higher level of excitement than he would alone. . . . Eric's self-experience or higher-than-usual excitement is, in fact, largely achieved and regulated by his mother's behavior. His experience of his own higher levels of excitement occurs only in the lived episodes in which her augmentary antics are a crucial

attribute. She thus becomes for him a self-excitement-regulating other. Eric's self-experience of high positive excitement never occurs unless mother is there participating in it. Specific episodes coalesce to form a RIG. [p. 193]

This vignette is consistent with what we call a selfobject—probably a mirroring selfobject. The mother is an integral part of the psychological regulation of the child. How does the pattern become established here? By repetition. The participation of the mother in the child's excitement and her repeated augmentation of it eventually lead to the establishment of an inner state that can be reevoked and with which the world is experienced. Repetition and participation, *not absence*, lay down governing patterns.

The elements of repetition and participation are even more evident in the process Stern calls "attunement," which comes a little later, when the child is about 9 months. The mother responds to the child by matching, cross-modally, the feeling state of the child. This is a crucial phenomenon in its own right, for, Stern holds, this kind of experience shifts attention away from simple external behavior to "what is behind the behavior, to the quality of feeling that is being shared" (p. 142). Hence, attunement is a way of perceiving or sharing internal states.

The shaping, molding, and structuring of internal states may then occur by way of the vicissitudes of attunement. By selectively attuning, for example, the parent underlies and selects some experiences over others. As Stern notes:

> Parents have to make a choice, mostly out of awareness, about what to attune to, given that the infant provides almost every kind of feeling state. . . . This process of creating an intergenerational template is part of ordinary everyday transactions. . . . In being themselves, parents inevitably exert some degree of selective bias in their attunement behaviors and in doing so they create a template for the infant's sharable interpersonal world. [p. 208]

Both the data and the thought of these developmentalists show us over and over and in many contexts that the creation of pattern occurs in significant transactions. And pattern is structure. Hence, the focus of our inquiry shifts. We were interested in internalization as the sine qua non of structure formation; but as we examine the issue more closely, we see that the essential question is not so much internalization, but creation. What makes the pattern in the first place? The experience itself seems to make the pattern. The formation of structure seems not to be a two-step process. That is, it is not something that happens and then is separately transposed inside. Rather the participation itself changes the child's inner construction.

Freud's abandonment of the seduction hypothesis directed him to the vicissitudes of the *internal* construction of pattern and meaning—that is, fantasy. With the emphasis on both internal generation of meaning and its accrual through frustration or loss, our attention has been drawn from the contextual *creation* of pattern in transaction. The concept of the selfobject has, of course, turned our attention back to these transactions. For self is maintained, generated, brought into existence, shaped in the experience of selfobject.

Let us turn now to some clinical data to examine these ideas further. If we look at the vicissitudes of the mirror transference, for example, we will see that we participate in the formation of important aspects of the patient's experience of self by our interpretations, by the framework of psychological values with which our interpretations are given, and by our therapeutic stance in general.

I have chosen to look at a fragment of one of the cases in a casebook (Goldberg 1978) to illustrate these issues.

> Mr. E., a 26-year-old married man, presented symptoms of anger with his wife, boredom, sensitivity to slights, and a work inhibition. His history included his having been born prematurely to a mother who was depressed and ill at his birth and experienced a progressive illness until her death when he was 15.
>
> The analysis, begun after several months of psychotherapy, centered on a mirror transference in which exhibitionistic impulses and wishes for a variety of responses were expectably engaged and stimulated. Weekend separations and vacations also played an important role in his feelings of coherence and his level of energy. An important voyeuristic perversion emerged only after the analysis was under way, and the symptom became part of the process in response to the separation from the analyst. The patient revealed the symptom during the hour after he had given his analyst a Christmas card. The analyst had taken it and said thank you. The patient expressed gratitude that

the analyst didn't interpret it. He said that he felt that it would have reduced the "genuineness of my behavior." In the next hour, he first told the analyst about his peeping at penises in men's bathrooms.

This sequence was paradigmatic for important aspects of the analytic process. In this exchange, it was the patient's experience of the analyst as accepting that permitted a deepening of the process—the patient was first able to tell of an important symptom and begin engaging it and his underlying needs more deeply with the analyst. In this instance the participation—the analyst's act of acceptance—led not to a structural change, but to a deepening of the process rather than to a defensive repression of his underlying needs.

Exhibitionistic wishes became mobilized shortly thereafter in a dream in which the patient was in the analytic room, but elevated in the center of the couch. At the same time he began to feel depressed during the weekend separations, and his voyeuristic perversion was enacted. In one poignant Monday hour he reported frequenting the men's rooms. The analyst (Goldberg 1978) said, "He reported a sense of feeling bizarre." In a desolate voice, the patient reported having spent the time he was not in men's rooms painting empty chairs in his apartment. Suddenly he shouted, "I demand to know what you are thinking. You think I'm psychotic, don't you?" The analyst replied, "I think you must have been very lonely." The patient then burst out crying and said, when he recovered himself a bit, "That was the first time anyone ever realized that." He paused and added, "And I think that includes me" (p. 271).

Here was an interpretation that obviously had enormous immediate impact, and as one reads the case one sees repeated instances of this kind together with profound structural changes in the patient. What was the meaning of this kind of intervention? It certainly made the patient aware of a feeling that had been previously unavailable to him. Perhaps it made the experience into an affect and hence more symbolically transformable. But what seemed most important to the patient was the fact of being understood. His inner state was accurately perceived and accepted. He experienced himself as the center of the analyst's attention (as indeed he was). By implicitly understanding the patient's need for the analyst and explicitly noting the loneliness, the analyst helped create an experience in which the patient did not feel alone or unattended. This occurred in the context of the revival of the experience of aloneness and lack of investment (weekend separation). I contend that the building of structure, the acquisition of pattern, occurred by virtue of the analyst's response, understanding; and the creation of that new pattern followed from the experience of the understanding and was not created by the absence of understanding. The internalization was implicit in and dependent on the construction—the presence of the understanding.

But one can raise an immediate objection. Was it not, after all, the *frustration*, the weekend separation, that was integral to the experience? Does this not follow Kohut's formulation, as we stated in the beginning, that is, need activation and optimal frustration via nonfulfillment of the need and substitution of direct need fulfillment with the bond of empathy? The separation functioned as the frustration of the need, and the interpretation of loneliness constituted the empathic bond. If one looks at it that way, what was the nature of the archaic need consistent with this explanation? Was it the need to be with the parent physically all the time? If it were that, the formulation would fit, at least in the sense that something else was offered for it. But that is a rather concrete understanding of the nature of the need. Rather, the patient needed the analyst's interest and investment and acceptance. These were certainly absent as far as the patient was concerned, at least over the weekend. But the interpretation did not then *substitute* for the fulfillment of the need; the interpretation satisfied the need. If the requirement was interest and investment, being the center of the analyst's attention, the need has been met. Hence, one could say that frustration was, indeed, the stimulus for the subsequent satisfaction, but the satisfaction was not a substitute.

The central question still remains: What is responsible for the creation of pattern? Could the experience of analyst-as-understanding-paying-attention and patient-feeling-valued (or cohesive) exist without the analyst's interpretation? No. Could it have occurred without the antecedent frustration? It seems not. Is the enduring quality of that experience dependent on the antecedent or subsequent-absence of the experience? No. I submit that such absences or interruptions provide the occasion for the experience of the analyst-as-understanding. It is the *repetition* of the *presence* that builds new structure. (The repetition of the *absence* reevokes the old patterns.) And this is much of the reason for and substance of the working through.

In many subsequent transactions, one sees more clearly the importance of the experience of the analyst as understanding and sustaining as *longings* for consistent responsiveness were mobilized without antecedent frustration. The patient had two homosexual dreams with overt and disguised transference manifestations about several frustrations and rejections from women. The patient became both aware of, and embarrassed by, the homosexual wishes for the analyst. The analyst interpreted them in a genetic context—a turning to the father after a disappointment with the mother.

The patient then had a dream that he reported the next day. His chairman had looked at several reports he had done and said, "I'll take it down to the bindery." The analyst reported the following:

> He associated to psychoanalysis and how it had helped him—that he now understood the "authority" of his experiences. He was not sure what he meant by that, but thought of a leader holding the diverse elements of a country together. "Here [referring to the analysis] both fact and fantasy are treated with respect. That is a comfort to me—you accept what I said about my sexual behavior." He felt that this made him less of a stranger to himself and that he felt less lonely as he saw that "there is understanding to be had. You are helpful because you are not threatened by my needs." [p. 276]

In this instance, it is more clear that the analyst's understanding, and, if anything, facilitation, of the patient's yearnings are the heart of the patient's experience. The stimulus for the yearnings is not a frustration by the analyst. Neither the interpretation nor its effect are frustrating. The patient felt bound together—more cohesive—as the result of both. He felt the analyst was not threatened by his needs for him. He could experience, express, and find satisfaction of many levels of need. Surely the need for understanding his feelings and the awareness of, and interest in, his inner state was amply fulfilled. And this was at the same level as the childhood experience. The inner experience and the transactions establishing them are not so different from what the child most centrally needs.

The feeling that the analyst was not threatened, that he accepted the patient's needs, may also serve a regulatory, integrative function that had been warded off or not yet given coherent form. This analytic act changes existing structure or creates structure anew—that is, it helps form a pattern of experience of self-acceptance, or self-existence. And it is the presence of the act that creates pattern. Will it then be internalized? I think it is being internalized in the making.

The patient's experience of acceptance, and the analyst's communicating acceptance through his interpretations, seem to be an essential part of the patient's construction and reconstruction of himself.

The vacation at some point after this episode produced a sense of impending fragmentation. The analyst reports: "He reported feeling decrepit, complained he was lacking compared to others. He thought of lizards, rats and a guillotine. He could actually see heads rolling and hear the squish of dead bugs on the pavement" (p. 276). The analyst called attention to his upcoming vacation, to which the patient responded with embarrassment over his wishing for the presence of the analyst. His awareness of the feeling, and, again, of the analyst's understanding of it, seemed to lead to a reintegration and further recall of, and connection with, his mother's deterioration and death.

Here the impending absence—the prospective vacation—restimulated the experience of loss of attention and loss of self; but after the interpretation of his feeling and the reintegration of the interpretation, the patient had further access to the memory and affect around his mother's deterioration. Something had changed in the patient—both the control of the regression and the useful reexperience of the past—that permitted a reproduction of the old experience in a new framework. (This is nothing new, of course. We all see this every day in every functioning analysis. Indeed, the whole analytic process is viewed this way.) I contend that the interpretation here supplied exactly what the patient was missing in reliving the past: the alive, understanding presence. It did so also by virtue of the structure that had already begun to grow and consolidate—a self, if you will, that was vital, continuous, even lovable—and acquired in the experience of the analyst's interpretations, presence, and acceptance.

Certainly vacations and weekends, in this case, provided the opportunity to reexperience aspects of the past, but I am maintaining that the reintegration and new integration around those periods depended on understanding and responses that were not substantially different from what was required in the past, and that the reformation of the old and formation of the new patterns grew out of the fulfillment of the requirements, not their frustrations.

*   *   *

There are obvious and enormous differences between development and the therapeutic situation. First, as I noted, the developmental data to which I have referred are from infants under 2. Stern (1985) makes the interesting assumption that such infants mainly experience reality. He writes, "Their subjective experiences suffer no distortion by virtue of wishes or defenses, but only those made inevitable by perceptual or cognitive immaturity or overgeneralization" (p. 255). Hence, the complexity of acquired inner structure and the processing of experience by such a more complex structure are missing. Second, the situation of newly developing structure—of laying down for the first time—is, of course, quite different from the therapeutic encounter with, and mobilization of, preexisting structure. The raison d'etre of the transference is the reevolution of such preexisting and other-wise inaccessible structure. Indeed, the way the patient experiences us as participating is already determined by such preexisting structure.

Yet the core of *change* of that structure—or the creation of a new structure, the resolution of the transference—always entails an experience of the analyst that is different from the past. Classically, this has meant only a change in the perception of the analyst because of the change in inner organization effected by the altered defensive structure—that is, it has been viewed as an internal change from purely internal factors. The concept of the selfobject, however, has permitted us to examine the therapeutic process and systematically explore the role and meaning of our responses in the genesis and change of those inner structures. And when we turn to these phenomena and examine them, the parallels are suggestive, even striking.

We do not "frame" precisely the way Kaye (1982) observes in the parent–child relationship. We do not, for example, supply memory or effect the various cognitive functions; we do not create a cognitive dialogue. However, we do participate in an *affective dialogue* in which the inner structure that we call self changes or emerges. In the case described, the analyst's interest, investment, understanding, and acceptance—especially of the patient's longings for precisely those qualities from the analyst—constituted the responses in a dialogue in which the analyst was an essential member and in which the experience of a whole, alive, and lovable self emerged. I suspect the process is not unlike Stern's RIG—representation of interactions that have been generalized. Often in relation to the old RIG—the experience of the depleted mother and the dying weak self—the new or changed self is created. But it is also created anew as in the episode in which the longings for the analyst were by implication validated and accepted. That was a new opportunity in which a new experience of self was generated. The analogy, if not homology, between this process and Stern's (1985) description of the development of a state of self-excitement in Eric, is highly suggestive.

A theory of structure formation that emphasizes our participation is indicated. Socarides and Stolorow (1984/85) have pointed to the same issue. Confining their concerns to cases of early selfobject failure, they postulate that "the central curative element may be formed in the selfobject transference bond itself" (p. 112). It is the intactness of the selfobject tie that permits the resumption of growth in these cases. Similarly, in discussing the metabolism of depressive affect, they shift the emphasis on the mechanism of change from optimum frustration to the centrality of affect attunement.

In Chapter 1, Bacal offers the term *optimal responsiveness* to emphasize the appropriate ways the analyst can respond in accordance with the patient's phase-appropriate and individually specific requirements for growth or repair. This felicitous term emphasizes the necessity for participation and response in the formation of pattern, and helps us look beyond the narrow confines of the concept of frustration to consider a much richer and broader spectrum of experience—both in development and the therapeutic process.

The emphasis on participation in the formation of pattern is not to deny that frustration also creates pattern. It does. Further, not all participation leads to adaptive, harmonious pattern; some leads to distorted, maladaptive structure. And, in fact, more of the distortions of structure are due to mismatches of responses of many sorts than are due to nonresponse. But to make frustration the central mechanism of pattern creation distracts our attention from the variety and significance of an enormous spectrum of transaction that is so far suggested in both developmental and therapeutic fields.

Bacal (Chapter 1) states, "We cannot assume that all internalizing processes occur through frustration. In a good enough situation, for example, identification and assimilation occur" (p. 31). I would be more emphatic. I suspect that internalization and structure formation have little to do with frustration, and I do not think identification and assimilation quite account for the power and pervasiveness of a system of communication, affective dialogue, in which pattern is generated.

I suggest the term *dialogue of construction* to characterize this process of structure. The doing is the making. The dialogue is the structure. The repetition—not the absence or interruption—creates the enduring pattern.

This is the essential stuff of which we are made—and remade. And this is what we must continue to study.

References

Goldberg, A., ed. (1978). *The Psychology of the Self: A Casebook*. New York: International Universities Press.

Kaye, K. (1982). *The Mental and Social Life of Babies*. Chicago: University of Chicago Press.

Kohut, H. (1984). *How Does Analysis Cure?* Chicago: University of Chicago Press.

Socarides, D., and Stolorow, R. (1984/85). Affect and selfobjects. *Annual of Psychoanalysis* 12/13:105–119.

Stern, D. (1985). *The Interpersonal World of the Infant*. New York: Basic Books.

Vygotsky, L. S. (1978). *Mind in Society*. Cambridge, MA: Harvard University Press.

4

Optimal Responsiveness and a Search for Guidelines*

MORTON SHANE AND ESTELLE SHANE

EDITOR'S COMMENT

In this wide-ranging consideration of the conceptualization and implementation of what is most favorable in psychoanalytic therapy, Morton and Estelle Shane concur with David Terman and John Lindon and me that frustration and abstinence cannot constitute a basis for understanding and treating patients. They conclude that *optimal responsiveness*, as I have defined it in Chapter 1, provides an encompassing concept that reflects the therapeutic goal of the clinician.

In this chapter, the Shanes review the perspectives of a number of significant psychoanalytic thinkers whose ideas, in their view, constitute guidelines for optimal responsiveness in the clinical situation. Thus, they cite the work of Bowlby (attachment theory), Terman (dialogue of con-

---

*An earlier version of this chapter was presented at the 17th Annual Conference on the Psychology of the Self, 1994, and was published in *Basic Ideas Reconsidered: Progress in Self Psychology* (1996), edited by A. Goldberg.

struction), Lichtenberg (motivational systems), Lindon (optimal provision), Stolorow and colleagues (attunement to affect states), Basch (attention to pathological affect states), Beebe and Lachmann (mutual and self regulation), and Goldberg (interpretation of Kohut's (1977) vertical split) that is relevant to the optimal responsiveness concept.

The Shanes introduce a concept of their own—*optimal restraint*—as a substitute for the principle of abstinence ("transference gratification"). This guideline can usefully serve as a reminder of the asymmetry of the therapy situation and draw our attention to the ethical and professional responsibility of the therapist in responding optimally to the patient.

————————— ❖ —————————

In 1985 Howard Bacal published a paper entitled "Optimal Responsiveness and the Therapeutic Process" (see Chapter 1) that proved to be seminal for self psychology. With this paper, and the introduction of a new concept, *optimal responsiveness*, as well as a new way of viewing the analyst's participation in the therapeutic process, a conversation was begun among us that is still going on. New psychoanalytic concepts appear when we want to discuss certain clinical problems with each other, but we perceive ourselves to be unable to discuss them adequately in the language and conceptual framework familiar and available to us. This has been the history of psychoanalysis from its beginnings. As Charles Spezzano (1993) states, based on his own application to psychoanalysis of the philosopher Richard Rorty's (1989) work,

> The evolution of psychoanalytic theory [is] an ongoing conversation in which a person's psychology was once thought to be most usefully discussed in a repression/resistance/neutrality/[abstience] language, but is now believed by many to be more usefully discussed in an affect/communication/conarration language. This does not mean that it was a mistake to use [the old theories] when [they] held center stage in psychoanalytic discourse, any more than it means that this discourse suffers from a relativism in which anything anybody says about human psychology is just as acceptable as anything else, because after all it is just a conversation. [But] it does mean that conversation is at the heart of human psychological evolution, and that the exchanges that make up

the psychoanalytic conversation are evolving in a rational and critical
fashion [yielding] more useful clinical concepts. [p. 20]

In this chapter we enter into the conversation about the optimal in the
clinician's response. We focus on guidelines that may help direct us in our
search for the appropriate and the useful in the therapeutic moment. We do
so with full understanding that any contribution we may make, if useful at
all to our community of self-psychologically informed clinicians, will lead
at best to no more than a temporary solution to the clinical problem at
hand, or, as Spezzano put it, a temporary rest in the dialogue.

The chief participants in this conversation about the optimal in
psychoanalysis have included Sigmund Freud (1911–1915), Anna Freud
(1965), Heinz Kohut (1971, 1977, 1984), Ernest Wolf (1976, 1989),
Robert Stolorow, Bernard Brandchaft, and George Atwood (1987), Howard
Bacal (see Chapter 1), David Terman (see Chapter 3), and, most recently,
John Lindon (1994). In this chapter we focus mainly on Bacal, Terman,
and Lindon, who themselves have referenced and amply discussed the
important contributions of the others. We begin with our assessment of
where the field rests at the present time, and where the conversation has
stopped thus far.

Bacal's challenging 1985 presentation (see Chapter 1) called into
question Kohut's generative contribution concerning the role of optimal
frustration via transmuting internalization in fostering the structuring and
restructuring of the self. As optimal frustration was so central to Kohut's
thesis on how analysis cures, the challenge to it had to be made with care
and with great persuasiveness, and Bacal was eminently successful in
achieving these requirements. In effect, what Bacal accomplished was to
demonstrate that Kohut's covert tie to classical analysis hampered his
capacity to break free of some hidden assumptions of classical theory.
Kohut's remarkable observation that clinical work with self disordered
patients is punctuated by disruptions that require repair, and that following
such repair the patients seem improved, was confounded with the sense
that it was the frustration itself, requiring that the patient assume functions
heretofore supplied by the analyst, that was responsible for the improvement, for the growth of structure.

In contrast, Bacal reasoned that just because structure building followed optimal frustration and its repair did not mean that there was an
inevitable cause-and-effect relationship between moderate frustration and

structure building. Bacal argued that what created new structure was the patient's sense of being understood that had followed the disruption attendant to the frustration and its repair. Optimal responsiveness, leading to a resumption of harmony in the relationship, is therapeutic not because understanding of the disruption is therapeutic, but because understanding in itself is therapeutic, that is, it leads to psychological growth. The valorization of frustration had been linked in classical theory to beneficial results because the Freudian model of secondary process thinking and structure building was related to and depended on the frustration of primary process drive discharge and gratification (Rapaport 1960). While Kohut was able to drop the drive model, he could never relinquish the idea that frustration in itself was beneficial, viewing it as adding to the establishment of what he had originally termed the "narcissistic equilibrium" of the patient, and later, harmony, strength, and cohesiveness of the patient's self. Bacal was able to persuade many in our community of analysts to believe otherwise, leading to the introduction into our clinical vocabulary of the concept of optimal responsiveness and, as well, to a set of new questions regarding what it means to be responsive, and, especially, what is meant by "optimal."

Noting that Kohut himself had posed the question about what is optimal in optimal frustration, but could never arrive at a satisfactory answer, Bacal defines "responsiveness" as the therapist's act of communicating his understanding of the patient to the patient, and "optimal" as the response that for a particular patient will be most suited to the patient's developmental capacity and selfobject needs for human relatedness. Further, optimal responsiveness was presented by Bacal as the umbrella term that would subsume optimal frustration, gratification, and provision. Bacal noted that while frustration and gratification are both inevitable in the clinical relationship, neither serves as appropriate treatment goals for the analyst; the analyst should seek neither to deliberately frustrate, however optimally, nor to deliberately gratify. Rather, the proper goal in the clinical situation is that the analyst, having understood his or her patient, should then communicate that understanding through an optimal response.

Bacal offers to the analyst in this same paper two guidelines toward the optimal response. The first derives from Kohut's concept of a developmental line of empathy, an advance from understanding to interpretation to be offered by the analyst in response to a progression the analyst has observed in the patient. This progression has moved from a lower form of the patient's capacity to feel the analyst's empathy, so that a literal holding environment or an experience of merger is required with the analyst, to a higher form of the patient's capacity to feel the analyst's empathy, where now a more metaphoric holding environment provided through verbal understanding or explanation is most appropriate to serve the patient's selfobject needs. Kohut had illustrated this progression by speaking of the young child's needing bodily contact, and then the child's developing to a capacity wherein words alone could achieve the same result. This was translated into the clinical realm by Kohut with his famous and final demonstration of empathy with a severely disturbed patient to whom he offered his hand, or, more accurately, a restrained two fingers, and also, again more metaphorically, in the distinction Kohut made between the understanding phase of interpretation and the explaining phase. Thus, developmental line of empathy serves as the first guideline offered by Bacal for optimal responsiveness.

The second guideline Bacal offers for optimal responsiveness also derives from Kohut's writings: the state of self–selfobject relatedness falling along a continuum of disruption and repair. At a time when the patient is in a disrupted state, and the self–selfobject relationship is at an impasse, a different sort of response is called for from the analyst than at a time when the selfobject tie has either been reinstituted or is perceived as smoothly ongoing. A third guideline for optimal responsiveness is only hinted at by Bacal in his 1985 paper in which he alludes to the limitations of the analyst inherent in the analyst's level of understanding, the degree and depth of the analyst's empathy, personal or technical inflexibilities of the analyst in response to the patient's needs, or the analyst's unconscious countertransference experiences.

Recently, in a paper written with Peter Thomson (1996) which has been revised and elaborated for this book in Chapter 12, Bacal elaborates on countertransference in a self psychological framework, building on Wolf's insight that the patient serves necessary ongoing selfobject needs for the analyst by being, in effect, a successful patient, and affirming thereby the analyst's sense of competence and sense of effectance. Bacal and Thomson focus on instances wherein the patient is experienced as failing to serve the analyst in this way, and wherein as a consequence, the analyst becomes embroiled in unconscious, *non*optimal exchanges with the patient based on the analyst's own unmet needs, which lead to impasses or disruptions in the therapy. By self-reflecting on the unexplored needs that the analyst has for the patient, or, indeed, for the analyst's entire population of patients, a third guideline to help the analyst become more optimally responsive to the patient is provided.

With this comprehensive, indeed groundbreaking, statement, it is interesting to note that the conversation about the optimal didn't rest there. A year after Bacal's paper was published, David Terman appeared at the Eighth Annual Conference on the Psychology of the Self, in 1986, to address the audience on Optimal Frustration: Structuralization and the Therapeutic Process. The paper is presented in this volume as Chapter 3. Terman's paper is a useful addition to Bacal's original thesis, providing more than just supporting evidence for it. Terman's own opposition to Kohut's concept of optimal frustration derives primarily from two sources: First, there was the evidence from his psychoanalytic practice, which to him clearly did not conform to Kohut's theory of structure building via optimal frustration and transmuting internalization, but instead convinced him that in the clinical situation, understanding of the old and creation of the new had nothing to do with the experience of frustration, it was, rather, the experience of satisfaction that had opened new pathways for the patient, and that had remade old ones. The second source for Terman's opposition was drawn by him from developmental studies, the findings from which preclude the concept that structures can arise or develop from absence in the dyad, or interruption of the dyad, as would seem to be inherent in a frustration model of development. On the contrary, findings from developmental studies emphasize that structuralization of the mind grows only out of the presence of human relationships, not apart from them.

Terman cites the Russian psychologist and linguist Lev Vygotsky, who stresses the interpersonal genesis of language. He also cites the developmentalist Kenneth Kaye, who stresses the two-way process of creating and structuring the infant's mind, the parent continuously drawing the child forward in the dyad, in the zone of proximal development, eventually toward a full partnership. The child's parents, Kaye writes, frame the child's behavior, providing functions and regulations for him. Finally, Terman refers to Daniel Stern to demonstrate that it is the repetition and participation of the caregiver in the child's activities, not the absence of the caregiver, that lays down governing patterns. Terman argues that the shaping, molding, and structuring of internal states occurs by way of the vicissitudes of attunement, not by way of frustration. Again, his point is that frustration does not build structure, and he refers to Socarides and

Stolorow, who contend that it is the intactness of the selfobject tie that permits the resumption of development, not its disruption following frustration.

Supportive of Bacal's position, then, Terman goes beyond him with an important addition to our understanding of how structure is formed, both in development and in the clinical situation. Bacal says that not all internalizing processes occur through frustration, but that in fact, in the good-enough situation, identification and assimilation occur and build structure through internalization. But Terman emphasizes that, first of all, frustration has little to do with internalization and structure formation, and that, in addition, even identification and assimilation fail to describe and capture the process, that it is power of the affective dialogue in its repetition, not in its absence, that creates structure, in both development and in analysis. Terman argues that the concept of frustration leading to structure has distracted us from the variety of transactions between caregivers and child and between analyst and patient; that these transactions, taken together, create patterns, adaptive or maladaptive; and that it is the repetition of the pattern itself that ultimately builds structure. Anticipating the Darwinian neurophysiologist, Gerald Edelman (1992), as well as Arnold Goldberg (1991), Arnold Modell (1993), and Colwyn Trevarthan (1994), Terman asserts here that "the doing is the making," the dialogue of constrඃtion between parent and child and between therapist and patient, *is* the structure; there is no need to posit a two-part process wherein one first experiences and then internalizes to build enduring function; rather the structured schema is created by the transaction itself, in real time, at the same time as the transaction is occurring. Finally, Terman states emphatically that it is repetition, not absence or interruption, that creates the enduring pattern.

Thus, Terman uses experimental findings from infant and child observation to support his own clinical experience, and while he is well aware that such developmental findings cannot be depended on to prove analytic theory, he obviously believes that such findings can be used to bolster, shape, and delimit theory, providing, as we ourselves see it, an important external coherence (Strenger 1991) and confirmation from related disciplines.

Bacal (1988) responded to Terman's paper by finding himself in essential concurrence with him. He specifically refers to a point Terman makes that interpretation serves to make the patient feel understood, being tantamount to providing what was missing in the patient's past. But, Bacal adds, a good interpretation is nevertheless but one component of the analyst's optimal responsiveness, and perhaps not even the most therapeutic one. There are noninterpretive responses, responses that are out of the ordinary, that the analyst may or may not be willing or able to provide. Bacal notes that the patient says "be who I need you to be; don't just interpret it," and if the analyst cannot find a way to be that, the patient may have to accept the limitations of analysis, at least with that analyst. Bacal emphasizes that noninterpretive responsiveness may be just what the patient needs, and while most analysts do know this, they hesitate to discuss it or to write about it freely.

Thus, we see how, in Bacal's remarks, an invitation can be heard to continue the conversation on the optimal. When in 1993 John Lindon addressed the Sixteenth Annual Conference on the Psychology of the Self, he entered the dialogue with his own paper in which he asserts that we should replace the rule of abstinence with his concept of optimal provision. Lindon's particular emphasis is on the rule of abstinence, which he contends is both pan-theoretical and universally obstructionistic to the unfolding of the analytic process. He asserts that the analyst, rather than having a withholding, frustrating stance, designed to enhance the patient's verbalization and ultimate insight through interpretation, should instead tailor his or her response in accordance with the patient's requirements. To perceived developmental needs on the part of the patient, the analyst should respond with optimal provision; to perceived urgent desires on the part of the patient, the analyst should respond with optimal gratification. While gratification and provision exist in every analytic relationship, these concepts cannot be encompassed by a rule, such as had existed in the rule of abstinence, but must be approached instead by what is optimal for the particular patient. This inevitably leads Lindon back to the central question, What is optimal in optimal provision? Optimal provision is then defined by Lindon with a paraphrase of Atwood and Stolorow's definition of psychoanalysis itself, as any provision that, by meeting a mobilized developmental longing, facilitates the uncovering, illuminating, and transforming of the subjective experiences of the patient. Providing many clinical illustrations of what he means by "optimal" and what he means by "provision," Lindon warns that provision may become subverted in clinical work to an addiction in a mutual enactment process. On the other hand he notes that while abstinence may be the optimal provision for some patients, he nevertheless cautions against the relentless abstinence to be found in classical analysis.

At this point we would like to enter into the conversation more directly, hoping to further an understanding of the optimal in the therapeutic dyad. We are persuaded by Bacal that optimal responsiveness, defined by him as the responsivity of the analyst that is therapeutically most relevant at any particular moment in the context of a particular patient and his or her particular pathology, does reflect the therapeutic goal of the clinician; that is, the clinician does not seek to frustrate, nor even to gratify, but only to respond in such a fashion as to communicate to the patient that he or she has been understood. We would add to Bacal's statement that the response may be either direct (i.e., interpretive) or indirect (i.e., noninterpretive), that the response is optimal if it serves ultimately to enhance the patient's self development, and that what guides the clinician to the optimal response is one's particular theory of development and pathology.

From our perspective, the other terms traditionally used to guide the therapist's interventions are subsumed under optimal responsiveness, including Lindon's optimal provision (the response to the patient's need) and optimal gratification (the response to the patient's desire). We would, along with Lindon, eliminate the rule of abstinence, and, in fact, replace the term altogether, since it connotes an absence, or shutting down of response. Still, we believe there is some need for reserve, so to supply that function we would offer the term *optimal restraint*, that is, a response within the two-person dyad that is neither in excess of what is needed or desired by the patient, nor so withholding or nonresponsive that it serves to derail the process. As with provisions, restraint should be tailored, insofar as possible, to the clinical moment with the particular patient, ideally negotiated and co-constructed by both participants. As for the concept of optimal frustration, we are in agreement with the tenor of the conversation focused on thus far that optimal frustration is a relic of the past, that while the patient may at times be frustrated, this is not an appropriate or desirable treatment goal for the therapist to have. We feel this altered view of the process has profound meaning for how all analyses will be understood in the future, allowing us not only to proceed differently, but to reflect differently on the analyses we have already completed. This leads us to a brief discussion of our own perspective on an aspect of self psychology that influences our view of the optimal.

As we have stated elsewhere (1992), self psychology as a single homogeneous entity does not exist; there are now many self psychologies. We ourselves integrate current self psychological theory with intersubjectivity, in an effort to modify the direction of self psychology toward a more truly relational perspective. While we retain as singularly important the idea of selfobject relatedness, equating it more or less with Daniel Stern's core self in relation to a self-regulating other, we don't believe that the selfobject concept is sufficient to explain all types of relatedness either in development or in the clinical situation, and we don't find that the concept of mature selfobject relatedness, as distinct from archaic, answers our concern. We find it essential to postulate as well another dimension of relatedness, an intersubjective relatedness, that encompasses a subjective self in relation to an intersubjective other wherein each subject in the dyad can appreciate the other as a person in his or her own right, each possessing a separate and distinct mind, and a set of motives, and emotions, leading in the direction of a mutuality and intimacy between two persons. In Stern's (1994) terms, it is the interactive state of "I know that you know that I know," and "I feel that you feel that I feel," and most importantly, we would add, "I care to know and feel all about us, about you, about me, and about our 'we-ness'" (Emde 1988a,b).

While we appreciate and borrow from the contributions of Stolorow, Brandchaft, and Atwood to self psychology, in particular their concept of intersubjectivity as defining the mutual influence of each person upon the other in the intersubjective matrix between them, as well as their concept of unconscious (sequestered) organizing principles that underlie character, symptomatology, and character pathology in both patient and analyst, requiring the analyst's articulation and interpretation, our difference with them is that we choose to view the concept of intersubjectivity in a less global fashion than they do, reserving the capacity to interact in an intersubjective fashion to a relationship wherein each member in the dyad is concerned with the subjectivity of the other. By maintaining this distinction, we can better conceptualize and delineate the quality of selfobject relatedness from the more mature capacity for a self-other relatedness wherein the other is appreciated as a person in his or her own right. We would conceptualize, then, only the dimension of experience that corresponds to the subjective self and the intersubjective other as truly intersubjective, in that in such a case, each person in the dyad is vitally interested in the subjectivity of the other. In contrast, the patient who is relating to his or her analyst in the selfobject dimension is not relating to his or her analyst as a subjective entity, but, in selfobject terms, this patient is relating to the analyst as a provider of functions, or experiences requisite for self-sustenance, with little or no involvement in the other's complex inner world and with little or no capacity for or interest in mutuality or intersubjective intimacy. In our view, then, in the clinical situation, the selfobject dimension of relatedness is distinctly one sided, the analyst, ideally, fully concerned with the intrapsychic world of the patient via empathy, as well as being concerned with his or her own intrapsychic world, and the intersubjectivity between them, while the patient uses the relationship in a more one-sided way, via selfobject functions. This more focused view of intersubjectivity inherent in our clinical theory is not meant to detract from what Stolorow, Brandchaft, and Atwood have described concerning the significant impact of each member of the dyad on the subjective experience of the other; this important insight holds whether that other, the analyst, is experienced by the patient in the intersubjective dimension or in the selfobject dimension.

One pathway to optimal responsiveness, then, stems from the therapist's attention to which dimension of relatedness is in the foreground at any point in the analysis.

A young woman who suffered from a developmental impairment wherein she could, in effect, only relate to others as providers of selfobject functions complained bitterly to her analyst one day about a good friend's slighting her by canceling a small dinner the woman had been planning to celebrate the patient's birthday. The patient had been depending on the dinner to ameliorate her sense of being alone, and was now faced with the prospect of being deserted on her birthday. The depth of her pain, genuine and understandable, was the center of her focus, and it was only in passing that she noted to her analyst the reason for the cancellation, that the friend was pregnant, having struggled for years to achieve this, and was now at risk of losing her child and was ordered by her physician to remain in bed. The patient could talk about this situation, and note her own reluctance to commiserate with her friend's distress, which she had understood intellectually, but not emotionally. She said, "I tell her everything about myself, and I always expect her to feel for me, but I cannot and I am not interested in, hearing about or feeling for her." The patient, then, was able on her own to see the irony of the situation, the lack of symmetry in the relationships she establishes. Her analyst responded to the patient by an affirmation of her feelings without any attempt to interpret the patient's discomfort with her own perception of this imbalance. The analyst did not confront her with her developmental incapacity, interpret its origins, or in any way bring it into the transference, or relate it to the analyst's own experiences of being similarly unresponded to and unappreciated by this patient; in other words, a garden variety self-psychological response was offered by the analyst, informed by knowledge of this patient's archaic selfobject neediness.

Our point is that optimal responsiveness for this patient would require taking into consideration the dimension of relatedness currently at the forefront of her experience.

In contrast, in another analytic dyad, a depressed female patient whose parents have been unhappy with one another, and distant and controlling with her, commented to her male analyst who is in supervision with one of us, that she knows he is subtly but distinctly interested in her, both as a person, and, more pertinently, as a sexually desirable woman. She told him as well that she feels he is unhappy in his own personal life, and that she knows she adds with her presence in his life some essential vitality and interest to his existence. As it happens, the patient's perceptions are absolutely correct on all counts, including her assertions about her analyst's sexual interest in her, and even, at times, his sexual excitement. Moreover, the patient told her analyst that she feels sorry for him, that she wishes to comfort him, knows that he really desires her comfort, and would like a romantic involvement, but understands that such an affair is out of the question. On his side, the analyst knows she knows all of this, he appreciates her for it, feels a poignancy in the intimacy of their relationship, and is able to use all of this to respond in a respectful, insightful way that does not deny her reality, and yet shows optimal restraint. He could have interpreted her sense of his unhappiness genetically, in terms of her parents' troubled marriage, but chose more authentically and more optimally to stay with her in the here and now, despite his own discomfort at being so exposed, cognizant of this patient's capacity to relate on a fully intersubjective level and to resonate accurately with his self state. Aware that he is hewing a fine line between optimal and nonoptimal, even dangerous, responsivity, he proceeds nevertheless to explore her experience of him, never denying her reality and perceptiveness, and knowing that such risks constitute the occupational hazard of all well-functioning, self-attuned analysts. This analyst, while appreciative of his patient's selfobject needs that indeed have come to the fore many times, did not mistake this particular instance of intersubjective mutuality for a need on her part for a one-sided provision of self-regulating functions.

It is our contention, then, that both dimensions of relatedness must be kept in mind as guidelines to the quality of optimal responsivity, as well as those constructs we perceive to be subsumed under the optimal responsive umbrella, namely optimal provision, optimal gratification, and optimal restraint.

Another guideline in our search for the optimal is attention to a comprehensive organization of motivational systems, such as the one Lichtenberg (1989) delineates, or the one offered by John Bowlby (1988). By detecting in a given patient precisely what motive is most prevalent in the therapeutic moment, we can come closer to identifying the "main meaning," to use Lawrence Friedman's (1996) apt phrase, and with that understanding, respond most optimally. For example, an anorexic bulimic patient who has severe problems in regulating her physiological need states, particularly her eating and defecating, works together with her analyst in a way that highlights the patient's physiological disregulation. The analyst does not translate her patient's difficulty into classical dynamic motivational formulations such as forbidden oedipal wishes to bear a child, or oral aggressive wishes to destroy a hated mother within, trends that could certainly be found, if one seeks them, in what the patient brings in. Nor does the analyst address the problem in the attachment realm, though this longing, too, can be discerned quite easily in the patient's associations. Rather, the analyst goes directly to the patient's urgent inability to deal with the psychological effects of her chronic eating and bowel disregulation, which inability is analyzed within both present and past disturbed relationships, especially the relationship with her mother, her thin and beautiful mother who always felt that the patient was too fat. The analyst will deliberately inquire as to how and what the patient eats, both in her periods of bulimia and in her periods of anorexia. She actually shares with her patient information about what she herself eats, and how she herself attempts to maintain her own weight and health. The analyst continues to focus on this motivational system irrespective of its more or less obvious connections to other motivational systems more salient in the analytic literature. She abides her own discomfort at not acting like a "real analyst" because she has detected that the main meaning in this patient's disturbed relatedness is encompassed in physiological regulation motivational-functional system. She therefore relates to the patient directly in this dimension, in order to respond optimally, using provision, in Lindon's sense (i.e., dietary direction, shared nutritional needs, and the like) and, again in Lindon's sense, gratification (i.e., self-revelation of her own private battle in the same arena so as to provide a sense for the patient that the patient is not alone in her difficulty, but shares it with her much admired, idealized analyst). By recognizing multiple motivational systems, then, and by choosing the one that has more relevance in the particular clinical situation at hand, the therapist has a greater chance of responding most precisely to the patient's predicament in an optimal fashion.

An example follows wherein the main meaning for the patient is found in the attachment motivational system. This foreground need was confounded because for the analyst, a confused state of feeling sexual stimulation, and then guilt and shame for it, interfered for a time with his capacity to respond optimally.

> Some years ago a woman patient was in the middle of an analysis that had gone on for five years when she developed an eye pathology that led over the period of the next year to marked diminution in her vision. Understandably distressed, the patient in time requested that the analyst hold her hand while she was lying on the couch, at least at the beginning of each hour, and that upon leaving, she be allowed to stroke his arm for some moments, and at times to feel his face. These requests appeared quite understandable in view of the patient's need to augment through touch the perception of her analyst and her vital attachment to him, but the analyst, who was overly rigorous in regard to allowing any physical contact with patients, or to put it more simply, was uptight, found himself, while without question acceding to his patient's request, in a state of discomfort; he unavoidably and involuntarily experienced his interaction with his patient, when either holding her hand or being stroked by her, as sexually charged. This dissonance within himself had to be resolved quickly in order to allow

him to be optimally responsive to his patient, to be, that is, attuned and available to his patient's need for special provision in the attachment sphere, which is where *she* was. As he came to be able to respond more authentically to her touch, with a less divided internal state, the analyst was then also able to reflect upon his exceeding rigor, his need to do the right thing, to be the proper analyst, and he was able as well to look back on previous experiences with patients where he might have been more optimally responsive in this same way. The change in him was facilitated in part by an appreciation of the fact that the attachment motivational system was separate from, not derivative of, the sensual-sexual system as he had originally been taught. Were the main meaning of the patient's desire for physical contact within the sensual-sexual sphere, then the analyst, to respond optimally, might still have acceded to this blind patient's request, but he would have pursued the inquiry into its main meaning for the patient in a different direction. Thus, detecting as closely as possible the salient motive in the clinical moment facilitates an understanding of the most helpful way to be with a given patient.

As a final example of the use of motivational systems to aid in the achievement of optimal responsiveness, we provide an instance derived from the assertive exploratory mode.

The analyst greets her patient in the waiting room, and is struck by the beauty of the patient's jacket, which is lying on the chair next to where the patient was sitting. The analyst spontaneously remarks about it, commenting on the lushness of color, and they enter the office together talking of other things. At the end of the session, which was filled with the patient's emotion concerning her relationship with her mother, who had been inadequately responsive to her and who had died when she was 21, the patient and analyst get up together. The patient lifts her jacket from the couch, and, quite suddenly, extends her arm and says, "Here. You admire this greatly, I really don't, and I want you to have it." The analyst, nonplussed, completely taken off guard, and striving to remain an analyst with an appropriate degree of optimal restraint, after first spontaneously reaching out to take it from the patient's hand, and noting, without wanting to, the pure pleasure of its expensive, silken feel, again just as spontaneously, returns it to her patient, saying, "I simply can't just take your jacket; let's talk about it tomorrow."

The next day the patient returns furious, ready and fully energized to explore the encounter with her analyst. She jumps right in with, "How can you be so stupid and unfeeling? You of all people know how hard it is for me to feel I have anything of worth to offer. You know how hard it is for me to take a chance and do something risky and experimental. You know how hard it is for me to assert myself at all. And yet, you humiliate me by rebuffing my offer of something that belongs to me and that you like. I can only think it is because it is *mine* that it is distasteful to you, and I feel ashamed, and angry with you that you caused me to feel this way." At this point, the analyst feels remorseful, confused, disturbed, and humiliated herself. Now she is *truly* uncertain as to what to do, and uncertain also about what she should have done the day before. Groping for the optimal, she responds by telling her patient that the patient's offer was only made, after all, in response to herself having admired it, that it was not something the patient would otherwise have intended to give her, that it wasn't as if it were a gift she had brought in with the full expectation of presenting it. She also tells the patient that she feels remorse for how she had handled the situation up until now, that certainly she had no intention of squelching the patient's experimental mood, and that, in fact, the analyst's response was based on her own awkwardness, her own being thrown off balance. By these statements the analyst had intended to support the patient's new and tentative effort to assert herself. And the analyst's remarks did seem to repair the moderate impasse, for the next day the patient, exhibiting a new resourcefulness and a fine sensitivity and irony, ceremoniously presented her analyst with an elaborately gift-wrapped box, which of course contained the jacket. The analyst this time acted with grace and with proper, optimal responsiveness, accepting both the gift and the joyful and humorous spirit with which it was offered.

We turn now to a consideration of guidelines toward the optimal response inherent in specific diagnostic categories as recognized by various self psychological contributors. Michael Basch (1988) discusses the clinician's determination as to how affect is subjectively perceived and integrated, or not integrated, in a given patient, which Basch conceptualizes as contributing to the development of different pathological states. In his system, the pathological state itself serves as a guideline to the therapist's most appropriate and useful response. For example, Basch has identified pathological self states that result from an initial failure of the affective bond between the infant or very young child and his or her caregiver, wherein the normal regulation and self-regulation of affect is interfered with, requiring from the clinician a specific type of responsiveness, namely a responsiveness that enhances the patient's capacity to be soothed and regulated, as well as to self-soothe and self-regulate.

> A patient who has had a history of maternal deprivation begins her treatment with her therapist by coming in so late to each scheduled session that only five or ten minutes remain. The therapist responds initially by just accepting her lateness, and using what is left of their time together for attempting to deal with the patient's anxiety, which anxiety increases predictably during the session. This pattern leads the therapist to deduce that the patient's lateness is a function of the degree to which being with him causes her unbearable stimulation, so that she, either consciously or unconsciously, titrates the time with him and thereby self-regulates her anxiety within the therapeutic matrix. The strategy of not interpreting the lateness, or even questioning it, works, as the patient feels increasingly comfortable with her therapist, and can allow herself increasingly to spend more of the allotted time with him, coming less late as the therapy progresses.

This clinical vignette exemplifies the need, with patients who have suffered from a significant failure in the affective bond, for the therapist to attend first and foremost to that patient's need for soothing and regulation. Basch has also identified self states that result from failures of the caregiver to attune to and name for the child particular affect states, leaving the individual unable to identify his or her own feelings and emotions, and requiring of the clinician that he or she empathically sort out and name these feelings and emotions for and with the patient as the optimal response. Basch asserts that such pathological self states are not usefully addressed through affirmation but that this response should be reserved for the patient who recognizes his or her affect states, and feels shame in relation to them.

While Basch particularizes in this way individuals who suffer from pathological affect states and the response from the therapist that is most optimal, Stolorow and his colleagues (1987, 1992) write more inclusively about affect integration, about conditions wherein affect is rendered inaccessible to the individual. Stolorow's contribution to our understanding of the optimal response is his focus on affect attunement, offering to the therapist an approach encompassing close attention to and empathy with the patient's feeling states as they manifest in the transference.

And for another brief example of the use of diagnostic categories as guidelines toward the optimal, Arnold Goldberg (1995) has offered a comprehensive approach to the treatment of perversions. His understanding of the pathology leads him to address an interpretive mending of the vertical split viewed by him as etiologically significant in these narcissistic behavior disorders. Thus, the guideline to the optimal response offered by Goldberg is to actively interpret aspects of the vertical split, especially within the transference.

There is a final guideline toward the optimal that is to be found in an important contribution authored by Beatrice Beebe and Frank Lachmann (1994) that concerns data from infant observation as to how structure is developed, or how an infant learns in a normal parent–child relationship. They identify what they term three principles of salience to describe interaction structures in the first year of life, and include the familiar concept of disruption and repair, as well as the concept of heightened affective moments, borrowed from Fred Pine's (1990) revision of Mahler's (Mahler et al. 1975) symbiotic phase of development. But the most salient of these three avenues toward structure building observed in the infant–caregiver dyad is that of ongoing regulations, a concept developed by Beebe and Lachmann, which serves as the most overarching of these three principles. The ongoing regulations construct captures the characteristic patterns of repeated interactions, the patterns of mutual and self regulations that the infant comes to recognize and expect. This going-on-being in the infant–caregiver dyad is characterized not by dramatic moments, either disruptive or epiphemal, but by the quiet, uneventful experiences of well-being in the relationship that have largely escaped attention because of their background quality. In an earlier presentation of the ideas contained in this paper, a fourth principle of salience was noted, that of the familiar frustration-gratification sequence, but Beebe and Lachmann ultimately decided that these experiences, although present and observable in the experimental situation, were merely secondary to the other three principles noted here. This conclusion, drawn from the arena of infant and child observation, confirms the clinical sense of all of the contributors to the conversation about optimal responsiveness considered here: frustration is not a useful guide for the clinician as a method of enhancing developmental progression and structure building.

We believe that a conclusion can be drawn from this convergence of clinical and observational data; not only in the clinical importance of frustration as a vehicle for meliorative change diminished, as we just said, but more than this, the significance of ongoing mutual and self regulations in the analytic dyad is confirmed. Being safe and in sync with one's caregivers, whether in childhood or in analysis, is important for normal development and for therapeutic change.

It would seem that if these findings from the clinical situation and from the laboratory are taken seriously, one will see more reports in the literature than currently exist wherein analysis is described with less attention to disruptions that frustrate and dismay the patient, but that do make the analyst feel that he or she is truly doing analysis. If our theory doesn't focus especially on frustration and impasse, perhaps our clinical work, both as experienced and as reported, will take on a different look. We think of analyses we ourselves have conducted that are characterized by a minimum of disruption and impasse, and which have seemed to us, at moments of uncertainty and self-doubt, for that very reason, to be inadequate, incomplete, and insufficiently deep, even though the therapeutic results appear to be as good, or even better, than analyses that look like the picture a theory of optimal frustration would seem to dictate.

A patient in the field, finishing seven years of a successful training analysis, successful, that is by any measure of symptomatic and character improvement and conflict resolution, told her analyst that she cannot help but feel that something must have been missing, that both she and the analyst must have overlooked deeply buried conflicts of aggression, murder, envy, and the like. The patient would be concerned about this from time to time during the analysis, whenever she would compare her own experience with certain of her contemporaries, and especially when she would be taught by analysts who had a particular dramatic flair for the "deep"; and her analyst himself could not help but wonder whether this concern might have some validity, but try as they may, the pair could do no more than work together in a general atmosphere of calm, cooperation, and friendly feeling, despite occasional misunderstandings and disruptions.

Another analytic pair is currently completing eight years of analysis wherein the work is characterized throughout by a similar ongoingness, smooth developmental progression, and an articulation of an increasingly illuminated life narrative. In this instance the patient doesn't have any doubts about the value and depth of his analysis, but then, the patient is not in the field. The analyst, however, does worry at times that something must have been missed or overlooked—it seems on the whole to be too simple, too easy, and too pleasant an experience to be *real* analysis.

We wonder if the result of this entire contemporary psychoanalytic conversation about the optimal response might be to even further relax self psychologists, in concert with Kohut's (1984) original observations about the relative ease with which the self psychologist does his or her work.

Here is the direction we ourselves propose to take in regard to this felicitous concept of the optimal. We are in the process of completing a book, written with our colleague Mary Gales (1997), that incorporates a developmental nonlinear dynamic systems approach to self psychology. In this framework, the nonlinear aspect is specifically investigated, and through such investigation we believe the search for the optimal is facilitated. We make the underlying, broad assumption that identifying the components and patterns, including expectations, actions, and outcomes, enhances the likelihood of effectiveness of clinical work. We are speaking here, at one and the same time, of both the unique, idiographic nature of the analytic venture, and of the attempt to create within that analytic venture more lawful, nomothetic aspects as the patient and analyst gain experience with one another over time, and as the analyst gains experience with many patients over time. Like many of our colleagues, then, in their search for the optimal, we attempt to distill from within the psychoanalytic situation ways of conceptualizing emergent order among the complexities that pertain there, and it is toward this end that we have formulated a theory of developmental systems self psychology in which we focus on the centrality of self, of trauma, and of positive new experience.

References

Bacal, H. A. (1988). Reflections on "Optimum Frustration." In *Learning from Kohut*, vol. 4, ed. A. Goldberg, pp. 127–130. Hillsdale, NJ: Analytic Press.

Basch, M. (1988). *Understanding Psychotherapy: The Science Behind the Art*. New York: Basic Books.

Beebe, B., and Lachmann, F. M. (1994). Representation and internalization in infancy: three principles of salience. *Psychoanalytic Psychology* 11:127–166.

Bowlby, J. (1988). *A Secure Base*. New York: Basic Books.

Edelman, G. M. (1992). *Bright Air, Brilliant Fire: On the Matter of Mind*. New York: Basic Books.

Emde, R. N. (1988a). Development terminable and interminable. 1. Innate and motivational factors from infancy. *International Journal of Psycho-Analysis* 69:23–42.

––––––– (1988b). Development terminable and interminable. 2. Recent psychoanalytic theory and therapeutic considerations. *International Journal of Psycho-Analysis* 69:283–296.

Freud, A. (1965). *Normality and Pathology in Childhood*. New York: International Universities Press.

Freud, S. (1911–1915). Papers on technique. *Standard Edition* 12:89–171.

Friedman, L. (1996). Main meaning and motivation. *Psychoanalytic Inquiry* 15:437–460.

Goldberg, A. (1991). *The Prisonhouse of Psychoanalysis*. Hillsdale, NJ: Analytic Press.

––––––– (1995). *The Problem of Perversion: A View from Self Psychology*. New Haven: CT: Yale University Press.

Kohut, H. (1971). *The Analysis of the Self*. New York: International Universities Press.

––––––– (1977). *The Restoration of the Self*. New York: International Universities Press.

––––––– (1984). *How Does Analysis Cure?*, ed. A. Goldberg and P. Stepansky. Chicago: University of Chicago Press.

Lichtenberg, J. (1989). *Psychoanalysis and Motivation*. Hillsdale, NJ: Analytic Press.

Lichtenberg, J., Lachmann, F. M., and Fosshage, J. L. (1992). *Self and Motivational Systems*. Hillsdale, NJ: Analytic Press.

Lindon, J. A. (1994). Gratification and provision in psychoanalysis: Should we get rid of the rule of abstinence? *Psychoanalytic Dialogue* 4:549–582.

Mahler, M., Pine, F., and Bergman, A. (1975). *The Psychological Birth of the Human Infant*. New York: Basic Books.

Modell, A. (1993). *The Private Self*. Cambridge, MA: Harvard University Press.

Pine, F. (1990). *Drive, Ego, Object and Self: A Synthesis for Clinical Work.* New York: Basic Books.

Rapaport, D. (1960). *The structure of psychoanalytic theory. Psychological Issues Monograph 6.* New York: International Universities Press.

Rorty, R. (1989). *Contingency, Irony, and Solidarity.* Cambridge, MA: Harvard University Press.

Schlesinger, H. (1988). A historical overview. In *How Does Treatment Help?*, ed. A. Rothstein, pp. 7–27. Madison, CT: International Universities Press.

Shane, M., and Shane, E. (1992). One self psychology or many? *Journal of the American Psychoanalytic Association* 41:777–797.

Shane, M., Shane, E., and Gales, M. (1997). *Intimate Attachments: Toward a New Self Psychology.* New York: Guilford.

Spezzano, C. (1993). *Affect in Psychoanalysis: A Clinical Synthesis.* Hillsdale, NJ: Analytic Press.

Stern, D. (1995). *The Motherhood Constellation: A Unified View of Parent–Infant Psychotherapies.* New York: Basic Books.

Stolorow, R., and Atwood, G. (1992). *Contexts of Being: The Intersubjective Foundations of Psychological Life.* Hillsdale, NJ: Analytic Press.

Stolorow, R., Brandchaft, B., and Atwood, G. (1987). *Psychoanalytic Treatment: An Intersubjective Approach.* Hillsdale, NJ: Analytic Press.

Strenger, C. (1991). *Between Hermeneutics and Science.* New York: International Universities Press.

Trevarthan, C. (1994). Intersubjectivity in parent–infant interaction. Presented at the Institute of Contemporary Psychoanalysis, Los Angeles.

Wolf, E. (1976). Ambience and abstinence. *Annual of Psychoanalysis* 4:101–115.

———— (1989). *Treating the Self.* New York: Guilford.

5

Optimal Responsiveness from Abstinence to Usability*

KENNETH M. NEWMAN

EDITOR'S COMMENTS

In this chapter, Kenneth Newman affirms the views of David Terman (Chapter 3), Paul Tolpin (1988), John Lindon (1994), and myself (Chapter 1; also see Bacal 1992) that *abstinence* and *optimal frustration* are concepts that should be retired. Newman also extends our understanding of the theoretical, developmental, and therapeutic aspects of optimal responsiveness.

Newman describes how Winnicott's emphasis on the importance of the presence and availability of the maternal object to meet primary needs also constitutes a strong challenge to existing tenets regarding the beneficial effects of optimal frustration on development. Drawing on Winnicott's idea of the "usability" of the object, and illustrating his views with many

---

*This chapter originally appeared in the *Annual of Psychoanalysis* (1992), volume 20, pp. 131–144.

clinical examples, Newman conceptualizes optimal responsiveness as the quality of the analyst's responsivity that enables the patient to "use" him therapeutically. I agree with Newman's depiction of therapeutic usability as comprising responses of the analyst that variously include the verbal and the nonverbal. The verbal includes a host of utterances in addition to interpretation, and much of the nonverbal entails what has been variously called the analytic atmosphere by Balint (1968) or the analytic ambience by Wolf (1976). Newman agrees with Winnicott (1958) that "many patients . . . cannot dare to express their hurts and needs until some part of these needs are in some symbolic or even tangible way met"; (p. xxii) and he concurs with Kohut (1984) that selfobject connectedness is a necessary precondition for the patient's therapeutic use of the analyst. Newman in particular emphasizes the therapeutic importance of establishing a selfobject connection prior to the interpretation of the patient's dysphoric and negative affects toward the analyst. We may note that a similar view was put forth by Fairbairn when he asserted that in order to breach the patient's "closed system" that is constituted by transference, and enable the release of bad objects, analyst and analysand must first establish a good, genuine relationship (Bacal and Newman 1990).

Newman especially emphasizes that an essential aspect of the optimal responsiveness of the analyst entails the management of affect states. Referring once more to Winnicott's work on the "holding" environment and his concept of the importance of the object's "survival of destruction," he underscores the importance of the parent's and the analyst's ability, respectively, to accept the infant's and the patient's negative, rageful reactions to their selfobject failures. In other words, the failure to do this optimally in development or treatment constitutes a critical aspect of selfobject failure. Newman makes significant contributions to how the understanding of a variety of countertransference feelings may be therapeutically useful and thus constitute important challenges to the optimal responsiveness of the analyst.

References

Bacal, H. A. (1985). Optimal responsiveness and the therapeutic process. In *Progress in Self Psychology*, ed. A. Goldberg, vol. 1, pp. 202–226. New York: Guilford.

————— (1992). Optimal responsiveness: the patient's experience of the analyst's therapeutic function. Lecture presented at the Department of Psychiatry, University of Cincinnati, May 20, 1992.

Bacal, H. A., and Newman, K. M. (1990). *Theories of Object Relations: Bridges to Self Psychology*. New York: Columbia University Press.

Balint, M. (1968). *The Basic Fault*. London: Tavistock.

Kohut, H. (1984). *How Does Analysis Cure?* Chicago: University of Chicago Press.

Lindon, J. (1994). Gratification and provision in psychoanalysis: Should we get rid of "The rule of abstinence"? *Psychoanalytic Dialogues* 4:549–582.

Tolpin, P. (1988). Optimal affective engagement: the analyst's role in therapy. In *Learning from Kohut: Progress in Self Psychology*, ed. A. Goldberg, vol. 4, pp. 160–168. Hillsdale, NJ: Analytic Press.

Winnicott, D. W. (1958). Masud Khan's introduction to *Through Paediatrics to Psycho-Analysis*. New York: Basic Books.

Wolf, E. (1976). Ambience and abstinence. In *The Annual of Psychoanalysis* 4:101–115. New York: International Universities Press.

———————— ❖ ————————

Most of our patients live in an internal atmosphere chronically peopled by malignant introjects or by failing selfobjects. The environmental failures that contribute to the creation of these internal figures compose a twofold trauma. First is the inadequate parental response to primary needs, which leaves the self in a state of vulnerability with varying degrees of deficiency in self-regulation and with a pervasive sense of frustration. The second, equally important, problem is a failure on the part of the early caregivers to help the child sufficiently in the management of intense affect states consequent to the failure to gratify primary needs for mirroring and tension regulation. Often, the critical step producing pathological character formation and constricted or "frozen" objects is the secondary failure in the holding environment. The resultant crippling character defenses can be considered to be the product of heroic but distorted efforts to quiet the dangerously seething internal environment. This pathological environment contains the presence of the caregiver who failed or was in some way unreliable as a good-enough object, that is, who was in some way unable to enhance the self of the child or help it contain its painful affects.

If we are to alter this pathological atmosphere, I believe the most vital issue to be the provision or creation of a "usable" object capable of modifying the nature of this pathological state. This can best occur through the experience of an analytic relationship that differs in significant ways from one based on more traditional thinking. In the next section I briefly review contributions by Winnicott, Kohut, and others that highlight crucial ideas and background components of my thesis.

BACKGROUND CONCEPTS:
A BRIEF LITERATURE REVIEW

Before work on deeper conflicts can be confronted safely and new structures developed, the patient must achieve a connection to the therapist, whom the patient experiences as "usable." This term, first referred to by Winnicott (1971), implies an object whom the patient views as separate and as a source of emotional sustenance for the matrix of the self. The patient must be able to experience this new object (relationship) as relatively free of the compromise solutions characterized by the pathological bonds (false self) established as a reaction to the original environmental failure. How patient and analyst establish a usable connection to create something mutative and new can only be learned by trial and error, over time, and often only after stalemates, countertransference lapses, and empathic breaks. Bacal's concept of *optimal responsiveness* (see Chapter 1) is especially helpful in thinking about the quality that helps establish such a relationship. As Bacal and others (e.g., Lindon 1994, Terman [see Chapter 3], Tolpin 1988) attempted to counter old ideas about the benefits of abstinence, they naturally had to clarify the meaning of gratification as it relates to optimal responsiveness.

The troublesome issue of gratification in clinical theory can be introduced by starting with Winnicott's (1958) observations on those factors that lead to growth, enhancement, and strengthening of the self-matrix. He emphasized that the capacity to recognize an external object and place it outside comes in the context of gratifying experiences with an available mother who can adapt herself to the primary needs of the infant. Frequently using almost poetic or vague terms, Winnicott underscored the importance of the availability and presence of the maternal object, thus challenging existing tenets regarding the beneficial effects on development of optimal frustration. Application of this developmental view to the clinical situation involves the therapist's providing an environment of "usability" to facilitate the forging of a new object experience. Winnicott recognized that often the patient's resistance to accepting this provision was manifest in the rigidity of the false-self character; considerable creativity was often required on the part of the therapist to offer a mutative new object experience. In keeping with this developmental view, Winnicott (1958) advocated the selective provision of components of need satisfactions. The various ways in which he imagined the therapist might accommodate the patient were not always clear, but he did speak to a major controversial issue when he stated that "many patients . . . cannot dare to express their hurts or their needs until some part of these needs are in some symbolic or even tangible way met" (p. xxii). This is clearly a marked departure from the classical view that frustration promotes the verbal expression of wishes, fantasies, and needs. Terman offers compelling evidence from infant research that it is the presence of a gratifying object that leads to new structures in the growing infant. In the clinical situation it is the analyst's understanding, attunement, and responsiveness to the patient's needs that strengthens and enhances the self, thus making it possible for new pathways to grow and old ones to be explored. I share Terman's view that frustration plays a secondary role in the building of structure or the acquiring of patterns. Terman acknowledges Kohut as the source for the concept that positive connectedness is a necessary precondition for the patient's use of the analyst for constructive self-cohesion as well as conflict resolution.

Kohut's influence on our current thinking on the needs of the self and how it develops must be underscored. In positioning the developing and vulnerable self as the core of much of pathology, Kohut (1984) explicitly sanctions the therapist's role as transforming selfobject. By stressing the importance of permitting the self–selfobject relationship to be established as the foundation of the clinical encounter and by decentralizing the role of drives to a secondary consideration, Kohut (1977) moved closer to a nonadversarial position with respect to his patients.

The shift in clinical theory of psychoanalysis to a less adversarial, less drive-oriented relationship was further elaborated by the concept of intersubjectivity, that is, transference as a two-party system. Hoffman (1983) addresses the importance of the patient as interpreter of experience—both his own and the analyst's. This requires a revision of the classical tenets that considered the therapist merely as a receptacle for distortions and as the interpreter, as well as arbiter, of reality. The recognition that the therapist plays a crucial role in effecting the patient's immediate experience and, in turn, is himself influenced emotionally by the patient's conscious and unconscious productions changes our understanding of the overall clinical environment, largely by shifting the site and focus of therapeutic action.

These newer concepts regarding the role of the analyst are reflected in a reconsideration of the issue of management of affects and of the role of the early parent's "container" function. I refer especially to Winnicott's work on the "holding environment" and his concept of survival of destruction. Like many later clinicians (e.g., Basch 1984, Krystal 1977, Newman 1988, Stolorow and Socarides 1985), Winnicott was interested in the management of affect states, especially those activated by frustration or injury. He saw the role of the early caregivers as involving tolerance for the intensity of the infant's feelings while still remaining available and psychologically alive for the infant. This holding function could then provide the containment and integration necessary for even painful feelings to be embraced within the matrix of the infant's subjective self. I believe that faulty responses by objects to the infant's negative, rageful feelings are a critical, developmentally ominous aspect of selfobject failure. These authors have made more or less explicit the watershed effect whereby pathological defenses become instituted when the object's failure renders the fear of affects a threat to *both* the subject's psyche and his tie to the object. In many ways this reasoning parallels Winnicott's motivational explanation for false-self development.

CLINICAL EXAMPLE 1

A few years ago I held to a technical approach that often ignored the crucial significance of the atmosphere necessary for a patient to safely relive intense feelings. Let me offer an example.

A patient quickly permitted herself a therapeutic regression that opened up early developmental failures and needs. When I returned from a vacation, she requested more frequent appointments and often some extra phone contact. I was hesitant to fulfill these requests and chose instead to interpret them as an attempt to have us collude to cover over the depth of her hurt, loneliness, and accompanying rage. These interventions were always met with varying degrees of despair and protest, but fortunately the patient retained enough positive alliance to indicate to me in compelling terms the ways in which I was misguided. The gist of the matter was that while she recognized that rage was embedded in her overall reactions, she in no way could safely face these intense feeling states until I first made the steps necessary to gather our relationship back in. These steps usually included a brief period of time devoted to understanding how difficult the separation had been because it was accompanied by memories of "ruthless" abandonment by her mother and left her with a disorganizing sense of alienation. In the first few years of treatment the patient needed to feel that I was glad to be back as a way of providing an antidote to the constant potential for the dreaded anxiety that I was all too happy to have been away from her. While the patient was nearly always available to participate in verbalizing these experiences during the time immediately after a vacation, it was necessary for her to feel reimmersed in the reconnection before explanations and the acknowledgment of other affects (rage, for example) could be broached. It was only from a position of feeling reconnected (a self–selfobject union) that she could feel more secure in expressing her rage.

The issues may be illuminated by a comparison: How do our own children behave after a separation from us, and how do we relate to them? When we return from a vacation most of our children express the need for more immediate and prolonged contact, and trouble begins if we treat this as spiteful, manipulative, or otherwise illegitimate. But it would be ludicrous to say to a 4-year-old who was left behind for one or two weeks, "Come on now, don't be so clinging or insist on spending more time with me; you know it's only a reaction formation against your rage." Similarly, it is becoming more apparent that if we want to help our patients integrate intense affects, we do so best by first providing the frame to allow them to regain a sense of union both with us and within themselves. This is the security position from which they can begin to express their hurt, their loss, and their anger, both currently and as these feelings connect to the past.

In recent years the notion that we need to provide an atmosphere for safety prior to the exploration and interpretation of deeper conflicts pivoted around the concept of the therapeutic alliance. Early diatrophic (parental) components of development that contribute to the formation of the self and the maturation of the ego serve as the foundation for therapeutic and analytic work. Support for or responsiveness to these issues was seen as a necessary prerequisite for later interpretive work.

Self psychology has extended the idea of the therapeutic alliance (see Brandchaft 1990) with the addition of the idea that the vulnerable self needs a more complex connection to a selfobject in order to feel safe enough to access its deeper, more threatening reaches. Furthermore, this connection is not only a prerequisite but constitutes the beginning of the emergence of a core transference in itself.

It is the acceptance of the need for this vital transference connection that leads to the stability as well as the expansion of the self. The yield to the patient of this self–selfobject connection is the improved capacity to gain an understanding of his inner world and the acceptance of needs and hope for a new response. This then permits deeper regressions to unfold, setting the stage for more work on conflicts and primitive affect-laden material.

CLINICAL EXAMPLE 2

Another clinical vignette offers an opportunity to contrast a more traditional therapist's approach with some of the modern views just outlined.

> The patient, a divorced woman in her thirties, came for analysis because of recurrent depressions and a history of misadventures with a series of uncaring men. She had been seeing her male analyst for several weeks when she reported the following dream: the patient was to meet her analyst after regular hours on the balcony located just outside the latter's office and felt an anticipatory pleasure at the thought of the meeting.
>
> In her associations the patient thought of her compulsive mother, who brought her up by strict rules. She remembered a specific incident that occurred when she was 4 years old: she had been put outside and was not allowed to come in until a prescribed time had passed despite the fact that it was winter and extremely cold that day.
>
> The analyst's interpretation was that the patient wanted him to meet her in a special place and time as a way of breaking the rules; that is, the patient wanted to feel special in order to avoid the rage she had at her mother. Several months later, the patient requested that the therapist change a particular hour in order to accommodate a new job

schedule. The therapist remained silent at first and finally, again, interpreted the patient's wish to break the rules. In both instances the patient responded with a period of silent withdrawal followed by a determined feeling that the analyst was withholding and was, in fact, as bound by rules as her mother had been.

The technique the therapist used to address this material may seem caricatured, but it does represent the essence of a sanctioned and familiar traditional approach. The therapist's interpretation was designed to undermine what he saw as the emergence of a transference defense designed to block access to the underlying hostile maternal transference. Although it was quite early in the treatment and little work had been done on establishing a working alliance, let alone recognizing the importance in this regard of a self–selfobject relationship, the therapist's assumption was that the patient's ego would be able to manage a direct confrontation with her anger without the assurance of a solid connection with the therapist. Many analysts (Kernberg, for example) could argue convincingly that an authentic alliance can only be established after the negative transference has been made conscious and then interpreted. While conflict over hostility is surely prominent in this woman's dynamics, I believe (along with Fairbairn) that care should have been given to the establishment of a more solid therapeutic relationship before expecting such negative affects to be usefully integrated.

Whether we refer to it as attending to the therapeutic alliance or following self psychology's model (that the patient needs a reliable self–selfobject relationship as a precondition for more regressive work), a different approach might have characterized the response of many clinicians to this dream. I would rather consider the patient's communication as a desire for a new experience (unlike that with her mother), one that transcended the therapist's agendas based on arbitrary evaluations of what was good for the patient. I would have spoken to the nature of her inner world and to her chronically feared and hated relationship with her mother. By responding at this level, I think I would convey my understanding both of what she hopes for in the treatment and of what she fears being repeated. If through my grasp of the patient's inner experience I hope to "seed" the possibility of a different relationship with me, I must first convey to her some evidence of my reliable understanding of her aims. By accepting and even verbalizing what the patient is trying to attain, rather than focusing on what is being covered over, I avoid the danger of automatically being experienced as the attacking mother. To focus at this time on what is being avoided can only be experienced as criticism. Incidentally, we might reflect (at least silently) on the creativity of the patient's constructing a dream that described a new space (open but dangerous?) in which to frame a new experience.

COUNTERTRANSFERENCE: THE THERAPIST'S DILEMMAS

Having established the importance of the newer attitudes, which may best be condensed in the term *optimal responsiveness*, we need to consider the therapeutic complexities that refine the concept.

Many of our patients, having suffered the twofold selfobject failures described earlier, have had to organize protective character armor that makes our recognizing and providing optimal responsivity more difficult, if not tumultuous. Our patients naturally have erected defenses and other protective barriers that, for at least a time, make direct access to their core needs impossible. Not only do they suffer from unfulfilled needs, but they have the memory traces of needs that in their original form were thwarted; hence, the promise of reawakening hopes for fulfillment is also a threat. Why? Because it reawakens the stored-up frustration/rage/helplessness of previous encounters. The initial presenting character patterns of such patients may prevent them from making significant use of us; nor can simple empathy or logic alone help. We may be forced to stumble through a long period of trial and error before we can learn what they really need from us—and under what circumstances they will accept it. What is common to all these revisions in theoretical understanding is a recognition that however troublesome the impact on us, at root the patient is not an implacable or hostile adversary but is acting with the hope of fulfilling legitimate needs and claims. The patient should be trusted to have an ultimately reliable prescription for new constructive experience. It nearly always takes considerable time and creative effort on the part of the therapist to learn how best to provide the framework and nidus for new responsiveness.

On the way to this goal the pathological character of the patient's old solutions and restitutive (defensive) object relations will create massive obstacles that may temporarily ensnare the therapist. But out of this seemingly difficult morass of conflicts and affective storms the therapist may learn with increasingly fine sensitivity just how to be truly helpful. At a tactical level, just how does this occur?

Sampson and Weiss (1986) have referred to the unconscious plan of the patient to achieve a "non-confirmation of toxic introjects." The authors describe how the patient's character pathology confronts the therapist with a stiff test, yet the patient's ultimate hope is that the therapist will find his way out of the neurotic enmeshment and be able to offer a new, positive experience. This is a thesis that acknowledges in the patient an unconscious ally whose needs for a new constructive object—while often encoded in complex, if not contradictory, messages—can be viewed as a legitimate plea for optimal responsiveness. Like Racker (1968), these authors also see the stages of our colluding with the patient's old objects as forms of countertransference reaction. These reactions are potentially the most affectively immediate ways of tasting the patient's failed and frozen internal world. If we are willing to learn from our inevitable failures evolving out of the interaction between the patient's character with our humanness, then this troublesome "way in" may often turn out to be the most therapeutically useful "way out" (Newman 1988).

Let's look at a spectrum of clinical examples that illustrate the obstacles created by our patients' character and the challenges they raise as we attempt to recognize what therapeutic conditions are needed to achieve optimal growth.

The more benign-appearing presentations, where we see the patient's compliant, false, or performing self (the "good" patient), can prove very gratifying to the therapist in the initial stages. If we are tuned into ourselves, disquieting noises will eventually signal us to be alert to messages from the patient's unconscious. When properly deciphered, these communications, often encoded in extratransference allusions, dreams, or even symptomatic acts, convey the patients' fear that they have been or will be seduced into a compromise bond. The critical issue here is not a matter of whether we have in reality accepted this role and hence are identified with aspects of the faulty introjects but how gracefully we accept our patients' view of the situation. When we become aware that we have been unconsciously replicating these identifications and enjoying too gladly our patients' intuiting our agendas, we then have a chance to provide a constructively new experience. We first have to listen for our patients' protests, and we must validate as correct in some way their perceptions about our participating unwittingly in a collusive bond similar to that of their childhood relationships. When we allow the patient to be the interpreter of our countertransference reaction (Hoffman 1983), we set in motion a number of new and vital psychic events. By accepting our role in the current transaction, we are offering a new paradigm of "comfortable acceptance" for affect management. If we can absorb and contain without retaliation in some form the negative feelings that accompany the patient's disappointment, we can provide a holding environment that can help an internalizing process to begin. Because this leads to a deepening of the transference, in certain patients it will result in the emergence of new demands and other "regressive" manifestations. As a major player in this occurrence, we need to be prepared to consider the multilayered management issues with which this "progress" confronts us, issues that are illustrated in the following scenario.

The patient, in the context of unfolding selfobject needs or rising tension, may request or insist upon some extra contact with the analyst. Most often the patient seeks some symbolically special experience with the analyst, such as a phone call (and may even require a protracted interaction before he can hang up). The patient usually expresses conflict over this "intrusion," which he fears burdens the therapist. This has been described as an "archaic transference crisis" (Gunther 1984). While endeavoring to handle the situation with grace, at some point or on some occasion the therapist will feel oppressed but remain silent. It is here that the first serious self–selfobject disruption may occur. The patient may quickly sense the therapist's reaction. Several outcomes are now possible. The patient may simply withdraw and become emotionally detached. Or, out of anxiety, he may become more intensely demanding and plead for reassurance. If the therapist already feels put upon, he may now become openly angry or withdraw. In spite of this deteriorating situation, I believe we can use this as an opportunity to both identify with the patient's malignant introjects and work our way out to a constructive therapeutic position based on a careful understanding of the patient's world.

How to do this can be illustrated by looking at the transaction from the patient's vantage point. If the therapist is prepared to provide an atmosphere suitable to meeting regressive needs, then shouldn't he be welcoming these heretofore walled-off strivings? If we believe that significant therapeutic regressions bring forth these demands, then shouldn't we understand that we may have to not only accept being used as a new target of old object needs but also accept (willingly) for a time our own feelings of being so burdened? When we become overwhelmed and irritated by our patients and can taste the wish to criticize or even rid ourselves of them, we are getting a first-hand sample, albeit unwelcome, of their internal objects with whom we have unconsciously identified. We might silently think, "Now I know the kind of inner world you live in and why you dread showing needs and fear being rejected for being a burden, because for the moment I felt you were a burden and wished to be rid of you, too; but does this period of enactment, which I find so burdensome, even qualify as therapy?"

This interaction also represents a potential new beginning (Balint 1968) and a chance to neutralize the toxic introjects. For once we can gain some separation from this temporary, if not inevitable, countertransference reaction, we may reclaim our positive tie to the patient.

However, we must learn to discriminate between the therapeutically regressive events—involving newly awakened, albeit intensely expressed, needs on the one hand, and the repetition of old solutions that have no potential as new beginnings on the other. By the latter, I mean those addictive-like and exploitive behaviors (often described as manipulative) organized early in life in collusion with parents who were unable to meet the child's original needs in an optimal manner. These restitutional structures that represent a kind of maladaptive expedient while severely compromising made psychic survival possible for the child. Such discriminations between the emergence of unfulfilled needs and repetitive solutions are difficult to make, as illustrated by the following example.

CLINICAL EXAMPLES 3 AND 4

A single woman in her late thirties began and continued her treatment with the insistence that her therapist be responsive to her feeling that she was constantly being frustrated by men who did not conform to her specifically stated requirements. The woman therapist thoughtfully empathized with what appeared to be her patient's indirectly expressed longings for an idealizable male, whose own excitement and panache could serve as a counter to a self deadened and suffocated in an enmeshment with a distant, compliance-demanding and form-bound mother. But after a period of several years of apparent stalemate, the therapist sought supervision, and a different picture began to emerge. As the therapist became witness to her patient's rejection of almost every man who attempted to court her, we began to imagine the patient's enacting a fantasy of being a "princess," high in her fortress, viewing her would-be suitors as toads with offending warts. We began to see that her manifest character was forged out of an identification with her critical mother and, while it preserved her own sense of "specialness" and buffered her from the awareness of her own chronic sense of inadequacy, it cost her dearly in finding any real sense of satisfaction. Empathy directed at her complaint of never finding the right man actually only confirmed her defensive grandiosity. Her addiction to this hollow identification and the character pathology it sustained were difficult to discern and even approach in treatment. They required a more direct interpretation of the pathological solution and the price it exacted, leaving her isolated and lonely, before a breach could be made and genuine empathy with her fragile and neglected self could be heard. In other words, the analyst's responses that were initially optimal for this patient did not echo her subjective experience; rather, they invalidated her defensive/addictive requirement that every man who desired her was beneath her consideration.

Bearing the sometimes burdensome aspects of adapting to the needs of those patients who are reliving newly awakened needs enables us to provide a new experience that can provide new patterns and structures for affect management. Part of the new experience is the therapist's availability for tension regulation. He adapts to the patient's prescription, which sometimes includes the need for almost immediate responsivity at times that may be quite inconvenient. By so adapting, I believe we are laying the groundwork for important structural accretion. How? The patients who require and even allow themselves this form of regression also need our inherent trust that they will not misuse this auxiliary maternal function we offer. The beneficial yield in these admittedly unique cases is that the patient's psyche does use our presence, as well as our capacity to bear the painful affects and storms, to gain strength and learn new pathways for tension discharge. In time, we begin to work on certain core conflicts.

A patient of mine needed an immediate responsiveness on the phone if inevitable separations, such as a weekend break, strained the self–selfobject bond after a prolonged immersion in a fairly consistent responsiveness, before she could begin to brook tolerable delays. Previously, if I were ill and had to be away from the office, the prospect for the patient of feeling separated and experiencing my unavailability had led to unbearable tension states. These events revived so concretely the memory of a mother who was irresponsible, exposed herself to accidents, and simultaneously removed herself from my patient in what seemed to be an unfeeling fashion, that only an immediate responsiveness could help stave off traumatic anxiety. However, as confidence developed that I was understanding of the meaning of these episodes and was empathic to the urgency of her need, I could, one day when I was not really able to talk, offer a *brief* response that confirmed her need but took into account my temporary indisposition. This understanding could "hold" the situation until I could get back to her and restore the connection. Then we could talk about how the current situation was a too similar reminder of the original trauma, but she could call upon our experiences together to keep it from being identical. In retrospect, the patient could say that the enactment of the availability and reassurance of my presence were necessary as a prestage to being able to give words and then meaning to these episodes—episodes that evoked the core traumata of her earlier life. In the context of repeated experiences of having been understood, there are now periods where the patient permits delay and thereby makes it possible for us to explore and discriminate between the current reality and his conviction of having been abandoned or otherwise misused in the past. As we become more selective in our availability and responsiveness, we can introduce interpretations that take up the old issues of burden and rejection, as well as the repetitive use of maladaptive solutions in a vain attempt to heal old injuries.

CLINICAL EXAMPLE 5

The following case illustrates an especially common dilemma into which well-intended, empathically attuned therapists occasionally fall. Our usual method of providing a therapeutic atmosphere sufficient to create a new experience rests on a presumption of our available empathy, utilized to understand the inner world of our patients. I would emphasize how the nature of patients' "resistances" makes this technique eminently more complex. Sheldon Meyers (1988), in writing about a supervised case with Kohut, presents a patient who reacted with extreme irritable sensitivity and bristling rage to many of his early interventions.

> The patient was especially enraged at those interpretations that, from the therapist's point of view, were attempts to explain his current resistances to the therapist's efforts in terms of his chronic frustration with disappointing past objects. These interpretations were viewed by the patient as attempts by the therapist to force him prematurely into a "transference" relationship motivated primarily by the therapist's own needs. By having his constant negativism labeled as resistance to the therapist's interpretations, the patient felt not only rebuked but openly justified in his criticism of the therapist. He believed that his therapist's vulnerability to his repeated attacks caused the latter to both misunderstand him and to use genetic interpretations to distance himself from the validity of his accusations.
>
> A rapidly evolving stalemate was recognized and reversed, with some collaborative help from Kohut, so that a therapeutic process could develop. To place the problem conceptually, this patient needed to have his current experience validated even though it was in large part transference-based. He needed a "holding experience" that could tolerate his criticism of the therapist, who did not sufficiently understand this patient's intense need for a totally empathic selfobject. Yet while doing this, the therapist had to restrain himself from identifying this transference. A further requirement involved the therapist's accepting the patient's need to negate his attachment to the therapy without labeling it as resistance. In essence, the therapist had to contain and absorb the angry affect, validate the patient's feelings of being misunderstood, and refrain from pushing the patient to acknowledge his need for the therapeutic relationship.
>
> The early stalemate occurred because the therapist had unwittingly duplicated the role of the toxic parental introjects. Specifically, the patient was experiencing the therapist as the parents who didn't understand sufficiently his hurt feelings and who wanted to focus his hostility and negative perceptions away from themselves and onto someone or something else. When the therapist attempted to recast the persistent hostility as some form of resistance or negative therapeutic reaction, the patient experienced this as parallel to the self-

centeredness of his parents. For him, the demand that he drop his suspicion and see the therapist as meaningful and important only reproduced for him the sense he had that his parents needed him to focus on them.

This patient represents a number of patients who have reorganized their vulnerable selves around a specific kind of protective character armor. They have retreated from directly engaging their deeper emotions in meaningful contact with others. Their acute sensitivity to slight and mis-understanding is both a transference and a defense. What they require most of the therapist is that he see their world, and accept it, as emotionally valid. They especially need to have the therapist understand and tolerate (1) their massive needs for empathy, (2) their need to not have the therapist insist on the patients' acknowledgment of their multilayered transference needs prematurely, and (3) their need to have the therapist renounce his usual urge or zeal to interpret their denials as transference or resistance to insight.

For the therapist to adapt to and meet this form of need requires considerable awareness and acceptance of the inevitable countertransfer-ence, which universally accompanies the deprivation and its defensive adaptations, especially the narcissistic insult of not being considered im-portant. But if one can transcend these countertransference affects and view the patient as frozen in a state of self-protection unconsciously awaiting the finding of a new object, one who can manage not being needed, then, paradoxically, in time an interpretable transference and an analytic alliance can emerge. These issues are addressed in more detail by Bacal and Thomson in Chapter 12.

Philip Bromberg (1983) extends the conceptualization of the thera-pist's problem in accepting the patient's inability to consider him in any way other than as an extension of his own defensive grandiosity. In contrast to Kohut's view of the "understanding" phase, Bromberg feels that explana-tions about the motive for the patient's resistance can be tactfully offered. But the overall atmosphere in which the therapy is conducted is one in which the therapist meets the patient's need not to have to be forced to recognize the transference. Requiring such a premature recognition by the patient would reduplicate his feelings regarding his early caregivers' narcis-sistic needs for centrality in the relationship. Bromberg stresses that these patients have a brittle tension-regulating system dependent on their own omnipotent control. By denying the separate existence of the other, they view the other as existing simply to confirm their ability to control input. Too early or active attention to the patient's need for the therapist may seduce him into a relationship of vulnerable dependence, which may activate a regression for which the patient's fragile structure is unprepared. Allowing the patient to set the agenda is also a crucial form of holding, Bromberg suggests. It offers an object, the therapist, who will be attentive and affectively available for new pathways for structural growth while preserving the patient's illusion of self-sufficiency until the capacity for genuine dependency can be better tolerated.

In keeping with a growing understanding of the meaning of optimal responsiveness is the recognition of the copartnership perspective on treatment. Viewed from this vantage point, the therapist's interventions, both verbal and nonverbal, often will be shaped by the patient's particular need. It is therefore vital that we keep old shibboleths from interfering with our recognizing that the patient's unconscious prescription for treatment is not violating some theoretical precept of what is therapeutic. Despite some room for controversy, I hold that it is crucial to recognize that certain patients need us not to be a significant object. If, in addition, we provide the proper setting of a usable object, the matrix of the self may silently begin to expand and acquire new pathways for affect integration and a gradual ability to accept and see us as separate and eventually valuable.

References

Balint, M. (1968). *The Basic Fault*. London: Tavistock.

Basch, M. (1984). Selfobjects and selfobject transferences: theoretical implications. In *Kohut's Legacy: Contributions to Self Psychology*, ed. A. Goldberg and P. Stepansky, pp. 21–42. Hillsdale, NJ: Analytic Press.

Brandchaft, B. (1990). Varieties of therapeutic alliance. *Annual of Psychoanalysis* 18:99–114.

Bromberg, P. (1983). The mirror and the mask: on narcissism and psychoanalytic growth. *Contemporary Psychoanalysis* 19:359–387.

Gunther, M. S. (1984). The prototypical archaic transference crisis. In *Psychoanalysis: The Vital Issues*, ed. G. H. Pollock and J. E. Gedo, pp. 69–95. New York: International Universities Press.

Hoffman, I. (1983). The patient as interpreter of the analyst's experience. *Contemporary Psychoanalysis* 19:387–422.

Kohut, H. (1977). *The Restoration of the Self*. New York: International Universities Press.

———— (1984). *How Does Analysis Cure?*, ed. A. Goldberg and P. Stepansky. Chicago: University of Chicago Press.

Krystal, H. (1977). Affect tolerance. *Annual of Psychoanalysis* 3:179–218.

Lindon, J. (1994). Gratification and provision in psychoanalysis: Should we get rid of "the rule of abstinence"? *Psychoanalytic Dialogues* 4:549–582.

Meyers, S. J. (1988). On supervision with Heinz Kohut. In *Learning from Kohut: Progress in Self Psychology*, vol. 4, ed. A. Goldberg, pp. 43–60. Hillsdale, NJ: Analytic Press.

Newman, K. M. (1988). Countertransference: its role in facilitating the use of the object. *Annual of Psychoanalysis* 16:251–275.

Racker, H. (1968). *Transference and Countertransference*. New York: International Universities Press.

Sampson, H., and Weiss, J. (1986). *The Psychoanalytic Process*. New York: Guilford.

Stolorow, R., and Socarides, D. (1985). Affects and selfobjects. *Annual of Psychoanalysis* 12/13:105–119.

Tolpin, P. (1988). Optimal affective engagement: the analyst's role in therapy. In *Learning from Kohut: Progress in Self Psychology*, vol. 4, ed. A. Goldberg, pp. 160–168. Hillsdale, NJ: Analytic Press.

Winnicott, D. W. (1958). Masud Khan's introduction to *Through Paediatrics to Psychoanalysis*. New York: Basic Books.

———— (1971). The use of an object and relating through identification. In *Playing and Reality*, pp. 109–111. London: Tavistock.

6

Optimal Responsiveness and Listening/Experiencing Perspectives[1]

JAMES L. FOSSHAGE

EDITOR'S COMMENT

In this chapter, James Fosshage elaborates his perspective on a dual mode of analytic listening and describes how this facilitates the analyst's optimal responsiveness to the patient. Fosshage also enhances our appreciation of the theoretical and clinical utility of the optimal responsiveness concept and, drawing on his work with Lichtenberg and Lachmann, further elucidates its goals. In addition, Fosshage proposes a spectrum of relatedness that constitutes a guide to optimal responsivity.

Kohut (1959) trenchantly observed that "[although] introspection and empathy . . . are often linked and amalgamated with other methods of observation . . . the final and decisive observational act [in

---

1. Portions of this paper appear in "Listening/Experiencing Perspectives and the Quest for a Facilitating Responsiveness," presented at the 18th Annual Conference on the Psychology of the Self, San Francisco, October 22, 1995, and published in *Progress in Self Psychology*, vol. 13 (1997).

psychoanalysis] . . . is introspective or empathic" (pp. 209–210). In contrast to the recommendation by Kohut that has now become second nature to self psychologists, but that was revolutionary when Kohut first advocated it in 1957 (see Kohut 1959)—namely, that the analyst should consistently maintain an empathic stance vis-à-vis the patient—Fosshage proposes that the analyst should instead adopt a *dual* listening perspective. He suggests that the analyst should vary his stance, back and forth, between an empathic vantage point and a point that he calls "other-centered," as this will provide more comprehensive data about the patient's experience. These data include a series of attachment needs and needs for relatedness, which are similar to the Shanes' intersubjective relatedness (see Chapter 4) and Jacobs's subject-subject relating (see Chapter 9). Fosshage thus agrees with the Shanes and with Jacobs that the term *selfobject relatedness* does not capture the range of needs for relatedness that can generate experiences of vitalization. Fosshage puts these needs on a continuum that entails self needs or concerns (selfobject relatedness), needs for or concerns about self-with-other (intersubjective relatedness, or subject-subject relating), and needs to focus on or concerns about the other. Fosshage avers that when any of these various relational, or attachment needs are met, selfobject experience (defined as experience of vitalization) is generated. I concur with this completely, yet I would add (as I indicate in Chapter 7) that it is important to recognize a special meaning that is implied by the term *selfobject relationship*. It embodies selfobject experience, but also implies a bond with another that includes an expectation of responsiveness with regard to the need to receive—or to provide—selfobject experience.

It is interesting to consider how Fosshage's other-centered perspective might arise, and how it functions. Since what we know as we experience and relate to our patients constitutes the impact on our own subjectivity, the "other" that experiences what it is like to be in relationship with the patient is, of course, the analyst. Insofar as the analyst is attuned to his own subjectivity as reflecting or resonating with, or reacting to, the patient's "other," the analyst hears a multiplicity of complex sounds that inform the analyst about the patient's subjectivity, which variously include the spectrum of experience that Fosshage describes (the patient's self needs or concerns, needs for or concerns about self-with-other, and needs to focus on or concerns about the other). I also believe that the analyst's mode of apprehending the patient shifts with his psychical distance from the patient and that these shifts, which are reflected in the analyst's subjectivity, are variously determined by complex interactions between the subjectivities of both participants in the analytic process (Bacal in press).

In my view, Fosshage's suggestion that we add an other-centered mode of listening as well as a spectrum of modes of relating to a self-psychological way of working extends a useful bridge back to concepts and perspectives that are intrinsic to the theories and practice of (British) object-relations (Bacal and Newman 1990). I believe that Fosshage's other-centered mode of listening as well as his spectrum of modes of relating should be carefully incorporated into self-psychological theory and practice because, as he convincingly details, they provide data and perspectives that can enhance therapists' optimal responsivity to their patients.

References

Bacal, H. A. (1997). The analyst's subjectivity: how it can illuminate the analysand's experience. *Psychoanalytic Dialogues*, pp. 669–681.

Bacal, H. A., and Newman, K. M. (1990). *Theories of Object Relations: Bridges to Self Psychology*. New York: Columbia University Press.

Kohut, H. (1959). Introspection, empathy, and psychoanalysis. In *The Search for the Self*, vol. 1, ed. P. Ornstein, pp. 205–232. New York: International Universities Press.

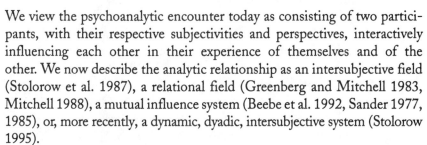

We view the psychoanalytic encounter today as consisting of two participants, with their respective subjectivities and perspectives, interactively influencing each other in their experience of themselves and of the other. We now describe the analytic relationship as an intersubjective field (Stolorow et al. 1987), a relational field (Greenberg and Mitchell 1983, Mitchell 1988), a mutual influence system (Beebe et al. 1992, Sander 1977, 1985), or, more recently, a dynamic, dyadic, intersubjective system (Stolorow 1995).

To view the analytic relationship as a complex interactive system (Fosshage 1995a) requires a far-reaching reconceptualization of the analyst's activities of listening and responding. No longer is the analyst seen as an objective listener, but as a subjectively organizing perceiver of events. No longer is the analyst seen as a removed nonparticipant, but as an interactively influencing participant. No longer is the analyst seen as a mere observer of transference, but as a variable co-determiner of transference. No longer is the analyst seen as anonymous, but as a perceived and palpable presence. No longer is the analyst seen as striving to be abstinent, but as attempting to be facilitatively engaged and responsive. No longer is the analyst seen as solely an interpreter, but as a responsive person who interprets. No longer is the analyst seen as totally neutral, but as intricately involved in attempting to help the patient.

In an effort to contribute to this ongoing reconceptualization, I will (1) delineate two listening/experiencing stances and their use in facilitating analytic work; (2) briefly address the expanded range of the analyst's responses and the striving for optimal responsiveness; and (3) examine the distinction between selfobject relatedness and intersubjective relatedness and their relationship to the two listening perspectives, as a guideline for an analyst's optimal responsiveness.

I begin my discussion of listening/experiencing perspectives in the quest for optimal responsiveness with a clinical vignette.

J. was a highly articulate, good-looking man in his mid-forties who had recently suffered a mild heart attack. The heart attack precipitated his seeking psychoanalytic treatment, for it had brought into bold relief his dissatisfaction with himself and his life, specifically that he was not living at an emotionally deep level. He described how he often felt as if he were performing and not fully present. There were those rare moments of freedom, primarily on treks away from his home in New York, when he felt more fully himself. He had never married and the heart attack intensified his desires for an intimate relationship and a family. He had dated one woman on and off for the past six years, but could not bring himself to marry her, for the relationship seemed lifeless. He kept searching for the perfect woman with whom he could sustain a passionate engagement. Similarly, while successful in a variety of career pursuits, he often found himself, after the initial excitement of a new career endeavor, becoming bored in what felt like monotonous work. He envied those who were able to sustain a meaningful involvement in their work.

J.'s parents, coming from an aristocratic European background, worked tirelessly in the father's professional business in New York City. Apart from his father's frightening violent rages primarily aimed toward J.'s older siblings, especially his brother, the atmosphere was formal and unemotional, even "deadly." The sterility of the home environment was sharply etched in a model scene (Lichtenberg et al. 1992) where J., as a boy, set up a fix-it shop in the doorway to his bedroom and waited longingly for hours for someone in his family to stop by and use it. Even in his attempt to connect through work, which had premium value in his family, he failed to elicit the recognition and sense of importance he so desired.

The issue I wish to focus on is that J. articulated with considerable urgency his search for lasting vitalizing involvement with a woman and his work. He often repeated this theme, conveying a sense that he was determined, yet totally stymied and frustrated as to how to bring it about. I was aware of feeling moved by his impassioned expressions to feel more vitally alive and, on those occasions, found myself deeply engaged and speaking with a heightened intensity as well, spontaneously matching his affect level. In light of this, it took me initially by surprise when J. first complained of my lack of emotion. He felt that I was too laid back, not passionate enough, and not really caring. As I reflected on the origins of J.'s experience, I thought that on occasion my moments of fatigue or laid-back self states could easily have contributed to his perception. I was also aware that, at certain times, J.'s routinized discussions and difficulty in being in touch with and expressive of affective experience had a deadening effect on me, a scenario that we gradually unraveled. I remained convinced, however, of my own intense emotional expressions to J. that he seemed to miss and wondered about what were the meanings and origins of the discrepancy in our subjective experiences.

While we were able to use, to a very limited extent, the discrepancy in our subjective experiences (Fosshage 1994, Wolf 1998), to further exploration of the origins of J.'s experience, we noted, with far greater effectiveness, the discrepancy between his more frequent experiences of me as emotionally "dead" with his occasional experiences of me as passionate. We used this discrepancy in his experience of me to gradually identify his proneness to experience me as indifferent and "lifeless" based on a thematic experience with his parents. More specifically, it became clear that J. wanted to impact me, wanted to feel that I cared. Yet, his lacking just this sort of relational selfobject experience appeared to make it difficult for him to experience me in this manner and, on those occasions when he did, to be able to "hold onto" the experiences, for they seemed to drift into oblivion. Based on his expectations of the affectless other, he was, I believe, often unable to register expressions of my emotional involvement with him. And, in anticipating deadness, he often affectively shut down, which, in turn, contributed to a "deadening" of me. While we identified his experience of me as "emotionless" to be thematic by noting its frequent occurrence in other relationships as well as its familial genesis, his contribution to his experience of me as lifeless could not be meaningfully addressed until he had an alternative experience of me. In order for us to create that needed alternative experience, I had to be sufficiently emotionally expressive so that J. could feel that I was meaningfully engaged with him, that he could impact me, and that he mattered. To talk about this did not suffice; words alone were too pale.

To provide the requisite affective responsiveness cannot be considered simply a matter of technique. It involved, as Kohut (1977) suggested, an empathic resonance with J.'s feelings and strivings. When I spoke more intensely, J. gradually was able to experience me as alive, caring, and emotionally engaged with him. While my affective responsiveness perhaps communicated understanding of his plight, it, in my view, provided a specific needed responsiveness (Lindon 1994) that enabled us to create together new relational selfobject experience.[2]

This new vitalizing relational experience was not sufficient, however, for J. could not store in memory these new experiences without establishing new memory categories (that is, new organizing patterns). To facilitate the establishment of new categories of experience, we noted the new experiences in contrast to his thematic expectations, that is, the old organizing patterns (Brandchaft 1994, Fosshage 1994, Lichtenberg et al. 1996, Stolorow and Lachmann

---

2. I use the term, relational selfobject experience, to refer to vitalizing attachment experiences. Kohut's (1971, 1977, 1984) mirroring, idealizing, and twinship selfobject experiences all occur within the attachment arena. Lichtenberg and colleagues (1992) posit that selfobject experience can occur in any one of five proposed motivational arenas. For example, cognitive mastery can be a vitalizing (selfobject) experience.

1984/85). We also attempted to help J. gain and maintain a perspective on his patterned view of the other as lifeless through tracking closely his experience, specifically what followed ongoing selfobject experience and what precipitated ruptures. We discovered that the older and more firmly rooted view of the lifeless other, offering a cohesive sense of familiarity, easily reemerged and usurped psychic space. In addition, we discovered that J., at times, retreated from experiencing and expressing his feelings for fear of the retaliatory "father," for fear that he would be hurtful (like father), and for fear that his feelings would not be responded to (a dreaded repetition of past experience [Ornstein 1974] with his mother and father).

Here is a synopsis of what I believe were the facilitative treatment features. The analysis of the transference and the analyst's sufficient responsiveness to selfobject needs combined to create new self-enhancing relational experiences. These new experiences, in turn, gradually established new and more vitalizing percepts of self, other, and self-with-other. More specifically, the analysis of the transference involved two central parts. First, we were able to identify through empathic inquiry the repetitive organizing pattern of the "lifeless" and deadened other. Through my "deadened" experience as the other, using the other-centered stance (described below) we were able to observe the impact of this organizing pattern on his relationships. Second, through empathic inquiry, we were able to create an analytic ambiance (Wolf 1976) of safety, acknowledgment, and understanding that facilitated his expression of his determined search for the developmentally requisite mirroring selfobject experience. In response to these relational selfobject needs, I became, through affect resonance and role responsiveness (Lichtenberg et al. 1992, Sandler 1976), more emotionally expressive and affirming to enable us to create together the needed selfobject experience. In other words, my interpretation (understanding and explaining) of the transference served both to expand awareness and to provide interactionally a needed mirroring response. Additional responsiveness to J.'s striving for needed mirroring selfobject experience, however, was required.

THE ANALYST'S LISTENING/EXPERIENCING PERSPECTIVES

Relativistic science clarified that (1) an analyst's observations are not only shaped by the patient, but also by the analyst; and (2) there are two perspectives in the analytic arena, neither of which is objective. In response to this paradigmatic shift, Kohut, updating psychoanalytic epistemology, formulated and recommended the consistent use of, what he called the empathic mode of observation. When using the empathic mode, an analyst's task is to hear and to understand the analysand's experience from within the analysand's perspective, recognizing that the analyst still shapes, more or less, what is heard. While all analysts variably use the empathic mode of perception, self psychologists, following Kohut, stipulate that we need to listen consistently from within the patient's perspective.

The use of the empathic mode of perception, in my view, needs to be primary in the pursuit of understanding the patient's subjective experience; yet, the empathic listening stance does not fully encompass how analysts listen to and experience their patients. Instead, I have proposed that analysts can shift experientially between two principal listening vantage points (Fosshage 1995b). I refer to these as listening/experiencing vantage points, for, as we listen, we experience the patient.

An analyst can resonate with the patient's affect and experience from within the patient's vantage point, the *empathic mode of perception* (what I also call the subject-centered listening perspective), self psychology's emphasis; and an analyst can experience the patient from the vantage point of the other person (in this case, the analyst) in a relationship with the patient, what I call the *other-centered listening perspective* (also referred to as "as-the-other" listening stance), frequently an emphasis in object relations and interpersonal approaches. While both listening/experiencing modes are variably shaped by the analyst's subjectivity (including the analyst's theories), the other-centered mode, frequently being less near to the patient's immediate experience, potentially lends itself to more idiosyncratic shaping by the analyst. When an analyst inquires as to a patient's feeling about a transaction that occurred in the analysis, the analyst is attempting to hear the patient's perspective, the empathic or subject-centered mode. When we view patients, for example, as seductive, controlling, humorous, or sensitive, we are listening and experiencing the patient as the other in a relationship with the patient, the other-centered perspective. When we listen, for example, to so-called extra-analytic situations, we make assessments not in an objective fashion, but through oscillating from the within and as-the-other perspectives with both the patient and the other person to decipher what is occurring.

I have proposed that in psychoanalysis the empathic and other-centered stances are the two principal methods of listening to our analysands' experiences and that important data are gathered through each listening stance. While it is primary and crucial to understand from within the patient's perspective, listening and experiencing as the generic other in a relationship with the patient (keeping in mind our variable shaping of our experience) is also useful in understanding how the patient tends to construct relationships. While we cannot safely infer motivation on the basis of the effects on others, the effects on others can inform us about relational scenarios. In oscillating between these two listening perspectives, an analyst can learn more about the patient's self and self-with-other experience. With J., for example, I learned about his fear and experience of deadness in relationships through empathic inquiry. Apart from my contributions to J.'s experience, I learned through my experience as-the-other in a relationship with J. about how J., through his aversiveness to affect, currently contributed to the deadness of the other that he readily experienced in his relationships. The data gathered through each listening stance was used interpretively to provide a more comprehensive understanding of J. and his relationships.

THE ANALYST'S RESPONSES

Apart from exploratory questions, Freud (1911–1915) designated interpretations to be the principal form of psychoanalytic intervention, for the aim of interpretation is to bring about insight, the principal change agent within the classical model. In contrast, Ferenczi began a long lineage, developed in British object relations and here in the various relational approaches, of emphasizing the relational experience as being central to the therapeutic action in psychoanalysis (Friedman 1978). From an interactive systems perspective, the focus shifts to the patient's relational experience within the analytic encounter, which includes but is not limited to insight. A patient's relational experience emerges within the ongoing interaction and reflects more accurately the impact of that complex interaction. It also opens the door to investigate the wide range of analyst's responses that are facilitative of a therapeutic experience.

Let us briefly follow the shift of emphasis from interpretation to relational selfobject when considering therapeutic action from within self psychology. True to his classical roots, Kohut initially viewed interpretation as the principal form of intervention. In the 1970s and 1980s Kohut and many self psychologists recommended that we interpret selfobject needs, not "gratify" them (Goldberg 1978). As a legacy of classical theory, this dichotomy between gratifying (that is, responding to) and interpreting (that is, understanding and explaining) the patient's selfobject needs was created, and interpretation became, for a number of years, in self psychology the singular acceptable analytic intervention. Ironically, interpretation still carries remnants of positivistic purity. Viewing interpretation as "objective" obfuscated the idea that interpretation was a response of the analyst (Gill 1994, Namnum 1976), that could gratify selfobject needs (Fosshage 1995a; also see Chapters 1 and 3).

Kohut, in concurrence with Ferenczi (1932), Alexander (1956), Fairbairn (1958), Winnicott (1965), Balint (1968), and Guntrip (1968), among the most notable, recognized, however, that interpretation alone is insufficient. An analyst cannot be a computer, using Kohut's language (1977), but must be engaged at the deeper levels of his or her personality. An analyst must be sufficiently responsive (akin to Winnicott's [1965] notions of a "good-enough mother" and of a "facilitating environment") to enable the analysand to make use of the analyst for developmental and regulatory purposes. A patient, for example, may need his analyst to be sufficiently affirming to establish a positive sense of self. Kohut (1977) called this modulated responsiveness, the "average expectable empathic responsiveness" (p. 252) or, more simply, "empathic responsiveness." By empathic responsiveness, he was referring to an analyst's human warmth and emotional responsiveness emanating from a deep involvement in working analytically from an empathic perspective.

While Kohut never deviated from the importance of interpretative work, when considering therapeutic action, the center of gravity gradually shifted away from insight, the product of interpretation, to self development occurring within the "self–selfobject" matrix of the analytic relationship. Kohut (1984), in his last book, suggested that change does not take place in the cognitive sphere per se, but occurs principally through the emergence of selfobject needs in the transference and the reparation through interpretation of the inevitable and optimally frustrating selfobject ruptures. While reparation of selfobject ruptures was the principal route to self development, he also included (although mentioning it only once in his last book) ongoing selfobject experience within the analytic relationship as structure producing. To use Kohut's (1984) words, "[the analyst's] on the whole adequately maintained understanding leads to the patient's increasing realization that, contrary to his experiences in childhood, the sustaining echo of empathic resonance is indeed available in this world" (p. 78). Embracing the relational selfobject experience more fully, Kohut responded to the anticipated "ill-disposed critic" who would call this process a "corrective emotional experience" with an unabashed acceptance, "So be it" (p. 78).

It is this internalization of the ongoing selfobject tie that Marion Tolpin (1983) suggested, and this repetitive "experience of the analyst-as-understanding" that Terman (Chapter 3) subsequently emphasized as structure building. And emerging out of infant research, Beebe and Lachmann (1994) conclude that the most salient avenue of structure building observed in the infant–caregiver dyad is that of ongoing regulations, that is, the characteristic patterns of regulatory interactions. Thus, from Kohut's emphasis on rupture, optimal frustration, and repair, our model of analytic change is shifting to an emphasis on the patterns of regulatory interactions that occur in the analytic relationship, of which rupture and repair is only one and not necessarily the most important. Examples of regulatory interactions (in this instance, regulatory for the patient) that through their consistency typically (depending on their meaning to a patient) facilitate analysis and a patient's development include (1) the implicit affirmation inherent in an analyst's concentrated listening and interest in a patient's experience, (2) the patient's self-empowering experience of impacting the analyst, (3) the calm and safe ambiance of an analytic relationship, (4) the mutual self-reflection, (5) the validation of a patient's experience, (6) the experience of the analyst-as-understanding, (7) the analyst's interpreting that expands awareness, (8) the patient's efficacy experience of change, and (9) the analyst's efforts to help the patient, offering a fundamental underpinning of emotional support.

Recognizing that analytic cure does not occur solely in the cognitive sphere and increasingly emphasizing the curative importance of new relational selfobject experience have gradually broadened the view of the analyst's activity beyond the bounds of exploration and interpretation

(Fosshage 1991). These shifts have enabled us to recognize the analyst's complex interactive involvement in the analytic relationship. These movements within self psychology have reciprocally influenced and been influenced by developments within relational approaches to psychoanalysis at large (Fosshage 1992, 1995a, Greenberg and Mitchell 1983, Mitchell 1988, Skolnick and Warshaw 1992).

A new term was needed that would better capture and help us to conceptualize the broad range of the analyst's activity, specifically the analyst's responsiveness that facilitated self development. To capture the broad range of analysts' responses, Howard Bacal, in 1985 (Chapter 1, this volume), provided us with the needed inclusive term, *optimal responsiveness*. Bacal broadly defines optimal responsiveness "as the responsivity of the analyst that is therapeutically most relevant at any particular moment in the context of a particular patient and his illness" (p. 5). Bacal initially emphasizes his description of optimal responsiveness as "the therapist's acts of communicating his understanding to his patient" (p. 5). Yet, interpretation, for Bacal, is only one form of communicating understanding to a patient, and not necessarily the most therapeutic. Expanding the interactive avenues for communicating understanding, Bacal notes that frequently a patient requires some noninterpretive action to feel understood. Bacal (1988) has aptly described this as the patient saying to the analyst, "Be who I need you to be; don't just interpret it."

> In a session some years ago I was making an interpretation and was priding myself over what I thought to be a particularly astute formulation. When I finished, my patient said, "Oh Jim, your words are so soft and comforting, just pour them over me." It was the affective tone of my words, not the content, that carried the day. I do not think that my patient was defending against what I was interpretively addressing, nor that she was aversive to my agenda to convey "insight." Rather, I believe that I became who she needed me to be at that moment by intuitively regulating my vocal tonality in keeping with her need for soothing and comfort.

Understanding involves the analyst's interest, acknowledgment, validation, and acceptance of the patient's experience and, on occasion, an explanation that expands awareness. While communication of understanding is central to the analytic process and therapeutic action, it falls short, in my view, in capturing the full range of what patients seek and developmentally need. For J., my more intense engagement and heightened affect may have conveyed my understanding to him about his need for others to be emotionally present. More importantly, however, my actions significantly contributed to developmentally needed relational experience. While in such instances understanding of the patient may serve as the basis for an analyst's action, understanding is a background feature for both patient and analyst in the action itself. Similarly, when an anxious patient is in need of a calm, protective person, an analyst's calm and soothing attitude conveys more than understanding—in Lindon's (1994) terminology, the analyst's attitude "provides" the responsiveness needed for self regulation.

Perhaps in response to such considerations, Bacal, in 1990, importantly both broadened and particularized his concept of optimal responsiveness as "the therapist's acts of communicating to his patient in ways that that particular patient experiences as usable for the cohesion, strengthening, and growth of his self" (p. 361). In other words, optimal responsiveness refers to the therapist's responses that facilitate a patient's selfobject experience and, therein, encompasses the Ornsteins' (1984) empathic responsiveness, Paul Tolpin's (1988) optimal affective engagement, Stolorow's (1993) affective responsiveness, Lindon's (1994) optimal provision, and the Shanes' (chapter 4) optimal restraint.

While "responsiveness" reflects the asymmetry of the analytic relationship in that the patient is in the forefront of focus and more often takes the lead in action, it needs to be understood, as Bacal makes clear in Chapter 7, that optimal responsiveness emerges within and is particular to each patient–analyst interactive system.

The term *optimal responsiveness* addresses the fact that the complex interaction within the analytic process entails, and requires, subtleties and varieties of analytic response, far beyond our notions of interpretation, to facilitate a therapeutic process.

Let us consider Kohut's (1984) well-known example of a "confrontative" intervention. In the third year of treatment, his analysand, a psychiatric resident who often drove "like a bat out of hell" (p. 74), was describing with anger and "a trace of challenging arrogance" his having received a speeding ticket. After forewarning him that he was going to give him the deepest interpretation yet, Kohut said firmly, "You are a complete idiot" (p. 74). After a second of silence, "the patient burst into a warm and friendly laughter and relaxed visibly on the couch" (p. 74). Why was this intervention facilitative? The patient had been viewed as the genius in his family, causing his father to pull away and form an alliance with the elder brother. Kohut's "confrontation," I believe, provided a needed relational experience wherein Kohut, as a caring father, was not intimidated and avoidant of this man's superior attitude and braggadocio, but was able to take the patient on man-to-man. Perhaps Kohut's comment implicitly conveyed an understanding that the patient needed an involved father, but, more importantly, Kohut through his comment was, in action, as the patient needed him to be, in creating a developmentally requisite relational experience.[3]

NEEDS AND RELATEDNESS INVOLVING SELF, SELF-WITH-OTHER, AND OTHER

While self psychology has focused principally on selfobject needs, that is, the use of the other for self-regulatory purposes, the selfobject dimension of relatedness is only one dimension of relatedness (Shane and Shane, Chapter 4, Stolorow 1986). More recently, based on Stern's (1985) infant research, there has been an emergent emphasis, both within and outside of self psychology, on the patient's need to relate to a separate other and to experience the other's subjectivity, what has been referred to as intersubjective relatedness (Aron 1991, Benjamin 1988, Shane and Shane 1989, also see Chapter 4, Slavin and Kriegman 1992), subject–subject relatedness (Jacobs, Chapter 9), or self-with-other relatedness (Fosshage 1995a,b).

In describing intersubjective relatedness, the Shanes first quote Stern (1994): "It is an interactive state of 'I know that you know that I know,' and 'I feel that you feel that I feel'" (p. 11). Emde's (1988) description follows, which I sense to be a progressively fuller interest in the other's subjectivity: "I care to know and feel all about us, about you, about me, and about our 'we-ness.'"

An analysand, who was in the field and savvy about these issues, sat down and exclaimed: "Jim, I am going to ask you a question. Enough of this empathic shit, I want your opinion!" While I am aware that

---

3. Bacal (1995) independently arrived at a very similar conclusion.

there are a number of ways of understanding this comment, I believe that she was addressing my proclivity (and, incidentally, hers when she functioned as an analyst) to understand from within the other's perspective. On this occasion, she desired input about herself from me as a person with a different subjectivity and perspective—input to be reflected on and considered. I, thus, gave her my opinion.

When, as an adult, an individual's motivation for attachment gains priority, attachment needs and forms of relatedness, in my view, are best conceptualized as ranging along a continuum involving self needs[4] *or concerns* (what the Shanes call selfobject relatedness), needs for or concerns about self-with-other (what Stern, Benjamin, Aron, and the Shanes call intersubjective relatedness; what Jacobs calls subject-subject relatedness), and needs to focus on or concerns about the other (an area of relatedness that has not been sufficiently acknowledged). For example, in a state of self fragility, self concerns and the need for a mirroring or idealized other are in the forefront. In the mid-range of the continuum, when one is feeling more centered, concerns and desires about self-with-other emerge, along with a mutuality and a different quality of intimacy. And at the other end of the continuum, a more exclusive focus on the concerns and subjectivity of the other has still another quality of relatedness that is more like a parent to a child, a teacher to a student, and a friend to a friend in need, and is highlighted in Erikson's (1959) stage of generativity. Yet, who the other is and what the other's subjectivity is are important throughout the entire range of self, self-with-other, and other concerns—it is a matter of degree and of focus. On those occasions when we are feeling vulnerable—for example, an important decision is about to be made—and self concerns are in the foreground, the opinion of the other may be sought out to expand one's awareness (the self-with-other dimension) and to shore up the self (the selfobject dimension). Even when one's self concerns and the need for mirroring are in the forefront, it matters who the other is and the nature of

---

4. Self needs, in a broad sense, traverse the whole continuum of needs, concerns, and relatedness. Yet, when I refer to self needs here more narrowly, I am designating when one's sense of self, and its regulation, is in the forefront of experience and involves, more poignantly, the mirroring, idealizing, and twinship selfobject needs that Kohut delineated.

the other's subjectivity—for example, Does the person like us or not? How significant is he or she to us?

When any of these various attachment needs are met, selfobject experience is generated. While we know well that an adequate response to a needed mirroring experience is vitalizing, to encounter another's subjectivity when one is feeling sufficiently consolidated also promotes a vitalizing (selfobject) experience. The so-called antagonistic or adversarial selfobject, as delineated by Wolf (1980) and Lachmann (1986), is, for example, one type of vitalizing experience with an intersubjective other. And generative acts of parenting a child and guiding and helping another can be vitalizing and self-enhancing. Accordingly, to speak of selfobject relatedness does not capture the range of relatedness that can generate selfobject experience.

Each experience of relatedness tends to activate expectations and constructions based on lived experience. Viewing these concerns or forms of relatedness on a continuum and always emergent within an intersubjective matrix positions us clinically, as Stolorow and colleagues (1987) have stressed, to remain alert to the problematic organizing patterns that are triggered.

The clinical implications of this relatedness continuum are profound. When self needs are in the foreground, the other's subjectivity is important to the extent that it can be used for self-regulatory purposes. Other aspects of the other's subjectivity can be experienced as intrusive and rupturing of the selfobject connection. On the other hand, when self-with-other needs are in the forefront, the insufficient presence of the other and the other's subjectivity can be experienced as frustrating and rupturing of the selfobject connection. One patient, for example, exclaimed, "I need to know your reactions to me as a person, how you experience me in a relationship." And when a patient is genuinely focusing on concerns for the other—for example, a patient inquires about the analyst's disturbed mood or ill health—the analyst needs to gracefully accept the patient's concern, rather than viewing it necessarily as a problematic relational pattern or as resistance to analytic work (for example, as solicitous or switching the focus).

Each of the two listening/experiencing stances positions the analyst advantageously across the spectrum of attachment needs and forms of relatedness. When self needs are in the foreground, the empathic mode, in its singular focus on a patient's self experience, provides a basis for optimally responding to the patient and for facilitating self cohesion. When a patient shifts to self-with-other concerns, listening and experiencing as the other in a relationship with the patient—the other-centered perspective—can provide needed information about a patient's relational experience. This other-centered information involves how a patient contributes to his relational experience, not only through his organization of experience but also through his impact on others. While a patient who needs primarily a mirroring experience can easily be thrown into self disequilibrium by the intrusion of the analyst's remarks based on the other-centered perspective, to remain exclusively in the empathic mode of listening can result in depriving a patient of information needed to understand his relational experience. Moreover, when self-with-other needs are in the foreground, to remain in the empathic mode exclusively will deprive the patient of the necessary subject-to-subject interaction. Lastly, when a patient is focused on the need to be concerned with the other, the empathic mode can help an analyst tune into the patient's inner experience, and the other-centered mode can help an analyst to experience the patient's empathic gestures, providing a fuller understanding of the patient.

I present the following brief clinical vignette to illustrate the interweaving of self and self-with-other dimensions of relatedness, and the analyst's use of the two listening perspectives to enhance understanding.

Several years ago I had begun psychoanalytic treatment with a woman who was extremely sensitive, perceptive, and reactive. She was quite labile in mood and prone to fragile self-states. Easily feeling impinged upon, she experienced natural light in my office as painfully too bright, for which, at her request, I regularly adjusted the blinds. Both of her parents had been remarkably absent, with her mother often feeling overwhelmed. She had a prolonged incestuous relationship with her older brother and, when she would cry out to her mother for protection, her mother pushed her away with "leave me alone, you're killing me." She felt that her life had been saved by her previous analyst, who had been her first real caregiver. His move to another city unfortunately aborted treatment and forced her to find another analyst, a very painful process.

During a session toward the end of the first month, I experienced the room as uncomfortably warm and went to the window to adjust the ventilation. At the following session she related how upset she was with me for my getting up in the middle of the session, when she was talking, to stare out the window. Being taken aback by what, to me, was a very idiosyncratic perception and knowing that our capacity to share humor often helped her to regain perspective, I, in a somewhat humorous self-mocking vein, said, "The mark of a good analyst—get up in the middle of a session and stare out the window." In this instance, it was a misjudgment, for she was far too hurt with her particular framing of the event to join in. Instead, she felt invalidated, and perhaps even ridiculed. Recapturing my empathic stance, I inquired about her experience when I had gone to the window (what Lichtenberg and colleagues [1992] call wearing the attributions). She had felt that I was uninterested in what she was saying. I reflected that her feeling that I went to stare out the window while she was talking and was uninterested in her understandably was quite hurtful to her. She appeared to feel better that I had heard, understood, and validated her experience; yet, she was still consumed by the injury and her particular organization of the event. Clearly she needed to be able to free herself from this particular pattern of experiencing the event in order to regain more fully her self-equilibrium. To that end, I inquired toward the end of the session if she would like to hear about my experience as to what prompted me going to the window. Possibly the use of the discrepancy of our experiences, I thought, would be useful in illuminating her view of the uninterested other and offering an alternative perspective. She declined.

In the following session, two days later, she told me that she had not wanted to hear my point of view at the previous session and somewhat humorously, yet pointedly, remarked, "Jim, when I come into the room, just check your subjectivity at the door." I smiled and told her that I would try my best, although it could prove difficult on occasion. We then proceeded with her experience and were able to focus on how precarious she felt my interest in her was. At one point it dawned on me what was occurring when she felt overwhelmed by my subjectivity, and I interpreted in a general manner, "I think I understand that when I do something suddenly, like go to the window, or bring my subjective viewpoint in here, that it feels like I am taking up all the space in here, that there is no room for you, for your thoughts and desires, and I sense that you must have felt just that way with your brother." She notably relaxed and acknowledged that she thought I was right. Shortly afterward, she smiled and said, "Now, you can let me know what was happening for you at the window." I then explained that I was uncomfortably warm, had assumed she was too and did not ask her, thinking that it would be more disruptive, and had adjusted the window to get more air. She smiled and felt reassured.

In light of the rupture and her fragile self-state, she needed me to hear and understand her feelings—self-relatedness was in the forefront. It was also crucially important to make sense out of her experience by illuminating the particular relational scenario or organizing pattern that had been triggered—an aspect of self-with-other relatedness—for her to feel fully understood and to enable her to restore self-equilibrium. So long as she framed the events as indicative of my lack of interest in her, she surely would be unable to feel fully restored. My interpretation of the transference in the here and now, and its origins, was based on both listening stances, that is, on my empathic grasp of her experience of me and on my other-centered experience as the intrusive, overwhelming other in relationship with the patient. Following the interpretation, she felt, through a sense of being heard and understood, sufficiently consolidated to be able to relate self-with-other more fully and inquired about my experience. Airing the discrepancies in our experiences further illuminated her particular organization as well as served as a basis for the establishment of an alternative perspective.

CONCLUSION

The emergent contemporary view of the psychoanalytic arena that increasingly is gaining momentum and definition is of two people, patient and analyst, interactionally engaged in pursuit of fostering the patient's development. Patients enter treatment hoping for the requisite developmental experiences. They also enter treatment with problematic expectations based on thematic lived experience. Traditionally, analysis has focused on the repetitive transferences or, what is called from a contemporary perspective, problematic organizing patterns. Self psychology has contributed to our understanding that an analyst must be sufficiently available so that patient and analyst can find a way of creating the necessary developmental experiences. While understanding and explaining the problematic transferential experiences provides one basis for needed experience, patients often require more poignant interactions with analysts to create needed relational selfobject experience. Even the analysis of transference requires experience with the analyst that contrasts with deeply embedded convictions about the nature of reality (that is, patterns of organization) in order to enable their illumination. Accordingly, the range of responses required of an analyst has expanded far beyond the bounds of exploration and interpretation and is more adequately captured by the term *optimal responsiveness*. I have proposed that the use of both empathic and other-centered listening perspectives enhances understanding of a patient and enables an analyst to relate more flexibly and facilitatively depending on whether a patient's self, self-with-other, or other concerns have motivational priority. Based on this understanding, an analyst uses a complex and subtle tapestry of verbal and nonverbal responses to facilitate the patient's development.

References

Alexander, F. (1956). *Psychoanalysis and Psychotherapy*. New York: Norton.

Aron, L. (1991). The patient's experience of the analyst's subjectivity. *Psychoanalytic Dialogues* 1:29–51.

Bacal, H. (1988). Reflections on "optimum frustration." In *Progress in Self Psychology*, vol. 4, ed. A. Goldberg, pp. 127–131. Hillsdale, NJ: Analytic Press.

——— (1990). The elements of a corrective selfobjective experience. *Psychoanalytic Inquiry* 10:347–372.

——— (1995). The essence of Kohut's work and the progress of self psychology. *Psychoanalytic Dialogues* 5:353–366.

Balint, M. (1968). *The Basic Fault*. London: Tavistock.

Beebe, B., Jaffe, J., and Lachmann, F. (1992). A dyadic systems view of communication. In *Relational Perspectives*, ed. N. Skolnick and S. Warshaw, pp. 61–81. Hillsdale, NJ: Analytic Press.

Beebe, B., and Lachmann, F. (1994). Representation and internalization in infancy: three principles of salience. *Psychoanalytic Psychology* 11:127–166.

Benjamin, J. (1988). *The Bonds of Love: Psychoanalysis, Feminism, and the Problem of Domination*. New York: Pantheon.

Brandchaft, B. (1994). To free the spirit from its cell. In *The Widening Scope of Self Psychology, Progress in Self Psychology*, vol. 10, ed. A. Goldberg, pp. 209–230. Hillsdale, NJ: Analytic Press.

Emde, R. N. (1988). Development terminable and interminable: 2. Recent psychoanalytic theory and therapeutic considerations. *International Journal of Psycho-Analysis* 69:283–296.

Erikson, E. (1959). *Identity and the Life Cycle.* New York: Norton.

Fairbairn, W. R. D. (1958). On the nature and aims of psycho-analytical treatment. *International Journal of Psycho-Analysis* 39:374–385.

Ferenczi, S. (1932). *The Clinical Diary of Sandor Ferenczi,* ed. J. Dupont. Cambridge, MA: Harvard University Press, 1988.

Fosshage, J. (1991). Beyond the basic rule. In *The Evolution of Self Psychology, Progress in Self Psychology,* vol. 7, ed. A. Goldberg, pp. 64–71. Hillsdale, NJ: Analytic Press.

——— (1992). Self psychology: the self and its vicissitudes within a relational matrix. In *Relational Perspectives in Psychoanalysis,* ed. N. Skolnick and S. Warshaw, pp. 21–42. Hillsdale, NJ: Analytic Press.

——— (1994). Toward reconceptualizing transference: theoretical and clinical considerations. *International Journal of Psycho-Analysis* 75(2):265–280.

——— (1995a). Interaction in psychoanalysis: a broadening horizon. *Psychoanalytic Dialogues* 5(3):459–478.

——— (1995b). Countertransference as the analyst's experience of the analysand: the influence of listening perspectives. *Psychoanalytic Psychology* 12(3):375–391.

Freud, S. (1911–1915). Papers on technique. *Standard Edition* 12:89–171.

Friedman, L. (1978). Trends in psychoanalytic theory of treatment. *Psychoanalytic Quarterly* 47:524–567.

Gill, M. (1994). *Transitions in Psychoanalysis.* Hillsdale, NJ: Analytic Press.

Goldberg, A., ed. (1978). *The Psychology of the Self: A Casebook.* New York: International Universities Press.

Greenberg, J., and Mitchell, S. (1983). *Object Relations in Psychoanalytic Theory.* Cambridge, MA: Harvard University Press.

Guntrip, H. (1968). *Schizoid Phenomena, Object Relations and the Self.* London: Hogarth.

Hoffman, I. Z. (1992). Some practical implications of a social-constructivist view of the psychoanalytic situation. *Psychoanalytic Dialogues* 2:287–304.

Kohut, H. (1971). *The Analysis of the Self.* New York: International Universities Press.

——— (1977). *The Restoration of the Self.* New York: International Universities Press.

——— (1984). *How Does Analysis Cure?* Chicago: University of Chicago Press.

Lachmann, F. (1986). Interpretation of psychic conflict and adversarial relationships: a self-psychoanalytic perspective. *Psychoanalytic Psychology* 3:341–355.

Lichtenberg, J., Lachmann, F., and Fosshage, J. (1992). *Self and Motivational Systems: Toward a Theory of Technique.* Hillsdale, NJ: Analytic Press.

——— (1996). *The Clinical Exchange: Technique from the Standpoint of Self and Motivational Systems.* Hillsdale, NJ: Analytic Press.

Lindon, J. (1994). Gratification and provision in psychoanalysis: Should we get rid of "The rule of abstinence"? *Psychoanalytic Dialogues* 4:549–582.

Mitchell, S. (1988). *Relational Concepts in Psychoanalysis*. New York: Basic Books.

Namnum, A. (1976). Activity and personal involvement in psychoanalytic technique. *Bulletin of the Menninger Clinic* 40:105–117.

Ornstein, A. (1974). The dread of repeat and the new beginning. *Annual of Psychoanalysis* 2:231–248.

Ornstein, A., and Ornstein, P. (1984). *Empathy and the therapeutic dialogue.* Presented at the Fifth Annual Psychotherapy Symposium on "Psychotherapy: the therapeutic dialogue," Harvard University, The Cambridge Hospital, Boston, MA, June 28–30.

Sander, L. (1977). The regulation of exchange in the infant–caretaker system and some aspects of the context-content relationship. In *Interaction, Conversation, and the Development of Language*, ed. M. Lewis and L. Rosenblum, pp. 133–156. New York: Wiley.

——— (1985). Toward a logic of organization in psycho-biological development. In *Biologic Response Styles*, ed. K. Klar and L. Siever. Washington, DC: American Psychiatric Press.

Sandler, J. (1976). Countertransference and role-responsiveness. *International Review of Psycho-Analysis* 3:43–47.

Skolnick, N., and Warshaw, S. (1992). *Relational Perspectives in Psychoanalysis*. Hillsdale, NJ: Analytic Press.

Slavin, M., and Kriegman, D. (1992). *The Adaptive Design of the Human Psyche*. New York: Guilford.

Stern, D. (1985). *The Interpersonal World of the Infant*. New York: Basic Books.

——— (1994). The maternal constellation. Presentation at Cape Cod, MA.

Stolorow, R. (1986). On experiencing an object: a multidimensional perspective. In *Progress in Self Psychology*, vol. 2, ed. A. Goldberg, pp. 273–279. New York: Guilford.

——— (1993). Thoughts on the nature and therapeutic action of psychoanalytic interpretation. In *The Widening Scope of Self Psychology, Progress in Self Psychology*, vol. 9, ed. A. Goldberg, pp. 31–43. Hillsdale, NJ: Analytic Press.

——— (1995). *Dynamic, dyadic, intersubjective systems: an evolving paradigm for psychoanalysis*. Presented at the American Psychological Association Division 39 Spring meeting, Los Angeles, CA.

Stolorow, R., Brandchaft, B., and Atwood, G. (1987). *Psychoanalytic Treatment: An Intersubjective Approach*. Hillsdale, NJ: Analytic Press.

Stolorow, R., and Lachmann, F. (1984/85). Transference: the future of an illusion. *Annual of Psychoanalysis* 12/13:19–37.

Tolpin, M. (1983). Corrective emotional experience: a self psychological reevaluation. In *The Future of Psychoanalysis*, ed. A. Goldberg, pp. 363–380. New York: International Universities Press.

Tolpin, P. (1988). Optimal affective engagement: the analyst's role in therapy. In *Learning from Kohut, Progress in Self Psychology*, vol. 4, ed. A. Goldberg, pp. 160–168. Hillsdale, NJ: Analytic Press.

Winnicott, D. W. (1965). *The Maturational Processes and the Facilitating Environment.* London: Hogarth.

Wolfe, E. (1976). Ambience and abstinence. *Annual of Psychoanalysis* 4:101–115.

———— (1980). On the developmental line of selfobject relations. In *Advances in Self Psychology*, ed. A. Goldberg, pp. 117–132. New York: International Universities Press.

———— (1988). *Treating the Self.* New York: Guilford.

7

Optimal Responsiveness and the Specificity of Selfobject Experience

HOWARD A. BACAL

EDITOR'S COMMENT

During the past twelve years, since I introduced the idea of optimal responsiveness to describe both the analyst's therapeutic function and the patient's therapeutic experience, there has been an increasing awareness of the interactive, relational nature of the psychoanalytic process. This chapter updates the concept of optimal responsiveness in the light of these insights. The chapter highlights the hallmark of what I believe constitutes a therapeutic process in which optimal responsiveness defines the therapeutic task: *the specificity of selfobject experience in therapeutic relatedness.*

My chapter begins with the work of a number of important psychoanalytic thinkers that anticipated the idea of optimal responsiveness. It concludes by describing the factors that determine the limitations of optimal responsiveness, which I believe are located in the complexity of the particular reciprocal dyadic system that constitutes every psychoanalytic endeavor.

❖

The search for the essence of the therapeutic in psychoanalytic[1] treatment continues to intrigue us and to challenge us, both clinically and theoretically. Accurate understanding of the analyst's contribution to the therapeutic process has been equally elusive. Currently, we are looking more and more closely at what is happening in the patient–analyst relationship in our quest for a deeper appreciation of both. I have suggested in Chapter 1 (also see Bacal and Newman 1990) that the analyst's therapeutic function can usefully be conceptualized by the term *optimal responsiveness*. I have defined this, variously, as the responsivity of the analyst that is therapeutically most relevant at any particular moment in the context of a particular patient and his illness, and as the therapist's acts of communicating to his patient in ways that that particular patient experiences as usable for the cohesion, strengthening, and growth of his self. This definition owes much to what I learned from Michael Balint, who, along with Maurice Levine, emphasized the necessity of identifying the responses that are specifically useful for the particular individual. Balint (1964), in addition, emphasized the importance of appreciating that the specific needs of the individual cannot be divorced from an understanding of the relationship between who the patient is, what the illness is, and who the therapist is that is attempting to treat them. In other words, Balint, although a committed psychoanalyst, was cognizant of the importance of a systems perspective on the therapeutic process.

The concept of optimal responsiveness must also be understood as centrally denoting the analyst's responsivity that facilitates the experience of certain kinds of *therapeutic relatedness*, and that this relatedness operates within an *interactive, reciprocal system*. I will elaborate on this shortly, but I will first briefly outline the perspectives of a few well-known analysts that anticipated the idea of optimal responsiveness in its relational aspects prior to the emergence of self psychology.

---

1. I include here, under the rubric of "psychoanalytic" treatment, not only so-called formal psychoanalysis but also much dynamic psychotherapy that is, in effect, virtually indistinguishable from analysis.

SIGNIFICANT ANTECEDENTS TO THE OPTIMAL RESPONSIVENESS CONCEPT

The Freudian vision of analytic treatment holds that interpretation is the essential contribution of the psychoanalyst, and insight constitutes its therapeutic effect on the patient. In contrast, the work of Sandor Ferenczi, Franz Alexander, and certain others whom we have come to call object relations theorists, in particular Michael Balint and Donald Winnicott—as well as, more recently, Heinz Kohut and other self psychologists—emphasizes the importance of a therapeutic relationship in which experience, which may or may not be evoked by interpretation or mediated by insight, is central to the curative process.

Certain British object-relations theorists significantly anticipated the relational aspect of what Kohut later identified as selfobject experience (Bacal 1987, Bacal and Newman 1990). Ian Suttie's (1935) emphasis on the importance of companionship, security, and the psychological responsiveness of the mothering figure resonates strongly with a relational view of selfobject experience as self sustaining. Balint and Winnicott, in particular, described certain characteristics of archaic relatedness that appear almost identical to those of Kohut's archaic merger or mirroring selfobject relationship in patients who were in deeply regressed states in analysis (Balint 1968, Winnicott 1954). For further illustrations of analogous conceptualizations to the selfobject relationship in the writings of the British object relations theorists, see Bacal and Newman (1990).

Aspects of Bowlby's attachment relationship are strongly reflected in the selfobject concept—a similarity that Lichtenberg (1989) has acknowledged in his schema of motivational systems. Bowlby's idea of the attachment figure also indicates the specificity of the selfobject; it implies the experience of a *relationship* with a particular important other—in other words, not any selfobject will do. It is *that* therapist that the patient misses, or whose absence results in the patient's falling apart.

Sandor Ferenczi

Ferenczi was the first to introduce an approach to the patient that anticipates certain aspects of optimal responsiveness. He underscored the many ways in which the analyst normally functions therapeutically in addition to providing insight through interpretation. He emphasized, in particular, the importance of the "psychological atmosphere" (Ferenczi 1929, p. 116) in analysis, and he attempted to account for it in terms of the analyst's personality and his style. Ferenczi (1931a) described, for example how

> the expectant silence [of the analyst] had the effect of disturbing the freedom of [the patient's] free association. The patient [had] barely reached the point of really forgetting himself and yielding up everything that [was] going on in his mind, when he suddenly [roused] himself with a start from his absorbed state, and [complained] that he really [could not] take the current of his emotions seriously when he sees that I am sitting tranquilly behind him, smoking my cigarette and at most responding coolly and indifferently with the stereotyped question: "Now what comes into your mind about that?" [p. 129]

In other words, Ferenczi understood that the demeanor of the therapist may affect the nature of the patient's transference as well as what we call his resistance. He questioned whether it is always the patient's resistance that causes failure in treatment rather than the therapist's unwillingness to be inconvenienced and thus his disinclination to adapt his methodology to the special needs of regressed patients.

Ferenczi had an abiding respect for the validity of the *patient's* experience. He advised that we offer our understanding to the patient tentatively, for we may be wrong, and the patient may have a better theory about himself (1928). He may even have a better suggestion as to how he should be treated (1931b). Ferenczi also recommended that the analyst acknowledge his mistakes (1928), as it would increase the patient's confidence in the analyst, which he considered to be a major factor in the therapy.

Michael Balint

Balint, a psychoanalytic pioneer in his own right, as well as Ferenczi's analysand and his major literary executor, significantly furthered Ferenczi's examination of how the analyst's noninterpretive behavior subtly but significantly alters the analytic atmosphere, and thus the patient's experience of the therapy. Balint cautioned analysts to consider whether the consistent maintenance of an attitude of benevolent, passive objectivity recommended by Freud—and which we now know that Freud himself observed mainly in the breach (Haynal 1989, Lipton 1977)—might sometimes constitute the repetition of a major traumatic factor, namely, the adult's indifference to the child's experience of overstimulation, rejection, or disappointment (Balint 1969). Balint was especially interested in developing effective ways of treating regressive states. He suggested that, at the level of what he called "the basic fault" (Balint 1968)—a geological metaphor denoting the effect on the infant of traumatic disruption of an archaic experience of harmonious relatedness between itself and its primary caregiver—the analyst's therapeutic function is not to provide insight, but rather to be there to be used relationally as a kind of pliable, primary, indestructible substance. If this process is successful, it can, according to Balint, provide the basis for a healthier, more trustful start in life—what he called "the new beginning." Balint did not, however, elaborate this idea into a theory of therapy that could be generally applied in psychoanalytic work.

Donald Winnicott

Winnicott also struggled with comparable therapeutic problems presented by the regressed states of his analysands. According to Winnicott, the failure of the mother to adequately "hold" her infant—that is, the absence of a sufficient amount of "good-enough" early mothering (Winnicott 1960a)—interferes with the development of a true self (Winnicott 1960b), produces a defensive false self based on compliance, and underlies much of the psychopathology that psychoanalysts see in their practice. Winnicott quite seriously draws the parallel between the good-enough mother and the good-enough analyst who, within the limits provided by his setting, can enable the patient, in the relationship with the analyst, to reach back and redress the early disturbance. In effect, the analyst must provide a "holding environment" (1960a) for the dependently regressed patient. The analyst must be aware, like the mother who holds her young infant, of his regressed patient's tendency to disintegrate or even cease to exist. The analyst needs to communicate with his regressed patient in ways that the patient experiences as therapeutically useful. Like Balint, Winnicott recognized that what is important in these situations is not what the analyst interprets but how the analyst behaves.

Franz Alexander

Alexander's (1950, 1956, 1961; see also Bacal 1990b) attempt to reconceptualize the analyst's therapeutic function was generally ill-received by the psychoanalytic establishment, but was tacitly accepted without much ado by the nonanalytic psychodynamic community. In my view, aspects of his contributions to our understanding of the therapeutic process deserve more consideration. Alexander coined the term *corrective emotional experience*, the essence of which was that the efficacy of analysis depended on a certain kind of emotional experience, whether or not it was accompanied by the acquisition of intellectual understanding (that is, "insight"). He believed all analysts intuitively appreciated this point but were reluctant to publicly acknowledge it. The corrective emotional experience was that, in the context of the reactivation of his central childhood psychological problems in the relationship with the analyst (which, Alexander noted, was itself usually an emotional experience), the patient experienced the analyst's reacting differently from those figures whose reactions were instrumental in determining his difficulties in the first place. Alexander drew attention to the fact that the usual analytic attitude of "objective detachment . . . is itself an adopted and studied attitude and not a spontaneous reaction to the patient" (Alexander 1956, p. 94). He also pointed out that, since the analyst cannot be a blank screen, certain of his personal qualities will be evident to the patient and will affect the climate of their relationship. Alexander was not advocating that the analyst attempt to hide the true nature of his personality from the patient and attempt to play the role of a significant figure of his past in a better way. Rather, he was recommending that the analyst deliberately modify his attitudes according to his understanding of the patient's original conflict situation, in order both to reactivate the patient's early attitude and to create an interpersonal atmosphere that will provide the patient with emotional experiences in his relationship with the therapist that would correct, or alter, reaction patterns that are currently maladaptive (Alexander 1956, Alexander and French 1946).

It is possible that the bad press that Alexander received from the analytic community about the corrective emotional experience and his technical recommendations for effecting it had as much to do with the package in which he wrapped his ideas as the contents themselves. He recommended brief analysis, varying and reducing the number of sessions per week, and using planned interruptions to minimize a factor that he regarded as antitherapeutic in the standard analytic procedure: encouragement of a resistive dependency on the analyst. Thus, he was, in effect, criticized for manipulating the transference and significantly altering the nature of the analytic process.

There is a popular misconception that Alexander's corrective emotional experience was a kind of synonym for gratifying the patient. Nothing could be further from the truth. Interestingly, the clinical examples that Alexander uses to illustrate his idea of the corrective emotional experience are predominantly instances in which the therapist, in contrast to an indulgent parent, frustrated the patient, and pointed out an unpalatable reality to him.

THE EVOLUTION OF OPTIMAL RESPONSIVENESS IN THEORY AND PRACTICE

My starting point for defining optimal responsiveness was the rejection of Kohut's (1977, 1984) theory of optimal frustration as an explanation of how analysis cures (see Chapter 1); but the conceptualization of optimal responsiveness went beyond the refutation of Kohut's theory of cure. In effect, I suggested that optimal responsiveness could serve as an overarching principle that usually characterizes the analyst's job. I did not, however, rule out the possibility that, although frustration is not an inherent ingredient of therapeutic responsivity, the analyst's optimal responsiveness may sometimes entail the patient's experiencing frustration. I discuss this issue later in the chapter.

The central observations that guided my efforts to understand the analyst's therapeutic function in this way are that

1. everything the analyst says or does not say, does or does not do, is experienced by the patient as a response that may or may not be specific to his needs, defenses, and conflicts;
2. the responsiveness on the part of the analyst that is experienced as therapeutic by the patient encompasses a considerably wider spectrum than we have traditionally regarded as effective.

The analyst's therapeutic functioning constitutes much more—and sometimes much less—than what our theories or some of our teachers have told us it does. John Lindon (1994) has tellingly illustrated this as entailing a wealth of provisions that patients variously experience as specific to their therapeutic needs.

The concept of optimal responsiveness accords therapeutic legitimacy to a wide variety of communications whereby analysts regularly provide their patients with therapeutic experience. To name only a few, they include interpretation—transferential, dynamic, or reconstructive; clarification; confrontation; support; recognition; validation or invalidation; self-disclosure; and a variety of so-called enactments. These communications are ubiquitous in the therapeutic interventions of the analyst. The responses of the analyst that the patient experiences as therapeutic include a remarkably wide range of the verbal and the nonverbal. The verbal includes a host of utterances in addition to interpretation, and much of the nonverbal entails what has been called the analytic atmosphere (Balint 1968) or the analytic ambience (Wolf 1976). We know that all of these variously play a therapeutic part in the conduct of all analyses, but we have been reluctant to grant them official legitimacy. To regard none of them except interpretive intervention as psychoanalytically appropriate except as temporary necessities, or "parameters" (Eissler 1953), is to blind ourselves to the range of therapeutically effective responsivity that patients commonly experience their analysts as providing.

In other words, the salient elements in the idea of a responsiveness that is optimal for the patient are its specificity and its potentially variegated nature. To these elements I would now add that of therapeutic relatedness, which variously operates within an interactive, reciprocal system.

SELFOBJECT EXPERIENCE AND THE VARIETIES OF THERAPEUTIC RELATEDNESS

What Kohut discovered, with the use of a sustained empathic listening perspective, was that his patients did not seem to experience him as an object toward whom they directed their conflictual wishes over the discharge of instinctual drives; rather, they appeared to need responses from him that would evoke and positively affect their sense of self. In short, this is selfobject experience.

Kohut's concept of the selfobject transference (Basch, personal communication) implies selfobject need, "a transference of need," which, when met, constitutes selfobject experience. Kohut delineated three primary selfobject experiences, which are associated with the self-affecting responsiveness of the other: the experience of acceptance and confirmation of the self in its grandness, goodness, and wholeness; the experience of merger with the sense of the other as a figure of calmness, power, wisdom, and goodness; and the sense of the presence of the essential likeness of another's self (Wolf 1988). We have subsequently added extensively to these three formalized constellations of mirroring, idealizing, and alterego selfobject experiences, such as experiences of self-delineation, experiences of being a center of initiative through responses of a respectful adversary, and the experience of efficacy. All of these evoke the sense of self in significant and important ways; that is, they are selfobject experiences.

I would like to identify two aspects of selfobject experience that have not usually been noted: (1) The vigorous engagement of creative activity can evoke integration and vitalizing self-experience, with or without the sense of participation of the other. It is noteworthy in this regard that Balint (1968) referred to "the area of creation" as possibly not being object related. (2) An important and sometimes essential aspect of the patient's selfobject experience may be the experience of providing it to the other. The experience of giving, as Suttie (1935) has indicated, can be as important to the development of one's emotional health as the experience of receiving. An example of this in the therapy situation would be the discovery that giving something to one's analyst who enthusiastically receives it can be a vitalizing selfobject experience (see Chapter 4, pp. 89–90, for a good illustration of this).

I would agree with Wolf (personal communication) that the term *selfobject* properly connotes "any experience that enhances the strength of the self or, in more 'experience-near' terms, any experience that enhances the feeling of well-being." Wolf and I also concur that *selfobject* is an unfortunate term in that it does not always correctly describe the experience that it has come to denote; but that at present we are, as it were, stuck with it so as to preserve a sense of continuity in our theoretical language.

Selfobject Relatedness and Non-Selfobject Relatedness

Psychoanalytic self psychology has made significant contributions to the conceptualization of therapy as an experiential process in a relationship. Prior to this, the only acceptable theoretical conceptualizations we had about the contribution of relationship in the therapeutic process were

Zetzel's (1958) "therapeutic alliance" and Greenson's (1965) "working alliance," concepts that relegated relationship to the background as a therapeutic factor. I have described in a series of papers (Bacal 1990a, 1991, 1994, 1995a,b) and in a book with Kenneth Newman (Bacal and Newman 1990) why I consider self psychology to be, in its essence, relational. I can but touch on the arguments for this here: "The self 'knows' itself only in the context of the experience of the self-other relationship" (Bacal and Newman 1990, p. 2). The *selfobject* concept gives expression to a centrally important form of this relatedness. Stern (1985), though not a self psychologist, regards the selfobject as a "term for a variety of ongoing functional *relationships* with others that are necessary to provide the regulating structures that maintain and/or enhance self-cohesion" (p. 242, my emphasis). Stern's view of the normal infant is that "[her] life is so thoroughly social that most of the things the infant does, feels, and perceives occur in different kinds of relationships" (p. 118). In effect, the selfobject concept defines relationship psychoanalytically in a way that constitutes a bridge from an "object-relational" theory to a "self-psychological" theory (Bacal 1987, 1990a, Bacal and Newman 1990). On the object relations side of the bridge, the focus is on the development of the capacity for concern, whereby the other (the "object") comes to be apprehended and related to as having a life of his own distinct from that of the self. Ernest Wolf (1985) pithily describes the focus on the self psychological side of the bridge: "Strictly speaking, selfobjects are neither self nor object; they are the subjective aspect of a function performed by a relationship" (p. 271).

Recently, self psychologists have been directing attention to forms of therapeutic relatedness in which the analyst is experienced by the patient as another whose self and its subjectivity are recognized as discrete, rather than as functioning to meet the patient's needs. These are in fact forms of therapeutic relatedness that have characterized the technique of object-relations therapists, but were ignored by self psychologists in their repudiation of the maturity morality of the object-relations perspective and in their enthusiasm for the therapeutic yield provided by focusing on selfobject relatedness. Yet, there is general agreement, among self psychologists, that all these forms of therapeutic relatedness entail selfobject experience, defined as experience that enhances the strength of the self. Kohut (1984) conceptualized the goal of psychoanalytic treatment not only as the attainment of a cohesive self but also as the capacity to seek out appropriate selfobjects—that is, to form appropriate selfobject relationships—

throughout the life cycle. Self psychologists are now beginning to reach back across the bridge (see Bacal and Newman 1990) to incorporate certain non-selfobject relationships into their theoretical and clinical perspectives.

Recent reference by self psychologists to the functioning of the self-object relationship in the clinical situation have largely been as background against which therapeutic work is carried out in the foreground (Lichtenberg et al. 1996, Stolorow et al. 1987). In my view, selfobject relatedness is to be regarded more than simply a static background experience against which therapy is effectively conducted, and more than as an issue that emerges in the foreground when it is disrupted. I suggest that it constitutes a continuous dynamic experience that arises from a complex interaction between analyst and analysand. It is integral to the ongoing therapeutic process (Bacal 1994).

I would reserve a distinct meaning for the term *selfobject relationship* (or *selfobject relatedness*). A selfobject relationship includes selfobject experience, but it implies something more. It implies a bond[2] with the other that permits an expectation of responsiveness with regard to the need for self-object experience. That is, a selfobject relationship refers to the expectation of reliability and a sense of natural, or basic entitlement to the selfobject responsiveness of the other (Bacal and Newman 1990). The archaic prototype of this would be, in health, the infant's relationship to the mother's breast, or her "holding function."

CURRENT PERSPECTIVES ON OPTIMAL RESPONSIVENESS

Today, some twelve years after I introduced the term *optimal responsiveness* to denote that therapeutic efficacy necessarily embraces diverse and differential responsivity to individual therapeutic need, I believe that it continues to usefully describe the analyst's job. However, I offer the following emphases and additions, some of which I have discussed in the preceding pages:

---

2. Lessem and Orange, in "Emotional Bonds: The Therapeutic Action of Psychoanalysis Revisited" (unpublished) discuss extensively the centrality of the selfobject bond in psychoanalytic therapy.

1. The analyst's responsiveness must be centrally informed by his awareness that the therapeutic process comprises the operation of a complex, more-or-less unique, relational system for each analyst–patient couple, in which the analyst's task is to discover and, if possible, to respond in ways that are optimal for that particular patient. Doctors's (1996) view of analyzability, with which I would agree, is relevant here: "From a dyadic systems view . . . each dyad is unique and there are a range of different, successful analyses conceivable for any one person. The question expands beyond 'what the patient needs' or even 'what the analyst is capable of' to the question of goodness-of-fit in the dyad" (p. 61). In a recent paper Slavin and Kriegman (in press) assert that "[the therapeutic relationship] becomes a more real relationship as the 'one size fits all' structures, rules, and experiences set in place before the two parties even met are re-negotiated in the specific relationship between two individuals."

2. Therapeutic relatedness in such a system is, I believe, accurately understood preeminently as a selfobject relationship, and its impact on the patient accurately described as corrective selfobject experience (Bacal 1990b, Bacal and Newman 1990). A selfobject relationship constitutes a link with a significant other who is expected to respond in ways that promote self-cohesion or self-enhancement, or self-restoration (via the analysis of what went wrong following disruption of the relationship). Therapeutic relatedness can also entail a relationship in which analyst and patient may at times—in some instances, even pervasively—experience each other therapeutically in a variety of ways as having distinct subjectivities of their own. (These ways are described by various authors: the Shanes [Chapter 4] describe intersubjective relatedness; Fosshage [Chapter 6] describes needs or concerns about self-with-other and a need to focus on or concerns about the other; Lynne Jacobs [Chapter 9] describes subject-subject relatedness. Lynn Preston [in press] elaborates a similar idea—expressive relating.) Yet I would maintain that these forms of relatedness also centrally entail selfobject experience, defined as the vitalizing evocation of the sense of self (Bacal 1995b).

3. The test of the analyst's optimal responsiveness is the patient's

experience of specific, needed therapeutic relatedness with the therapist.

4. Optimal responsiveness that facilitates therapeutic relatedness is always to some extent bidirectional, though not necessarily symmetrical.

5. The responsiveness of the analyst that is optimal for the patient's therapeutic experience must change when the patient's self development permits or requires a different kind of therapeutic relatedness. In other words, the principle of optimal responsiveness implies a theory of therapy that is relational, specific, and reciprocal.

CASE EXAMPLES

The following two case examples variously illustrate these points. The first example, an analytic treatment described by Jeffrey Trop and Robert Stolorow (1992), demonstrates how the therapist's interpretive responsiveness that was optimal in the context of a mirroring selfobject relatedness became disruptive when the therapist failed to recognize the change in the patient's self-organization, which required an idealizing relatedness and a different kind of interpretive responsiveness.[3] The example also strikingly demonstrates how the analyst's optimal response must change from offering attuned responsiveness to the patient's subjective experience to a confrontation with external reality under certain conditions (see also Chapter 13).

> Alan, a 34-year-old attorney, sought treatment because of confusion about his sexuality, and depressive feelings about himself. His major sexual activity had been a series of isolated contacts with men, but he had had a few experiences of heterosexual intercourse.
>
> Alan's mother was a highly critical, intrusive, but apparently distant and cold person who could not tolerate any disagreement from

---

3. This was not the stated intention of the case report when presented; rather, it was offered as an illustration of the shift in defense analysis that follows development.

her son. Alan repeatedly experienced humiliation and despair at her hands both as a child and as an adult. The father, although a warm and affectionate person, stood by without interceding on his son's behalf. Although intensely interested in and proud of his son's academic success, he was absorbed in his business, and had little time for him. He died when Alan was 20.

Women seemed to be attracted to Alan; he sometimes returned their interest. He wanted to have a permanent heterosexual relationship and have a family. However, he felt unattractive and defective as a man, and invariably became depressed and withdrawn whenever a woman was the slightest bit critical of him or when she seemed to be at all demanding of his attention. Although intercourse with the woman was exciting, he would soon begin to experience her essentially like his mother—controlling and selfish and more interested in her own satisfaction than in him, and he would have to leave her. He regarded his feelings about the women, however, as his problem in that he was looking for the perfect woman who didn't exist, and that he was inadequate and loathsome because he could not give the woman what she wanted. He would then seek the company of men, whom he would allow to admire him and perform fellatio on him. Occasionally he would masturbate the man, but without enthusiasm. He would experience the man as attractive, however, and would want to be like him.

Interpretive intervention centrally included the understanding that the patient longed to have his father, and now the analyst, help him maintain his sense of himself and of his value in the face of his mother's criticisms; that the patient's homosexual activities seemed to substitute for the alignment with him that his father had been unable to provide. The homosexual enactments were thus understood as concretely encapsulating the patient's hope of restoring and consolidating his fragile sense of self when it disintegrated in reaction to criticism, intrusion, or rejection by his mother or mother-surrogates.

Alan's homosexual activity eventually stopped and he began to struggle to maintain a relationship with a woman. The authors felt this was due to the strengthening of his uncertain and somewhat fragile sense of self due to the establishment of a selfobject bond with the analyst. Although there were clearly idealizing components to this relationship, it would seem to have been primarily a mirroring selfobject relationship, which enabled Alan to begin to delineate his sense of self. It should also be noted that, in the case of Alan, interpretations evidently mediated the therapeutic effect of the relationship (although the data from the case presentation do not permit consideration of other therapeutic factors).

Alan continued to find fault with every woman in the same way as he previously had and needed to leave all of them. However, he would invariably doubt the validity of his perceptions, and would turn to the analyst to help him retain his confidence in his inner experience. If the analyst deviated at all from articulating Alan's perspective, it would result in Alan's becoming acutely depressed and attacking himself cruelly. For example, at one point when he wanted to end a relationship with a woman because he felt she was critical, he became acutely downcast and suicidal when the analyst suggested that he might be misinterpreting as criticism the woman's strong wish to discuss their relationship. Following this disruption, Alan gave his telephone number to a man who seemed attracted to him. Alan reported to the analyst that his comments had made him feel as if his whole world had been turned upside down and that he felt completely alone. The selfobject bond with the analyst was restored when the analyst interpreted that it had been undermined when he had abandoned his function of validating the patient's affective perceptions and unwittingly allied himself with the woman's point of view. He added that the reactivation of homosexual desires reflected the patient's longing for the lost mirroring relationship with the analyst (very likely, as quite a different sort of mother than the one he had) in order to counter his sense of invalidity and self-loathing.

A second phase in the analysis began when the patient had a negative therapeutic reaction to the analyst's usual response of conveying Alan's need for the analyst's validation of his feelings in the face of criticism from a woman! Alan had become depressed when a female colleague told him that she would not continue to introduce him to women because he always found fault with them. The analyst persisted in his customary way, interpreting the patient's need for validation of his point of view. Alan reacted more and more angrily, and eventually indicated his wish to terminate the analysis. In the days that followed, the analyst recognized, and conveyed to Alan, that his anger reflected his dissatisfaction with the analyst's response, now, in continuing to help him establish the validity of his inner experience of women. He had become strong enough to remain grounded in his own subjective reality, and perhaps he now needed the analyst to help him examine what validity there might be in his colleague's comment about his always finding fault with women, that this fault-finding was a way that Alan protected himself from the dangers of being involved with women—dangers that he now wanted the analyst to help him face and understand.

In other words, at first unnoticed by the analyst, the patient's self had firmed up considerably, and the nature of his central selfobject need had shifted. The patient now had no use for a mirroring selfobject relationship but rather needed a relationship with the analyst as an idealizable father whose strength, support, and encouragement would help him deal with the dangers of involvement with women. The analyst then focused his interpretations on the patient's defensive retreat from engagement with women whom he found dominating and dangerously controlling. In effect, he now began to help the patient to see what *he* was doing that contributed to the failure of his relationships with women rather than validating his experience of how they were treating him badly.

Alan resumed his progress, substantially increasing his ability to become deeply involved in an emotional and sexual relationship with a woman. Quite recently (the analysis was continuing at the time), he became involved in a deeply intimate and satisfying relationship with a woman colleague. At one point, she surprised him by arranging a weekend for them together, indicating that she "had plans" for him. He complained to the analyst that he felt she was "pressing in" on him sexually. The analyst said that the patient was evidently experiencing her as a controlling mother who needed him to do her bidding so that she could feel good about herself. But the analyst also asked Alan: Did his girlfriend wish to control Alan or was she anticipating a sense of joy in being with him? Alan replied that he realized that she wanted to enjoy him and that, when he reflected on it, he could see that she had no desire to control him.

In this treatment, the therapist's optimal response to the patient shifted from validating his subjective reality to the examination of the patient's possible distortion of his view of the other. The vignette vividly illustrates how the optimal response of the therapist must shift with the need for change in the nature of the selfobject relationship. That is, changes in the patient's self-organization and corresponding need for selfobject relatedness determine the specific nature of the therapist's optimal responsiveness. When the patient's self had not been consolidated and delineated, the analyst's optimal response was to validate the patient's subjective reality. As the patient's sense of this reality became stronger, he sought a different kind of relatedness with his analyst. He was looking for an idealizing relationship with a mentor who would guide him. Interestingly, the optimal response now included the analyst's proferring a view that was at variance with the patient's articulated subjectivity, and concomitantly introducing him to another's (the woman's) possible reality, which could also be different from his own. In effect, the analyst confronted his patient with how he was protecting himself from the woman, and how his perception of her might be distorted by his previous experience.

Thus, the patient's requirement for optimal responsivity may change, sometimes quite dramatically, as he makes analytic progress. The following vignette illustrates a variation of the same process: how the patient and analyst usefully engage a form of therapeutic relatedness that entails the experience of each other as having distinct subjectivities. It also demonstrates the bidirectionality or mutuality of optimal responsiveness that obtains within a particular relational system. In this particular system, optimal responsivity significantly consisted of certain actions, or "enactments" as well as interpretations.

I have described the case of Dr. M. (Chapter 1), in which a persistent blockage in the analytic process was relieved through the effect on the patient of lowering her fee.

The patient presented a dream in her first session that she had had not long after our initial consultation a few weeks previously. She introduced the dream by what was, in effect, an association to it: how much she appreciated the generous gesture of her friend—an analyst—who called her prospective analyst to prepare the way for her referral. In the dream, the friend appeared as a taxi driver and drove her to a bridge where he said that he had forgotten the analyst's phone number and address. As she searched in her purse for the directions, the contents, her money, and things she had on her mind fell out. Her son called,

"Mummy" to her and, as at home, everything was once again pulling at her.

The dream reflected her fear that she would become caught up in a relationship with me that would repeat traumatic experiences with her parents: that she would be emptied by the selfish needs and demands of the mother, and abandoned by the father, to whom she imagined she was special, but who left the home when she was 5 and contacted her on only sporadic occasions thereafter. Her associations also expressed her hope that her relationship with me would enable her to enter a world in which she might receive the care and generosity that she felt significantly deprived of by both her parents.

Not long after Dr. M.'s analysis began, the relationship between us became disrupted. This patient, a divorced, single parent with three small children, receiving a meager allowance from her estranged husband, became increasingly anxious about her financial situation, which threatened her modest standard of living. My initial response was to acknowledge her financial difficulty, but also to attempt, over a period of several weeks, to analyze the nature of her anxiety. None of this helped, and since her intensifying anxiety about funds was seriously compromising her ability to make use of the analytic sessions, I told her I would accept the insurance payment, which was well below my fee, as full payment for the sessions. I also told her that I felt she needed me to do this not only for financial reasons, but also for psychological reasons, which I did not fully understand at the time, but which I felt that she needed me to respond to if I could. That is, rather than viewing her experience as an optimal frustration imposed by myself as part of the frame of the analysis and continue to analyze it, I responded to her anxiety symptoms as representing a transference of need based on antecedent trauma. The dream, in particular, illustrated her experience that the trauma of exploitation was being repeated in the transference, and her anxiety about the fee, in effect, communicated a plea that I mitigate this trauma by putting her "real" needs, experienced in relation to money, to some extent before mine. (The transference meanings were not apparent at the time; they were elucidated in a later stage of the analysis.) Theoretically, one could regard this as an attempt on the patient's part to change the analyst from a figure whom she experienced in the repetitive dimension of the transference into a figure whom she experienced as a selfobject; or, to apply the term that Newman and I have recently introduced, to transform the *bad selfobject* analyst into a good one (Bacal 1995a).

The result of my response was that the impasse disappeared, a stable selfobject relationship became established, and analytic work resumed, with the progressive unfolding of the meaning of significant, related events of her childhood. The patient and I went on to experience and work through many selfobject disruptions in our selfobject relationship as the analysis progressed. As Dr. M. contacted a sense of her natural entitlement to myself as archaic selfobject, she became able to express her disdain for my "financial generosity" as personally motivated and a drop in the bucket of her psychological need. She could criticize my conservative political views as sometimes socially unfair, and identify my male chauvinistic shortcomings—all quite accurately. It was important that I could survive these attacks, and that we remained on friendly terms, although I occasionally needed her to "right" me by some recognition (selfobject mirroring) of my value, say, as a writer of papers (especially this chapter and chapter 1, in which Dr. M.'s case is reported with her permission), when my professional self-esteem and my ability thereby to stay on her side were significantly endangered. I will say more about this shortly.

This patient made many gains as time went on, particularly in her relationships with her children and her parents and in her academic career. I will summarize a session that occurred many years into the analysis. There was a transit strike, and she telephoned to say that she would be late, as she would be driving her (now teenage) children to school. She arrived with about 20 minutes left in the session. The theme of the session was her growing recognition, as a result of our work together, that choices in life really do involve some renunciation of other wishes. When I indicated that our time for the session was up, she protested that this was not fair, noting that the next patient had not yet arrived, and would likely not arrive right away because of the transit strike. I said that no one would ordinarily arrive now, since, at this time, I usually took a 15-minute break, but that I had things to do, and therefore could not extend the session. She angrily walked out, without saying good-bye. My afterthoughts were, I don't think it was such a bad thing to be putting myself first, now. I think we will both survive—she from my selfishness and unfairness, and I from her anger and criticism. I also thought to myself, It's not a matter of fair, as she'd asserted. She is stronger, and I don't think she needs the same kind of responsiveness now, despite her frustration and anger.

Initially, for this patient, the therapeutic experience of a particular kind of relatedness was mediated by a specific response on the part of the analyst. The patient's felt need for a substantial lowering of the fee was met after an interpretive approach failed. The meaning of this response to the patient was profound and therapeutic. It not only diminished the undermining and traumatically disruptive experience of transference that was precluding a therapeutic process from taking place for her. It also enabled Dr. M. to experience her analyst as providing an archaic selfobject relationship (which embodied both mirroring and idealizing components) in which she could expect her needs to come first, before those of the "caregiver," which she had experienced as always coming first. Eissler (1953) would have described the analyst's action as a "parameter." I regarded it as an expression of the analyst's responsiveness that was therapeutically necessary for this patient, given the vulnerable nature of her self-organization at the time. The working through of selfobject disruptions in these spheres additionally strengthened her self. Later, when she became stronger, she did not always need this kind of relatedness to sustain her self. At these times, the analyst's self-abdicating responsiveness was not only sometimes unnecessary, the optimal response was to interact with her in a way that would respect this kind of progress. This kind of interaction entails the provision of responsiveness that vitalizes the patient's self through the analyst's recognition of her growing capacity to respect the needs of the other that are different from the needs of the self. It is this sort of interaction that Shane and Shane (Chapter 4), Fosshage (Chapter 6), Jacobs (Chapter 9), and Preston (in press) describe, respectively, as intersubjective relatedness, self-with-other relatedness, subject-subject relating, and expressive relating. As I indicated earlier, these forms of relatedness constitute a technique that is pervasively characteristic of object relations therapy. I would emphasize, however, that to the extent that patient and analyst related in a way that enhanced the patient's sense of well-being, these forms of therapeutic relatedness centrally provided what we call selfobject experience.

FRUSTRATION, ANGER, AND OPTIMAL RESPONSIVENESS

Some self psychologists would use the sequences I have just described as evidence for the therapeutic relevance of optimal frustration. To be sure, my denial of Dr. M.'s request to extend the session frustrated and angered her, as did the selfobject disruptions that occurred prior to my early accession to her need for a reduction in the fee, when I failed to respond adequately to her requests for archaic selfobject relatedness. But her experiences and expression of frustration and anger were not, in my view, of therapeutic significance. When the archaic selfobject needs were frustrated, she would become enraged and momentarily fragmented. When her request for sacrifice of my time for hers was denied when she was stronger, she became angry and frustrated, without fragmenting. But apart from the importance to her that I accept her affective reactions, none of her experiences or expressions of frustration or anger constituted a therapeutic experience. What she experienced as optimal at the time when she was more primitively organized was that I understood the injury that she sustained through our interaction. What was optimal at the time when she was stronger was her experience of my denial of her request as a recognition of that strength and of my respect for her ability, now, to tolerate a relationship in which discrepancy existed between us in which her own sense of need would sometimes be frustrated. It was instructive to note the difference in the quality of her affect between the earlier situation in which she required a reduction in fees from the later situation in which she was making a demand for provision of more time. In the early situation, she was narcissistically vulnerable and was threatened with fragmentation anxiety. Later, she was much less vulnerable. Her anger, then, was not the rage of an endangered self, but rather reflected the frustration of a more resilient self whose wish for more time with her analyst was rejected. That is, my response indicated my recognition that she could now manage my reality, a reality that had earlier corresponded to her traumatic experience of the archaic selfobject's failure ever to put her first—the result of cumulatively traumatic (Khan 1963) experience of this sort with her mother. More anger followed in subsequent sessions, but also more progress toward mutual understanding, in which our differing views and experience of the analytic situation could be engaged and analyzed (Wolf 1986).

This is, however, not the whole story. To provide the patient with the selfobject relatedness she required in the early stages of the analysis, I had to set aside, for the most part, any comparable expectations from her. In effect, I committed myself to a lived experience of putting her needs for valuing and consideration before mine for prolonged periods. This affected me in ways that, at times, I did not entirely appreciate.

OPTIMAL RESPONSIVENESS: ITS MUTUALITY AND ITS LIMITATIONS

The therapeutic process is much more mutually organized than we are usually prepared to admit. While we are there to treat the patient, and it may be said with some accuracy that we are paid not to act on what we call our countertransference, optimal responsiveness, in practice, is always to some extent a two-way street. In Chapter 1 I drew on Winnicott's (1952) aphorism that "there is no such thing as a baby, [there is rather] a nursing couple" (p. 99) and suggested that "there is no such thing as a patient; there is rather an analytic couple" or, as Shelley Doctors (1996) has recently conveyed, optimal responsiveness is a property of a "well-functioning dyad" (p. 61). That is, if we consider the treatment process as an optimal analytic interaction,[4] or system, we will be impressed by the evidence that it signifi- cantly entails a reciprocal selfobject responsiveness between patient and analyst. In this exchange, the therapist's experience of optimal responsive- ness from the patient is usually provided via the patient's meeting a mixture of spoken and unspoken, conscious and unconscious expectations of the analyst, such as paying an agreed-upon—mutually agreeable—fee, attend- ing sessions, arriving and leaving on time, talking, responding to interpre- tations, evincing some gratitude, perhaps some affection, and making some progress. All of these, in effect, meet various of the analyst's selfobject needs; they preeminently affirm the usefulness of what the analyst has to offer and how he offers it.

For the most part, Dr. M. and I were able to be optimally responsive to

---

4. Marian Tolpin (1983) calls this a "corrective developmental dialogue [involving] the establishment, interpretation, and working through of a new transference edition of the self–selfobject unit [between child and parent]" (p. 366). Terman's "affective dialogue" and "dialogue of construction" (Chapter 3) and Paul Tolpin's (1988) "optimal affective engagement" characterize a similar process.

each other's needs for mutual selfobject relatedness. What I was consciously aware of, in terms of the meeting of Dr. M.'s selfobject needs, was that I was proud of providing something special to a worthy, burdened, and vulnerable analysand. However, I gradually realized that I had been unconsciously expecting a certain measure of gratitude as a reciprocal response. I felt a mixture of guilt about this expectation, as well as some reluctance, at times, to respond with more affective generosity when I felt this gratitude was not forthcoming. Thus, while Dr. M. generally experienced me as acknowledging her efforts and encouraging her achievements, I did not always respond optimally in this regard.

Peter Thomson and I (Chapter 12; see also Bacal and Thomson 1996) have described the effect of the analysand's unresponsiveness to the analyst's selfobject needs on the analyst's capacity to be optimally responsive to the analysand. Thomson and I consider this process as delineating a new view of the phenomenon that is commonly identified as countertransference. While we would agree with Fosshage (1995a,b) that we must address all the feelings/experiences of the analyst that are usually subsumed under the term, *countertransference*, we believe that the term itself obscures more than it clarifies, and that we should stop using it. In other words, the ongoing responsivity of the analysand to ordinary ongoing selfobject needs of the analyst is ubiquitously a precondition for the analyst to respond optimally to the analysand. The withdrawal of this responsivity is likely the most frequent determinant of so-called countertransference reactions, which would, from our point of view, more accurately be called relatedness reactions. My relatedness reaction to my patient decreased as I learned to become more accepting of my need for reciprocity, and as I came to understand how important it was to her, at times, not to have to feel grateful, so that she could experience a sense of natural entitlement to my caring and generosity—an experience that was, for her, significantly therapeutic. Another, reciprocally determined relatedness reaction occurred with regard to mutual needs for affection. Dr. M.'s experience in life made it very difficult for her, in the early stages of the analysis, to convey her needs for affection and intimacy to me; and at those times when my self state was vulnerable, my ability to respond optimally to these needs may have been affected by her difficulties, which I unconsciously experienced as a frustration of my comparable needs from her.

There is no doubt that these issues are understandable as unanalyzed aspects of what is commonly designated as transference and countertransference, which should be addressed in consultation, or in further personal analysis for both analyst and analysand. They may even be clarified somewhat by writing about them, and sharing them with others as I am doing here. Yet, as useful as any of these may be, it is important not to lose sight of the particularity and limitations of this or of any other analytic dyad. "*Everyone*," as Sullivan (1953) has wisely observed, "is much more simply human than otherwise" (p. 32, my emphasis). No therapist is ever entirely immune to relatedness reactions—a better term, I think, than reactions that we designate as countertransference—no matter how well analyzed we are. (For a further discussion of "relatedness reaction," see Chapter 12.) As Stolorow (personal communication) has aphoristically put it, the recognition (by Thomson and myself) of the ubiquity of the effect on the analyst of the patient's unresponsiveness to universal selfobject needs of the analyst puts paid to the myth of the perfectly analyzed analyst. In other words, the limitations in the optimal responsivity of the therapist to patient lie in the complexities of the particular dyad, which need to be understood, and responded to, as far as possible, as optimally as possible. In this sense, the therapeutic relationship is not dissimilar to any other relationship, whether we, as professionals, would like to admit it or not.

I also believe that some of the so-called mis-fits between the personality of the therapist and that of the patient could be usefully understood in the same way; that is, the therapist and the patient are consistently unable to respond to the other in ways that meet certain essential needs for selfobject relatedness. These problematic forms of interaction can sometimes be relieved through supervision, and may be helped by some personal analysis or even self-analysis (Thomson 1991); but in some instances, the analyst may actually need the patient to help "right" him by modifying his or her behavior a little, which is to say, dropping some of her defenses momentarily in order to help restore the selfobject relationship between them. Occasionally, none of these modifications work, and then the patient will have to seek another analyst, and the analyst will have to find another patient.

CONCLUSION

The concept of optimal responsiveness simultaneously denotes the wide range that encompasses what analysts normally do and/or could do to help their patients heal, as well as usefully focuses our consideration on how that particular analyst can enable that particular patient to use him/her at that moment in order to have a therapeutic experience. Lichtenberg and colleagues' (1996) goals of shared expansion of awareness, self-righting, and symbolic reorganization imply certain kinds of responses that are optimal on the part of the therapist. Yet, these should be recognized for what they are—a series of criteria and goals that generally indicate that the analyst's responsiveness has been optimal.

I have presented two case examples that illustrate that the changing need for therapeutic relatedness requires a definitive shift in the responsiveness of the therapist. I would recommend caution, however, about offering general criteria or goals for improvement that imply certain kinds of responsivity to be optimal. Ultimately, it is the systematic particularity of mutual responsiveness that is experienced by both participants in the analyst–patient interaction that determines therapeutic effect; and we will rediscover what this is afresh, with each patient, if we are open to perceive it. That is, as dearly as we would like to have general guidelines about how to conduct therapy, the specificity of individual psychological need and the complexity of the dyadic therapeutic system that attends it underscore the limitations of generalizing about what is optimal for whom.

The closest that I would come to making any generalizations about what centrally constitutes a responsiveness on the part of the analyst that is therapeutically optimal for the patient is the experience of significant disconfirmation of the expectation that the analyst will react in ways that repeat the problematic or traumatic experiences that led the patient to seek help in the first place, and the experience of the analyst as responding in ways that facilitate the strengthening, growth, and vitality of his self. I believe that this experience constitutes the true essence of Alexander's idea of corrective emotional experience; it is what I have, in my own clinical work, found useful to identify as corrective selfobject experience (Bacal 1990b).

It is true, of course, what Fosshage (1995a) suggests, that there is no single response that will be useful for the patient. But this observation does not vitiate the appropriateness of searching for what may be most helpful to the patient. The principle of optimal responsiveness, as I have described it, disciplines us to consider carefully what is best for our patients; however, it also frees us to be more of who we can be (Mendenhall, personal communication) in order to help them heal. Because optimal responsiveness as a principle that guides therapeutic work accords legitimacy to a wide range of responses that may be therapeutic for the patient, it is fully consonant with the exercise of flexibility and spontaneity on the part of the analyst. In effect, the concept is intended to articulate a principle that expresses how good therapists actually work.

Optimal responsiveness as a guideline for therapeutic work is therefore not a counsel for perfect performance on the part of the analyst. While we are committed to doing the best we can for our patients, we not infrequently learn what is most therapeutic for them through their reactions to our responses that are anything but optimal. At these times, the careful analysis of what went wrong constitutes the experience of optimal responsivity. This process will now be as valuable as the experiences of the patient when the analyst's responses felt just right.

In this connection, it is important to recognize that when disruptions in selfobject relatedness occurs, the analyst's attempts at that moment to provide the selfobject function that was frustrated will usually not be effective; that is, an attempt to right the wrong, then, will usually not work, at anything beyond a superficial level. The responses that will be experienced by the patient as optimal, at that time, are the acceptance of the patient's experience as valid—"wearing the attribution" (Lichtenberg et al. [1996])—and the attempt to understand what went wrong. And, as Newman points out in Chapter 5 (see also Bacal and Newman 1990, Stolorow et al. 1987) a related, important aspect of the analyst's optimal responsiveness, underemphasized until recently, is the acceptance of the validity of the patient's negative affective reactions to the analyst's failure to respond optimally, as the patient experiences them. Only after all of these disruptive experiences are worked through can the analyst effectively respond by attempting to provide the therapeutic experience for the patient that was missing.

Judith Vida (1993) states, "Ferenczi (1988) wrote that the analyst must make adaptations to his patients 'as far as he is able'" (p. 629). An important implication of this is that, while it is our job to try to do the best we can for the patient, there should be no shame attached to the inability of the analyst to provide an optimal response. Another implication of the wise recommendation by Ferenczi that the analyst make adaptations in his responsiveness as far as he is able, is that the analyst will not act a part. The further implication of this is that, while we may feel inclined to stretch ourselves in the therapeutic interests of a patient, we must take care—again, as far as we are able to—not to promise more than we can deliver. Ultimately, the analyst must be himself or herself in the best way that he or she can in order to enable the patient to use him or her therapeutically. I believe that we cannot ask for more—or less—from ourselves. This is the essence of optimal responsiveness. This is what I believe will heal the patient.

References

Alexander, F. (1950). Analysis of the therapeutic factors in psychoanalytic treatment. *Psychoanalytic Quarterly* 19:48–500.

—— (1956). *Psychoanalysis and Psychotherapy: Developments in Theory, Technique, and Training.* New York: Norton.

—— (1961). *The Scope of Psychoanalysis.* New York: Basic Books.

Alexander, F., and French, T. M. (1946). *Psychoanalytic Therapy: Principles and Application.* New York: Ronald Press.

Bacal, H. A. (1987). British object-relations theorists and self psychology: some critical reflections. *International Journal of Psycho-Analysis* 68:81–98.

—— (1990a). Does an object relations theory exist in self psychology? *Psychoanalytic Inquiry* 10:197–220.

—— (1990b). The elements of a corrective selfobject experience. *Psychoanalytic Inquiry* 10:347–372.

—— (1991). Notes on the relationship between object relations theory and self psychology. In *The Evolution of Self Psychology. Progress in Self Psychology*, vol. 7, ed. A. Goldberg, pp. 36–44. Hillsdale, NJ: Analytic Press.

—— (1994). The selfobject relationship in psychoanalytic treatment. In *A Decade of Progress: Progress in Self Psychology*, vol. 10, ed. A. Goldberg, pp. 21–30. Hillsdale, NJ: Analytic Press.

—— (1995a). The essence of Kohut's work and the progress of self psychology. *Psychoanalytic Dialogues* 5(3):353–366.

—— (1995b). The centrality of selfobject experience in psychological relatedness. *Psychoanalytic Dialogues* 5(3):403–409.

Bacal, H. A., and Newman, K. M. (1990). *Theories of Object Relations: Bridges to Self Psychology.* New York: Columbia University Press.

Bacal, H. A., and Thomson, P. G. (1996). The psychoanalyst's selfobject needs and the effect of their frustration on the treatment: a new view of countertransference. In *Basic Ideas Reconsidered: Progress in Self Psychology*, vol. 12, ed. A. Goldberg, pp. 17–35. Hillsdale, NJ: Analytic Press.

Balint, M. (1964). *The Doctor, His Patient, and the Illness*, 2nd ed. London: Pitman Medical.

—— (1968). *The Basic Fault.* London: Tavistock.

——— (1969). Trauma and object relationship. *International Journal of Psycho-Analysis* 50:429–435.

Doctors, S. (1996). Notes on the contribution of the analyst's self-awareness to optimal responsiveness. In *Basic Ideas Reconsidered: Progress in Self Psychology*, vol. 12, ed. A. Goldberg, pp. 55–63. Hillsdale, NJ: Analytic Press.

Eissler, K. (1953). The effect of the structure of the ego on psychoanalytic technique. *Journal of the American Psychoanalytic Association* 1:104–143.

Ferenczi, S. (1928). The elasticity of psychoanalytic technique. In *Final Contributions to the Problems and Methods of Psycho-Analysis*, pp. 87–101. London: Hogarth.

——— (1929). The principle of relaxation and neocatharsis. In *Final Contributions to the Problems and Methods of Psycho-Analysis*, pp. 108–125. London: Hogarth.

——— (1931a). Child-analysis in the analysis of adults. In *Final Contributions to the Problems and Methods of Psycho-Analysis*, pp. 126–142. London: Hogarth.

——— (1931b). Notes and fragments: on the patient's initiative. In *Final Contributions to the Problems and Methods of Psycho-Analysis*, p. 235. London: Hogarth.

Fosshage, J. (1997). Listening perspectives and the quest for a facilitating responsiveness. In *Conversations in Self Psychology: Progress in Self Psychology*, vol. 13, pp. 33–55, ed. A. Goldberg. Hillsdale, NJ: Analytic Press.

——— (1995b). Countertransference as the analyst's experience of the analysand: influence of listening perspectives. *Psychoanalytic Psychology* 12(3):375–391.

Greenson, R. (1965). The working alliance and the transference neurosis. *Psychoanalytic Quarterly* 34:155–181.

Haynal, A. (1989). *Controversies in Psychoanalytic Method: From Freud and Ferenczi to Michael Balint*. New York: New York University Press.

Khan, M. (1963). The concept of cumulative trauma. In *The Privacy of the Self*, pp. 42–58. New York: International Universities Press, 1974.

Kohut, H. (1977). *The Restoration of the Self*. New York: International Universities Press.

——— (1984). *How Does Analysis Cure?* Chicago: University of Chicago Press.

Lessem, P., and Orange, D. *Emotional bonds: the therapeutic action of psychoanalysis*. (Unpublished.)

Lichtenberg, J. (1989). *Psychoanalysis and Motivation*. Hillsdale, NJ: Analytic Press.

Lichtenberg, J., Lachmann, F., and Fosshage, J. (1996). *The Clinical Exchange: Techniques Derived from Motivational Systems*. Hillsdale, NJ: Analytic Press.

Lindon, J. (1994). Gratification and provision in psychoanalysis: Should we get rid of "The rule of abstinence"? *Psychoanalytic Dialogues* 4:549–582.

Lipton, S. (1977). The advantages of Freud's technique as shown in his analysis of the rat man. *International Journal of Psycho-Analysis* 58:255–273.

Preston, L. (in press). Expressive relating: the intentional use of the analyst's subjectivity. In *Progress in Self Psychology*.

Shane, M., Shane, E., and Gales, M. (1996). *Optimal responsiveness: a developmental nonlinear systems self psychological approach to the patient–analyst relationship*. Presented at the American Psychological Association Conference, Denver.

Slavin, M., and Kriegman, D. (in press). Why the analyst needs to change: toward a theory of conflict, negotiation, and mutual influence in the therapeutic process. *Psychoanalytic Dialogues*.

Stern, D. (1985). *The Interpersonal World of the Infant*. New York: Basic Books.

Stolorow, R., Brandchaft, B., and Atwood, G. (1987). *Psychoanalytic Treatment, An Intersubjective Approach*. Hillsdale, NJ: Analytic Press.

Sullivan, H. S. (1953). *The Interpersonal Theory of Psychiatry*. New York: Norton.

Suttie, I. D. (1935). *The Origins of Love and Hate*. London: Kegan Paul, Trench, Trubner.

Thomson, P. (1980). On the receptive function of the analyst. *International Journal of Psycho-Analysis* 7:183–205.

Tolpin, M. (1983). Corrective emotional experience: a self psychological reevaluation. In *The Future of Psychoanalysis*, ed. A. Goldberg, pp. 363–379. New York: International Universities Press.

Tolpin, P. (1988). Optimal affective engagement: the analyst's role in therapy. In *Learning from Kohut: Progress in Self Psychology*, vol. 4, ed. A. Goldberg, pp. 160–168. Hillsdale, NJ: Analytic Press.

Trop, J., and Stolorow, R. (1992). Defense analysis in self psychology: a developmental view. *Psychoanalytic Dialogues* 2(4):427–442.

Vida, J. (1993). Ferenczi's clinical diary: road map to the realm of primary relatedness. *Journal of the American Academy of Psychoanalysis* 21(4):623–635.

Winnicott, D. W. (1952). Anxiety associated with insecurity. In *D. W. Winnicott, Collected Papers*, pp. 97–100. London: Tavistock, 1958.

——— (1954). Metapsychological and clinical aspects of regression within the psycho-analytical set-up. In *D. W. Winnicott, Collected Papers*, pp. 278–299. London: Tavistock, 1958.

——— (1960a). The theory of the parent-infant relationship. In *The Maturational Processes and the Facilitating Environment*, pp. 37–55. London: Hogarth.

——— (1960b). Ego distortion in terms of true and false self. In *The Maturational Processes and the Facilitating Environment*, pp. 140–152. London: Hogarth.

Wolf, E. (1976). Ambience and abstinence. *Annual of Psychoanalysis* 4:101–115.

——— (1985). The search for confirmation: technical aspects of mirroring. *Psychoanalytic Inquiry* 5:271–282.

——— (1986). Discrepancies between analysand and analyst in experiencing the analysis. In *Progress in Self Psychology*, vol. 2, ed. A. Goldberg, pp. 84–94. New York: Guilford.

———— (1988). *Treating the Self: Elements of Clinical Self Psychology*. New York: Guilford.

Zetzel, E. (1958). The therapeutic alliance. In *The Capacity for Emotional Growth*, pp. 182–196. New York: International Universities Press, 1970.

Part II

---

*Optimal Responsiveness
in Clinical Practice*

A. New Modes of Relating

8

Optimal Responsiveness and the Experience of Sharing

BRUCE HERZOG

EDITOR'S COMMENT:

In this chapter, Herzog delineates and describes *sharing* as a distinct selfobject transference and selfobject experience. He also demonstrates how the communication by the therapist that he or she shares the patient's experience and its associated affective state may constitute an essential optimal response in psychoanalytic treatment.

Herzog distinguishes between two types of sharing experiences that may occur in the clinical situation: *descriptive sharing* and *active sharing*. Descriptive sharing involves the sharing of memories through descriptions of past experience. Active sharing entails a shared activity within the therapy setting. The latter constitutes participation in a particular enactment in which a mutual experience occurs that includes a sharing of affect between therapist and patient. As we shall see in the next two chapters, Herzog's views on sharing have significant points of contact with what Jacobs calls *subject–subject relating* and what Lazar describes as "facilitating enactments." Lynn Preston's concept of *expressive relating* is in certain ways similar to both Jacobs's concept of *subject–subject relating* and Herzog's idea of *active sharing*.

Herzog also discusses and illustrates the ways in which patients may attempt to communicate their need for a sharing responsivity and how the therapist may become more attuned to this need.

---------------❖---------------

The enjoyment of sharing between two people is a phenomenon so common in human relations as to be taken for granted, and thus it is not surprising that it is seldom elaborated upon in the psychoanalytic literature. The sharing of experience between people may involve a wide range of interactions, some being as casual as discussing the weather, and some involving an intense, deeply attuned affective connection. I believe that the need to share both experience and affect with another is a universal human requirement, potentially constituting a distinct selfobject function that has manifestations in the treatment setting.

The need to share can be expressed in various ways in the analytic environment. It might involve (1) sharing memories with another by relating stories of past experience, a major component of the therapeutic process that can be considerably gratifying to the patient, and (2) attempts at engaging in a sharing of present experience via specific enactments, which can include anything from the sharing of the analytic process itself, to attempts to directly influence the therapist's behavior in or out of the treatment setting. The goal in both cases is to have the therapeutic benefit of an interaction that involves the sharing of an experience and its associated feeling state. I believe that the need to engage in the sharing of affect with a significant other is one of the specific components involved in the establishment of an empathic connection in therapy. The phenomenon of empathy has been an area of interest to therapists of many persuasions, and it is hoped here that by focusing on the affective sharing involved between empathically connected people, it will help to expand the range of optimal responses available to the therapist.

Although the importance of empathy has been an integral part of Kohut's ideas, emphasis was originally placed on its use as a therapeutic technique in listening (Kohut 1977). The empathic connection was seen primarily as a mode of observation in the gathering of data from the patient in order to facilitate understanding. Later, however, Kohut (1982) acknowledged the phenomenon of an empathic experience as having its own therapeutic properties.

Bacal (Chapter 1) helped expand on the uses of the therapist's empathic knowledge by pointing out that the therapist may use it to maximize the efficacy of his interventions, achieving what he calls an "optimal response." Thus, empathic immersion is initially used to gain knowledge of what is occurring in the transference, allowing the therapist to subsequently choose the most suitable response. This use of an empathic connection to inform the therapist of the necessary therapeutic response had been previously explored, leading to various attempts at adjusting analytic technique (for example, Ferenczi 1928, Winnicott 1965). When Bacal (1990) more recently examined Alexander's contribution to therapeutic technique (see also Chapter 7), specifically the oft-misunderstood "corrective emotional experience," it led to his elaborating on the concept of the optimal response, clarifying that its mutative effect involves a "corrective selfobject experience." These formulations help to enhance our awareness of the therapeutic effect of our responses to the patient and how they can, in the right circumstance, result in a therapeutic, structure-enhancing, selfobject experience.

This chapter deals primarily with the patient's indication that his or her experiences and their associated feeling states need to be shared with another, and discusses some situations where the necessity for a sharing response from the therapist can present itself in the clinical setting. It suggests that not only is it important to know that the therapist truly understands an experience, but as well there is a need to know that the related affect has been actually felt or shared by the therapist. This sharing of affect is, arguably, a reworking of the phenomenon of empathic resonance; however, the focus here will involve (1) an assumption that there is a need in the patient to know his affect has been shared by another, and (2) that the optimal response may involve the therapist's communication to the patient that this sharing has occurred. Previously, the formation of an empathic connection to the patient by his therapist had been acknowledged as an indispensable technique for gathering and validating information, and could be a significant aid in a therapeutic intervention, but what is further being suggested here is that the communication of that connection has a capacity to function as an essential optimal response in its own right.

Patients have various ways of informing us of the response they need, and their attempts can elicit a variety of countertransference feelings in the therapist. When the need for affective sharing is activated in the therapeutic setting it may evoke an attuned empathic state in the therapist. Thus, on the occasion where the therapist feels himself to be strongly connected to the patient's affect, he might consider whether his feelings of empathy may have resulted from the patient's attempt to evoke an empathic connection. If this is so, then an optimal response might demonstrate to the patient that the therapist had felt the connection. Requiring more than simply stating an understanding, it may be necessary to provide a clear indication to the patient that the therapist has "felt" with him. In this way the patient knows that he and the therapist have shared his affective state together.

These sharing experiences that may occur in clinical practice can be divided into two distinct types. The first type occurs when a patient can share with the therapist his emotional state when detailing the former events of his life. Through the description of his past memories, the patient can enable the therapist to become involved in a past experience as an observer who is capable of feeling the same affect that the patient himself feels during the recollection. The therapist who feels engaged in this type of mutual affective connection may then decide to communicate the feeling state that he is sharing. This communication can be delivered in a variety of ways, including those as subtle as a change in vocal inflection or an attuned silence. Regardless of the means, the result is that the patient becomes aware of himself and the therapist sharing an affective state, one that emanates from within the patient and is authentically felt by the therapist. I would call this sort of sharing experience *descriptive sharing*, involving the sharing of memories and their associated affects through descriptions of past experience.

The second way in which a patient may try to elicit a sharing experience involves trying to engage the therapist in a shared activity within the treatment setting. He may attempt to encourage the therapist to participate in a particular enactment, hoping to evoke a mutual experience that will include a sharing of affect between him and his therapist. He might bring into the therapy valued objects or gifts to help the therapist share in his feeling state (perhaps a sense of excitement, horror, or comfort). The patient could ask the therapist to listen to a piece of music, read a poem, or look at a meaningful photograph. The goal here is to share the activity with the therapist and to share the affective state involved in doing it. This is a specific sort of enactment that may lead to an achievement of mutual interest with the therapist and the sharing of the pleasure that the interest gives. This is *active sharing*.

The following two case examples are presented to illustrate occurrences of both descriptive and active sharing experiences.

CASE 1

Over the course of several years I saw a woman who came from a background of severe emotional deprivation. When I first met with her she told me she had no experience whatever of any feeling, except a constant and overwhelming desire to die, which had been with her since she was 11 years old. She related incidents with much confusion, often asking me to tell her what I thought had actually happened to her. It appeared that she had little sense of her own reality. I felt that she needed to achieve a connection with me, but had no idea of how it was to be done. Occasionally she would try by fixing a long intense gaze on me, attempting to make it appear to be sexual in intent. Instead, I was left with a feeling of eerie emptiness and a sense of her desperation.

The stories of her past were very upsetting to hear, although she exhibited little emotion in recounting them. For example, one particular childhood incident she recalled was of having cut her finger while playing outside and returning home for help. Upon seeing the blood, her mother told her to stay outside as the blood could stain the rugs in the house. No help was offered and the door was shut in her face, but the little girl thought this was reasonable, knowing how important her mother's cream-colored rugs were. Although she had acted as if her mother's behavior was quite acceptable, the story was told in a way that made me feel hurt and angry for her. Other "model scenes" such as this one were presented, stories that effectively served as a metaphor for her whole life experience (Lachmann and Lichtenberg 1992), and often involving her mother or the patient's physically and emotionally assaultive ex-husband. I began to see that her way of recounting the past was a means of demonstrating to me how she had dissociated herself from her feelings, and a way to have me feel for her, in order to have her repressed affect validated.

There were frequent discussions of her daily suicidal thoughts and her visits to various locations where she planned to commit the act. It was profoundly distressing to hear how casually she spoke of doing violence to herself, and to have to suppress my own anxious thoughts of being called upon to account for her death. After some time, however, it became apparent that the idea of suicide was her way of soothing herself. Having lived with a competitive mother and then a domineering husband who both communicated in various ways that they wished her dead, she found the thought of killing herself an oasis in a hostile and confusing world. Her thoughts of dying provide us with a good example of how negative selfobject experiences can eventually become an integral part of the self. Early repeated incidents demonstrated to this patient that she was not wanted, leading her to transform her chaotic feelings of despair into the more harmonious belief that she should be dead. Self psychology often discusses deficits in growth-prompting selfobject experiences by caregivers, but it is necessary to further clarify the phenomenon of the patient's incorporation of negative selfobject experiences. Bacal and Newman (1990) have suggested the introduction of the term *bad selfobject* to describe the relatively bad selfobject experience, and Bacal (1995) has developed this idea further. I would suggest as well that repeated negative selfobject experiences can be incorporated into the self and may provide both comfort and a sense of self-cohesiveness. In this woman, her experience of not being wanted became organized into thoughts of dying, which calmed her when she felt unloved. In order to be understood, she needed the therapist to know the adaptiveness of these suicidal wishes. In fact, she told me of her frustration with how previous therapists were often made visibly uneasy when she spoke of her suicide plans. Being watchful and worried that I would not be able to tolerate her suicidality, she gave a clear message: I was to suspend all judgment and try to understand the solace she felt in the idea of her suicide. The wish to die not only gratified the requirements of others but also brought her relief from having to rationalize her own life to herself. It took me almost two years to get comfortable enough with the idea of her fantasied death to openly tell her that I could understand how soothing the idea was to her. (I found it helpful to remember that she'd made no serious attempts in over twenty years.) There came a time when I achieved a deeper understanding about how important the wish to commit suicide was, and how much relief it gave her to focus on such thoughts when she felt bad. I was even able to experience some of the calm that she felt at the thought of her death and told her so. Following this, the incidence of suicidal wishes began to decrease in frequency and eventually stopped.

Past events that we had discussed before were recounted, but now with greater detail. She began to tell me her stories in a way that made me feel more and more upset and hurt for her. I noticed that she was now expressing some emotion in her tone of voice, and that we were starting to feel angry or sad together about the unfairness of things that had happened in her life.

Although her expression of affect was still often restricted, I was convinced that the increasingly detailed content of her narrative was directed at helping me to feel what she herself wanted to feel. This was necessary for her because she had blocked her ability to either re-experience or communicate about how she felt, as the verbalization of feelings had never been tolerated by her parents. Basch (1988) has described this type of "repression of affect." The feelings that I experienced for her were, I believe, a natural countertransference reaction, but my communication of them to her was a technical decision. At the time, I felt that reflecting back to her what I thought she was trying to communicate would help move her toward an increasing awareness of her own affective reality. Thus, I attempted to remain in touch with the affect she was communicating through the content of the story, even if she appeared not to feel anything. Then I would openly comment on how hostile, damaging, or simply unfair I felt others in her life had been to her. I allowed myself to continue expressing the affect that I felt in response to her descriptions, largely because when I did so she would observe me with a fascinated, pleased appearance. It seemed she wanted me to feel for her, and to articulate the feelings for her. This eventually evolved into my feeling with her, as the details of her history became infused with more affect.

I began to conceptualize the necessity of affective sharing because of something she said around the time of termination. Her forthrightness in telling me what she thought about the therapy showed how far she had come from the woman whose sense of being involved little more than thoughts of suicide. She began one of our final sessions by suggesting that I might enjoy her "consumer's report" on our work. This is part of what she said: "I felt as if I'd gone back to my past, relived the scenes of my life, and that I wasn't alone anymore; that we were there together. When I knew that you could feel how it felt to me, then I knew that things had really happened. . . . I don't feel as alone as I used to."

It occurred to me then that my articulating her repressed affect had a function that went beyond the validation of her experience. Her summary of our work made me realize the importance to her of my genuinely experiencing her feeling states, and of our being able to share them together. She had benefited from knowing that I had felt what she had felt. Thus, having me experience the affects that she had long ago discarded was, for her, necessary to her developing both a sense of her own reality and a feeling of togetherness with another, and was a crucial part of our work. It had been insufficient to simply interpret, understand, or affirm her. Being able to share her affect and communicate it to her had a profound therapeutic effect.

As a footnote to the case, this patient had also attempted to engage me in an active sharing experience in the later stages of therapy. While discussing her pleasure in playing the piano at home, she asked and I confirmed that I played the piano as well. The next session she showed me the music she'd been working on. After my appreciating its difficulty she said that the music was actually a gift for me, and that she hoped that I would learn to play it myself. I remember trying not to feel annoyed since learning to play it would have probably taken me many hours of work, and I did my best to appear interested. She looked very let down. I had wondered at the time why my initial response was not enough. After all, I had admired her perseverance in completing such a difficult work, so why would it be important to her that I must learn to play the music as well? Over the next few sessions I discovered that only through my desire to play the piece could she be assured that her enthusiasm for the piece had been genuinely shared, a sharing that would be further elaborated upon once I had tried to play it. I had clearly disappointed her with my indifferent response. Consequently she gave me another gift a few weeks later; a small pressed flower decoration inscribed, "Feelings are everywhere, be careful." The gift was given in good humor, as a permanent reminder of how I had let her down. It continues to instruct me to remember the importance of choosing my responses carefully. In our ensuing discussions, we determined that my anxiety about her musical request caused me to be politely dismissive of her, leading her to feel ashamed of having made the suggestion. I had hurt her in response to her trying to share something important with me, and temporarily disrupted her sense of being in a safe environment. As with other selfobject transferences, the frustration of the need to share can lead to a disruption of an empathic connection, and as with any disruption, the empathic connection can be restored again after exploration and interpretation of the meaning of the empathic error. Her giving of the gift and my accepting it and understanding its meaning was part of the restoration process.

This situation demonstrates that patients who seem intent on engaging in certain enactments may be trying to elicit a sharing of mutual experience and affect with their therapist. In addition, the reason why some are curious about their therapist's personal lives might not only be because they are engaged in an alterego or idealizing transference, but also because they may wish to test out whether their therapist can "feel together" with them. For example, my patient needed to know whether I could play the piano in order for her to attempt to share a musical experience with me. Their hope may be that similarities between themselves and their therapist will increase the likelihood that they can share their experiences and affective states and not feel alone in the analytic environment.

CASE 2

When I first met this retired gentleman I was very impressed with his ongoing effort to engage in an active and cultured life. He had been a reasonably successful freelance writer in the past and continued to write for pleasure. He also pursued his interest in oil painting as well as music performance and composition. All in all, he was quite lively and charming and I was pleased to be able to work with him. It wasn't long, however, before we discovered his powerful and sustained selfobject transferences. He began to ask me numerous probing questions about my personal life and interests and was very gratified when he felt he had discovered similarities between us. Following this, his need for affirmation from me grew to be seemingly insatiable, and I had difficulty responding in the way he needed because his grandiosity about his abilities was often hard for me to bear. This was a man who believed he could compose better than Beethoven, write better than Joyce, and paint better than Picasso, and he wanted me to acknowledge the truth of these assertions. Much of the first few months of our meetings was spent in my interpreting disruptions of the mirroring selfobject transference.

After a year of therapy, he told me that some of his friends often found his behavior offensive, and at the time I had little difficulty empathizing with both him and his friends. We both understood then that his questioning of his own behavior was an important sign of progress. He also stopped presenting himself to me as a perfect father, and started to become concerned about his attitude regarding his children. He began telling me that he wished he could have it "all together" the way he imagined I did, idealizing my life as a father and a professional man.

With this man, the knowledge of safety within a particular active selfobject transference had to be established before moving on to another. Thus, he needed to know there was a sufficient likeness (in the alterego transference) between us before he could look for affirmation (in the mirroring transference). Once alterego and mirroring needs were dealt with, he could then move on to an idealizing transference.

Memories of the early relationship with his father surfaced. His father had been easy to admire, because he was handsome, bright, and successful in business. Some additional "successes" also involved women outside of marriage. The unfortunate result was that his father developed a fatal venereal disease. During his father's final years he lost his business, his strength, and his mental faculties while mother and son watched. The patient recalled how his "wonderful dad" deteriorated into a "drooling, raging idiot." While recounting these memories, it became apparent that the patient was reinvesting in me as someone who could replace his lost father. In the transference he now needed me to respond to the idealizing alterego and mirroring selfobject needs that were being activated.

During this period in the treatment, there was a particular session that demonstrated his need for both a mirroring selfobject experience and the sharing of affect in an activity with me. He was working on a story that tried to capture the horror of what he knew was going on in Bosnia. It was a project that was very important to him. In the previous session, he had asked to show it to me and I had agreed. The next time we met I was surprised to see him carrying the thick manuscript of an epic work, along with a tape recorder. As I silently read along, he played for me a tape of his own voice reading it. Initially I felt little else beyond irritation. It was obvious that it would take more than a couple of sessions to get through; the work was massive, the writing unwieldy and complex, and it demanded a lot from the reader. I recall him stopping the tape at times and asking, "What do you think?" "Is it okay?" "Do you like it?" I tried to respond (to his mirroring selfobject needs) encouragingly. About halfway through, however, something happened in the reading. His voice on the tape became more solemn, and he sat with his head bent in concentration. Surprisingly, I found myself engrossed in the content of what was being read, which was

so touching that I had to stifle a sob. Without looking at me, he turned off
the tape recorder and asked quietly, "Did you feel it?" His tone seemed very
sad and resigned; he was expecting to be disappointed. I was able to tell him
that I had indeed felt it, whereupon he became immediately vitalized and
told me, "That part was really very important to me." When I told him I
could tell, he was buoyant. He turned off the recorder and then asked that
we go over the more meaningful sections of the work together. It was clear
that he enjoyed this part of the session immensely, with both of us sharing
some excitement together over what could be done with his writing.

The particular timing of his decision to read me some of his writing
came following his having satisfied himself that I was someone who could
respond to his alterego and idealizing selfobject needs continuing the
selfobject functions provided for him by the father who eventually disappointed him and died. Once this corrective selfobject relationship was
established, he felt free to risk showing me something very important to
him. The resurgence of his mirroring selfobject needs and the fear that they
would not be met was demonstrated by the unwieldiness of the work. In
most of his writing he tried repeatedly to gain admiration through using
complex phraseology and massive scale. He later told me that his need for
the work to impress me led it to become one of the worst things he'd ever
written. However, the central portion of the work expressed something he
deeply felt, and the change in his demeanor confirmed that his selfobject
need at that point had changed. Once he knew that he had made me
reverberate with his emotional state, his enjoyment at having shared this
with me was evident. Having me work further with him on the story was a
way of extending the experience of sharing, with our continuing to express
mutual excitement at his writing's potential.

In addition to illustrating active sharing, this case demonstrates something of the motivation for artistic expression that goes beyond what can be
explained by applying our current knowledge of other selfobject functions.
Primarily, it involves the capacity for successful artists to access genuine
feelings within themselves and work at trying to compel the observer to feel
with them, thus sharing their feeling states.

A musician, for example, may select a work where he feels connected
to the emotions expressed by the composer. He allows these various
emotions to reverberate within himself when playing the piece, which
induces the audience to share in these feeling states. In this way the
audience can provide a sharing selfobject function for him. In addition, the

playing of music can result in a sharing experience for the performer in yet another direction. When playing alone for himself, a musician can find great personal joy at being able to express how he feels, through music that he chooses to resonate with his feeling states. When he is able to express himself in isolation, the experience of shared affect can occur without the need for someone else's physical presence. The absent composer or the maker of his instrument can provide this selfobject function, or even the music or the instrument itself. Anything that can resonate with his own feeling state can be experienced as responding to the need to share affect. The opportunity that artistic activities can provide for affective sharing is an important aspect of why they can be so fulfilling to do, even when done in isolation.

DISCUSSION

The experience of the therapist as an optimally responsive other, and the interpretation of self–selfobject disruptions are both potentially mutative therapeutic events (Bacal 1990, Wolf 1988). Consequently, we need to make choices in trying to respond to what we perceive are the patient's predominant needs, while interpreting to the patient our view of the source of the inevitable disappointments.

This position has important clinical consequences. It suggests that the therapist must attempt to adjust his interventions according to what he determines to be the patient's most predominant need at the time. This may be a complex matter, involving multiple verbal and nonverbal cues. In the situation where the patient encourages the therapist to make a specific response to a need to share affect, there is a risk of the therapist's feeling that a so-called enactment may occur, requiring a type of gratification that may be inappropriate to the consultation room. It is recommended here that the therapist reconsider the role of the enactment as having a potential therapeutic function in treatment, and respect such requests on the part of the patient as being legitimate indicators for how the therapist can make the most helpful therapeutic intervention. Thus, a description of a powerful scene from the past, the display of an article, or presentation of a gift to the therapist may now be considered in the light of (1) whether or not there is an attempt to share an affective state, (2) whether or not the therapist has experienced this shared affective state, and (3) how to best communicate this to the patient as an optimal response.

In choosing his or her correct response, the therapist might also consider whether the patient is experiencing conflicting needs that require contradictory responses. When this occurs, an optimal response to one selfobject need may still constitute an inadequate response to another. For example, with particular regard to the sharing of affect, there are instances where a response that may be useful within the mirroring selfobject transference may also inadvertently demonstrate that the patient's affect has not been shared, leading to an experience of empathic failure.

A hypothetical situation might help to illustrate this. When a patient presents a story of feeling unfairly treated at work, one might consider saying, "You feel your boss is being unfair to you." This response could be appropriate if the predominant selfobject transference is a mirroring one. However, if the patient is also in need of sharing his affect with another, the use of "you feel" in the sentence could imply that the therapist is somewhat experience-distant from the patient's affect and the phrase could be felt to be disruptive.* A preferable comment, which would bridge the gap between the patient's need to share affect and his mirroring selfobject needs would be, "It hurts when you're treated so unfairly." Further, if the patient has been successful in communicating a deeply felt sense of outrage in such a way that the therapist can feel it, then the response of the therapist to the predominantly sharing selfobject need could be, "It's infuriating that you have been treated this way." The therapist who wishes to respond optimally wants his intervention to reflect the current balance between the predominant selfobject transferences.

I would suggest that the wish to share one's experience and its associated affective state is a need that functions similarly to other selfobject needs. Its importance is manifest throughout a person's life, and in early life this experience of affective "sharing" is one of the necessary interactions

---

*Katy Pastierovic (personal communication, 1996) has similarly observed that the therapist, in responding to the patient's mirror selfobject transference, may risk inadvertently distancing himself from the patient. She suggests that some patients have a need to know more about the therapist's experience, in addition to having their own experience understood. In her words, they need "to see behind the mirror."

crucial to normal development. For example, an early prototype of the sharing experience involves the child's knowledge that his comfort in being in his parent's arms is *felt* by the other (shared) in addition to being affirmed (mirrored). Stern (1985), in regard to the observed infant, comments that it is hard to imagine a situation in which there is no interaffective sharing. Lichtenberg (1989) has also observed the presence of affective sharing between parent and child. This experience of affective sharing becomes generalized later in life to include social experience as well. We may express our mature needs to share by having someone else taste our meal at a restaurant, listen to a piece of music we enjoy, or simply engage with us in ordinary conversation. It exhibits itself whenever we search for a companion to feel interested in the things we ourselves find interesting, being one of the motives that moves us toward intimacy and the search for a soul mate.

The normative yearning people have to share something that is important to them is a sign of the mature vestiges of earlier sharing needs. In people who suffer from a deficiency in affective sharing, this yearning can overwhelm them with a sense of aloneness. Conversely, people who have had sufficient sharing experiences in their development will remain cohesive and not feel abandoned when alone, since a togetherness feeling with the selfobject is an integral part of their self.

All positive self–selfobject interactions are crucial to the development of an integrated self, and each of these experiences can potentially satisfy different overlapping selfobject needs. In clinical practice it is necessary to separate out the active participants in a multiple selfobject transference in order to recognize and thus respond optimally to each one when possible. Because elements of the sharing selfobject transference bear a resemblance to both mirroring and alterego selfobject transferences, it should necessarily be differentiated from them. To do this, it might help to define them briefly: *Alterego* selfobject experiences involve a feeling of sameness between self and selfobject ("There are others like me"). *Mirroring* selfobject experiences involve a sense of affirmation emanating from the selfobject toward the self ("Others accept and understand me"). *Sharing* selfobject experiences verify that the self can make the selfobject reverberate with its feeling state ("Others feel with me what I feel").

It is my hope that developing the theoretical concept of a sharing selfobject will help further position the phenomenon of empathic resonance in the realm of mutative therapeutic experiences by giving it a specific selfobject function necessary to the formation of a cohesive self. Clinically, the suggested use of affective sharing in treatment supports Bacal's (Chapter 1) stance that we need not worry that a patient's requests of us are necessarily inappropriate demands for gratification. Rather, such directives can be used to lead the therapist to the most helpful response. This kind of thinking allows us to reconsider what some therapists call enactments as possibly being important therapeutic maneuvers, sometimes resulting in the active sharing of mutual experience. It may also recommend the adjustment of a therapist's response to evocative descriptions to include communication of having shared in his patient's affect. The empathically attuned therapist may now consider that, in order to be optimally responsive to the patient, he might indicate in one way or another that he can not only understand the patient's experience, but that he is actually sharing in that experience.

References

Bacal, H. A. (1990). The elements of a corrective selfobject experience. *Psychoanalytic Inquiry* 10:347–372.

——— (1995). The essence of Kohut's work and the progress of self psychology. *Psychoanalytic Dialogues* 5(3):353–366.

Bacal, H. A., and Newman, K. (1990). Reply to Estelle Shane's review of *Theories of Object Relations: Bridges to Self Psychology* by H. A. Bacal and K. Newman. Presented at the 13th Annual Conference on the Psychology of the Self, New York, October.

Basch, M. F. (1988). *Understanding Psychotherapy: The Science Behind the Art*. New York: Basic Books.

Ferenczi, S. (1928). The elasticity of psychoanalytic technique. In *Final Contributions to the Theory and Technique of Psycho-Analysis*, ed. S. Ferenczi, pp. 87–101. New York: Brunner/Mazel.

Kohut, H. (1977). *The Restoration of the Self*. New York: International Universities Press.

——— (1982). Introspection, empathy, and the semicircle of mental health. *International Journal of Psycho-Analysis* 63:395–407.

Lachmann, F. M., and Lichtenberg, J. (1992). Model scenes: implications for psychoanalytic treatment. *Journal of the American Psychoanalytic Association* 40(1):117–137.

Lichtenberg, J. (1989). *Psychoanalysis and Motivation*. Hillsdale, NJ: Analytic Press.

Stern, D. N. (1985). *The Interpersonal World of the Infant: A View from Psychoanalysis and Developmental Psychology.* New York: Basic Books.

Winnicott, D. W. (1965). *The Maturational Processes and the Facilitating Environment.* London: Hogarth.

Wolf, E. (1988). *Treating the Self: Elements of Clinical Self Psychology.* New York: Guilford.

9

Optimal Responsiveness and Subject–Subject Relating

LYNNE JACOBS

EDITOR'S COMMENT

The starting point for Jacobs's explication of subject-subject relating is to identify Martin Buber's "philosophy of dialogue" as a theoretical support for extending intersubjectivity theory into the arena of "otherness." She draws special attention to Buber's view that, to promote the development of selfhood in the patient, the analyst must not only "enter into the world of the other as the other experiences it" (what Buber calls "inclusion"), but also be present as an "other." She draws attention to Buber's views that selfhood emerges in genuine relations; thus, to be optimally responsive, the therapist must be prepared not only to respond to the selfobject needs of the patient, but also be available, if needed, to respond as a subjective other, a presence in her own right vis-à-vis the patient.

We may note that the consideration of subject-subject relating as an optimal response also includes but transcends the more narrow consideration of whether the therapist's self-disclosure will be therapeutic for the patient. Herzog's theoretical and clinical depiction of sharing as an optimal response (Chapter 8) is, in effect, similarly inclusive.

Jacobs's work with Jerry, in which she responds as a substantive other-in-relationship who shares (discloses) painful affects and limitations with her patient, preeminently illustrates four important aspects of optimal responsiveness that I have variously described in Chapters 1 and 7: its breadth, specificity, reciprocity, and an effective mode of *therapeutic relatedness*. Jacobs's responsiveness to Jerry, which was in some ways quite at variance with the traditional ways we have been trained to work with patients, was not a parameter but rather centrally constituted a profound therapeutic effect for the patient. In other words, Jacobs tellingly demonstrates how a certain kind of optimal responsiveness—a subject–subject responsiveness—enabled this patient to have a selfobject experience in the context of what I have defined (Chapter 7) as a selfobject relationship: the expectation that he could count on his analyst to respond optimally—as Jacobs puts it, "a reliable sense that [the analyst] is in [the analysand's] corner." The clinical data in Jacobs's paper is especially compelling in that the author speaks in support of her thesis not only from her experience as a therapist but also from the depths of her experience as a patient.

Jacobs's views join up directly with Lynn Preston's (n.d.) "expressive relating." Herzog's "active sharing" as an optimal response, which he describes in Chapter 8, is a broader concept that includes subject-subject relating as well as the meaningful sharing of other phenomena, objects, events, and their associated affective states. Susan Lazar's description of certain kinds of activity as optimal responsiveness, which we shall consider in Chapter 10, also implies subject-subject relating but it, too, has a wider conceptual connotation. Subject-subject relating also has significant points of contact with Fosshage's "self-with-other" (Chapter 6), Morton and Estelle Shane's "intersubjective relating" (Chapter 4), Terman's "dialogue of construction" (Chapter 3), and Paul Tolpin's (1988) "optimal affective engagement." I consider all of these as constituting diverse modes of therapeutic relatedness that variously constitute the therapist's optimal responsiveness (see Chapter 7) to the patient.

References

Preston, L. (in press). Expressive relating: the intentional use of the analyst's subjectivity. *Progress in Self Psychology*. Unpublished.

Tolpin, P. (1988). Optimal affective engagement: the analyst's role in therapy. In *Learning from Kohut: Progress in Self Psychology*, Vol. 4, ed. A. Goldberg. Hillsdale, NJ: The Analytic Press, pp. 160–168.

❖

Psychoanalytic theories that purport to embody the paradigm shift from a one-person to a two-person psychology must account for many dimensions of relatedness between two interacting subjectivities. A generally neglected dimension is that of subject-subject relating, in which the subjective worlds of *both* participants are considered meaningful to *each* participant. That is, each participant in an interaction is concerned with "otherness."

Intersubjectivity theorists have not yet developed a theory of otherness, despite having asserted strongly that all facets of development and living are inherently social—specifically intersubjective—processes. As with self psychology theorists, they refer to the needed other (specifically, the subject's perception of, and valuing of, the other as having his or her own meaningful subjective world independent of the subject) only in terms of the self-regulating functions the other performs by listening and responding in an empathically attuned manner. Such a description refers only to the meanings and functions of the other as an *object*. Object has a storied history and multiplicity of meanings in psychoanalysis. In this chapter, object means to perceive of, and relate to, another as though the other has no subjectivity, or as though the other's subjectivity has no meaning to the perceiver. The meanings and functions of the other as a *subject* have not yet been elaborated. Intersubjectivity theory has much to contribute to understanding subject-subject relating by elaborating the developmental longings for, and meanings of, the other. This chapter is a beginning exploration.

Arguments abound from various sources that subject-subject relating is a developmental necessity, as much as self-to-object and self–selfobject relating. From infant research (Lichtenberg 1989, Stern 1985) come hypotheses about affect sharing and other phenomena of intersubjective relatedness as being central to the development of a sense of self. Intersubjective relatedness makes possible the experience of having a sharable inner life, the development of a sense of belonging, and the development of the capacity to understand and relate empathically with others. From modern psychoanalysis, the voices of Hoffman (1992) and Aron (1991) have recently joined those of earlier advocates for the centrality of subject-subject relating, many of whom can trace their roots back to Ferenczi's influence. From the realm of philosophy, Martin Buber spoke eloquently of the necessity of "I-Thou" relating for the development of one's awareness of one's humanity. Buber (1970) wrote, "There is no I as such but only the I of the basic word I-Thou and the I of the basic word I-It. (p. 54) . . . Without it a human being cannot live. But whoever lives only with that is not human" (p. 85).

In fact, Buber's philosophy, called the "philosophy of dialogue," provides a suitable philosophical underpinning for intersubjectivity theory. Atwood and Stolorow (1984) looked to existentialist philosophers for such an underpinning and found them lacking, largely because the existentialists were embedded in the isolated "monadic mind" perspective. But Atwood and Stolorow did not examine Buber's philosophy, and Buber has some of the same criticisms of the other existentialists that Atwood and Stolorow raised. Hycner and Jacobs (1995) state:

> Buber, in a quote almost forty years before there were intersubjective self psychologists, could be easily mistaken for one: "He can know the *wholeness* of the person and through it the wholeness of *man* only when he does not leave his *subjectivity* out and does not remain an untouched observer" (1965, p. 124). . . .
>
> In regard to the label "existentialist," it should be noted that though Buber's philosophy of dialogue was certainly within the broad thrust of existential thought, he did not view his philosophy as "existentialist," in the vein of Heidegger's or Sartre's outlooks. He criticized most of the existentialists because in their philosophies individual existence often was overemphasized at the expense of human inter-existence—there was little room left for the possibility of genuine dialogue and relatedness between persons. Buber was primarily concerned with an intersubjective existentialism, or what he preferred to call the "interhuman" dimension of existence. [pp. 115–116]

There are some striking similarities between Buber's "philosophy of dialogue" and intersubjectivity theory. In both systems of thought, self and other are an indissoluble unit. Intersubjectivity theory posits that one's sense of self is an emergent phenomenon of intersubjective relatedness. In a very similar vein, Buber says one's selfhood emerges in what he calls "genuine relations" with others, often referred to as "I–Thou" meetings (1970). His entire philosophy is a radical affirmation of "self-in-relation" as the only meaningful characterization of human existence. For instance, in writing about psychological problems, he says that sicknesses of the soul are sicknesses of relationship. That is a poetic precursor to Stolorow and colleagues (1987) assertion that such pathological phenomena as border-line states are emergent phenomena of an intersubjective field rather than solely the property of the subject.

Another similarity between the philosophy of dialogue and intersub-jectivity theory is that the epistemologies of both theories eschew efforts to describe objective knowledge. In Buber's thinking, I–It and I–Thou relationships are phenomenological events, having no objective reality that can be assessed by an outside observer. Those relationships can be under-stood only from within the perspective of the participants.

Another crucial similarity between the philosophy of dialogue and intersubjectivity theory is that Buber believed quite firmly that for a genuine dialogue to occur—and only genuine dialogue promotes the emergence of selfhood—the ground of the dialogue must be an immersion in the subjectivity of the other. He called this immersion "inclusion" (1965). Buber defined inclusion in analysis in this way: "The analyst must feel the other side, the patient's side of the relationship, as a bodily touch to know how the patient feels it" (1967, p. 173). Inclusion means to enter into the world of the other as the other experiences it. He described, in evocative language, the stance of empathic inquiry that has been explicated in self psychology and intersubjectivity theory. Buber claims that inclusion is the basic scaffolding on which genuine dialogue in analysis stands. He ac-corded it the same central place that empathic inquiry holds in self psychol-ogy and intersubjectivity theory. However, Buber emphasizes an additional dimension of dialogue, which he believes to be a necessary companion to inclusion: the presence of the analyst as an other. I agree with this premise, that subject-subject relating is a necessary companion for empathic inquiry. It is the context within which the empathic inquiry unfolds.

The subjectivity of the therapist as an other is an important dimension of the developmental process of therapy. Subject-subject relating is differ-ent from the usual conception of selfobject relatedness. Our attention is drawn not just to the self-regulating, self-restorative, or self-enhancing function that is being served, but more to the fact that such functions are being served by one who is a separate other person. Thus, the analyst does not only serve selfobject needs for the patient. She[1] is also an other who can be met and known. Through meeting and knowing the otherness of the same analyst who serves selfobject functions, the patient develops a fuller apprehension of the world of human relatedness, and a fuller sense of his own selfhood.

While I have found Martin Buber's philosophy of dialogue to be a useful theoretical support for stretching intersubjectivity *theory* into the arena of otherness, I have found Howard Bacal's clinical theory and method of optimal responsiveness to be a useful guidepost for understanding clinical interactions. For if the experience of subject-subject relating is necessary for self-development, then the analyst who is open, in principle, to the patient's wish for engagement with the analyst-as-subject will have the potential to respond to the patient's developmental strivings in a facilitative manner. To be able to respond optimally, the analyst needs an understanding of clinical interaction that can include the therapist's presence as an other. The principle of optimal responsiveness, which has emerged from self psychology and intersubjectivity theory, provides the necessary framework.

The impetus for my interest in this topic derives in part from my own experiences as a patient, as well as from my experiences as an analyst. I kept encountering this simple experiential fact from my two analyses: that whatever deeply moving, facilitative selfobject experiences I had with my analysts, the transformative power of these interactive events resided, it seems to me, in the fact that they were offered voluntarily, by separate other people who willingly engaged their own subjectivity with mine, and used their subjectivity as a tool to serve my development. My awareness of this dimension—the otherness of the analyst—was crucial to rendering the selfobject experiences meaningful to me.

To date, the literature of intersubjectivity theory does not reflect my own experience as a clinician and as a patient. Intersubjectivity theory does not elaborate upon the developmental necessity of encountering the other as a subject. It is true that the literature is peppered with clear assertions that the consulting room is an intersubjective arena wherein reciprocal mutual influence shapes the experience of both participants. Stolorow and col-

---

1. For simplicity, the analyst will be referred to as female. Patients will be male, except when I am referring specifically to my own experiences as a patient.

leagues (1987) do not ignore the fact that the analyst is a subject as well as an object. They point out that the analyst, through her own subjectivity, is a co-constructor of the selfobject and repetitive transferences. Nowhere, however, do they suggest that the patient may seek out, and need, awareness of the analyst as a subject in her own right in order for his development to proceed. To date, with rare exceptions (Fosshage 1995, Shane and Shane 1989), references to the analyst's subjectivity address only the potential problems associated with the analyst's lack of ability to "de-center" from her own perspective. I believe that the analyst's subjectivity is also a positive ingredient in the patient's development. Orange (1995) makes a compelling and thoughtful case for emotional openness on the part of the therapist. Such openness is one dimension of subject-subject relating.

An example of where intersubjectivity theory falls just short of appreciating how the therapist's "otherness" plays a positive role in the therapy process is in the area of affect attunement. I think the methodology of affect attunement has effects on two levels of communication with a patient, only one of which is explicitly addressed in the theory. On the one hand, it is the ground from which a sense of affect validity, articulation, and integration occurs. We have seen that such integration enhances and strengthens the patient's sense of self to a great degree. But the second level of communication may be even more crucial. Affect attunement serves also as a recognition of the wholeness of the patient. The analyst, in attempting to attune to the patient's affects and needs, and to understand them in the context of this patient's history and present life, is recognizing a unique and yet understandable person. The therapist is also first and foremost a human being, and can only attune to the patient from the depths of her own subjectivity. I think patients often apprehend—if mostly unconsciously— the significance of the fact that the analyst must process their communications through her own subjectivity, and her successes as well as her struggles to be as accurate as possible are affirming. We see signs of this awareness in our patients' struggles and hesitations as they endeavor to communicate their experiences to us, as well as their noticeable relief when we understand them deeply.

An example from my experience as a patient may be illustrative.

It was my first session with a new analyst. I was in the process of interviewing analysts to find one with whom to work. I was already in tears, describing the recent death of one who was very dear to me. I felt shattered, lost, and was struggling to regain my footing in the difficult aftermath of this person's death. At one moment the analyst sighed and said with great feeling, "What a nightmare!" I was surprised and warmed by the vehemence of his remark. The affective tone was certainly attuned to my story and my state of mind. But more, he seemed to be expressing a spontaneous reaction of the impact of my story upon him. His remark did not seem to be aimed solely at communicating to me what he thought was my state of mind. Rather, he seemed to be balanced between being attuned to my state of mind, and expressing *his* state of mind as he was affected by being immersed in empathic listening. My reaction was an immediate, twofold sense of recognition. First, a bit of tormenting confusion lifted as I recognized that I *was* describing a nightmare. Second, I recognized that he was allowing my story to reverberate within him strongly enough to be deeply affected. I felt affirmed and grateful, and knew that I wanted to work with him. In a sense, one could say that his tone of voice—in which he expressed *his* state of mind as well as trying to capture my own—was well attuned to a need (and doubt) of mine to know that I can have an emotional impact on another.

My point here is that the attunement was useful and affirming to me not merely in and of itself, but as much because of the metacommunication that such attunement was being proffered by a discernibly separate other who was available for engagement with me. My analyst's response could be considered optimally responsive because he seemed to find the right balance between communicating something of his own experience, and staying within my experience at that moment. Bacal's notion of specificity (see Chapter 7) suggests that such a response was facilitative for me in that it was responsive to my longing to know that another can be moved by my experience. Such a longing is one among many that revolve around the otherness of the analyst.

I am not saying that *all* attuned responses to a patient must carry this metalevel message overtly in order to be usable. In fact, at other times, it has been very important in my own analysis for my analyst to stay very close to my experience, without intruding any hints of his own experience. Yet that first experience let me know that this analyst would have no objection to allowing his presence to be part of the analytic ambience, and I needed such a sign before I could begin. That first experience also enriched the meaning for me of those times when his own presence is kept further in the background. At those times I appreciate his commitment to his task, such that he is voluntarily holding more of his own presence in suspension, for my sake. By "presence," I mean an analyst's willingness to be open to a kind of engagement in which the patient can touch the therapist's subjective experience, both directly and indirectly.

Quite often the analyst's subjectivity is revealed indirectly, through tone of voice, choice of language, focus of interpretation, and so on. But at crucial points in the therapy, for instance, in efforts to address serious disruptions in the therapy relationship, or at certain developmental thresholds, the patient may be intensely interested in, and require, access to the therapist's experiencing. From a perspective that asserts that all experience is embedded in a relational matrix, it seems almost self-evident that self-development proceeds not only through the experiences gained through sensitive attunement to the patient's experience, but through the experience of that attunement coming from a discernible, personal other. Buber (1965) wrote:

> Man wishes to be confirmed in his being by man, and wishes to have a presence in the being of the other. The human person needs confirmation because man as man needs it. . . . Secretly and bashfully he watches for a Yes which allows him to be and which can come to him only from one human person to another. It is from one man to another that the heavenly bread of self-being is passed. [p. 71]

In effect, in certain, sometimes subtle, ways, the therapist's presence is a continuous phenomenon, sometimes more in the foreground of the patient's experience, sometimes more in the background. For in the analyst's efforts at empathic inquiry, her presence is always, more or less subtly, coming forth. She does not simply parrot what the patient says, with the same inflection. She uses different words. She often articulates the affect that is only implied by the patient. She changes inflection. In each of these slight (or perhaps not so slight) alterations of his original communication, the patient may find himself affected as much by the other's attempts to live in his shoes as by the relative accuracy and depth of the attempt. This is the second level of meaning that is embedded in affect attunement; whether or not the analyst's attunement is accurate, she confirms the patient's existence as a live, feeling other, merely by her attempts to understand him. In fact, an attuned response based on empathic inquiry is an enactment of the analyst's otherness. Attuned responsiveness carries not only her understanding of the patient's communication, but her understanding and response to the affective interplay between the patient and analyst. An obvious example of optimal responsiveness in the context of affect attunement is when the analyst adjusts her tone of voice toward gentle softness in response to the patient's expressions of hurt and shame.

All analysts are aware that a specter of otherness hovers as a constant presence in the consulting room. But we are used to thinking of the power of otherness and its influences on the patient in two negative ways. First, as I described above, is the therapist's otherness as a countertransference impediment when the analyst cannot de-center from her own perspective. Second, the patient is all too aware of the analyst's predilection toward having her own responses, and that awareness frightens and constricts the patient. In intersubjectivity theory, when otherness is feared, we might say the patient is in the repetitive dimension of the transference. The patient tends to expect that the analyst's subjectivity will be perilously similar to the subjectivity of traumatizing caregivers in his life. But many patients also struggle toward an engagement with their analyst not just as a repetitive figure, and not even as someone who merely serves their developmental needs. I think they strive for a more complex experience of the analyst in her subjectivity. I think the deep gratitude we so often hear from our patients is a sign of their recognition that we *are* a separate center of initiative, we have our own aims and needs and organizations of our subjective worlds, and yet we volunteer to suspend our aims and needs where possible to make room for our patients.

It is not uncommon for clinicians to talk of a developmental sequence in the analytic process, whereby the patient begins the analysis with little or no awareness of, or interest in, the otherness of the analyst. As the analysis proceeds, the patient moves from his self-centered original position to one with a greater appreciation of the mutuality of relatedness. As Bacal and Newman (1990) have pointed out, sometimes such apparent blindness to the otherness of the analyst may reflect the patient's lack of confidence that appropriate selfobject responsiveness will be forthcoming. Patients may need to forcefully blot out the subjectivity of analysts in order to ensure that there is room for their own. For such patients, the discovery of a mutuality that is enriching to them—rather than leaving them bereft and depleted—while they explore the otherness of the analyst is often powerfully moving.

I have also encountered the opposite situation, where patients have needed to be able to contact me as a separate subject at the start of the analysis. For such patients, the lack of the analyst's accessible presence was akin to being lost in a terrible empty darkness. One such patient feared a repetition of rote caregiving activities similar to his experience with his distant parents. Another patient began his analysis with me by saying that his deepest longing regarding the analytic process was that he wanted a place to be completely true to himself, and yet where the other person would not have to compromise herself in order to provide room for him. In these cases, it appears that an optimally attuned response was one wherein my reactivity as an other was apparent to them, along with my attempt to understand their particular longings for contact with my otherness in the context of their developmental strivings.

Sometimes the achievement for such a patient is not the discovery of otherness, but rather the discovery that the analyst's otherness can remain intact even if the patient does not keep his eye on it. These patients come to find an other in the analyst who can be used unself-consciously, an other whose otherness does not disappear, but is sturdy enough to be left in the background for long periods of time, to be refound at a later point, unharmed and available for engagement.

Below I will present a case example from a patient who needed to know my subjectivity in order to differentiate me from others who had been exploitative and cruel to him. But first I present some brief ideas of ways in which patients have sought and benefited from access to my subjectivity. One example is a man who fears that empathy, tenderness, and compassion all render him vulnerable to derisive dismissal. We have worked together for many years. A few years ago he knew I was grieving, and shyly and tentatively inquired as to how I was faring in my grief. It was obvious to him that I was moved by his interest, and this provided a new, relatively safe setting for him to explore relating to someone with compassionate interest. Another patient often asks how I react to various life situations. He grew up in a chaotic family where responses did not appear to be linked to events. He uses my answers as a foil for finding his own reactions. He often says, "That's interesting. My reaction is different. I feel more———." This is the patient I described above who wanted a place to be true to himself. He wants to find room for two subjects in the room, and he seems to be using me well toward that end when he differentiates between his reactions and mine. Someone else, who has had little sense of his own inner life, and none at all of others' inner lives, is discovering something about the relativity of subjectivity by asking me about my own. I once suggested to him that he pretend to be an anthropologist from Mars. He should interview some of his friends about their feelings and thoughts that were not apparent to him. He turned the tables by making me his first interview subject, and has come to feel quite liberated by the discovery that everyone's inner world is both the same and different from his own, and that even someone as functional as his analyst has vulnerabilities and conflicts.

PRESENCE AND OTHERNESS

Therapy is, in large part, a developmental process. At different points in the process, different qualities of otherness are sought and required for the patient's growth, or for the patient's healing. This is a view of interaction in therapy that goes beyond understanding and interpretation, and into the areas of affect attunement and optimal responsiveness. One of the arts for the analyst is to bring one's presence forward in a way that addresses the patient's current particular relational strivings. I believe that the impetus for various forms of engagement arises from the pushes and pulls one experiences when attempting to listen systematically from the patient's frame of reference and to be optimally attuned in one's responses. There often comes a time when the empathic inquiry into the patient's experience leads to an apprehension that the patient seeks to meet the analyst's otherness. If the analyst does not recognize that her otherness is central to the analytic process (that is, a central factor in promoting the self-development of the patient), then she may miss the signals of the patient's interest in her subjectivity. She may also underestimate the place of her subjectivity in the process of exploration, preferring to think of exploring *only* when she believes her subjectivity is a hindrance to the patient's progress.

On the other hand, as Hoffman (1992) asserts so eloquently, we cannot always know when to reveal ourselves more fully and when to recede. So much of the analytic process is constructed by the seat of our (unconscious) pants, that it is only in retrospect that we can speak with some certainty of our motivations, assessments, reactions, and technical judgments. The case I describe below fits Hoffman's description well. Yet, as an intersubjectivist, I think the moments about which Hoffman speaks emerge from the overall discipline of sustained empathic inquiry as the primary listening perspective, and of course the relational event that occurs is then examined from the stance of empathic inquiry.

In my opinion, presence and the listening perspective of empathic inquiry exist in a direct relation to each other. We can only understand the subjectivity of another by allowing our own subjectivity to come into a kind of free play with the other's. Also, through empathic inquiry we arrive at an understanding of how our presence is being experienced by the patient. Finally, we come to understand what kind of otherness the patient seeks. We can adapt our presence to be optimally responsive to the patient's emergent developmental needs. The constant interplay between listening via empathic inquiry, attuned responsiveness (of which empathic inquiry may be one form), and the ever-shifting adaptations of one's presence are all played out in a therapeutic dialogue.

CASE EXAMPLE[2]

This patient has, from the very beginning, insisted in a myriad of ways that my subjectivity be easily accessible to him. Many of the initial disruptive interactions between us occurred when he experienced me as hidden or opaque. It appears that the experiences that are most therapeutic—at times even transformative—for him, are those moments when I am most revealed to him in my heartfelt but excruciatingly difficult attempts to be emotionally available to him, and to be true to myself at the same time. It is just such an experience, which occurred in his third year of treatment, that I wish to describe.

These moments derive their compelling power in no small part from the context in which they arise. The context is one of steady, persistent, and disciplined attempts to articulate and understand the terrible demons that dominate Jerry, and the faint whispers of hope that keep him tenuously attached to his analysis. The demons and the hopes have woven themselves tightly into our relationship, so that every meeting between us is a terrifying struggle for him. Dare he trust me? From his perspective, I give him so

---

2. The gender and sexual orientation for this patient were selected by a random coin toss to protect confidentiality. The patient has read this chapter and has given permission for publication.

many reasons not to. We spend much of our time trying to understand and repair the wrenching dislocations caused by my myriad betrayals of him, such as a poorly chosen word that signals that I have contempt for him, a tone of voice that says that I wish to be rid of him, or a subdued response at a time when he needs a firm loud sign that I am intensely engaged.

Jerry was sadistically beaten and sexually abused as a very young child. Both parents worked, and he was left every day in the care of a young couple who abused him. In the course of our work together we have pieced together a story that seems to fit with the body sensations, feelings, and images that have long tormented Jerry, along with newly emerging sensations and memories. His babysitters left him alone in his crib for extended periods of time. He would gaze wistfully at the door, hoping for some respite from his loneliness. But they would come in and harm him and cause him great pain, discomfort, and confusion. The details, as they have emerged, have horrified and appalled both of us. Among the many legacies of this background are severe sexual inhibition, terror of intimacy, and chronic suicidality.

In our first session, Jerry told me he was desperate to hold onto a relationship with a man that had lasted now for seven years but he was afraid he was "killing" it with his enormous problems. He was pessimistic that he could be helped because he felt so "alien." He was also deeply frightened of becoming dependent on me and then being betrayed or abandoned. He felt an intense attachment to me immediately, which exacerbated his fears and sense of vulnerability. Several times he has decided he must quit because he cannot bear the pain of needing me and having me fail him so often and so thoroughly. He has also had recurring periods of intense suicidal preoccupation.

Once, about eighteen months before the incident to be described, we reached such an impasse in our work that he sought an outside consultation. He was desperately needy of my wholehearted emotional involvement. He thought he could not survive from day to day without me. I had been struggling already with my countertransference difficulties. I often found myself retreating from him defensively, fearing some brutal humiliation from him. My stance increased his insistent search for a clear sign of my devotion to him, which increased my defensiveness. We were hanging on by our fingernails already, and then I suffered the unexpected and shattering loss mentioned earlier. I became emotionally incapable of rising to the challenge of remaining open and responsive to him. He said he was in a horrible limbo. He could not bear life without me, but life *with* me was killing him. After the consultation, which was enlightening for both of us, I was able to describe my countertransference difficulties to him, including the above, as well as my agonizing self-doubts about my work with him. He was deeply moved. We both felt humble. His trust in me and our work increased greatly.

Eighteen months later another impasse occurred. It seemed to follow from a deepening of trust and confidence in my abilities. The background for the "forward step" is too lengthy to describe here, but often an increase in any sense of trust, confidence, or intimacy with me gives rise in him to terrible fears of betrayal, or of being flooded with unbearably intense and repulsive (to him) longings for more contact and closeness with me.

We were then meeting three times weekly, for a full hour each session. In our first meeting of the week, he reported that he had spent the weekend hungrily wishing to throw himself into my arms and be gathered in. He was also convinced that, unlike the people of a group to which he belongs, I was simply too constrained and "immobile" as a person to be able to reach for him in the bold way he needed. For instance, he fervently wished I would be willing to cradle him and I was not willing to do so. He thought that in the absence of bold movement on my part he was doomed to an ice-shrouded isolated withdrawal. (In the first months of his analysis he had related to me primarily through pictures and collages. One frequent drawing was of an ice cave in which he huddled, turned toward the corner, and if I was in the picture at all I was in the opposite corner and did not seem to notice him.) He then moved on to talking about his love of roses. He had realized over the weekend that roses symbolized an antidote to his experience of himself as filled with garbage. He felt very sad. He began to see an image of a rose framed by purple flashes—the purple flashes he used to see when he was being beaten about his head. He said the image was a satisfying affirmation that there was a rose to be found amidst his garbage. I suggested that he needed to know that I, too, knew there was a rose in him, to be pulled from the garbage. I said I thought that together we must sift through his garbage and find his roses. At this point we were both teary. I also remembered his concern that I was too constrained, that he had not sensed from me a "permission" to connect more deeply. I said maybe he was not sure it was worth it to me to get my hands dirty. He was moved by that statement, feeling very close to me, and he became nauseous. I suggested, based on past work together, that the experience of intimacy with me stirred up his feeling of being full of garbage. He said intently, "Wear gloves!" I said no. I said I did not expect to be permanently soiled. I wanted to be able to feel the rose with my bare hands, and I knew that we would find a way to wade through the messes created by our intimacy, that together we would find ways to untangle and clean up the messes.

He began to realize that as miserable as he had been all his life, he had still kept his worst horrors hidden away. He was in agony as the session ended. He was terribly frightened over what else might emerge. As he left, so shaken, I instinctively reached out and squeezed his elbow. This was the first time I had touched him spontaneously. He had always wanted me to be freer with touch, and had to settle for the fact that at certain emotionally charged times, if he wanted to hold my hand I would do it. Those times were often packed with meaning for him, especially because he knew it was a stretch for me to do it.

He began the next session saying he did not know if he could survive the space between this session and our next. He was desperate to have me with him all the time to protect him from the horrors of his inner world. And the longings themselves were unbearably shameful and dirty. In the course of his anguished speaking I began to notice small changes in his physical state. We ended up attending to some unusual bodily sensations, and what developed was an experience that seemed to be halfway between a recovery of a memory and a flashback. The end of the memory involved lying desolate in his crib after being abused, and longing for one of his sitters to return and pick him up and soothe him. He remembered the awful confusion of wanting them to return, and yet being terrified of their return because it would lead to further abuse. Now we understood more viscerally how his longings to be gathered in by me were acts of self-betrayal that left him prey to me, and that turned intimacy into sickness. He felt horribly trapped, both by these awful people, and also by his longings for connection. He was crying very deeply now, more than he had ever done. I reached out and held his hand while he sobbed.

In the remaining minutes of the session he sought out a cabinet in my office and said he was leaving his tortures and his longings tucked into one drawer, and reserved the rest of the cabinet space for himself.

After that session, all hell broke loose. He called and left a tearful message on my machine. I returned his call and left a message on his machine (a long-standing pattern between us). We spoke on the phone later in the day, because he was dissatisfied with my return phone message.

He left several messages over the course of the next day, saying he must quit, that therapy could not possibly work for him if he felt worse after a phone contact with me than he did before the contact. His messages felt like blows to my stomach and head each time he called. He said he would return for one last session, only because it was the appropriate thing to do, but he was only coming in "to say good-bye." I reached his answering machine at one point and told him I was very concerned about his thoughts of quitting at this time. I offered a tentative interpretation about his need to protect himself as he became more vulnerable, and asked him to consider allowing for more than one session if need be, so that we could walk through what was happening between us slowly and carefully. I was befuddled, angry, humiliated, and crushed. From my perspective, I had risked reaching out in a way he had yearned for since the beginning of our work, only to be rebuffed. The rebuff simply confirmed for me a deeply embedded shame about myself: that at my core I was a disgusting toxin, and therefore spontaneous gestures of mine poisoned people and ruined relationships.

By the time of our session the next morning, I was filled with dread, and my chest was sore with the residue of hurt feelings that I had spent the night trying to work through. Jerry appeared willing to take whatever time was necessary to try to understand what had happened. We spent the first half of the session working out the problems that had occurred during our phone calls. We learned that I needed to make only a small adjustment in my way of handling his calls in order to permit him to feel more reassured of my availability. What had happened in the disruptive phone call was this: I had asked him what about my previous phone message had been so painfully unsatisfying to him. He had needed me to remember that he was a baby in a crib, and to know that "the baby" was calling me, not his more grown self. He felt rudely "dropped" and abandoned that I had not held in my mind that he was feeling like a desolate little baby in a crib, and had not simply assumed that "the baby" was calling me. It was generally my practice *not* to make assumptions, and instead to leave a more open space for patients to tell me of their experience, but I did think (and have found it to be true), that I could fairly easily respond to his calls with the assumption that the "baby self" was reaching out to me, if that dimension of his self-experience was present in our sessions.

In the course of working out the problem, I told him that I felt defensive, and that I found it difficult to listen well to him without also speaking from my point of view. There was a surprisingly relaxed atmosphere of serious purpose and humor in our exchanges. My defensiveness was obvious to him, and we had enough prior experience to know that if I spoke from my perspective—even when I was defensive—at times, it actually led to further clarification of his perspective. So with good humor, we forged ahead. I lamented, "Why must you throw the baby out with the bathwater? Why leave our face-to-face sessions because our phone contacts are problematic?" Jerry pointed out that all our contacts were part of a whole for him. He said he had never felt closer to me than in our last few weeks, and my failings on the phone meant that I had only seduced and betrayed him. It felt as though I had come into his room, lifted him from his crib, and as he breathed a sigh of relief, I had raised him over my head and smashed him to the ground! At another point I asked rather plaintively, "Why must you threaten to leave? Why not just say you *feel* like leaving?" Within a minute I answered my own question. I slapped myself across my forehead and exclaimed, "Of course! If you cannot at least leave me, then you are utterly trapped! That must never happen to you again." Our eyes teared up at this recognition, and at the same time we both laughed gently at my plaintive plea for him to be "rational and mature." By this point, we were thoroughly settled back into our relationship. I was no longer filled with dread, although I was still quite sore from what I had been through.

Jerry told me quietly and shyly that he loved me. We chatted for a few minutes about other parts of his life. Then in a pause, he asked how I was feeling about what had transpired. I told him I was greatly relieved that what he needed from me over the phone was something I could understand and readily provide. Then my eyes filled with tears. Jerry looked at me with curiosity. I told him I was still recovering from the emotional storm, and I said I was unable to talk about my feelings further without crying. But it was already too late. I *was* crying. Not just a tear or two, but streams of tears. I told him that I had been deeply hurt by his need to leave the therapy, that unfortunately he had touched upon a very painful core issue of mine. I explained (while he handed me two tissues) that at the very moment when I had jumped into our relationship with all my heart and soul he had snapped back that our relationship was no good, and that he was abandoning me (shared laughter at recognition of a familiar theme for him as well!). I also said I lived with a dread that my spontaneous touch of others, both physical and emotional touch, was destructive, and his behavior had only served to confirm that dread.

Jerry started to weep. He told me how much my touch had meant to him. For him my voluntary touch had meant there was more to him than just garbage and slime. He cried more deeply. I had touched his substance. Monday's touch had carried him through until our next meeting. He said my touch gave him life. At this point I handed him one of the tissues he had given me, and we both chuckled. He spoke tearfully of how different his experience was, compared to mine. For him, our relationship had been the most important, nourishing, positive thing in his life of more than fifty years. He wanted to protect and cherish it the only way he knew how. Since he had no hope of cleaning up the mess, his only option had been to leave in order to at least save what he had.

The session ended in what seemed to me to be a sweet, sad humility about our interwoven vulnerabilities, and a renewed sense of intimacy and optimism about our work together.

The next week he said he had experienced a massive shift in his internal world. He had decided that he could risk committing himself to his therapy. I asked if he had felt some pressure from me to make such a commitment to rescue me from my own vulnerabilities. He laughed and said no, and that he thought I would in fact still get hurt in the trenches with him. I said, "Because roses have thorns?" He said, "Of course," and that his reasons had more to do with the fact that he had been deeply moved that his leaving would have such an impact on me. This evident impact was once again an affirmation to him that I saw beyond the slime to the rose in him. If our work together meant so much to me, then perhaps he was safe in throwing his lot in with me. What surprised both of us was that he also said his sense of being suicidal changed. By committing himself to seeing the therapy through, he no longer found himself turning to the prospect of suicide as an escape. He felt more fully embedded in life than he had ever felt.

Approximately two years have passed since this incident. There has been a profound change in our work, which endures as a new underpinning for our efforts. Jerry now has a *reliable* sense that I am in his corner, no matter what might happen between us. He retains that knowledge even when repetitive transference fears are in the foreground. He no longer doubts my commitment to helping him achieve his aims, nor does he doubt (except when he is buried in shame) my deep affection for him. Needless to say, these are hard fought gains for him—for us, really—that appear to have been firmly consolidated by the incident I have described, and the subsequent analysis of his meanings.

The change has affected the flavor of our work in two discernible ways. First, when there are misunderstandings or other disruptions between us, he does not question the very foundations of our relationship. In fact, at times he uses misunderstandings between us as openings for him to reflect on his own defensive organization. In the past, these misunderstandings were so threatening that he could not afford the luxury of such exploration. All of his attention was directed to merely *surviving* the rupture through either "fight or flight."

The second change, a poignant one to me, was in the tone of his suicidality. His suicidal wishes did not disappear for long after the watershed incident. In fact, he plunged into his deepest despair to date shortly after that incident. The difference now was that he seemed to be bringing his suicidal despair into the room with me as perhaps the loneliest of all of his lonely experiences, and he was asking me to get to know him "in the darkness," just as he had struggled to let me know so much else of his tormented inner world. Prior to this point, his suicidal feelings peaked largely in reaction to my misattunements. Now, his suicidal despair emerged when our selfobject bond was intact, at a time when our bond had its deepest impact on him. As he struggled to discern, articulate, and identify with what it meant to love someone (me), he realized that "they got all of me." That is, no aspect of his inner world, not even his capacity for love, was unscathed by the abuse that he endured. Most recently, as we have continued to analyze how alien he feels even his love to be, he has spoken of feeling a sense of integration and a sense of belonging, both new experiences for him.

DISCUSSION

In the case of Jerry, my empathic inquiry has led me to the hypothesis that, at times, an optimally attuned response was one wherein I disclosed my own reactions, wishes, and fears to him. Such disclosures have had different meanings to him at different points in the evolution of our relationship. Early on, they were building blocks toward a safe climate for engagement with me. For him to be able to trust me, he had to know I did not need to hide my reactions from him. He also could not dare to begin to idealize me if I could not openly acknowledge my struggles in our relationship. At the current time my disclosures seem to serve two purposes. One, they concretize my willingness to be known by him (and my trust of him), and hence signify that he is a worthy member of the human race. Two, he uses his knowledge of me as a relatively safe place to discover that another person-as-subject can commit herself to helping Jerry develop. He is experimenting with his tenderness and other intimate feelings for an other, not just one who has helped him, but one who has her own subjective world as well, and daring even to idealize me, within the relatively safe world of our analytic relationship.

CONCLUSION

In the case described above, I endeavor to show that a patient seeks relatedness in differing ways, depending on past experiences and current developmental needs. Analysts can be guided by the developmental readiness of the patient in emphasizing or de-emphasizing their own otherness. The readiness of the patient is often discovered through systematic empathic immersion. The therapy process becomes a fluid process of alternation between affect attunement and presence. The guiding therapeutic methodological principle may be that of optimal responsiveness, and the understanding of what is optimal may be arrived at through a process of sustained empathic inquiry (which is also a response), as differing types of relatedness are sought by the patient at different stages in the therapy process.

ACKNOWLEDGMENTS

I am grateful to Elizabeth Loken-Egdahl, M.D., and Robert Stolorow, Ph.D., for their insightful criticisms and encouragement after reading an earlier draft of this chapter. Howard Bacal, Gordon Berger, Ph.D., Rich Hycner, Ph.D., and Estelle Shane, Ph.D. each improved this final draft immeasurably. However, I am solely responsible for the contents of the chapter.

References

Aron, L. (1991). The patient's experience of the analyst's subjectivity. *Psychoanalytic Dialogues* 1:29–51.

Atwood, G., and Stolorow, R. (1984). *Structures of Subjectivity: Explorations in Psychoanalytic Phenomenology*. Hillsdale, NJ: Analytic Press.

Bacal, H. A., and Newman, K. M. (1990). *Theories of Object Relations: Bridges to Self Psychology*. New York: Columbia University Press.

Buber, M. (1965). *The Knowledge of Man*. New York: Macmillan.

—— (1970). *I and Thou*, trans. W. Kaufmann. New York: Scribner.

Fosshage, J. (1995). Countertransference as the analyst's experience of the patient: the influence of listening perspectives. *Psychoanalytic Psychology* 3:375–391.

Friedman, M., ed. (1967). *A Believing Humanism: Gleanings by Martin Buber*. New York: Simon & Schuster.

Hoffman, I. Z. (1992). Expressive participation and psychoanalytic discipline. *Contemporary Psychoanalysis* 28:1–15.

Hycner, R., and Jacobs, L. (1995). *The Healing Relationship in Gestalt Therapy: A Dialogic-Self Psychological Approach*. Highland, NY: Gestalt Journal Press.

Lichtenberg, J. (1989). *Psychoanalysis and Motivation*. Hillsdale, NJ: Analytic Press.

Orange, D. (1995). *Emotional Understanding: Studies in Psychoanalytic Phenomenology*. New York: Guilford.

Shane, E., and Shane, M. (1989). The struggles for otherhood: implications for development in adulthood. *Psychoanalytic Inquiry* 9(3):466–481.

Skolnick, N. J., and Warshaw, S. C., eds. (1992). *Relational Perspectives in Psychoanalysis*. Hillsdale, NJ: Analytic Press.

Stern, D. (1985). *The Interpersonal World of the Infant*. New York: Basic Books.

Stolorow, R., Brandchaft, B., and Atwood, G. (1987). *Psychoanalytic Treatment: An Intersubjective Approach*. Hillsdale, NJ: Analytic Press.

10

Optimal Responsiveness and Enactments

SUSAN G. LAZAR

EDITOR'S COMMENT

Lazar's elucidation of the therapeutic value of certain kinds of activity on the part of the therapist continues the theme addressed by Herzog and Jacobs in the preceding chapters of exploring ways of relating that constitute optimal responsivity but that transcend traditional psychoanalytic interventions. Lazar calls these responses "enactments." She provides an extensive review of the literature on the subject, which demonstrates some recent movement away from its usual cautionary tone to examine the possibility that certain enactments might be valuable and even necessary to the treatment process. Lazar offers a classification of therapeutic interventions other than verbal interpretation and clarification that include limit-setting, opposing, confronting, directing, and taking charge, which she extensively illustrates with clinical examples.

For Lazar, as well as for myself (see Chapter 1), these responses are not to be regarded as "*parameters*" (Eissler 1953) that must unfortunately be employed temporarily until the therapist can once more resume "proper" analytic technique; they are no more or no less legitimate than any other responses that are therapeutically usable by the patient, and thus they must be given a place of respectability beside the more traditional psychoanalytic interventions. Lazar also addresses one of the major issues that has remained controversial in this area: whether these active responses always require interpretive analysis in order to be therapeutic. Lazar conveys that for some patients, a variety of enactments are sufficient in themselves, that is, they can constitute the optimal response, while for other patients, they must be the prelude to the more conventional therapeutic responses of empathizing, understanding, and explaining. Lazar's essay thus presents a vivid elaboration of the theory of specificity that underlies the principle of optimal responsiveness. So-called enactments are but one expression of the specificity that must characterize the responses of the therapist in order that the patient may experience them as therapeutic.

References

Eissler, K. (1953). The effect of the structure of the ego on psychoanalytic technique. *Journal of the American Psychoanalytic Association* 1:104–143.

---------------- ❖ ----------------

In recent years psychoanalysis has experienced an increasing openness of investigative spirit in its revisions and expansion of theory, and less self-conscious defensiveness about orthodoxy of tradition. Psychoanalytic theorizing has become more inclusive of contributions from competing psychoanalytic schools as well as data from related fields. The theory of psychoanalytic technique has also expanded with the widening scope of psychoanalysis for a broader range of clinical problems. Innovations in technical interventions can now be discussed in a freer atmosphere as we move toward a mode of greater scientific honesty and objectivity. We have more of a consensus that theory must now be altered to account for clinical reality as opposed to an earlier time when classical theoretical doctrine was valued over any new observations that the theory did not encompass and could not explain. Self psychology has played a trailblazing role in the revision and broadening of psychoanalytic theory and has set the tone for a willingness to consider openly all of the nuances, however challenging, of how treatment really works. Along with many other clinicians, I have repeatedly had to confront the reality in my own practice that a classical, passive-receptive, never-leading, abstinent technique has been inadequate to meet the needs of seriously regressed patients or to negotiate brief or protracted periods of regression in the treatment of those who are more intact.

Self psychology has done pioneering work in stressing interventions based on an empathic immersion in the inner world of the patient. Self psychology and intersubjectivity theory stress the use of the fluctuating transference/countertransference intersubjective field to inform verbal interventions that are both growth promoting and palatable to the patient. To be a complete psychoanalytic theory, however, self psychology is obliged to explain in its own terms all therapeutic interventions that are discovered to be helpful whether or not the clinical theory as it exists so far would predict their usefulness.

While self psychology has done well elucidating the selfobject transferences that evoke a purely empathic and resonating kind of response, I do not believe it has investigated in a systematic way patients' needs for a critically different kind of object from the self. Some of the forms this very different from self-needed other may take may include a containing, independent, actively reflecting, charge-taking, or even strenuously opposing and limit-setting other. I believe that these other, appropriate responses arise *spontaneously* in the analyst in the context of her countertransference (defined in the broad sense of the totality of her emotional responses to the patient). I also believe that these appropriate, spontaneous responses are both necessary and highly *specific* to the individuality of each patient.

There have been a number of recent articles in the psychoanalytic literature on the topic of enactments and countertransference responsiveness in the analytic situation. Perhaps the most commonly held modern view is that enactments in the analytic situation are inevitable as analysts are pulled by the transference into a piece of unwitting countertransference-induced behavior. While the prevailing view is that enactments as such are counterproductive to analytic progress, it is now also generally believed that examination of the enactment and its elucidation by interpretation furthers the progress of the analysis. This view is held by Boesky (1990), Chused (1991), and McLaughlin (1991), among others. Renik (1993) goes further, stating that "these interactions provide a crucial series of gratifications and frustrations to the analysand that form the basis for a successful analytic process" (p. 564). Ogden (1994) goes further still, introducing his concept of "therapeutic action" which is "understood as the analyst's use of action (other than verbally symbolic speech) to convey to the analysand specific aspects of the analyst's understanding of the transference-counter-transference which cannot at that juncture in the analysis be conveyed by the semantic content of words alone" (p. 219). Hoffman (1994), in fact, sees a source of considerable therapeutic power in the dialectical tension between the traditional, formal psychoanalytic posture and the analyst's personal responsivity and self-expressiveness. Thus, Renik, Ogden, and Hoffman introduce a subtle but crucial shift in the way some enactments may be valued within psychoanalysis. Their writing departs from the more usual cautionary tone in order to examine the possibility that certain enactments might be valuable and even necessary. Both Renik and Ogden, however, speak in the context of a relatively traditional analytic setting in which the enactments they describe are subtle and consist of such things as tone, deliberate silence, or an inner emotional response that skews the analyst's attention and responsivity. Hoffman (1994) goes a bit further in describing actual enactments, such as acquiescing to the demand of an analytic patient to call her internist to recommend tranquilizing medication.

In his summary of the more classical analytic views on enactments, Gabbard (1995) concludes that although the idea that countertransference enactments are useful is a controversial one, more theorists are beginning to agree that "both the events occurring in the relationship and the interpretations resulting from these events work synergistically to produce psychic change" (p. 482). Another author who has described the importance of enactments is Mendelsohn (1991), who writes, "Serious failures in negotiating developmental tasks often demand concrete experiences of involvement with a therapist—which are specific to what is lacking in the patient's representational world—before growth and progression can continue. Interpretations depend upon the viability of symbolic processes, and thus cannot be effective when they cannot completely reach what has not been symbolized" (p. 63). Similarly, Colson and colleagues (1985) note that some patients in the Menninger Foundation's Psychotherapy Research Project had negative outcomes when therapists failed to recognize the patient's inability to use exploratory techniques and the need for more supportive measures.

British authors have also discovered the therapeutic value of certain enactments. Lomas (1987) feels we stress interpretations because "our culture idealized words" (p. 56) and that a therapist has impact because "it is the totality of her behaviour that influences the patient" (p. 56). Furthermore, he states that a stress on interpretation alone "omits the fact that the force required to make a difficult change often derives from a *passionate* experience between therapist and patient" (p. 56). Stewart (1990) has also described the mutative power of some enactments and the need at times with regressed patients for the analyst to defend himself and to confront and limit the patient's destructiveness of the treatment. Symington (1983) describes a necessary "x-phenomenon" in some treatments, which he calls the "analyst's inner act of freedom" in which the analyst asserts his own autonomy and separateness from the patient.

Self psychologist Anna Ornstein (1990) succinctly summarizes and distinguishes the self-psychological perspective from both the confrontation recommended by Reich and from the defense interpretation advocated by ego psychology: "The difference in approach—and this difference cannot be sufficiently emphasized—is related to the fact that defense organizations, and their behavioral correlates, are not viewed in self psychology as being obstacles to unearthing 'the truth' from the depth of the psyche. Rather, they are viewed as performing the crucial psychological function of protecting a vulnerable self from further depletion or fragmentation" (p. 46). In his discussion of her paper, Lachmann (1990) concurs and cautions against a confrontive position because, "through this stance a dimension of authority-submission may be introduced into the analyst–patient relationship. Behavioral changes may be 'forced' upon the patient. A self-critical, self-judgmental stance, manifest in the patient's insensitivity to others would be perpetuated and substitute for self-reflection" (pp. 63–64).

London (1983), however, describes the necessity of confrontation in his treatment of a borderline patient. He found himself unable to engage his patient and further the treatment at turbulent periods of intense transference demands. He states, "Although it is often of crucial importance to contact the patient at his mature level of functioning, it is equally crucial to be able at certain times to contact the patient at his level of regression. Such contact is often established at a level of action quite different from any conventional psychoanalytic interpretive stance" (p. 262). He concludes that certain patients "often thrive on a treatment involving a high degree of confrontation" (p. 263) and he postulates that certain patients require confrontation in order to experience the therapist as an "independent center of initiative" (p. 264) or as a "firm center" (p. 265). He makes the crucial point that a confrontive "ally-antagonist" selfobject may not "necessarily be experienced as part of the self" (pp. 266–267) but may nonetheless provide a vital selfobject function in promoting and sustaining the patient's self. In his discussion of London's paper, Bach (1983) speculates that such a need for confrontation refers to an early developmental period antedating the formation of a cohesive self in "an identity that exists only in opposition to the object" (p. 275).

London's contribution is a more complex elaboration in a clinical setting of Wolf's (1980) notion of the experience of the adversarial selfobject "as an antagonist against whom self-assertion mobilizes healthy aggression that promotes the cohesive strength of the self" (p. 126). Lachmann's (1986) description of adversarial selfobject relationships is similar.

Bacal (Chapter 1), in particular, has written trenchantly about the need to conceptualize all of the interventions which further analytic progress. He cautions that in self-consciously constricting our repertoire according to rigid rules, we may "inadvertently deprive the patient of the experience of therapeutic relatedness" (p. 13). He writes, "The continuing controversy among psychoanalysts as to what constitutes a valid addition or alternative to interpretation is due to our failure to evolve a framework for the systematic consideration of the psychoanalytic nature of the therapeutic relationship and how it relates to the interpretive process" (p. 16). He reminds us of Winnicott's view that there are patients for whom the analyst is the first "to supply certain environmental essentials." Bacal also would drop the term *parameter* and focus instead on the idea of *optimal responsiveness* as the analyst's job of which "interpretation and relationship are its component aspects" (p. 32). A subsequent paper by Lindon (1994) expands on the ideas of both gratification and provision and recommends discarding the rule of abstinence. Lindon finds many things that both gratify and provide in all theoretical models of psychoanalysis. He defines provision as "anything that is experienced by the patient as meeting a need or a mobilized developmental longing" (p. 554) and that "facilitates the uncovering, illuminating and transforming of the subjective experiences of the patient" (p. 559). In his case material, Lindon presents examples of his technical flexibility. For one patient he was available seven days a week, from another he took frequent telephone calls, another patient he saw twice daily, another needed expanded session times, with another patient he answered direct questions, and for another he read a paper the patient had written. Lindon describes these interventions as "all in the service of uncovering, illuminating and transforming the patient's unconscious organizing principles and should quite properly be considered widening psychoanalytic technique to accommodate the widening scope of psychoanalysis today" (p. 576). At my suggestion, Lichtenberg has also included the role of enactments in his catalogue of useful interventions, referring in a general way to all helpful enactments as "disciplined spontaneous engagements" (Lichtenberg et al. 1996, p. 107).

In reading these recent contributions and in formulating the diverse interventions I have used with different patients, I have attempted to construct a tentative catalogue of interventions other than verbal interpretation and clarification. They seemed to fall into two broad general categories of (1) active containing and (2) active reflecting, resonating, validating, and informing. In active containing, the containing is provided by an extremely broad range of interventions within psychoanalysis, including more passive, purely listening modes that are not considered to be enactments. I stress the activity of reflecting, resonating, validating, and informing to highlight a more deliberate and thoroughgoing reflecting than what we normally assume as a part of the analytic process. Active containing can be subdivided into (a) limit-setting, opposing, and confronting, and (b) directing and taking charge. Active reflecting, resonating, validating, and informing can be thought of in regard to the patient's self and experience in the past or present with others or with the analyst. In addition to these two broad categories, the need for three pervasively required, important interventions include (1) a willingness to acknowledge the truth, be it of the patient's self, or of the patient's relationship with the analyst, or of the patient's relationship with others in the past or present, and acknowledging the truth might then also necessitate (2) judicious self-disclosure of the analyst's feelings and motives in the moment with the patient, especially as they are tentatively apprehended and reacted to by the patient; and (3) authentic and sincere affective connection with the patient, even occasionally explicitly expressed.

Again, as I catalogue these helpful and specific enactments, the very process of *retrospective* thoughtful description makes them begin to sound more like planned, noninterpretive interventions. To be sure, the boundary between these two types of responses cannot be an absolute one. Nonetheless, because of the emotionally driven spontaneity of their expression, I see these interventions as *enactments*, albeit *necessary* and *facilitating* ones.

ACTIVE CONTAINING: OPPOSING, LIMITING, AND CONFRONTING

Frequently in the treatment of seriously narcissistic and borderline patients and perhaps in the treatment of patients from other diagnostic groups, the patient becomes destructive of himself or of the ongoing treatment. Perhaps the majority of self psychology's technical recommendations and contributions apropos of this kind of clinical situation is to stress the need for empathizing with the thwarted developmental longings leading to the hostility and destructiveness. Otto Kernberg (1987), from an object relations perspective, has been in the forefront of those arguing for active elucidation and confrontation of the destructiveness itself. Is there wisdom to be distilled from each of these approaches or are they fundamentally and diametrically opposed? Object relations and self psychological theories differ dramatically in their respective formulations of the origins of persistent deliberate destructiveness. Kernberg (1975) uses the language of drive theory and implicates "the development of pregenital, especially oral aggression" and "a particular pathological condensation between pregenital and genital aims under the overriding influence of aggressive needs" (p. 43). On the other hand, self psychologists, who have been accused of neglecting patients' aggression, often understand rage and destructiveness as reactive to a felt or threatened injury, often to self-cohesiveness or self-esteem. A self psychologist would attempt to take a more empathic position in order to elucidate an underlying legitimate need. At times, self psychologists view rage in the clinical situation as iatrogenically derived, stimulated by an overly abstinent, sterile, or disengaged analytic stance. In addition to these approaches, however, I have come to feel that a judgment must also be made about the tenacity and subjective meaning of the patient's destructiveness in order to determine when it has become ego-syntonic and is pursued as a goal in itself. In such cases, actively pursued destructiveness and sadism conceal stubbornly the patient's thwarted underlying developmental needs while also serving a vitalizing function, albeit a pathologically organized one (Lichtenberg et al. 1992). In these situations, the optimal response first entails confronting the patient with her deliberate sadism in order to create eventually an opportunity to respond empathically to the thwarted longings underneath.

Clinical Example

A., a 44-year-old divorced professor, presented after a number of years of dynamic psychotherapy. She now wanted an analyst with a self-psychological approach because she understood herself to be suffering from lifelong, suffocating shame that permeated and inhibited all of her personal and professional ambitions. She had grown up as a lonely, shame-ridden, and bookish child. In the first year of treatment she was very quick to feel misunderstood and slighted and had a number of frank rage attacks when she felt I misunderstood her or that my posture and tone indicated a lack of appropriate interest and respect for her as a person. Much work was done on her exquisite sensitivity to feeling slighted and disrespected. Nonetheless, her rage with me continued to erupt and she threatened to report me to the medical society's ethics committee for a lack of sufficient sensitivity to her. Although the idea of making such a complaint was objectively ludicrous, I chose to take her intention very seriously and I informed her that in such an event I would discontinue the therapy since such behavior would constitute deliberately hostile and destructive action against me and against the treatment taken outside of the frame of the treatment situation.

She seemed quite stunned by my limit-setting position. Although she continued to profess that her rage was largely my responsibility because of my lack of exquisite attunement to her needs in a given moment, its intensity abated very gradually over the following year and a half. As elements of an idealizing and dependent transference developed, it was initially displaced and enacted in a series of brief romantic relationships in which A. would quickly become intensely demanding of the man's attention and responsiveness. She was hurt and puzzled when several men dropped her abruptly. When I drew her attention to the fact that she was also experiencing strong feelings about me, she became more aware and engaged but also at times nearly overwhelmed by her shame-ridden, intense need. She would then become newly enraged again, telling me she was paralyzed and silent with shame and it was my responsibility to speak when she couldn't and to make her feel comfortable and welcome in the sessions. While on one level I agreed with what she said, on another it became clear that I was to be friendly, admiring, and welcoming on command. For example, she would complain that a silence was terrible and she needed me to comfort and reassure her. At times, she would fall silent for a minute or two and then suddenly snort derisively, saying, "See, I told you, you have to help and you just sit there saying nothing! I told you I need to feel liked and accepted. I need friendly, welcoming, and admiring comments from you. Dr. X. used to do that for me and with him I could discuss anything because he understood shame and you don't."

My first reaction to the patient's challenge was to make a sustained attempt to empathize with the shame-filled and neglected feelings I felt she was shielding with her angry demands. While A. agreed that this was an important area to explore, she was emphatic that the primary issue was my failing in my obligation to make her feel comfortable, valued, and secure. Over time I could not escape my sense of A.'s intense pleasure in her continued battering of me. Finally, I began to clarify and to inquire into what seemed to me to be a vengeful and pleasurable sadism toward me. A. acknowledged that violent, sadistic sexual fantasies were a frequent preoccupation and she related reluctantly that as a child she had taken particular pleasure in endlessly tormenting a younger sister until she would explode.

I then moved more actively to confront the patient with her demandingness and contempt, which she at first simultaneously disavowed and rationalized. In addition I interpreted that she was also letting me experience the internal environment in which she so often experienced vicious criticism and contempt for herself although the antecedents for her attitude were not yet clear, since she herself had never been treated in this manner. I also clarified that one source of her intense shame was her awareness of her own sadism and cruelty, which were both exciting and gratifying to her. Since A. would often instruct me in a superior and condescending manner and then point out any subtle evidence of annoyance in my reaction, I also clarified that her aggrieved, belittling, and contemptuous manner was in fact quite insulting to others and to me and caused people to distance from her. Her intensely sadistic and self-critical position began to abate only after these interventions (all of which she agreed with).

My observations were completely new ideas for her and she subsequently interpreted that she had clung to her lifelong sense of being cheated, which then kept her suspicious, ungenerous, and thwarted in close relationships. She also reported becoming newly aware that she had been testing me to see if she could get me to "fire" her. Later she reported much more comfort socially and less fear of her own anger, shifts that she felt were a result of my confrontations, which she described with a deep chuckle as my "blasting" her. My confrontational intervention included both acknowledgment and self-disclosure of my emotional responses, which the patient had already perceived. How are we to square this sequence of events with an empathic approach to the patient's inner world? Clearly this confrontive, at times even combative, portion of the treatment was not characterized by an attitude of sustained empathic attunement. I believe that my specific response or enactment with this patient was optimal for her because it met a developmental gap in that in childhood her sadism had never been recognized or addressed. I do not believe my enactment met or dealt with the underlying unmet needs that gave rise to her sadism. Nor do I feel these needs could have become accessible in the treatment situation until her sadism was confronted and contained.

ACTIVE CONTAINING: TAKING CHARGE

The need to take charge in a gross way is more obvious with a hospitalized patient or an overtly regressed, disorganized outpatient. But the active structuring of daily activities, hygiene, and food intake often required in a psychiatric inpatient setting has more or less subtle derivatives that become necessary in the outpatient psychotherapy of even quite high-functioning patients, where taking certain positions vis-à-vis the patient's life is experienced as a needed selfobject function. A more subtle taking charge is often needed with more organized patients, which I feel has not been recognized or acknowledged in our theorizing. While these next two patients did not carry a borderline diagnosis, "taking charge" occurred during periods of regression in their treatment.

Clinical Examples

B. presented in the context of spousal abuse, about which she had no clarity, despite intense suffering. Her gifted, narcissistic, and impulse-disordered husband was unfaithful, condemning, demanding, and occasionally enraged to the point of gross verbal and frank physical abuse. Furthermore, he was verbally abusive to their children and neglectful and unhelpful in the context of a younger child's disability, leaving the burden of care on the patient. One of the very first things I said to this patient was, "You are in a crisis and need to attend to it." She referred back to this statement as a watershed moment over the many subsequent years of treatment.

After her divorce and increasing self-reliance, at moments of crisis this patient would again feel tempted to trust her ex-husband in ways that put herself and her children at risk. I would then intervene again, pointing out the history with the husband, and inquire about her deference to his judgment and compliance with his wish to control. It was clear that because of her history of being abused and exploited in her family of origin, B. had virtually no way of judging abuse in her current life; her only means of coping had been to blame herself and to try to adapt.

In highlighting my taking-charge intervention, I am not focusing on the accompanying, very important interpretive inquiry into the meaning of her dependency on an abuser and the genetic antecedents of her lack of self-reliance. I am focusing only on the need for a specific alerting intervention in the moment that the patient is about to ignore an emergency or is about to take a self-damaging action with consequences in her life outside the office. Despite the interference of my active intervention in this case, B. was able to develop an intense transference relatedness and to explore her anxious dependency, her rage, and her own struggle for autonomy in the context of her treatment relationship. How then do we theorize about the contribution of taking charge to this patient's psychic growth? Here again, as with A., I would invoke Bacal's idea that this particular enactment had specific value and relevance to this particular patient. In her case, she had parents who had never alerted her to the state of danger in which she lived, because they were themselves the source of the danger.

More active taking charge occurred in the treatment of C., who extricated herself from a bad marriage with a self-indulgent, narcissistic man and who was increasingly independent and self-reliant. The moment her life goals were in reach, however, in the increasing stability of her work and in a new relationship with a much more mature man, C. began to regress and on several occasions drank to excess in a manner clearly meant to alarm and alienate her new, somewhat straight-laced suitor. She expressed extreme self-doubt and self-loathing and the conviction that a stable and satisfying life were not possible for her and that her new man would reject her. There were many dynamic and genetic reasons for C.'s self-sabotage, all of which were actively explored. In addition, however, I emphatically confronted the patient with her own behavior as a deliberately destructive playing out of a defective self-image and a repetition of her mother's lifelong destructiveness as well as earlier regressive behavior of her own. I said I considered her behavior to be an emergency that needed to be addressed in her therapy, in extra sessions if necessary, and to be consciously avoided and controlled in her life outside of her treatment. My act of taking charge and redirecting was a more active step on a spectrum of interventions than the active clarification of abuse in the life of B.

Even more active taking charge interventions occurred in the treatment of a seriously regressed but brilliant and high-functioning borderline patient, D., who had a history of serious suicidality. He was the youngest of four and had been severely neglected and ignored in the first year of his life and had grown up in a family with an alcoholic and probably psychotic father who had abused his siblings. D. developed a rapidly fluctuating, frequently overtly paranoid transference in which he would skip sessions, inform me he was dropping therapy hours, and, often in a rage, give me abrupt notice that he was breaking off the treatment. After first making the error of acceding to his wishes to drop certain sessions, for instance, I gradually learned that what kept this patient on track was a constant emphatic refusal to cooperate with his sabotage. I kept his scheduled hours and would call if he did not appear. I adamantly disagreed with any plans for abrupt termination and would schedule an immediate emergency session whenever he would leave a message interrupting treatment. He said I "ordered" him to continue and he also valued my increasingly steadfast position.

As the years passed, his rage declined and the signs of a more trustful alliance emerged. He said that his early life had been so bad that he was not meant to survive it. However, with active and open combat with his conviction that I too wanted to abandon him and wished for him to die, he said he was beginning to feel like one of the few emaciated, surviving prisoners in Auschwitz liberated by the Allies, very nearly dead yet somehow, improbably, still alive. These overtly taking charge interventions also involved both active self-disclosures (affirming my investment and interest in him) in the transference/countertransference relationship as well as explicit acknowledgments of his often piercing insights about my states of distraction or states of greater emotional distance. Without these validating admissions, I am convinced this treatment would have been prematurely interrupted. Despite the stormy, frequently combative "noise" of this psychotherapy, a deep empathy was required as to what was really needed underneath the patient's demands to quit treatment. Reflecting or formulating to this patient was anathema. London's point about the need to meet the patient on his level of regression necessitated the "real," matching (in this case combative), response to D.'s provocative rages and flights.

ACTIVE REFLECTING, RESONATING, VALIDATING, AND INFORMING

This heading is meant to convey a very broad-sounding idea that boils down essentially to the analyst's willingness to step out of a more passive mode that reflects only a little more than the patient's judgment, ideas, and feelings about him- or herself, about others, and about events in his or her life. In this more active, if you will, enacting mode, the analyst acknowledges or even clarifies explicitly certain qualities about the patient or about others, or about events that the patient apprehends tentatively but needs to confirm. The analyst's active reflecting, resonating, and echoing lead to the amplification and integration of feeling. Validation is a result of successful reflecting and resonating. In addition, however, at times patients may initially have very little or no awareness of some important operative factor about themselves, others, or their environment, which the analyst feels constrained to point out. In other words, the analyst may then need to inform. One common example includes those patients (perhaps especially guilty and self-effacing personalities) who are increasingly symptomatic in the face of external life pressures that they find difficult to assess, and in the face of which they have trouble retaining their sense of intactness and self-esteem. Many depressed patients fall quickly to self-blame when they are attacked and are often quite unable to protect themselves. In such a situation it can be very important for an analyst not only to point out a patient's suppressed rage, which may underlie the depression and anxiety, but also to point out a patient's difficulty in self defense and in countering or even accurately assessing irrational attacks directed against him- or herself.

Clinical Examples

This patient had a borderline diagnosis, and was an intelligent and accomplished woman who had been raised by a highly critical and disapproving mother. Her psychiatric history included bouts of suicidal depression and one hospitalization following an extremely difficult overseas work assignment. She would regress when she was criticized or perceived herself to be failing. Accordingly, she would experience helplessness, disorganization, and terror whenever she was criticized by a superior. After I had begun to understand her pattern and something about its origins, on several occasions during such regressions I asked her to consider the behavior of her boss. Several times I told her it seemed to me that her boss did not sound objective or appropriate. On several other occasions I told her the criticism was not earth-shattering and asked if she was overreacting because of the intense rage and helplessness she felt in connection to her mother. I also reminded her of her own power to persuade and to press her own point of view, which she then would often become sufficiently mobilized to do. My interventions increasingly helped limit and contain what had previously been very serious regressions in such circumstances, including another brief hospitalization during the early years of her treatment with me.

Yet another much more intact patient had severe inhibitions in initiating and pursuing any career path despite her substantial gifts and impressive academic achievements. A child of accomplished World War II refugees, she had accepted her parents' pessimistic view of the world in which they viewed all organizations—corporate, academic, or political—as corrupt and potentially undermining and dangerous. Her "inherited" pessimism coupled with a crippling perfectionism kept her paralyzed in functioning in any substantial way outside her home. To question her parents' viewpoint felt disloyal and was intensely guilt-provoking, but to accept their vision stifled all of her ambition. We explored both her guilt and her great reservoirs of anger and resentment toward her parents. What she reported as truly liberating, however, was my suggestion that her parents' views seemed plausible in the face of the political system that had in fact sought to kill them and from which they had narrowly escaped. I also said that it was clear that her parents had never mourned their many dead relatives or ventilated their own grief, rage, and terror at the severe privations they had experienced themselves, thus perpetuating their pessimism and posttraumatic state. To view her parents as two human beings with unique histories that led to their own unique reactions and opinions was a completely new and freeing idea. Only then did the patient begin to experience some internal permission to form some new and unique opinions of her own, separate from the ideas of her parents.

A third patient was struggling with pathological grief over the cancer death of a dearly loved sister, five years after the suicide of another sister. In her late twenties, the patient felt helpless to move out of the parental home. While her parents chided her for her continuing dependence, it became clear to me that the aging, grieving parents were really subtly undermining and criticizing any attempt the patient made to regain her confidence and her will to separate from them. After two illuminating family meetings with the patient and her mother, I told the patient what I thought. She was subsequently able to move out and continued in her therapy with me to process each new debilitating wave of parental criticism until she herself became able for the first time in her life to perceive, point out, and protest explicitly her parents' unconscious sabotage. As her autonomy increased, her depression lifted. The explicit idea that her parents were sabotaging her independence came originally from me and was not evident in the patient's material. This is an example where the analyst felt constrained to inform and not to wait for the possible emergence of a crucial idea in the patient's own associations.

D., the gifted, high-functioning borderline patient mentioned above, was exquisitely sensitive to my mood and degree of affective attunement with him. He frequently diagnosed subtle shifts in my level of engagement and could always detect in me the presence of a latent preoccupation with some "out-of-the-office" issue. His astuteness was all the more remarkable because I found this extremely compelling patient always riveting and never boring or in any way to be taken for granted. Thus, despite my own subjectively complete attention to him, D. could still accurately perceive fluctuations in my degree of connection. He was especially sensitive to the fact that my mood never mirrored the depths of his frequent despair and he would upbraid me, saying I was "in la-la land," smug, and "bragging" that I was better off than he because I was claiming wordlessly to be "fine, just fine." At the depths of his regression, when he said he was "psychotic" and "fragmented," he experienced my concern as patronizing because I did not resonate sufficiently or expose in some way the most vulnerable, depressed, and "psychotic" parts of myself that he had no doubt were present. He experienced my silently expressed "superiority" as "violent" and "murderous" and as a message to him that he should die.

It took several years to spell out and appreciate fully how he experienced my affective state. Fully articulating this patient's experience with me was, however, insufficient to alleviate how excruciating it felt for him. Very particularly, he could not tolerate anything resembling a "passive," waiting, receptive, "analytic" posture. He derided this listening mode as completely worthless with "psychotic" patients like himself and as a pathetic therapeutic cop out. He emphasized how regressed patients need to be talked and responded to, preferably in the simplest way. With D., however, unlike A., the female patient who had made similar sounding demands, I did not feel I was being abused as a goal in itself. I felt rather that when I could tune in more precisely in the way he was requesting, there was a freeing-up of the atmosphere between us and much more possibility for an exchange. It was as if by my matching and mirroring him better, he experienced a firmer boundary around a more consolidated self, at least for a moment, which then allowed him to recognize and to deal with me more as a separate person. With A., similar dynamics were probably at work underneath, but her underlying "perversion" in her pleasure in torturing me made it in fact impossible for me to do what she seemed to be asking. There were, however, moments with both patients in which they reported a sense of feeling both more valid and somehow more real after my explicit repetition, or echoing, of their descriptions of feelings and perceptions about which they felt tentative and unsure.

I got nowhere with D.'s complaints about my repeated failures to resonate with him sufficiently when I attempted to understand them merely as transference repetitions of previously thwarted developmental need. I finally accepted all of D.'s observations as accurate in some important way. For example, it would at times be very settling to him if I would acknowledge the presence of a subtle preoccupation that might be distracting me, although at first it might be completely out of my awareness. Searles (1986), Gabbard (1995), Hoffman (1994), and others have made similar points about the reality of the patient's perceptions and the analyst's responsibility for the construction of the patient's transference. What I felt with D. was the necessity at times to acknowledge to him the accuracy of his perception of me. D. also persuaded me that to comment, however sympathetically, on someone else's distressed feeling state without resonating in some way with the disturbing affects often involves a projection onto the patient of disavowed disturbed affects in the analyst. Such a projection also contains an implicit expression of superiority and difference of place, "You are the ('sick') patient and I am the ('fine') analyst." Or as D. succinctly expressed it, "There's something wrong if the therapist is just a 'doctor' with a 'patient.'"

Simple, straightforward, affectively congruent reactions are indeed often the only effective bridge-building response to a regressed patient. Once when I got too abstract in my response to him, D. said to me, "I am in my crib over here and can't understand a word you're saying." On another occasion he expressed this principle most succinctly, "Everything you say to me is trash; the only reason I've stayed is because there's something right about the natural way you sit in your chair."

DISCUSSION

I have outlined and described a number of technical departures from the traditional psychoanalytic posture and technique that are necessary for specific patients at regressed periods in their treatment. These interventions fall into two categories, the first of which is more alien to the spirit of self psychology insofar as it constitutes active containing and uses strategies of opposing, limit-setting, confronting, directing, and taking charge. The second category is very much in the spirit of self psychology in its reflecting, resonating, and validating techniques, except that it is more active and includes the need at times to inform or to provide crucial information that the patient needs but has been missing.

One general principle that dictates a number of therapist enactments is that "actions speak louder than words." In other words, in the face of an intensely fixed or psychotic transference, a therapist may be compelled to counter the patient's percept with her own, never-contrived, genuine, but contrasting behavior to create the actual lived experience of an alternative to the patient's relentless expectation. I believe that more classical analysts are actually bowing to this principle when they invoke "analytic tact." McLaughlin relies on this explanation in his 1991 paper in which he describes adopting a more tentative and egalitarian tone to soften and reality test his patient's transference rage with him as an authoritarian figure. In my view, McLaughlin was in fact employing a necessary enactment but does not acknowledge it as such out of a widely shared allegiance to the idea of verbal interpretation as the one true mutative agent in psychoanalysis.

Another idea I have presented for the consideration of self psychologists is the need to confront actively a patient's pleasurable, entrenched, or ego-syntonic sadism and destructiveness when they are pursued as ends in themselves. This is a principle advocated by Kernberg and others, but I envisage it as a necessary prelude with certain patients in order to establish an alliance and an atmosphere in which a more mutative empathy can occur.

One important challenge to psychoanalytic therapists is to correlate what we can learn from infant and child development studies with our expanded panoply of technical interventions that constitute our optimal responsiveness. And as we expand our therapeutic repertoire, another extremely critical challenge and responsibility is to reconceptualize the maintenance of both our professional boundaries and our professional mission even as we are enlarging our receptivity, availability, and spontaneity.

CONCLUSION

I have catalogued a series of specific, facilitating enactments as needed therapeutic responses to regressed patients and to other more intact patients in regressed periods of their treatment. This "catalogue" or array of possible enactments lies outside the boundary of the traditional psychoanalytic posture and technique of passive, neutral, abstinent, evenly hovering attention, and inner processing of countertransference leading to clarification and interpretation. Clearly not all enactments or spontaneous countertransference actions are therapeutic. However, even for those that have been acknowledged as helpful, the psychoanalytic literature (with several notable exceptions) has focused on them as merely conducive to a deeper understanding leading to mutative interpretation that has been considered the sole true agent of structural change. The thesis of this chapter is that many patients in fact require specific enactments as interventions. The specificity of the needed enactment is dictated by the details of each patient's individual history.

References

Bach, S. (1983). Discussion of paper by N.J. London. In *Reflections on Self Psychology*, ed. J. Lichtenberg and S. Kaplan, pp. 269–275. Hillsdale, NJ: Analytic Press.

Boesky, D. (1990). The psychoanalytic process and its components. *Psychoanalytic Quarterly* 59:550–583.

Chused, J. F. (1991). The evocative power of enactments. *Journal of the American Psychoanalytic Association* 39:615–639.

Colson, D., Lewis, L., and Horwitz, L. (1985). Negative outcome in psychotherapy and psychoanalysis. In *Negative Outcome in Psychotherapy and What to Do About It*, ed. D. T. Mays and C. M. Franks, pp. 59–75. New York: Springer.

Gabbard, G. O. (1995). Countertransference: the emerging common ground. *International Journal of Psycho-Analysis* 76:475–485.

Gabbard, G. O., and Wilkinson, S. M. (1994). *Management of Countertransference with Borderline Patients*. Washington, DC and London: American Psychiatric Press.

Hoffman, I. Z. (1994). Dialectical thinking and therapeutic action in the psychoanalytic process. *Journal of the American Psychoanalytic Association* 43:187–218.

Kernberg, O. (1975). *Borderline Conditions and Pathological Narcissism*. New York: Jason Aronson.

——— (1987). Projection and projective identification: developmental and clinical aspects. *Journal of the American Psychoanalytic Association* 35:795–819.

Lachmann, F. M. (1986). Interpretation of psychic conflict and adversarial relationships: a self psychological perspective. *Psychoanalytic Psychology* 3(4):341–355.

——— (1990). On some challenges to clinical theory in the treatment of character pathology. In *The Realities of Transference: Progress in Self Psychology*, vol. 6, ed. A. Goldberg, pp. 59–67. Hillsdale, NJ: Analytic Press.

Lichtenberg, J. D., Lachmann, F. M., and Fosshage, J. L. (1992). *Self and Motivational Systems: Toward a Theory of Psychoanalytic Technique*. Hillsdale, NJ, London: Analytic Press.

——— (1996). *The Clinical Exchange: Techniques Derived From Self and Motivational Systems*. Hillsdale, NJ, London: Analytic Press.

Lindon, J. (1994). Gratification and provision in psychoanalysis: Should we get rid of "the rule of abstinence"? *Psychoanalytic Dialogues* 4:549–582.

Lomas, P. (1987). *The Limits of Interpretation*. Northvale, NJ: Jason Aronson.

London, N. J. (1983). Confrontation and selfobject transference: a case study. In *Reflections on Self Psychology*, ed. J. Lichtenberg and S. Kaplan, pp. 247–267. Hillsdale, NJ: Analytic Press.

McLaughlin, J. T. (1991). Clinical and theoretical aspects of enactment. *Journal of the American Psychoanalytic Association* 39:595–614.

Mendelsohn, R. (1991). *LEAPS: Facing Risks in Offering a Constructive Therapeutic Response When Unusual Measures are Necessary.* Northvale, NJ: Jason Aronson.

Ogden, T. H. (1994). The concept of interpretive action. *Psychoanalytic Quarterly* 63:219–245.

Ornstein, A. (1990). Selfobject transferences and the process of working through. In *The Realities of Transference: Progress in Self Psychology*, vol. 6, ed. A. Goldberg, pp. 41–58. Hillsdale, NJ: Analytic Press.

Panel, Enactments in Psychoanalysis (1989). Presented at the Annual Meeting of the American Psychoanalytic Association, San Francisco, Reported by Morton Johan, May 6, 1989. *Journal of the American Psychoanalytic Association* 40:827–841.

Renik, O. (1993). Analytic interaction: conceptualizing technique in light of the analyst's irreducible subjectivity. *Psychoanalytic Quarterly* 62:553–571.

Searles, H. (1986). *My Work with Borderline Patients.* Northvale, NJ: Jason Aronson.

Stewart, H. (1990). Interpretation and other agents for psychic change. *International Review of Psycho-Analysis* 17:61–69.

Symington, N. (1983). The analyst's act of freedom as agent of therapeutic change. *International Review of Psycho-Analysis* 10:283–291.

Winnicott, D. W. (1975). Hate in the countertransference. In *Collected Papers: Through Paediatrics to Psycho-Analysis.* London: Hogarth.

Wolf, E. (1980). On the developmental line of selfobject relations. In *Advances in Self Psychology*, ed. A. Goldberg, pp. 117–130. New York: International Universities Press.

B. The Management of Disruptions and Countertransference

11

Optimal Responsiveness and Disruption-Restorations

ERNEST S. WOLF

EDITOR'S COMMENT

Wolf regards *optimal* as entailing both a therapeutic experience that is maximally effective for that particular patient and simultaneously an experience of maximally enhancing the therapist's effectiveness. He carefully delineates the subjective and objective criteria for each. He thus identifies *responsiveness* in the therapeutic encounter—as in all relationships—in the same way that I have done in Chapter 7, that is, as reciprocal. Both patient and therapist, in effect, serve as selfobjects for the other. That is, both participants experience some enhancement of the sense of well-being and strengthening of the sense of self as a result of being therapeutically engaged. Wolf calls a well-established therapeutic dialogue an "ambient process" and asserts that such a process is characterized by optimal, mutual responsiveness.

Despite our commitment to respond therapeutically to our patients, we are not always effective in implementing this aim. We understand our patients' need for defense (some analysts still call it resistance) against expressing their needs for optimal responsiveness. And their fears that we will let them down and reactivate or exacerbate the pain in the wounds that they have sought our help to heal are, in fact, not infrequently realized. Put in another way, disruptions in selfobject relatedness between a patient and a therapist are a not unusual fact of psychoanalytic life. The "ambient process," Wolf says, will "almost inevitably" become disrupted as a result of nonoptimal responses; and in some instances the perception of the other as not quite attuned to his or her own self and its agenda will be enough to disrupt it.

Wolf emphasizes that an important aspect of what the therapist must do when selfobject disruptions occur is to "blamelessly" accept participatory responsibility for the production of the discrepant interaction. Wolf holds that the therapist's acceptance of responsibility usually has the salutary effect of generating a full discussion of what the patient experienced during the onset of the disruption—a discussion that has a good chance of restoring the self cohesion of both participants. I am here reminded of Ferenczi's (1928) pioneering recommendation that analysts acknowledge their mistakes as this would increase the patient's confidence in their analyst.

As I have indicated (Chapter 7), I would include this acceptance of responsibility on the part of the therapist for contributing to the disruption—as well as the provision of whatever else that is useful in order to engage the patient in an examination of what went wrong—under the rubric of optimal responsivity. In other words, it is the patient's experience of optimal responsiveness that is therapeutic, regardless of whether this experience occurs in the absence of frustration or disruption or—in Wolf's central focus—in the context of the repair of disturbances in the patient–analyst relationship.

In the wake of Wolf's avowal that the ambient process will "almost inevitably" become disrupted as a result of nonoptimal responses, I would pose two questions for further discussion: Are there respectably effective therapeutic processes in which the experience of optimal responsiveness without significant selfobject disruption occurs? And if so, under what conditions does this happen?

Reference

Ferenczi, S. (1928). The elasticity of psychoanalytic technique. In *Final Contributions to the Problems and Methods of Psychoanalysis*, pp. 87–101. London: Hogarth.

The theoretical elaboration and the clinical application of the concept of optimal responsiveness has become a vital concern for psychoanalytic self psychologists ever since Bacal (1985, see also Chapter 1, this volume) introduced this modification of the concept of optimal frustration. Sparked by Bacal's continuing evolvement of these concepts, the discussion in this volume bespeaks the abiding lively interest in various facets pertaining to the therapeutic process.

An important question raised by Bacal directs us to consider the impact of these contemporary ideas on our long-held views of the disruption-restoration process. To recapitulate briefly, nearly all of us have observed that in an ongoing therapeutic relationship there will almost inevitably occur, sooner or later, some disturbing ripples that threaten to disrupt the selfobject bonds between therapist and patient. Therapists usually are able to manage this vicissitude by properly responding. I have suggested (1988, 1993) that a blameless acceptance by the therapist of the responsibility for having precipitated these threatened or actual disruptions is a necessary first step in the correct conduct of therapy. The ensuing dialogue often leads to a restoration of the selfobject bond that is then reflected in strengthened selfs of both participants, analyst and analysand.

Optimal responsiveness is an important, perhaps essential, aspect of the therapeutic process in self psychology. However, it is just one of various aspects of that very complicated process. For an adequate discussion it is necessary to examine the therapeutic process in its totality. Such an examination implies a close look at all aspects, including a definition or redefinition of the various conceptualizations that guide our thinking.

Contemporary psychoanalytic self psychology consists of the theoretical and clinical modifications introduced by Heinz Kohut and his colleagues. Some of these modifications evolved initially from an effort by Kohut (1959) to define more precisely the field of psychoanalytic science and to examine the relationship between mode of observation and theory. Scientific fields are delimited by their methods of data collection. Kohut defined psychoanalysis as the science of complex mental states accessed systematically through introspection and empathy. A clinical psychoanalytic approach based on this fundamental view stresses the pivotal importance of empathically derived data (Kohut 1959). In other words, the core of the self psychological field rests on subjective experience even when we use experience-distant language to describe the observed psychological events.

People come into psychoanalytic treatment because they suffer the symptoms of a weakened or disorganized self. The goal of treatment is to strengthen the self (Wolf 1988). A milieu created by an empathic understanding supplemented by explanatory interpretations that illuminate the etiologic link between trauma and symptoms is often sufficient to strengthen the selfs whose pathology consists mostly of arrested development. The analyst is experienced as an understanding other who provides needed recognition and is available for idealizing, alter-ego, adversarial, vitalizing, and efficacy selfobject experiences. A frequent misunderstanding of self psychology by those not familiar with modern thinking concludes that the self psychologist merely dispenses sympathy or compassion. In fact, the facilitation of such an ambient therapeutic process rather often requires limit setting within a frame of realistic expectations. Self psychologists are not strangers to a well-timed confrontation. They know these not as an end in itself but as part of empathically derived clarifications in the service of mutual enhancement.

To examine the issues posed by Bacal's reconceptualization let us now look more closely at the nature and meaning of optimal responsiveness as he defines it. What does he mean by optimal? He defines it by anchoring it firmly to the therapeutic effect on the patient. Whatever had the maximum therapeutic impact on that particular patient, whether it had taken the form of a verbal intervention or of any other behavior or of the absence of any action at all on the part of that particular analyst, is, by definition, optimal for that particular patient. At first, therefore, optimal seems to describe a totally patient-centered point of view. However, that is not Bacal's vision. By insisting on what he labels the theory of specificity (see Chapter 7) he recognizes that the therapist is an essential part of the transaction. Optimal thus implies not only a therapeutic experience maximally effective on that particular patient but simultaneously also an experience of maximally enhancing the therapist's effectiveness. Furthermore, there is an implication that the patient experiences him/herself as a "good" patient and that the therapist experiences him/herself as a "good" therapist. This may sound like an unnecessarily complicated way of stating what goes on during this step in the therapeutic process. Indeed, it is complicated because in self psychology we often find it urgent to describe an event from at least two points of view simultaneously: from the point of view of an outside observer, that is, an objective scientific view, and, at the same time, from the point of view of the experiencing person, that is, a subjective phenomenological description that is no less scientific. Thus, the apparently simple transaction of a therapeutic event yields at least four descriptions, two pertaining to each participant, one of which is couched in objective observational terms, and one in subjective experiential terms. A fifth description would focus not on the participants but on the relationship between them: the intersubjective point of view.

Our examination of "optimal" has yielded four definitions/descriptions each of which aims at being maximal within its own objective or its subjective frame. We want a maximal therapeutic effect (objectively observable) and a maximal enhancement of the sense of self for the patient (subjectively experienced); analogously, we want a maximally effective functioning of the therapist (objectively observable) and a maximally enhanced self experience of the therapist (subjectively experienced). Bacal's theory of specificity tells us that we cannot choose just one of these four simultaneous events. The various interactions are so tightly bound to each other that either we achieve all four of them or none of them. I suppose this tight interactive bondedness leads into the considerations that have effectively been conceptualized as intersubjectivity. However, for certain purposes of which this chapter is an example, I find it useful to consider the various constituents of the therapeutic encounter separately.

Our observations of others in therapeutic interaction via empathic immersion, and of ourselves via introspection while being participants, has yielded data that match the above descriptions of the various aspects of the clinical encounter. I believe that such a close match between data and conceptualization is close to what Kohut meant by experience-near. And, on the basis of some decades of doing analytic treatment, I also believe those to be true descriptions of what we can observe. How do we best explain these phenomena with our self psychological theories? Or, better yet, how do we modify our theories to match these observations? First, we must recognize that self–selfobject relationships are always to some extent reciprocally mutual. There are no therapeutic encounters that proceed one way from therapist to patient without involvement of the therapist and without some alteration in the therapist's self. From this it follows that in any self–selfobject relationship both participants have an effect on the other that may not necessarily be therapeutic. This effect may be enhancing or tend toward being fragmenting, or it may be neutral in its implication for the other's self cohesion. In a self–selfobject relationship with therapeutic goals we obviously would want an enhancing effect on the other, that is, on both participants. Thus a therapist's enhancing effect on a patient would be experienced by the therapist as also enhancing to the therapist's self. And we can add quantitatively that the more enhancing on one, the more enhancing on the other. Optimal therefore means maximally enhancing for both therapist and patient.

In its most simple definition, *responsiveness* could mean the totality of responses of one subject to another. A description might include factors such as intensity, rapidity, and degree of being a focused attunement, whether affectively modal or cross-modal. However, such an analysis might easily miss the essential point that it is the subjective experience per se, not the mode of producing it, that counts in evaluating its therapeutic potential. And as soon as we bring in *subjective* and *experience* we are back to thinking of the other, the selfobject, and *its* experience of the response in question. Responsiveness, therefore, also cannot be grasped as a one-way phenomenon but should be looked at as part of a two-way, mutual, reciprocal series of events. This is true for all relationships, not just the therapeutic one.

Linked with Kohut's conceptualization of optimal frustration was also the concept of transmuting internalization. Kohut modeled transmuting internalization on Freud's conceptualization of mourning: memories of the lost object are brought into the foreground of consciousness and worked through in conjunction with identification with the lost object. The now introjected object becomes part of the mourner's ego. It is easier to detach (decathect) from an introjected object than from a real object. According to Kohut, numerous microfrustrations via transmuting internalizations lead to gradually transferring to the self the capacity to function as a substitute for the missing and, therefore, frustrating functioning of the selfobject. Kohut is correct in stating that the end result of therapeutically effective events is an acquisition by the self of new functioning capacities that carry out for the self what the selfobject had performed before. However, with our contemporary accent on subjective experiencing and on the interactive aspects of self–selfobject events, I prefer to conceptualize the acquisition of new capacities—in contrast to Kohut's concept of transmuting internalization—as an internal rearrangement of the self's constituents, a new configuration that thereby confers the potential for new experiences and for new responses. Such a rearrangement is facilitated by loosening of the configurational ties in connection with some regression (disorganization) that accompanies effective therapeutic as well some other regressive experiences. We see here the return of a favorite traditional psychoanalytic concept of regression in the service of the self. Later in this chapter I will return to the dynamic processes that produce this rearrangement.

I have taken a long detour of refining and clarifying definitions into redefinitions of much-used concepts that have been carried into contemporary self psychology from traditional psychoanalysis, ego psychology, and early Kohutian usage. We can now assess the impact of optimal responsiveness on the disruption-restoration process during treatment.

We can begin our consideration of the disruption-restoration process by looking at a productive working relationship between patient and therapist—a therapeutic alliance. How would one recognize that a therapeutically rewarding relationship characterizes the work of the two participants in the therapeutic endeavor?

An outside observer of these two people in interaction might notice them talking to each other, mostly relaxed but occasionally, in view of the contents of their dialogue, appropriately animated, perhaps even excited. Prolonged monologues by the patient might be punctuated by comments, questions and, from time to time, interpretations from the therapist. While one could observe periods of silence, generally these would not be very long and they would appear to be introspectively reflective in nature rather than directed at the other participant in a manner designed to elicit a reaction. The tone of the dialogue would sound mostly calm but interested and friendly in keeping with a joint cooperative effort. The neutral observer would probably judge the two to be feeling warmly appreciative of each other as well as each feeling good about his or her own participation. Of course, all of this might also be observed by each of the two participants.

What would be the subjective experience of the therapeutic couple (to paraphrase Winnicott) engaged with each other in the therapeutic relationship? Relatively speaking and compared to most extra-therapeutic relationships both participants are likely to have some enhanced sense of well-being. That is not to say that the patient now feels well or that the therapist can only feel good while therapeutically engaged. Yet there is some kernel of truth in noting that, when really engaged, the therapeutic engagement per se is experienced by both with some strengthening of self, that is, some increased self-esteem, some enhancement of the sense of well-being. In essence this is the experience noticed again and again by Kohut, when still a classical psychoanalyst, that led him to discover the self—selfobject relationship upon which he built his modifications of psychoanalytic theory and clinical practice. Using basic concepts of psychoanalytic self psychology we can formulate this experiential state by postulating that in this thera-peutic dialogue each participant serves as selfobject for the other, and they provide each other with cohesion-enhancing selfobject experiences. We need not specify whether these are mirroring, idealizing, alter-ego, adver-sarial, efficacy, or vitalizing experiences. I refer to a well-established clinical therapeutic dialogue of this kind as an *ambient* process, characterized by optimal and mutual responsiveness, a subject that Bacal and Thomson address further in Chapter 12.

Almost inevitably during the course of the usual psychoanalytic treat-ment, this ambient process will suddenly cease to function well or at all. The optimal and mutual responsiveness that had prevailed was based on a high degree of mutual attunement of patient and therapist to each other. But the therapist and patient are both imperfect. So in addition to their conscious intent, they have individual agendas that are unconsciously determined, at least to some degree. Thus, there exists an unconsciously determined discrepancy between the agendas of the two participants. Among the innumerable possibilities one common discrepancy might be the patient's anxiety-laden need to feel safer by hiding some shameful thoughts from the therapist versus the therapist's ambitious urge to know all about the patient. Despite, or maybe because of, the mutual commit-ment to therapeutic goals and method, the patient's fears and the therapist's frustration are going to be sensed by the other with some uneasiness. Both will perceive the other as not quite understanding, in other words, as not perfectly attuned to their own self and its agenda. That may be enough to disrupt the ambient process. The patient will experience the therapist as somehow estranged, perhaps as not caring or as being more interested in his own agenda than in the patient's. No longer is the therapist the source of all the needed self-enhancing selfobject experiences. Consequently, the pa-tient's self loses some of its cohesion; it becomes somewhat disorganized and regresses into a fragmented state. The fragmentation is evidenced by the patient's symptoms. Some of these may be subjectively uncomfortable such as anxiety or depression, some may manifest in acting out such as a self-protecting anger, and others may be the direct expression of a failing self that can no longer function fully effectively, for example, impaired cognitive judgment. The therapist is likely to notice the changed ambience in the consulting room, the sudden tension or coldness, however mild the particular patient's symptoms may be.

For his part, the therapist will also be subject to some degree of loss of sustaining selfobject experience, with the resulting tendency toward disorganizing fragmentation. One must hope that therapists by virtue of their own therapeutic psychoanalytic treatment as well as by their professional training will be able to cope with their own regressions well enough to limit the disorganizing process within and begin to do what is necessary to restore the prior ambient milieu in the treatment situation. That means the therapist has to do whatever is needed to again be experienced by the patient as optimally responsive.

The first step in this process of restoration has to be the acknowledgment of the therapist's role and responsibility in having precipitated the disruption by some action or lack of action. I do not mean that the therapist has to accept or feel blame, but by realistically accepting a participatory role in the mutual production of the discrepant interaction the therapist relieves the patient of some of the feeling of blame that patients usually suffer. In accepting a precipitating participatory role the therapist is acting in contrast to the usual acts of the parents of the patient's childhood. Perhaps, this is an updated contemporary version of Franz Alexander's corrective emotional experience. More importantly, the therapist's acceptance of responsibility will usually generate a full discussion of what the patient has experienced during the onset of the disruption. The chances are good that during the course of that discussion both participants will gain the courage to accept their own contribution and talk about it, with the result that the optimal responsiveness is restored and with it the cohesion of the selfs.

The disruption was characterized by regressive disorganization of the self with loss of cohesion (fragmentation, if we wish to use this terminology). Viewed from the outside we can conceptualize that the constituents of the self are no longer tightly bonded to each other but now are in a loosely held together configuration. The looseness makes it possible to rearrange the constituents into a slightly different configuration. During the formative, pre-cohesive self years of childhood the self's constituents in response to environmental circumstances configured themselves to be optimally adapted to the prevailing conditions, which included the parental selfobjects. Dynamically similar conditions prevail in the therapeutic situation during a disruption with the therapist now in the position of the archaic parent. The regressively loosened bonds now allow a rearrangement of the self's constituents that is adapted to the therapeutic milieu. This is true for the therapist as well as for the patient, and thus facilitates the therapist's change of self to become increasingly capable to respond optimally. The following vignette illustrates some of the conceptualization of the above discussion.

> A young lawyer, in his third year of analysis, reported that his cat had died. The cat had never been mentioned before, and rather perfunctorily, without any real feeling, I acknowledged the loss. A period of silence ensued and I said, "Let's go on." More silence, and I commented that the cat must have been quite important and the loss very painful to the patient. Yes, the cat—he used the cat's name—meant very much to him but he did not think I could understand that. He sounded upset. During the next session he still was upset as I could tell by his coldly angry voice. I interpreted that he was angry with me for not having been more sympathetic. Yes, he agreed, he did not think I really cared, but just like his mother I acted as if I did. Mother would put on a great show of concern, especially when other people were watching, but she didn't really care. I confirmed that I did not feel about pets the same way that he and many other people do but that he must have experienced my comments as pretending concern similar to his mother.

Looking at this vignette we can discern the various aspects that make up optimal responsiveness, or, in this case, fail to come together to yield optimal responsiveness. Observing the patient objectively, one notices that his responsiveness was impaired as evidenced by more than usual stretches of silence after the analyst acknowledged the loss of the cat. Perhaps, to the extent that the cat had provided important selfobject experiences, his self and responsiveness were already compromised by the loss itself. Such an acute loss of crucial selfobject experiences will not necessarily fragment the self completely but shatter it enough to make it much more needy to substitute other selfobject experiences. The increased need, therefore, results in increased sensitivity to the minor fluctuations that beset all relationships.

Subjectively, as we have just speculated, there may or may not have been an increased sensitivity on the part of the patient because of the painful loss of the cat, but the therapist's neutral, detached, and even cold "let's go on" could only have been experienced by the patient as an uninterested unresponsiveness or, worse, as a deliberately hurtful expression of unconcern. Some other patients might not have had the same experience; indeed, there might be patients who could experience such neutrality and detachment as optimal responsiveness, for example, individuals who had grown up in an environment of painfully excessive emotional concern of the parents for their offspring. They would usually welcome the calm, unemotional neutrality of the disinterested observer. However, this patient was different and wanted a warm emotional embrace to substitute for the lost experience with the loved and loving cat. The experience of pain and sadness was followed by anger expressed in a hostile silence, and then in the accusation that the therapist did not really understand such feelings.

The observable behavior of the therapist can never really be objective but always must include some values and judgment of the describing observer, whether the latter is the patient or some other, more scientifically distant and less participating individual. Also, the importance of the therapist's inner experience can hardly be overestimated. I can recall clearly what I felt. At first I was aware of a mild sort of sympathy reminiscent of my feelings at the time when dogs of mine had died. My attachment to these animals was friendly but never as intense as I have had occasion to observe in others. This attitude of mine has a long history going back to the early grades in grammar school. An admired old teacher, who even taught my father, had commented bitterly on some people giving money to the S.P.C.A. (Society for the Prevention of Cruelty to Animals). He told his pupils that as long as so many human beings were suffering in this world, any charitable money should be spent on ameliorating their fate as a first priority and not on animals. On principle, humans are more deserving than animals, he believed. That conviction of an idealized teacher has become a part of me. Added to that is a more general tendency to appear unemotional and not to express my feelings too openly, which grows out of other early experiences. Associated with this inexpressive posture is just a trace of arrogance vis-à-vis those who cannot resist showing and acting out their emotions. No doubt some of this inner experience was communicated to my patient via my detached "let's go on." In spite of my recognition of his having been injured by me, which I tried to heal by my commenting on the importance of the cat and painful loss he had sustained, the disruption continued.

When he angrily accused me of pretending like his mother, he revealed an important transference to himself as well as to me. Many of us might stress the value of such insights. In fact the disruption continued until I acknowledged my role in bringing it about. That was the point when the ambience in the room began to change. Subsequently, he was able to accept me as I am, flaws and all, and, by implication, was able to accept himself as well. The relationship had shifted in the direction of two people who have different outlooks on many things but accept each other as partners in the therapeutic enterprise. Mutually reciprocal acceptance means acceptance of being imperfectly human, accepting the inevitable up and down ripples in a relationship without avoiding painful issues and without placing blame but with seeking to understand. That is optimal responsiveness. Who could ask for more?

References

Bacal, H. (1985). Optimal responsiveness and the therapeutic process. In *Progress in Self Psychology*, vol. I, ed. A. Goldberg, pp. 202–227. Hillsdale, NJ: Analytic Press.

Kohut, H. (1959). Introspection, empathy, and psychoanalysis. *Journal of the American Psychoanalytic Association* 7:459–483.

—— (1968). The psychoanalytic treatment of narcissistic personality disorders. *Psychoanalytic Study of the Child* 23:86–113. New York: International Universities Press.

Wolf, E. (1988). *Treating the Self*. New York: Guilford.

—— (1993). Disruptions in the therapeutic relationship in psychoanalysis: a view from self psychology. *International Journal of Psycho-Analysis* 74:675–687.

12

Optimal Responsiveness and the Therapist's Reaction to the Patient's Unresponsiveness*

HOWARD A. BACAL AND PETER G. THOMSON

EDITOR'S COMMENT

Thomson and I contend that the patient–therapist relationship is much more extensively reciprocal in nature than psychoanalytic therapists have been willing to acknowledge, the implications of which for the therapist's optimal responsiveness we explore in this chapter. Thus, we extend and elaborate Wolf's idea that selfobject needs of patient and analyst are bidirectional, and that the analyst as well as the patient may experience disruption in his or her selfobject relationship with the patient when these needs are not met. In particular, we believe that the analyst normally has a variety of conscious and unconscious expectations of the patient, many of which constitute selfobject needs that are ordinarily responded to by the

---

*This chapter is based on "The Psychoanalyst's Selfobject Needs and the Effect of Their Frustration on the Treatment: A New View of Countertransference," by Howard A. Bacal and Peter G. Thomson (1996) in *Basic Ideas Reconsidered: Progress in Self Psychology*, edited by A. Goldberg.

patient during the course of therapy. Some of these needs are ubiquitous, others are particular to specific analyst–patient pairs. Many of them are hidden in the procedures and formalities of the treatment situation, with which the patient usually tends to comply.

When the therapist's selfobject needs are being responded to by the patient, the therapist may feel a variety of self-syntonic emotions as he or she empathically attunes to the patient. When the therapist's selfobject needs are unresponded to, the therapist may experience dysphoric affects along with self-disruption of varying degrees. This may result in an interference with the therapist's empathic capacity and his optimal responsiveness to the patient—a so-called countertransference reaction. This term, however, often does not adequately or accurately identify the disruptive selfobject experience that is occurring in the relational process, and we feel that a more appropriate designation for these reactions would be "selfobject relatedness reactions" or, more inclusively, "relatedness reactions." The authors provide examples from the clinical setting and the training situation that illustrate this perspective.

The understanding and acceptance of the psychological legitimacy of reciprocal needs for selfobject responsiveness will make it less necessary for the analyst to disavow his or her own needs for responsiveness from the patient, and more able to deal effectively with the patient's unresponsiveness. Specific proposals are offered that may assist the analyst in accomplishing these tasks. (We use the designation "analyst" to refer both to the psychoanalyst and to the analytically oriented psychotherapist.)

---------------- ❖ ----------------

The essence of this chapter can be stated in a few propositions:

1. From the perspective of our increasing comprehension of the psychotherapeutic process as a relational, intersubjective system,[1]

---

1. I refer here to the intersubjective relational perspectives elaborated by Stolorow and colleagues (1987, 1992), by Natterson (1991), and by the self and mutual regulatory perspective described by Lachmann and Beebe (see Chapter 15), which conceptualize in diverse ways the experience of interaction between subjec-

the analyst's therapeutic function is highly contingent upon reciprocal responsiveness on the part of the patient.

2. What this means, from a self-psychological point of view, is that the analyst's experience of the patient's selfobject responsiveness is ordinary and ongoing, and, in many respects, identical to selfobject experiences that are at the heart of the patient's experience of the optimal responsiveness of the analyst.

3. The withdrawal of the patient's responsiveness can precipitate a reaction in the analyst that interferes with his therapeutic function; this, in our view, constitutes one of the most common determinants of so-called countertransference. In other words, whether or not, with Searles (1979), we regard the patient as therapist to the analyst, the analyst's experience of the patient's responsivity can be as crucial to the therapeutic process as the patient's experience of the responsivity of the analyst.

Much of what obtains about optimal responsiveness as it refers to the experience of the patient in relation to the therapist (see Chapters 1 and 7) also refers to the experience of the therapist in relation to the patient. While it is the therapist's task to treat the patient, and not the other way around, each is variously sustained by the experience of the other's responsiveness. From a self psychological point of view, much of what each participant in the therapeutic relationship experiences as optimally responsive is the selfobject responsiveness of the other. When this responsiveness is unavailable, either participant may have a "relatedness reaction." We believe this term more accurately describes what has up to now been called "countertransference."

We postulate that every analyst normally brings a number of conscious and unconscious selfobject needs into the relationship with the patient that are differentially evoked as a result of interacting with the particular patient, and that these needs are ordinarily responded to by the patient as the therapy proceeds. The analyst also brings to the relationship with the

tively apprehended psychological organizations. None of them, however, nor the several relational conceptualizations that Bacal has described elsewhere (Bacal 1990, Bacal and Newman 1990) specifically place the notion of reciprocal sustenance at the core of a viable therapeutic process.

patient the expectation that the patient will validate—or invalidate—certain of the analyst's organizing principles—in effect, who the analyst feels himself to be. This, too, is usually responded to adequately by the patient. The patient's responses may be said to thus facilitate or even sustain the analyst in his work. They constitute what we would call the ordinary optimal responsivity of the patient to the analyst—a responsivity that, to an appreciable extent, "keeps the analyst going" (Beatrice Beebe, personal communication).

Much of the analyst's experience of the patient's responsivity is hidden, as it were, in the patient's compliance with the formal conditions for the viability of the treatment: that the patient attend the scheduled sessions and arrive on time; that the agreed-upon fee is paid in a timely manner; that the patient lie on the couch or sit in a chair; that the patient attempt to convey, as openly as possible, what is troubling or problematic, which has also been tacitly agreed upon. Some of the analyst's expectations in these matters arise from economic, organizational, and methodological considerations. Many of them derive from his training that decrees how analytic patients must comport themselves. Balint (1957) referred, somewhat pejoratively, to the "apostolic mission or function" of the doctor, "that every doctor has a vague, but almost unshakably firm, idea of how a patient ought to behave when ill. . . . It [is] as if he had a sacred duty to convert to his faith all the ignorant and unbelieving among his patients. . . . Although this idea is anything but explicit and concrete, it is immensely powerful, and influences. . . . practically every detail of the doctor's work" (p. 216). Although Balint identified the apostolic function as a characteristic of general practitioner psychotherapy, we believe that the expectations that underlie it also operate—perhaps largely unconsciously—even in the minds of trained psychoanalysts and psychotherapists. These expectations in part determine the style that the analyst has developed in working with patients over time. They derive to some extent from the analyst's training—some would say from his indoctrination. The analyst's reaction when the patient does not comply with these expectations, however, suggests that, in some measure, they also serve to maintain the analyst's self-cohesion, vigor, and balance (Wolf 1988). Many of these needs and expectations have more discernible psychological underpinnings.

Kohut (1971) described the "narcissistic countertransferences," the problematic reactions in the analyst to the archaic needs of the patient. Wolf (1980) was the first to explicitly recognize the bidirectional nature of these needs in the analytic relationship. He coined the term *selfobject countertransferences* (1979), to denote that the analyst, too, has selfobject needs that are mobilized as a result of participating in the analytic process (Wolf 1980). These needs are ubiquitous. They are commonly responded to by the patient, and when they are not, the analyst's therapeutic efficacy may become compromised. This kind of neediness in the analyst has not been generally appreciated, because it has not been openly acknowledged. While the patient's needs for selfobject responsiveness from the analyst have become increasingly accepted as psychologically legitimate, comparable needs of the analyst in relation to the patient, although they are understandable, have in practice continued to be regarded as largely undesirable. We are not supposed to have needs for the patient's responsiveness. Their occurrence is regarded, at best, as residua of inadequately analyzed issues during our training analyses. We are, in short, somewhat ashamed of them and we tend to disavow them. Yet, we believe it would be the atypical analyst who does not usually bring some sensitivities, vulnerabilities, and longings into the relationship with his or her patient that derive from personal and professional frustrations or injuries, both past and present (cf. Wolf 1979). We would plead for a measure of tolerance for the myriad of imperfections in the personalities of all therapists that continually influence his or her expectations of the patient but that do not necessarily disturb the therapy, partly because the patient is responding to them in one way or another. One may properly question whether, in any instance, this situation should be regarded as "intersubjective collusion" which should be analyzed. This question can only be answered by determining whether the situation is detrimental to the patient's treatment.

We believe that analysts regularly expect patients to respond in a number of ways that are, in fact, self-sustaining or self-enhancing. And our patients ongoingly meet a number of psychological needs that enable us to go on treating them. For the most part, we are unaware that this is happening. Our need for the patient's responsiveness becomes quite conscious, though, when it is significantly frustrated. (It is analogous to the effect produced when the flow of air to which one has become accustomed starts to become unavailable.) Put in another way, when the selfobject needs and expectations of both parties are being more-or-less responded to, a situation of mutual or reciprocal regulation is operating and a kind of harmony prevails in the analytic ambience. At these times, the analyst may feel a variety of syntonic emotions, such as friendliness, concern, mild idealization, sympathy, compassion, and sometimes anger or attraction of a regulatable degree toward the patient. The analyst's experience of the patient's unresponsiveness is in essence no different from the patient's experience of the analyst's unresponsiveness. When the patient experiences this, we call it a disruption. When the analyst has this experience, we call it countertransference.

Although some authors (e.g., Fosshage 1994, Heimann 1950) have good arguments for using the term *countertransference* to designate all the analyst's experiences of the patient, the most common usage of the term would appear to be the experience of feelings that tend to interfere with the analyst's therapeutic function. Used in either way, the term is a poor designation for the analyst's feelings, which do not arise only in reaction to the patient's transferences, as Racker has amply shown (1968). In this chapter we use its commonest meaning, since we are interested in the feelings of the analyst that may interfere with the analyst's therapeutic function. We introduce the term *relatedness reaction* to designate them. When our patients stop responding to certain of our selfobject needs or to our need to represent ourselves in certain ways, we may experience dysphoric affects along with self-disruption of varying degrees, which may interfere with our empathic capacity and our optimal responsiveness to the patient. (We believe that it is not uncommon for the analyst to experience the painful and even visceral sensations of disturbed self-states when the selfobject responses to which he or she had become accustomed are no longer available.) These experiences may include distancing, lack of interest, hostility and hatred, contempt, eroticism, prolonged boredom, sleepiness, or other somatic reactions. In self-psychological parlance we may speak, with justification, of the transient loss of cohesiveness of the analyst's professional self.

When we speak of failures in optimal responsiveness, we are placing these against the background of the expectable performance of a committed therapist at the level of his or her experience and training. Yet we must acknowledge that all of us attempt to defend ourselves from the repetition of disruptive experiences and their disturbing affects—especially that of shame—with anyone, including with our patients. Gunther (1976) emphasizes this perspective in his understanding of countertransference reactions. He sees them as enactments whose purpose is to restore the "narcissistic" equilibrium of the analyst, which becomes disturbed in interactions with the analysand. They are symptoms of the reassertion of the analyst's narcissistic needs.

We believe that these disruptions can be attenuated and sometimes averted as a result of the analyst's lessened requirement to protect himself or herself against the awareness of needs for the patient's responsiveness. We will suggest ways in which this goal may be attained—ways that centrally entail deactivating the sometimes disabling sense of shame that may accompany the awareness of these needs.

While the need of the patient and the analyst for selfobject responsiveness from each other is in essence the same, we recognize that those of the therapist are represented through his or her therapeutic function. A common selfobject need of the therapist is for mirroring of his function according to whatsoever way he conceives this function. If he conceives it as a benevolent attitude, he needs to be affirmed for this. If he needs to idealize the patient, then he can feel wonderful if he perceives his patient as having special attributes. The therapist may see his function as providing a holding, enlivening, reliably receptive, or whatever, ambience, for any of which he unconsciously needs affirmation. Perhaps the therapist's predominant need is for affirmation of his capacity to understand and for his caring, humanistic motivation. We suspect that this need by therapists to be seen by their patients as decent, well-motivated human beings is both pervasive and unacknowledged. This situation should be distinguished from the one in which the meeting of such needs is at the center of the general raison d'etre of the therapist. For these therapists, the patient's responsiveness may serve to repair defects in self-structure that arose from a requirement to accede to the archaic selfobject needs of their caregivers. For these therapists, their self-esteem and self-cohesion depend on their success in fulfilling the needs of their analysands (Stolorow and Atwood 1992). When a patient becomes seriously disrupted, this need may become significantly frustrated; in particular, the analyst may experience a loss of the sense of efficacy, along with a variety of dysphoric and disrupting affects, such as anger, inadequacy, disappointment in himself, and shame. According to Wolf (1988), "*Efficacy need* is a person's need to experience the self as an effective agent, that is, capable of eliciting a selfobject response" (p. 181).

CASE ILLUSTRATION 1: TINA

A situation that illustrates a number of these issues arose with Tina, an accomplished and successful young architect who had been in analysis for a little over three years. Tina had a mother who was continually and grossly out of tune with her affiliative-attachment needs, and who apparently had been so from Tina's early infancy. Tina had not felt this in the analysis. The analyst liked and admired Tina, and generally felt good about his ongoing work with her. The transference was, reciprocally, conspicuously idealizing.

In her analysis, Tina railed bitterly, angrily, and despairingly against her mother's overall insensitivity and cruelty as well as about her mother's near-total dismissal of the validity of Tina's complaints. As she regressed in the transference, she began to experience the holiday breaks as quite intolerable. And on more than one occasion, she experienced herself dissociating and fragmenting during breaks in ways that profoundly distressed her. However, she never appeared ill enough to justify hospitalization, nor was she at all interested in taking medication. The analyst responded by offering what he regarded as appropriate transference interpretations—essentially that she experienced him as repeating the neglect of her mother and deserting her like her mother and others had done in the past. Tina did not contest these interpretations, but they were of no help in relieving her painful symptoms. As time went on, and each break produced the same horrendous distress, Tina began not only to rebuke the analyst for leaving on his holiday, but to imply that he should not be going, because of what it did to her.

The analyst experienced a conscious resistance within himself to take his patient's request seriously—that the only way he could remedy the situation was never to take a holiday. In other words, although he was not aware of it at the time, he had already begun to repeat for Tina a deadly mixture of major experiences of suffering at her mother's hands: he was not only abandoning her, but also invalidating her experience, in this case, her experience of abandonment. He could not be aware of doing this because he needed to feel that, despite Tina's dissatisfaction, he was being a good therapist for Tina. The condemnatory quality of Tina's complaint about the therapist's vacation was making it even more difficult for him to become aware of his "wrongdoing." He felt a mixture of anger, shame, and guilt, as well as bewilderment about Tina's relentless reproaches. He also needed to feel free to take a holiday. Tina never appeared to want to go on holiday with him—in which case he would have had more problems— and she was quite uninterested in phoning him as a substitute for his being with her. In other words, Tina's ongoing responsiveness to the analyst's unconscious need for affirmation of his caring, generosity, and relative selflessness (a picture of himself that also reflected some of his central organizing principles) was now being withdrawn; indeed, it was being replaced by an escalating vilification of his professional self.

The analyst eventually stopped attempting to explain, that is, to interpret, the reasons for Tina's self-disruption during breaks. He thought that she had lost touch with reality around this issue and that it was time to draw her attention to it—that is, it was quite unrealistic of her to expect him not to go on holiday, and that he would simply not entertain the idea seriously. This did not help either. The analyst was now torn between a sense of outrage and a sense of inadequacy. This could conceivably have been the time for interpreting the patient's projection or projective identification of the parts of her that contained those feelings in an attempt to control him or to communicate her desperation in this way. The analyst did not experience the situation in this particular way, however, so he did not do this. He felt that Tina was being excessive and inappropriate in her demands; yet he also felt inadequate as a therapist. Nothing he could say was useful and his patient was, by her account, being made worse by the analysis and regarded him as a bad, cruel, and uncaring person. He did not know what to do to remedy the situation as she experienced it.

Tina left the analysis after four years but returned some months later for psychotherapy because she felt unable to hold onto a man. She consciously decided to avoid the regressive experience of analysis that would render her vulnerable to trauma at holiday breaks, but she referred, reprovingly, to the "failed" analysis, which failed, as she saw it, because of the analyst's inadequacies. Indeed, it would take several years more for the analyst to "get it," that is, to be able both to acknowledge to himself his need for responses from his patient that would confirm the efficacy of his therapeutic efforts and to accept— without experiencing a disabling sense of shame—that his responses to Tina were not good enough. Paradoxically, this achievement made him a better analyst for Tina. The analyst's recognition and acceptance of this need enabled him to begin to provide Tina with what she really needed from him — the deep-going validation that she had been right all along, that he *was* insensitive to her needs and, therefore, was cruel to her. He was putting his need for a holiday above her pain. He did not need to accede to her overt request to forgo his holiday, however, in order to alleviate her feelings of rejection and desertion. He did have to acknowledge, though, that she was right, he didn't care about her all *that* much. She was, as she put it, "only" a patient, and he was "only" an analyst. She didn't need to experience either his blame or his shame or his guilt. In taking his holiday, he had made the choice, at that moment, to put the needs of his self before those of Tina's. In other words, when she reproached him in these ways, all he had to do was to say, "Uh huh," and mean it, and she felt understood.

It is useful to discover, although it may not be easy to accept, that our need to be responded to by our patients as good-enough therapists is not only common to all therapists, but that this need never completely disappears. It took a long while for this quite experienced therapist to hear his patient's psychological need to be validated and to respond optimally to it. This was largely because of the disavowed shame that threatened whenever he began to experience his own need for his patient's selfobject responsiveness, especially when these needs were being thwarted. This came with the growing strength of the analyst's self over time, facilitated by some analytic consultations, which helped to decrease his vulnerability to shame in the face of perceived failure in his work.

Personal analysis or formal supervision can assist the therapist in accomplishing this. In our experience, this purpose may be significantly advanced when the therapist's relatedness reactions are dealt with in ways that provide more immediate access to the intersubjective issues that make them apparent. We will describe a training process (see below) that provides the opportunity to address them in this way. This process can enhance therapists' awareness of how their psychological needs and vulnerabilities have become organized into their professional working persona. It can both enhance therapeutic efficacy as well as, equally important, enable therapists to become clearer about the limits to their capacity for optimal responsiveness to a patient.

Some patients continue to associate, apparently doing their own analysis, but leave the analyst out of their associations for long periods. Such a patient not only tends to make the analyst sleepy (Dender 1993, McLaughlin 1975), but also tends to elicit transference interpretations, or interpretations about his or her resistance to transference. Interpretation has been accorded such a high and unquestioned value in analytic practice that we have lost sight of—or perhaps never saw—how intrinsic it is to the analyst's assertion of his role as an analyst. A little self-analysis will demonstrate that most of us tend, at times, to step up our interpretive activity when we feel less effective with our patient. We may then interpret simply to assure ourselves that we have a function.

One sometimes hears at analytic training committee meetings that such and such student seems to avoid making transference interpretations or has difficulty making transference interpretations. While in any instance this may be a problem for the student to consider, it may also reflect an analytic shibboleth. Even seasoned analysts sometimes feel a little edgy when they have not been able to make a transference interpretation for some time. Apart from this sort of pressure, we believe that transference interpretations are not infrequently offered when the analyst feels unengaged with the patient, and one of the determinants of this occurrence is the emotional disengagement on the part of the patient. The withdrawal of this familiar expected responsiveness can contribute to lethargy and devitalization in the analyst. In one such instance, an analyst found himself drifting off during a patient's silence. He then experienced the urge to interpret that the patient was removing himself from the analyst and was thus making it difficult for the analyst to stay with him. Fortunately, the analyst was able to recognize that his own need for stimulation and for a sense of functioning were at odds with the patient's need to use him through silence, and that the patient would only experience the interpretation as the analyst's need for the patient to accommodate to him; so he was able, in this instance, to control his urge to interpret.

CASE ILLUSTRATION 2: TOM

Tom, a young psychologist in analysis, regularly talked on without pause and without any reference to the analyst. His demeanor was invariably upbeat as he struggled bravely and insightfully with the many problems in his personal relationships. Central among these was a competitive struggle with his father-in-law who was chief of the department in which he worked—a man he had admired initially, but who had come to earn his contempt for his arrogance and ineptitude. Tom clearly liked and admired his analyst, and the analyst felt similarly about Tom. The central dynamics of Tom's selfobject transference constituted the developmentally restitutive idealization of the analyst to shore up a deflated self that derived from Tom's acute disillusionment with his father. He had idealized his father, who had been of central importance to him as a boy, although the father rarely appreciated Tom's abilities. Tom became acutely disappointed with his father when he lost his business and became depressed and discouraged and went to work for his older brother when Tom was in early adolescence. The analyst understood Tom's conduct in the analysis as subserving a defensive idealization of the analyst in order to preclude a repetition of this injury in the transference. In other words, Tom could not afford to allow the analyst to fail, so if he kept talking and doing the analysis himself, he wouldn't be able to discover the analyst's failings.

Rather than feeling buoyed up by this idealization, the analyst felt so bored and sleepy he could hardly keep awake. He rarely had the opportunity to make an interpretation, as Tom articulated everything the analyst regarded as relevant. Interestingly, Tom admired the analyst's skills, and he would, from time to time, refer to "our relationship," which he implied he valued very much. The analyst, however, felt himself to be a nonparticipant and irrelevant to Tom's therapeutic experience. He felt he needed to give at least some interpretations sometimes in order to be useful. He could have interpreted to the patient, in effect, confronted him with the assertion that Tom was resisting the transference, or competing with him; or he might have ascribed to Tom an unconscious intent to make him feel useless, if he did not question, with Brandchaft and Stolorow (1988), the validity of assuming that the analyst's disrupted affective reactions should be attributed to the hidden intentions of the patient. What no doubt helped him to refrain from interventions such as these, which was not always easy to do, was that Tom was improving steadily, which provided the analyst with a sense of satisfaction, if not a sense of efficacy. When he did, occasionally, offer interpretations that attempted to identify hidden negative transference, the patient would consider them respectfully, but briefly, and then offer his own, different viewpoint; thus, the interpretations were neither useful nor disruptive.

In our view, interpretations in such situations are sometimes motivated unconsciously by a specific deprivation in mirroring: a depletion has occurred in the analyst's experience of being recognized for what he has to offer, of being seen or appreciated for what he regards as important. An ongoing selfobject need—the tacit acknowledgment of the significance and utility of his existence as an analyst, which the analyst has generally come to count on his patients to meet (in the case of Tom, that he relate to the analyst in some measure and be at least somewhat interested in what he had to say)—is not being provided, and the analyst feels useless and devitalized. Tom needed to have an admired analyst/father mirror his efficacy. He was not interested in the analyst apart from this. At such times, the analyst is inclined to interpret in order to bring himself front and center. While some patients—like Tom—may be able to dismiss such interpretations as simply incorrect, or irrelevant, others may experience them as a disruptive transference repetition of the intrusive archaic selfobject needs of a significant caregiver.

Late in his life, Winnicott (1971) came to the conclusion that he had often prevented or delayed deep change in his patients by his need to interpret. And Casement (1985) states, "I was often tempted to interpret just to reassure myself that I was still able to think and to function in the session, when things seemed chaotic, but I had to learn to refrain" (p. 177). We would add, here, that when the analyst reassures a patient, sometimes his underlying need is actually to reassure himself.

Wolf (1980) has suggested that the analyst's experience of the intensification of his selfobject needs may be used as signals to alert him to an impending derailment of the therapeutic process. Such a disruption in the analyst may signal the analyst that his selfobject needs or self-representational needs are not being met, and that a relatedness reaction may be imminent. The next vignette illustrates the difficulty that an analyst may have in responding optimally to such a signal, because of the need to disavow the meaning of a professional expectation, which was imbued with selfobject and self-representational needs. It also illustrates the significance of shame in the therapist's experience of frustration and self-disruption and, in particular, the difficulties in facing shame.

ILLUSTRATION 3: DR. S.

Dr. S., a recently qualified analyst, briefly returned to her former training analyst after she experienced a distressing reaction to a psychotherapy patient who had been talking about terminating his recently begun once-weekly therapy sessions. Dr. S. had reacted to this by telling him that, in her view, he should not only not quit but that he should come five times a week. Immediately after saying this, she felt suffused with an inexplicable sense of intense shame. There is no question that her shame was partially in reaction to her sudden awareness of what she had done. That is, asking her patient to do something that she realized he was quite unprepared to do made her feel foolish both to him as well as to herself—and also to her analyst, when she reported it to him. She was also understandably reluctant at first to permit the analyst to include the vignette in this chapter, because, like most therapists, she did not quite believe that everyone, including her analyst, had had the same kinds of experience. There was more to understand, though.

Dr. S.'s patient had been suffering keenly as a result of the recent abandonment by his wife. His wife had begun an affair with her husband's boss and had moved in with him along with the patient's three children. He was trying, now, with considerable difficulty, to live a new life on his own, while continuing in his role as father on a part-time basis. Dr. S. had been empathically resonating with his strongly disavowed—and intense—feelings of shame about his wife's abandonment. Dr. S. was not new to experiences of abandonment. She had had similar feelings in comparable circumstances—some of which she had never completely owned. Prominent among them was the loss of her father—to whom she had believed she was special— who left home when she was a little girl. In addition, she was currently facing the painful possibility of losing her boyfriend. Her patient's talk of leaving stirred up disavowed feelings of shame that were associated with her experiences of abandonment. She could empathize with her patient and respond optimally to him as long as he did not do the same thing to her that others had done—and what his wife had done to him. When her patient announced his intention to leave her, she lost her empathic contact with him because she had in part unconsciously cast him as *the* selfobject who must not desert her. The shame surfaced when she tried to get him to be with her even more often. She was, in effect, expressing her unconscious, unrequitable love to her abandoning father, whose leaving she had been powerless to prevent.

Dr. S. also came to see that her disavowed sense of shame, as well as that of her patient, was due to a feeling of inadequacy. Neither of them had felt able to maintain sufficient regard for their idealized partners who had failed them (for the patient, this was Dr. S., his wife, and his family; for the therapist, it was her patient, her boyfriend, and her father, as well as, in part, her own analyst to whom she had returned for help) and, in consequence, Dr. S. and her patient were unable to retain their sense of self-respect. The commitment of her patient to the therapy unconsciously represented (that is, symbolized) for Dr. S. the partial, but significant redressment of a lifelong disillusionment of an idealizing need as well as that of a mirroring need to be special again. The therapist had made herself vulnerable to shame because she needed to disavow her selfobject needs in relation to her patient—selfobject needs that he had, in effect, been responding to all along, by staying with her and enabling her to feel worthwhile as a therapist. Had she been able to acknowledge them and accept them, she could likely have offered her patient a considered therapeutic response instead of reacting to the "signal disruption" that his talk of leaving elicited.

This therapist's experience is not unique. It is true that experience of desertion had a specific meaning to her that contributed to a need for certain kinds of selfobject responsivity. However, the occurrence of this sort of selfobject transference toward the patient on the part of the analyst is in itself not at all unusual. Indeed, we would claim that the patient's commitment to the treatment meets a universal idealizing selfobject need of therapists toward their patients as well as a universal need of therapists to be mirrored as being effective and special in relation to their patients.

Thus, the situation for the analyst is essentially the same as it is for the patient: if the analyst cannot accept the psychological legitimacy of her selfobject needs in relation to the patient, she will be affected in the same kind of ways as the patient. Her needs will intensify and she may act them out, very likely in relation to the partner who has frustrated them—her patient. That is, if we must protect ourselves from the shameful awareness of our needs in relation to our patients, we will not be able to engage these feelings through vicarious introspection or empathic resonance[2] with the patient or to respond optimally to the patient's comparable, disavowed needs. If, however, the analyst can accept the psychological legitimacy of these needs, it will significantly enhance her therapeutic function (Bacal and Newman 1990). That is, when the analyst's sense of shame about these needs and expectations in relation to the patient decreases, her defenses against them also relax, and she can then extend to herself the same empathy and acceptance she accords the patient. Gunther (1976) recommends the analyst use "selective empathy" with himself as a means of monitoring his defenses and disturbances. The discovery that this sense of shame is indeed universal will enable the analyst to be freer to respond therapeutically. What, in effect, appeared to be centrally useful for Dr. S. in her consultations with her former training analyst was the recognition and especially the developing acceptance of her selfobject needs in relation to her patient.

We believe that it is only recently, in particular because of the work of Broucek (1991), Morrison (1989, 1994), and Wurmser (1981), that the ubiquity of shame in human experience is becoming recognized. The therapist is no less liable than the patient to experiences of shame and to those defenses against shame experience that Morrison has described. But these experiences also offer us the opportunity for fresh self-inquiry, self-understanding, and self-acceptance. There are a variety of ways of pursuing this. More analysis is often the prescription for such problems— and it can help. Formal consultation or supervision is another. These tasks can also be effectively accomplished if the therapist's analyst is prepared to respond directly to the therapist's discussion of his or her therapeutic work during the analytic sessions. In this way, the analyst can offer his immediate understanding of his patient's counterrelatedness reactions that are precipitated by the frustration of her selfobject needs in the work with her patient. This, in effect, characterized the unique form of supervision that was offered by Ferenczi, Balint, and others to trainees at the Budapest Institute of Psycho-analysis, where this was the usual form of supervision. When Balint emigrated to England from Hungary in the late 1930s, he offered

---

2. I have drawn a distinction between empathic attunement, or vicarious introspection, and empathic resonance within the subjectivity of the analyst (Bacal 1997).

this form of supervision to his trainee analysands at the British Institute of Psychoanalysis. He supervised the student's first training case during the student's own analytic hours. In this way, the student's countertransference problems could be addressed with more immediateness, richness, and effectiveness than in the standard form of supervision, where the unconscious determinants of the student's countertransference can only be touched on by the supervisor.

Another way of approaching such problems is to seek out opportunities for open exchange with trusted colleagues. The exploring and sharing, in a collegial ambience, of experiences about the effects of disavowed selfobject needs and their frustration can be enormously helpful. The usefulness of such groups, which Balint started at the Tavistock Clinic in the 1950s and which have come to bear his name, is, we believe, augmented by a self-psychological perspective, which was not available in Balint's time. We regularly find that, as a result of these exchanges, we have less opportunity to feel ashamed of our "failures"; at least shameful feelings do not inhibit our self-inquiry. The ambience of acceptance in these groups, which meet on a weekly basis, facilitates the therapist's forthright engagement of such problematic issues that arose in the treatment of Tina and Tom, and the struggles of Dr. S. to help her patient. In such a setting, the discrepancy between the therapist who is faulty and the therapist who is supposedly not is greatly diminished. In addition, the evolving bond of trust between members mitigates the shame of disclosing one's selfobject needs and organizing principles and the defenses against them. Concomitant with such a process, one's self undergoes significant strengthening.

There are some difficult or adversarial situations, however, that may particularly strain an analyst's capacity to maintain an empathic stance and benign bond with his patient. "[W]hen . . . certain of the analyst's self-object needs surface and he perceives his patient as, so to say, 'violating' his expectations or acting upon him beyond the threshold of his tolerance, [t]his may precipitate a reaction in the therapist that can trigger or exacerbate a disruption of the patient's sense of selfobject relatedness to him" (Bacal and Newman 1990, p. 269). Such situations, when the patient becomes disrupted and perhaps enraged, may reverberate back onto the analyst, resulting in further frustration of his psychologically legitimate needs for self-enhancing or self-restorative responses from his patient. Now the analyst may experience a spectrum of painful feelings such as rage, hatred, anxiety, profound discouragement, and loss of self-esteem. He also experiences the pressure of the requirement that he de-center from such feelings in order to remain in empathic contact with the patient. This, however, may be easier said than done, for it may seem to him that it demands that he totally disavow authentic aspects of his affective experience.

We may ask whether self psychology demands too much of the analyst by requiring him to maintain the empathic stance at all times, which sometimes would seem to entail the complete renunciation of his or her selfobject needs. We allow, and indeed often encourage, children, parents, and patients to feel entitled to protest when their needs are not met. The long-suffering analyst tends to disallow himself such latitude. Moraitis (1993) states,

> In order to achieve his objectives the analyst must forfeit his personal needs to the maximum degree possible, so that he can place himself or herself in the service of his patient and his science.
>
> I believe such demands are unrealistic and unwarranted. They place the analyst in the defensive position of claiming altruistic motives he usually questions in others and of disclaiming in himself the very needs he helps his patients to acknowledge and satisfy. [p. 343]

Is it not the analyst's natural and perfectly human need to protest against the assault on his own sense of self? No doubt in the vast majority of instances such protest would not be expressed openly. But the right to give covert—and sometimes even overt—expression to his own aversive attitude may help protect the analyst from injury and, having acknowledged his legitimate needs, enable him to continue working with his patient.

For a long period in the analysis of a young woman, every interpretation the analyst made disrupted her. She angrily and contemptuously dismissed almost all his interventions. The analyst now, himself, became disrupted. He began to experience increasing degrees of mortification, shame, and disappointment in himself. He strove valiantly to restore both the patient's and his own self-esteem by searching for the "right" interpretation. This was all to no avail. Finally, he withdrew in discouraged silence. As his own vitality and cohesion were undermined, so this reverberated on the patient in a vicious circle. This analyst was unable to accord himself the right to protest, even inwardly, at the patient's failure to affirm him. It was only with the aid of a consultant that he was able to begin to tolerate her disillusionment. The problem of this analyst with this patient is one that might well lend itself to the kind of group discussion and support that we have suggested.

Winnicott (1947) recognized that the analyst will, at times, hate the patient, especially the regressed patient. He regarded it as important that the analyst acknowledge this hate to himself as well as tolerate both the patient's hate and his ingratitude. Winnicott was, in effect, implying a significant selfobject need on the part of the analyst that is being deeply frustrated by the patient. In our experience, if the analyst accommodates to the patient on an ongoing basis in order to avoid the patient's experiencing intolerable trauma in the transference, the hate engendered in the analyst by the prolonged frustration of his selfobject needs will inevitably interfere, at times, with the analyst's therapeutic function. We are referring here to trauma that tends to occur when the analysand regresses to pathognomonic genetically related disruptions in the transference—what Balint called "the basic fault" (Bacal and Newman 1990, Balint 1968).

We recognize that not all analysts find adversarial situations difficult or disaffirming. In fact some analysts feel mirrored or stimulated by the cut and thrust of an aversive encounter, as do some patients. The different personalities and theoretical approaches of analysts entail great variation in their selfobject needs and expectations vis-à-vis their patients. Stolorow and Atwood (1992) emphasize that sustained empathic inquiry must include the therapist's continual reflection on his ongoing subjective processes, that is, as part of the intersubjective field. We believe it should be possible for an analyst to become practiced in monitoring his self states as they are affected by those of the patient as well as by the effects of external factors on his life.

SUMMARY

We have asserted that the analyst's self states and, in consequence, his or her therapeutic work, are significantly affected by the patient's ongoing responsiveness. More specifically, we have suggested that what enables the analyst to carry out his therapeutic task routinely includes responses on the part of the patient that provide the analyst with selfobject experience. Lessem and Orange (n.d.) suggest that the mutuality of selfobject experience is associated with an increasingly solid bond of seeker and healer. That is, they imply that the therapeutic process is enhanced by the patient and analyst both experiencing the other as providing selfobject functions. The recognition that selfobject experiences are universal and that certain of them are probably experienced by most, if not all, psychoanalysts will tend to preclude their disavowal and so enable analysts to regulate their reactions more effectively when the need for these responses is frustrated. Stolorow (personal communication) states that the views we have expressed here usefully serve to dispel the myth of the perfectly analyzed analyst. We would agree, and would add that this will not only relieve the analyst of unnecessary strain but will also potentate more genuine and effective therapeutic interaction.

We are thus offering a new perspective on countertransference, insofar as this term is used to refer to the interference with the analyst's therapeutic function. When the patient is unresponsive to selfobject needs or self-representational needs—needs that the analyst may (perhaps quite unconsciously) have come to expect the patient to respond to—the analyst's therapeutic function may become disabled. In other words, countertransference reactions, or what we feel would more appropriately be called selfobject relatedness reactions—or simply, and more inclusively, relatedness reactions—may occur when these responses are significantly absent. We believe that a thorough appreciation of these processes increases our understanding of the mutual relatedness of the psychoanalytic enterprise and enhances our capacity to respond optimally to our patients.

References

Bacal, H. A. (1990). The elements of a corrective selfobject experience. *Psychoanalytic Inquiry* 3:347–372.

——— (1994). The selfobject relationship in psychoanalytic treatment. In *Progress in Self Psychology*, vol. 10, ed. A. Goldberg, pp. 21–30. Hillsdale, NJ: Analytic Press.

——— (1997). The analyst's subjectivity: how it can illuminate the analysand's experience. *Psychoanalytic Dialogues* 7(5): 669–681.

Bacal, H. A., and Newman, K. M. (1990). *Theories of Object Relations: Bridges to Self Psychology*. New York: Columbia University Press.

Balint, M. (1957). *The Doctor, His Patient and the Illness*, 2nd ed. London: Pitman, 1964.

———— (1968). *The Basic Fault*. London: Tavistock.

Brandchaft, B., and Stolorow, R. (1988). On projective identification: a reply. *Los Angeles Psychoanalytic Bulletin*, summer.

Broucek, F. J. (1991). *Shame and the Self*. New York: Guilford.

Casement, P. (1985). *On Learning from the Patient*. New York, London: Guilford.

Dender, J. M. (1993). *The phenomenon of sleepiness in the analyst*. Presented at the 16th Annual Conference on the Psychology of the Self, Toronto, October 31.

Fosshage, J. (1994). Countertransference as the analyst's experience of the analysand: the influence of listening perspectives. *Psychoanalytic Psychology* 12(3):375–391.

Gunther, M. S. (1976). The endangered self: a contribution to the understanding of narcissistic determinants of countertransference. *Annual of Psychoanalysis* 4:201–224.

Heimann, P. (1950). On countertransference. *International Journal of Psychoanalysis* 31:81–84.

Kohut, H. (1971). *The Analysis of the Self*. New York: International Universities Press.

Lessem, P., and Orange, D. (n.d.) Emotional bonds: the therapeutic action of psychoanalysis revisited. Unpublished.

McLaughlin, J. T. (1975). The sleepy analyst. Some observations on states of consciousness in the analyst at work. *Journal of the American Psychoanalytic Association* 23:363–382.

Moraitis, G. (1993). The analyst's quest for self-consciousness. *Psychoanalytic Inquiry* 13:333–347.

Morrison, A. (1989). *Shame: The Underside of Narcissism*. Hillsdale, NJ: Analytic Press.

———— (1994). The breadth and boundaries of a self-psychological immersion in shame: a one-and-a-half person perspective. *Psychoanalytic Dialogues* 4:19–35.

Natterson, J. (1991). *Beyond Countertransference*. Northvale, NJ: Jason Aronson.

Racker, H. (1968). *Transference and Countertransference*. New York: International Universities Press.

Rycroft, C. (1972). *A Critical Dictionary of Psychoanalysis*. New York: Penguin.

Searles, H. F. (1979). The patient as therapist to his analyst. In *Countertransference and Related Subjects*, pp. 380–459. New York: International Universities Press.

Stolorow, R. D., and Atwood, G. E. (1992). *Contexts of Being*. Hillsdale, NJ: Analytic Press.

Stolorow, R. D., Brandchaft, B., and Atwood, G. (1987). *Psychoanalytic Treatment: An Intersubjective Approach*. Hillsdale, NJ: Analytic Press.

Winnicott, D. W. (1947). Hate in the countertransference. In *Collected Papers of D. W. Winnicott*. London: Tavistock, 1958.

—— (1971). *Playing and Reality*. London: Tavistock.

Wolf, E. S. (1979). Transferences and countertransferences in the analysis of disorders of the self. *Contemporary Psychoanalysis* 15:577–594.

—— (1980). Empathy and countertransference. In *The Future of Psychoanalysis*, ed. A. Goldberg, pp. 309–326. New York: International Universities Press.

—— (1988). *Treating the Self*. New York and London: Guilford.

Wurmser, L. (1981). *The Mask of Shame*. Baltimore: Johns Hopkins Press.

C. New Perspectives on Empathy in Clinical Work

13

Optimal Responsiveness and a Systems View of the Empathic Process

MAXWELL S. SUCHAROV

EDITOR'S COMMENT

In this chapter, Sucharov describes the complexity and shifting nature of perspectives (which he notes is especially well expressed in Orange's perspectival epistemology) that are implied in his identification of the empathic process as bilateral. Sucharov suggests that, in listening to our patients, we go beyond the mode of listening via "empathic immersion" and attend to the mutually regulated empathic dance that is continually being choreographed by both patient and analyst. Sucharov's view of the empathic process as a bilaterally operating system lends significant substance to my elaboration (in Chapter 7 and with Thomson in Chapter 12) of optimal responsiveness as constituting the operation of a complex, more-or-less unique, reciprocal-relational system for each analyst–patient couple. Sucharov, in particular, underscores the patient's empathic understanding of the therapist, which he recognizes as complementary to the perspectives of Thomson and myself (see Chapter 12), that the therapeutic process is a relational, intersubjective system in which the analyst's therapeutic function is highly contingent upon reciprocal responsiveness on the part of the patient.

Sucharov draws attention to Searles's view that, in order to acknowledge to the patient that the therapeutic process involves both patient and analyst, it is important, particularly in the treatment of very ill patients, to accept the patient's attempts to cure the analyst of those aspects of himself that would interfere with the analyst's therapeutic function for him. In doing so, Sucharov not only invokes support for his contention that the empathic process is bilateral, he also adds significantly to the understanding of optimal responsiveness as both reciprocal and specific.

———————— ❖ ————————

I have, in recent years, written a series of four papers in which I have explored the penetration into psychoanalytic thought of a new quantum worldview generated by the discoveries of modern physics (Sucharov 1992, 1993a,b, 1994). I have focused on the overlapping epistemological journeys of Heinz Kohut, Robert Stolorow, and George Atwood. It has been my contention that self psychology and intersubjectivity constitute an important alliance for the integration of this new nonmechanistic worldview within the mental health field.

I have attempted to consolidate this alliance by articulating a central thesis that the evolving generalization of self psychology and the evolving clinical relevance of intersubjectivity is leading to a convergence of the two theories inside a common general systems paradigm (Sucharov 1994). Furthermore, this convergence reflects a shared commitment to a nonobjectivistic constructivistic epistemological base.

My objective in this chapter is to firmly anchor the psychoanalytic enterprise inside a bidirectional systems paradigm that embraces a nonobjectivistic relational epistemology. I respect that the success or failure of my stated objective is contingent not on the conceptual elegance of the theory but on its clinical utility to the pragmatic clinician, who will ask: In what way does systems theory help me with my daily empathic immersion in my patients' subjective experience?

The question, put in this way, is a paradox. Hidden inside its framework is an implicit rejection of a bilateral intersubjective systems view of the psychoanalytic process. Our pragmatic clinician harbors an assumption that the asymmetrical role distinction between patient and analyst gives the analyst a privileged monopoly on empathic understanding. "Empathic immersion" evokes a unidirectional process flowing from analyst to patient. We therefore need to search for a more appropriate question that does not contain, within its language, a negation of the bidirectional nature of the psychoanalytic encounter.

I will attempt to generate this new question by centering on my own clinical experience. My provisional acceptance of an intersubjective systems approach to my psychotherapeutic practice has facilitated my gradual recognition that my exclusive focus on my empathic immersion in my patients' experience in order to facilitate a selfobject experience in them, concealed a complementary process: the empathic striving of my patients, albeit at a sometimes rudimentary level, toward my subjective world, and the subsequent generation of a selfobject experience in me that would facilitate my entry into their world.

My emerging recognition of the above process was given conceptual clarity by Bacal and Thomson's (1993; also see Chapter 12) ideas on the selfobject needs of the therapist. Bacal and Thomson (1993) assert, "A therapist's experience of a selfobject relationship with his or her patient is not only pervasively operative in every therapeutic relationship; it constitutes a precondition for the therapist to respond in ways that will enable the patient to experience a selfobject relationship with him."

I would suggest that the therapist's experience of a selfobject relationship with his patient can only occur if there is a corresponding empathic grasp (conscious or unconscious) by the patient of the therapist's subjective world. A corollary to the above yields the central thesis of this chapter: *In the psychoanalytic encounter empathic understanding is bilateral. Understanding of the other and being understood by the other is an indivisible process that is mutually regulated on a moment-to-moment basis.* Selfobject countertransference has been described by Wolf (1979). The patient's empathic grasp of the analyst's subjectivity has been described by Wolf (1986) and Aron (1992). The moment-to-moment nature of mutual regulation in dyadic human systems derives from the infant research of Stern (1971) and Beebe and Stern (1977). Application to adult treatment derives from the work of Beebe and Lachmann (1993).

The patient's empathic understanding of the therapist therefore represents his/her contribution to the particular selfobject needs of that therapist, thereby facilitating his optimal responsiveness for that particular patient. This interdependent mutuality of empathy and optimal responsiveness was actually suggested (but not further developed) in Bacal's original paper on optimal responsiveness (Chapter 1). Drawing on the work of Wolf (1981), Bacal states, "Reciprocal empathic resonance took place between analyst and patient. . . . The interaction has been optimal from *both the analyst's and the patient's point of view* (p. 15, italics my own).

There is a more appropriate question for my skeptical pragmatic clinician: Is it clinically useful to postulate a bilateral systems view of the empathic process? This chapter constitutes a preliminary answer to this question by examining the empathic process in general, and the patient's empathic understanding of the therapist in particular. I begin by reviewing Harold Searles's pioneering work in this area. The integration of Searles's intuitive insights and Bacal and Thomson's work on the selfobject needs of the therapist with current theories of empathy provides us with a bilateral systems approach to the empathic process. Three prototypical clinical vignettes are reported that illuminate the clinical application of this approach. A reexamination of some clinical, structural, and epistemological concepts from within a systems perspective of empathy will culminate with the articulation of a new way of listening that transcends the unilateral limitations of empathic immersion.

THE CONTRIBUTION OF HAROLD SEARLES

Harold Searles's explicit acknowledgment of the contribution of both patient and analyst to the process anticipated the notion of the intersubjective field. Furthermore, his recognition that symbiotic relatedness (selfobject merger) is a normal dimension of adult experience anticipated Kohut's recognition of the ubiquitousness of selfobject experience: "Symbiotic relatedness is not confined to infancy and early childhood but forms at largely, though not entirely an unconscious level, the dynamic substrate of adult living" (Searles 1991a, p. 421).

In 1975 Searles wrote an evocative paper titled "The Patient as Therapist to His Analyst" (Searles 1981b). His central thesis was that "innate among men's most powerful strivings toward his fellow men, beginning in the earliest years and even earliest months of life, is an essentially psychotherapeutic striving" (Searles 1981b, p. 104). Furthermore, Searles contends that the patient is ill in part because his own psychotherapeutic strivings have been frustrated or not acknowledged. Searles integrates this thesis into the dynamics of the analytic process by illuminating the patient's unconscious attempt to cure the analyst of those problematic aspects that would interfere with the analyst's therapeutic function for that patient. With respect to technique, he emphasizes the importance of accepting the patient's strivings as an intrinsic part of the treatment process in order to acknowledge that the therapeutic process involves both patient and analyst. He also emphasizes that these issues are of particular relevance in the treatment of very ill patients (with whom he had extensive experience).

If we substitute empathic striving for psychotherapeutic striving, Searles's contribution encapsulates the following:

1. Empathic striving is a ubiquitous and powerful human motive that begins in infancy. Patients are ill, in part, because these strivings were ignored or actively suppressed.
2. In the psychoanalytic situation, the patient's empathic striving is a nonpathological constructive attempt to facilitate the analyst's therapeutic responsiveness.
3. The thwarting of the patient's empathic striving in the psychoanalytic encounter re-creates the original trauma for which the patient needs help.
4. The psychoanalytic situation is a bilateral process that facilitates the growth of both patient and analyst.

THE NATURE OF EMPATHY

Kohut's specification of the empathic mode of observation for psychoanalysis did not constitute the creation of a new phenomenon. He was simply harnessing a normal human capacity as a scientific instrument. In his last address several days before his death, Kohut emphasized the need to articulate a developmental line of empathy from its early archaic beginnings to more mature forms (Kohut 1991).

Here is a summary of current theories of empathy, based on infant observation (Beebe and Lachmann 1988, 1993, Kiersky and Beebe 1994,

Stern 1985), biology of human relationships (Maturana and Varela 1987), and studies in perception (Feiner and Kiersky 1994):

1. Empathic capacity has a developmental line from archaic infantile to complex adult forms.
2. Infants develop a capacity for empathy arising out of mutually regulated interactions with the caregiver. These interactions generate "interaction structures" that regulate experience along dimensions of affect, rhythm, spatial relationships, and arousal.
3. These early interaction structures are precursors to the nonverbal background dimension of adult empathic relatedness.
4. Mature adult empathy is a two-step process. The first step involves an emotional resonance that is immediate, holistic, and nonverbal. This emotional resonance probably involves unconscious coordinations at a presymbolic sensorimotor level. The second step consists in the assignment of meaning to the resonance via complex cognitive affective and conceptual structures. This step presupposes verbal capacity.

A SYSTEMS VIEW OF EMPATHIC UNDERSTANDING

The integration of Bacal and Thomson's work on selfobject needs of the therapist, Searles's clinical work on the empathic strivings of patients, and current theories of empathy provides us with a new systems view of empathic understanding in the psychoanalytic encounter:

1. In the psychoanalytic encounter empathic understanding is bilateral and mutually regulated.
2. It is a precondition for mutually regulated selfobject experiences.
3. Empathic understanding has a presymbolic and a conceptual dimension. A coordinated "empathic dance" (affective resonance) at the presymbolic level is a precondition for mutually regulated empathic understanding in the verbal conceptual dimension.
4. The presymbolic dimension is the adult transformation of the infant's archaic empathic capacities. It is ordinarily unconscious. For the difficult to engage patient, this dimension may occupy the foreground of the empathic process. This presymbolic empathic

coupling generates selfobject experiences for both patient and therapist that can sustain the therapy for long periods of time during which conceptual empathic engagement is either minimal or totally absent.

5. The patient's empathic understanding of the therapist represents his/her contribution to the particular selfobject needs of that therapist, thereby facilitating his optimal responsiveness for that particular patient.

6. Severe and repetitive early childhood trauma skews the development of empathic capacity. The mode, nature, and range of a patient's empathic understanding reflect both stabilizing defenses against retraumatization and transformational strivings for needed relationships.

CLINICAL APPLICATIONS

A bilateral view of empathic understanding has provided me with a useful clinical approach to patients of various developmental levels in a wide variety of contexts. I will focus on three prototypical groups of patients for whom this approach is particularly relevant.

The Hyperempathic Vigilant Patient

Hyperempathic, vigilant patients have coped with early and repetitive trauma by developing a deep and broad range of empathic understanding. Their precocious and enhanced empathic capacity shapes a vigilant approach to relationships that protects them from retraumatization. In the psychoanalytic situation the regulation of their self experience is rigidly contingent on their empathic grasp of the therapist as having a consistent and calm inner state. Abrupt disruptions occur with the slightest sense that the therapist is off his usual center. It is important to emphasize that a minor shift (from the therapist's vantage point) of the inner tension state of the therapist is amplified by the patient's enhanced empathic capacity and carries with it a meaning to the patient of impending trauma.

One patient begins every session by carefully scanning me for any sign of difference in my inner state. A perception of me as being angry, tense, or depressed typically triggers an immediate panic reaction. Over the course of the therapy, she has developed enough trust in me to share her perception of me and to inquire as to its accuracy. I have discovered that when I reveal to the patient just enough personal information that accounts for my changed state (invariably something is preoccupying me), she is able to calm down. An exploration of the meaning of the transaction reveals that her questioning me has nothing to do with invasive curiosity. It is motivated by the hope that I will share with her my inner state, thereby dissipating some of my tension. It is my belief that the above interaction reflects my patient's active and creative attempt to harness her enhanced empathic capacity to regulate my tension state and thereby facilitate my optimal responsiveness that will generate a soothing selfobject experience for her. I also believe that if I dealt with her observations and questions by simply asking for her fantasies, I would not only invalidate her perception but would also deprive her of a healing selfobject experience (achieved by regulating my self experience).

The Difficult-to-Engage Patient

Difficult-to-engage patients have coped with severe and early traumatization with a complex set of dissociative defenses that severely truncate the experience of an inner psychological life. Their profound difficulties in elaborating psychological experience, combined with a paranoid vigilance, make them very difficult to engage in the psychoanalytic process. These patients typically tax the legitimate selfobject needs of the therapist to feel affirmed and mirrored in his therapeutic function, thereby interfering with the therapist's optimal responsiveness to the patient. However, I have come to understand that even though these patients have minimal or absent empathic and introspective capacity in the conceptual domain, they nevertheless retain some empathic capacity in the more archaic presymbolic domain. In other words, their capacity to connect in a relationship of mutuality is restricted to and concealed in the archaic presymbolic empathic domain. This recognition enables us to search for their empathic strivings in this domain.

These archaic empathic strivings usually include, but are not restricted to the regularities of the therapy, such as appointment times, choosing a favorite chair, and any other behavior that becomes ritualized and repetitive and is connected with the routines of the therapy. Their archaic empathic signals may also contribute to mutually regulated processes connected with vocal tone, mood, rhythm, and arousal (Beebe and Lachmann 1993).

I would suggest that the therapist's discovery of the patient's archaic empathic strivings provides affirmation (to the therapist) that the patient values the relationship. The therapist's responsiveness can now be brought into congruence with the developmental level of the patient by monitoring the maintenance and disruptions of selfobject relatedness in this presymbolic domain of connectedness.

It is my contention that this archaic, empathic coupling generates selfobject experiences for both patient and therapist, thereby sustaining the therapy for a protracted period until more complex conceptual modes of empathy begin to evolve in the patient. It is important to accept and acknowledge the value to the therapist of the patient's empathic strivings. However damaged our patients may be, it is erroneous to assume that they are passive empty vessels that we fill up with psychological structure. They are always, from the very beginning of therapy, actively participating in the mutually regulated growth of both patient and therapist.

The Patient with Intense and Peremptory Empathy

These patients are often characterized as borderline. They have coped with their trauma by the retention of archaic selfobject needs, which they experience with a sense of urgency. The psychotherapeutic process with these patients often features tempestuous enactments. The collaborators of intersubjectivity have stressed that borderline phenomena cannot be understood apart from the intersubjective context in which they arise. They attribute these enactments to a disruption of an archaic selfobject bond in the context of empathic failures on the side of the therapist (Stolorow et al. 1987).

My own experience with these patients suggests that enactments during the therapy hour often begin with intense and peremptory empathic grasps of my own subjectivity that have as their purpose an attempt to cure me of those problematic aspects of my personality that interfere with my capacity for optimal responsiveness. My initial rejection of these strivings rationalized by classical technique would provoke escalating enactments. I gradually recognized that these patients were trying to help me with my obsessive preoccupation with proper technique, which I was using as a defensive maneuver against my own experience of feeling overwhelmed and invaded by the intense and peremptory nature of their empathic grasp of my inner experience. My acceptance and acknowledgment of their creative empathic striving thus facilitated the regulation of my own self experience (i.e., I became more relaxed and flexible), and a desperately needed archaic selfobject bond was reinstated. "Borderline" enactments therefore receded into the background.

My own amendment to the intersubjective understanding of border-line phenomena is that enactments are more than reactions to disruptions of an archaic selfobject bond reflecting the rage and fear of impending fragmentation. They also represent, particularly in the early phases of the enactment, the patient's active and creative empathic striving toward the therapist's subjectivity that have as their aim the self regulation of the therapist in order to reinstate a desperately needed archaic selfobject bond.

The above patient prototypes demonstrate that an optimally responsive psychotherapeutic process is contingent on bilateral mutually regulated selfobject experiences organized by bilateral mutually regulated empathic understanding. The patients' empathic strivings represent their active contribution to the co-creation of a healing selfobject bond. For those patients whose empathic conceptual capacity is absent or deferred (e.g., archaic mirror transference), their contribution to the empathic process is reflected in archaic presymbolic empathic strivings. The recognition, acceptance, and acknowledgment of these strivings by the therapist validates and deepens the collaborative nature of the therapeutic process. Similarly, Stern (1994) illuminates the healthy tendency of patients to evoke the experience of being responded to in ways they needed but never received.

CONCEPTUAL APPLICATIONS

Optimal Responsiveness and Optimal Restraint

It should be apparent that empathic understanding, selfobject experience, and optimal responsiveness (see Chapter 1) are interdependent phenomena. The bidirectionality of both empathic understanding and selfobject experience therefore requires a new understanding of optimal responsiveness consistent with a systems view of the psychoanalytic process. I would suggest that the term *optimal responsiveness* be used to characterize the emotional climate that is co-created in the intersubjective field in the context of mutually regulated selfobject experiences organized by mutually regulated empathic understanding. Optimal responsiveness is therefore a property of the intersubjective field and reflects an "optimally functioning dyad" (Doctors 1994).

It is important to underline that a bilateral systems view of empathy should not be used as a rationalization for therapists to engage in enactments in order to feed off the empathy of their patients. It is in this context that the idea of optimal restraint, articulated by Shane and Shane (1994; also see Chapter 4), is crucial. I would therefore suggest that optimal restraint reflects the special responsibility accepted by the therapist to act as a self-reflective guide to the therapeutic process, thereby guarding the asymmetry of the process inherent in the role distinction between patient and therapist. It is this restraint that protects the therapeutic process from deteriorating into a chaotic series of enactments, in which the distinction between patient and therapist could become dangerously blurred.

Empathic Structures

The nature, mode, and range of one's empathic understanding is shaped by the unconscious invariant organizing principles that structure experience. I would suggest the term *empathic structures* to refer to that particular set of organizing principles that shapes one's empathic capacity. This concept allows us to capture with a more experience-near language the intersubjective nature of the psychoanalytic process. The intersubjective field of the psychoanalytic encounter reflects a continually evolving empathic dance co-choreographed by the respective empathic structures of patient and analyst.

Complementarity and Perspectivalism

In a previous series of epistemology papers that draw on analogies from modern physics (Sucharov 1992, 1993a), I have articulated a new non-mechanistic descriptive framework for psychoanalysis. I have specified that the indivisibility of observer and observed in the analytic encounter precludes, in principle, an unambiguous objective description of the patient's experience. The embeddedness of patient and analyst in the constantly shifting intersubjective system denies the analyst a firm external ground from which he could gaze with objectivity at the patient's psyche and describe what he sees with a language that mirrors the contents of that psyche (correspondence theory of truth). (It is like trying to view a kaleidoscope when your eye is one of the pieces of glass that is constantly rearranging itself in relation to the other pieces.) Furthermore, the analyst's description of the patient is shaped in part by the analyst's language and theories that organize the empathic data in a particular way.

Any account of the patient's subjectivity can only emerge from a shifting series of perspectives, corresponding to different empathic moments organized by differing sets of concepts and/or metaphors. Each perspective is, in principle, subjective, contextual, language dependent, and incomplete. However, the perspectives, taken as a group, can provide a rich and textured understanding of the patient's experience. They complement one another. A single comprehensive and objective description is replaced with a series of complementary perspectives or "takes." The descriptive framework of complementarity reflects the quality of knowledge we obtain in any domain where the interaction between the observer and the observed forms an integral part of the phenomenon.

I have transposed the descriptive framework of complementarity from the field of quantum physics, where the need to take into account the interaction between the measuring instruments and the microphysical object preclude a single objective description of light. Depending on the experimental arrangement, light would manifest either as a wave or a particle, but never both at the same time. Wave and particle constitute complementary descriptions (or perspectives) of light. Kohut's awareness of the isomorphism between the observational situation in psychoanalysis and that of quantum physics shaped, in part, his nonmechanical views of mental life (Sucharov 1992, 1993a).

The bidirectionality of empathic understanding articulated in this chapter necessitates a reformulation of the above epistemological argument to conform with a dyadic systems view of the empathic process. The bilateral nature of empathy specifies that there are two observers in the analytic encounter. (There are two sets of eyes in the kaleidoscope.) Each participant to the encounter therefore forms his/her own series of complementary perspectives.

The emergence of truth in the empathic dialogue is therefore a highly complex coordination of shifting perspectives and shifting observers. We therefore need a transformational language that will capture the essence of the rule of complementarity for dyadic human systems. I believe that Orange (1992) supplies us with this language in her articulation of a perspectival epistemology for psychoanalysis: "One version of this communitarian or intersubjective realism might be a perspectivalism which would conceive a reality as a socially understood or socially articulated process in which each participant in the inquiry has a perspective which gives access to a part or an aspect of reality. There could be an infinite—or at least an indefinite—number of such perspectives" (p. 196).

The above quotation captures the spirit of complementarity as it applies to bilateral human social systems. Orange's perspectival realism also strikes a healthy balance between the solipsism of subjectivism and the mechanistic limitations of objectivism.

CONCLUSION: A NEW WAY OF LISTENING

A systems view of empathic understanding is a natural extension of Kohut's (1977) recognition that the empathic mode of investigation reflects the essential indivisibility of observer and observed in the psychoanalytic encounter. The bilateral nature of the empathic process is also a natural corollary to the acknowledgment of the bidirectionality of both transference/countertransference (Stolorow et al. 1987) and selfobject experience (Bacal and Thomson 1993). The placement of empathy inside a system of mutual reciprocal influence firmly anchors psychoanalysis inside a general systems paradigm and profoundly changes what we listen for and how we listen in the therapeutic encounter.

We are no longer the detached observers who listen to information (i.e., free associations) that is transmitted from patient to analyst. This tube metaphor of communication reflects a classical mechanistic epistemology. The concept of empathic immersion constitutes a giant step toward a more relevant listening stance, but nevertheless fails to capture the bilateral systems nature of empathic understanding. The concept contains a subtle but important remnant of isolated mind thinking (Stolorow and Atwood 1992).

I would suggest that the term *empathic immersion* constitutes a reification of the experience of an isolated mind of the therapist wandering around inside the subjective world of the patient. This reification obscures the embeddedness of empathic understanding in the highly coordinated mutually regulated empathic dance that is co-choreographed on a moment-to-moment basis by the empathic structures of both patient and therapist. It is therefore to this empathic dance of the intersubjective field that we direct our listening focus. Futhermore, our role as participant observers requires that we listen to the dance while we are dancing.

I think that we are still learning to listen in this new way. Whether or not this new listening perspective is clinically useful has constituted the central question of this chapter. It is my hope that I have made at least a modest contribution to an affirmative answer. Nevertheless, the question must remain open pending the accumulation of more data. We need more detailed clinical presentations in which the moment-to-moment contribution of both patient and therapist to the empathic process is explicitly demonstrated.

References

Aron, L. (1992). The patient's experience of the analyst's subjectivity. *Psychoanalytic Dialogue* 1:29–51.

Bacal, H., and Thomson, P. G. (1993). *The psychoanalyst's needs and the effect of their frustration on the treatment: a new view of countertransference.* Presented at the 16th Annual Conference on the Psychology of the Self, Toronto, October.

Beebe, B., and Lachmann, F. (1988). The contribution of mother–infant mutual influence to the origins of self and object representations. *Psychoanalytic Psychology* 5:305–337.

——— (1993). *Shifts in theory and practice.* Presented at the 16th Annual Conference on the Psychology of the Self, Toronto, October.

Beebe, B., and Stern, D. (1977). Engagement—disengagement and early object experiences. In *Communicative Structures and Psychic Structures: A Psychoanalytic Interpretation of Communication,* ed. Norbert Freedman and Stanley Grand, pp. 35–55. New York and London: Plenum Press, 1977.

Doctors, S. R. (1994). Discussion of *In Pursuit of the Optimal in Optimal Frustration, Optimal Responsiveness and Optimal Provision.* Presented at the 17th Annual Conference on the Psychology of the Self, Chicago, October.

Feiner, K., and Kiersky, S. (1994). Empathy: a common ground. *Psychoanalytic Dialogue* 4:425–440.

Kiersky, S., and Beebe, B. (1994). The reconstruction of early non-verbal relatedness in the treatment of difficult patients: a special form of empathy. *Psychoanalytic Dialogue* 4:389–408.

Kohut, H. (1977). *The Restoration of the Self.* New York: International Universities Press.

——— (1991). On empathy. In *The Search for the Self*, vol. 4, ed. P. Ornstein, pp. 525–535. Madison, CT: International Universities Press, 1991.

Maturana, H., and Varela, F. (1987). *The Tree of Knowledge: The Biological Roots of Human Understanding*. Boston and London: Shambhala.

Orange, D. (1992). Subjectivism, relativism, and realism in psychoanalysis. In *New Therapeutic Visions, Progress in Self Psychology*, vol. 8, ed. A. Goldberg, pp. 189–197. Hillsdale, NJ: Analytic Press.

Searles, H. (1981a). Concerning therapeutic symbiosis. In *Classics in Psychoanalytic Technique*, ed. R. Langs, pp. 419–428. New York and London: Jason Aronson.

——— (1981b). The patient as therapist to his analyst. In *Classics in Psychoanalytic Technique*, ed. R. Langs, pp. 103–135. New York and London: Jason Aronson.

Shane, E., and Shane, M. (1994). *In pursuit of the optimal in optimal frustration, optimal responsiveness and optimal provision*. Presented at the 17th Annual Conference on the Psychology of the Self, Chicago, October.

Stern, D. (1971). A microanalysis of mother–infant interaction. *Journal of the American Academy of Child Psychiatry* 10(3):501–517.

——— (1985). *The Interpersonal World of the Infant*. New York: Basic Books.

Stern, S. (1994). Needed relationships and repeated relationships. An integrated relational perspective. *Psychoanalytic Dialogue* 4:317–345.

Stolorow, R., and Atwood, G. (1992). *Contexts of Being: The Intersubjective Foundations of Psychological Life*. Hillsdale, NJ: Analytic Press.

Stolorow, R., Brandchaft, B., and Atwood, G. (1987). *Psychoanalytic Treatment: An Intersubjective Approach*. Hillsdale, NJ: Analytic Press.

Sucharov, M. S. (1992). Quantum physics and self psychology: toward a new epistemology. In *New Therapeutic Visions, Progress in Self Psychology*, vol. 8, ed. A. Goldberg, pp. 199–211. Hillsdale, NJ: Analytic Press.

——— (1993a). Psychoanalysis, self psychology, and intersubjectivity. In *The Intersubjective Perspective*, ed. R. Stolorow, G. Atwood, and B. Brandchaft, pp. 187–202. Northvale, NJ: Jason Aronson.

——— (1993b). *The wise man, the sadist, and cartesian anxiety: a tale of two solutions*. Presented at the 16th Annual Conference on the Psychology of the Self, Toronto, October.

——— (1994). *Self psychology and intersubjectivity: a converging alliance*. Presented at the 17th Annual Conference on the Psychology of the Self, Chicago, October.

Wolf, E. S. (1979). Transference and countertransference in the analysis of the disorders of the self. *Contemporary Psychoanalysis* 15:577–594.

——— (1981). *Empathic resonance*. Panel discussion at the Fourth Annual Conference on the Psychology of the Self, Berkeley, California.

——— (1986). Discrepancies between analysand and analyst in analytic experience. In *Progress in Self Psychology*, vol. 2, ed. A. Goldberg, pp. 84–94. New York: Guilford Press.

14

Is Empathic Attunement the Only Optimal Response?

HOWARD A. BACAL

EDITOR'S COMMENT

Empathy has been defined in many ways. The major differences between the various definitions (reviewed by Tuch 1997) appear to turn upon whether empathy should be understood as constituting solely the apprehension of the other's affective experience or whether it should include the other's cognitive experiences as well; and, correspondingly, whether the data that constitute the determinants of empathy are affective or cognitive or both. My own view is that empathy is variously constituted by cognitive and affective elements, in varying proportions. But I would emphasize other aspects of empathy as more significant. I suggest that the hallmark of empathy is the sense of a direct grasp of the subjectivity of the other. I believe that the definition of empathy must also take into consideration the obvious but important fact that it is a subjective experience (Bacal 1997). Empathy is the subjective experience of "knowing" who the other is or what the other feels at that moment. I agree with Basch (1983) that when we empathize, we are reading an aspect of our own subjective state as it is affected by the other. *How* we are affected is another question, which is in turn related to the further question as to how empathy differs from what analysts describe as countertransference and projective identification (Bacal 1997).

I distinguish between *empathy* and *empathic resonance*. Empathy constitutes a limited or circumscribed contact, through vicarious introspection, with who the other is or feels; empathic resonance constitutes a more or less full immersion, within oneself, in the other's subjectivity (somewhat similar to sympathy). And I contend that what determines whether the therapist contacts the other's subjectivity in the one or the other way is the result of complex psychological interactions that influence *physical distance* between therapist and patient (Bacal 1997).

In this chapter, I address the broader distinction between empathy, or empathic resonance, as an experience, and its application as an optimal response.

References

Bacal, H. A. (1997). The analyst's subjectivity—how it can illuminate the analysand's experience. *Psychoanalytic Dialogues* 7(5):669–681.

Tuch, R. (1997). Beyond empathy: confronting certain complexities in self psychological theory. *Psychoanalytic Quarterly* 66:259–282.

───────────────❖───────────────

There is a psychoanalytic truism that has rarely been explicitly acknowledged: empathy is not only the fundamental method of analytic data-gathering (Kohut 1959), it is also one of the most potent therapeutic responses that the psychoanalyst can offer the patient. This chapter will demonstrate the incorrectness of self psychology's tacit—and sometimes explicit—promotion of empathic attunement as the only response that is therapeutically effective.

Kohut's insistence that the analyst maintain a position of prolonged empathic immersion in the patient's subjectivity may have seemed to some to be an unremarkable restatement of what all analysts do anyway, but it led to nothing less than a revolutionary shift in psychoanalytic practice. In my view, this was Kohut's most important contribution to psychoanalysis

(Bacal 1995). Kohut himself regarded his paper, "Empathy, Introspection and Psychoanalysis: An Examination of the Relationship between Mode of Observation and Theory" (1959) to be his best. As Kohut saw it, analysts were no longer listening adequately to their patients. Rather, they were employing their theories without adequate regard for their patients' experience. Kohut's assertion that a sustained listening perspective from the vantage point of the patient should constitute the basic clinical Weltanschauung—in effect, an essential psychoanalytic procedure— constituted a vital antidote to authoritarian, omniscient attitudes that had pervasively crept into psychoanalytic work, attitudes that found their most pernicious expression in the view that the patient was "resisting" the analytic process. The concept of resistance, as it was generally employed by analysts, ensured that, if there was a difference between the analyst's subjectivity and the patient's subjectivity, the analyst was right and the analysand was wrong. Kohut, in effect, reversed this perspective. "If there is one lesson that I have learned during my life as an analyst, it is the lesson that what my patients tell me is likely to be true—that many times when I believed that I was right and my patients were wrong, it turned out, though often only after a prolonged search, that *my* rightness was superficial whereas *their* rightness was profound" (Kohut 1984, pp. 93–94).

Kohut described the therapeutic function of the psychoanalyst as entailing a two-step process. The first step is to empathically obtain understanding about the patient's psychological world. The second is to explain, that is, to interpret what one has first understood via empathy— which Kohut defined as *vicarious introspection*. However, if we look more closely at Kohut's descriptions of the treatment process and the analyst's contribution to it, a more complex picture emerges. On the one hand, Kohut officially identified vicarious introspection, or empathy, as the diagnostic methodology that defined depth psychology (i.e., psychoanaly- sis). On the other hand, much of Kohut's writing and his teaching, as well as his analytic work, overwhelmingly conveys that he also regarded empa- thy as one of the major curative factors in psychoanalysis. Perhaps Kohut's strongest and most explicit statement about this was, "Despite all that I have said . . . [about empathy being] an informer of appropriate action . . . empathy, per se, is a therapeutic action in the broadest sense. The presence of empathy in the surrounding milieu, whether used for compassionate, well-intentioned purposes . . . and even for utterly de- structive purposes, is still an admixture of something positive" (Kohut

1981, p. 530). In Chapter 1, I discussed how Kohut considered different forms of providing empathic attunement that were appropriate and usable for patients whose self is organized at different developmental levels. That is, unofficially, Kohut did appreciate that the therapist's empathic attunement alone could be experienced by the patient as a significant therapeutic response. As evidence for this, we could point to the dramatic example of his now famous patient, Miss F.—whose case is often cited as template for the discovery of self psychology—who required empathic echoing as the only response that provided her with a therapeutic experience. Anything else was catastrophically antitherapeutic!

Yet, most analysts—and most self psychologists, including Kohut— have been disinclined to bestow official recognition on empathy as a function that, in *itself*, constitutes an effective therapeutic response. I believe that this is a legacy of the classical Freudian perspective; that is, without explanation or interpretation, our function as analysts is somehow incomplete. The idealization of the analyst's interpretive activity and the relative depreciation of empathic attunement as a therapeutic factor are officially retained as analytic shibboleths by most self psychologists as well as by most other analysts. But we need go no further than our own consulting rooms to discover that it is the rule rather than the exception that people who seek our help experience our empathically reflective responsiveness to their suffering as preeminently therapeutic.

In effect, self psychology has given substance to what analysts have always known through clinical experience—that the provision of in-depth empathic attunement is crucial to the therapeutic process, and that it will often, and perhaps for the most part in relation to the majority of patients that we see in our practices, be the only response, or the central aspect of the analyst's response, that is experienced by the analysand as useful. Empathic attunement and optimal responsiveness are, in effect, synonymous in much of the work that we do. Is this always the case?

THE LIMITATIONS OF EMPATHY AS A THERAPEUTIC RESPONSE

Having recognized this, I believe we have gotten a bit stuck there. A kind of rigidity about empathy has insidiously crept into self psychology. In practice, self psychology has hierarchically promoted empathic attunement to a position of being the only appropriate response to the patient. Some of us would not even consider offering the patient any response that is not "empathic," that is, one that does not reflect the patient's conscious subjectivity or disavowed affective experience. Yet, not all patients always experience our responsiveness as therapeutic when it consists of only, or even mainly, empathic attunement. There are many situations in which this is the case. I will mention only a few. For example, when the patient struggles with certain schizoid problems (such as fear of exploitation, impingement, or even of being known) or employs schizoid defenses (such as distancing or hiding), or has difficulty in boundary-regulation—conditions that are not at all uncommon—the need for privacy may seriously conflict with his or her yearning for closeness and understanding. At these times, empathic attunement or even an attitude of empathic inquiry as a response may not be experienced as therapeutic, let alone an accurate interpretation, which could be experienced as seriously invasive and disruptive. Such a patient may experience anything other than the analyst's accepting presence as intrusive or dangerous; as Winnicott (1960) observed, the analyst will otherwise be a "witch" who knows the patient and what is good for him.

Ultimately, it is the meaning of the analyst's responsiveness that will determine its therapeutic effect.

> An analytic patient of mine, Ms. Q., was moaning miserably about the welter of depressing experiences in her life. As she described these in painful detail, I echoed her affect and conveyed my appreciation of her plight with compassion and understanding. After about 10 to 15 minutes of this, I noticed that she was speaking more slowly and haltingly and her voice was getting quieter and quieter. Finally she turned around and said, "You know, I don't feel very good about your doing this." For a while, it was hard for her to explain what she meant, or what she needed. Eventually she was able to say that my careful tracking of her affects also made her experience me as down there with her—it turned out, like she felt her mother was, all too much. "I think I need someone to be up there a bit more, while I am down here," she said. While she did need my empathic understanding of her unhappiness, the echoing of it had begun to disturb her. She also needed an ambient responsiveness that declared a sharable outlook that was quite different. (Herzoz [Chapter 8] illustrates how sharing can be delineated as a specific selfobject function.) She needed me to retain a

perspective that would enable her to question a relational organizing principle that one of the major elements of the connection between her and her partner must be a shared melancholy centering around the preeminence of defect. Otherwise, there could be no end to her despair that her "defects" could ever be fixed.

It has gone conceptually unnoticed that the therapeutic effect of the adversarial selfobject relationship, which promotes the experience of being a center of initiative through permitting nondestructive oppositional self-assertiveness (Lachmann 1986, Wolf 1978, 1988), entails the analyst's responding optimally from a vantage point that is directly at variance with that of the patient. The analyst's empathy might advise him of the therapeutic gain in enabling the patient to experience such an antagonistic or adversarial selfobject relatedness, and his therapeutic response to the patient will not, in this situation, reflect the patient's subjectivity.

Several of the authors in this book provide clinical examples that illustrate the therapeutic effect of offering a response that is not only not empathically attuned to the patient's articulated experience, but also at variance with it (see especially the case of Alan in Chapter 7, Kenneth Newman's clinical illustration in Chapter 5, and the case of A. described by Susan Lazar (Chapter 10) in which "[a] confrontive, at times even combative portion of the treatment was not characterized by an attitude of sustained empathic attunement" [p. 223]).

Sometimes an outright invalidation of the patient's subjectivity is more effective than an empathic echo or an empathically elaborated interpretation. Margaret Black (1987) has given us a vivid example of this, when she effectively invalidated her patient Christine's recurring self-disparaging presentation of herself. She had been consistently echoing her patient's subjective experience, and the patient had improved in many ways. Yet there were a number of areas of Christine's experience that remained unresponsive to the treatment, in particular, her fear of being assertive and being fully and visibly expansive. Detailed interpretation of the determinants associated with the crucial moments when the patient's self-esteem collapsed were helpful but didn't alter her self-presentation. While she would sincerely agree with the therapist's interpretations of her experience, she continued to report the same process, while at the same time her mood and attitude appeared considerably improved. Christine was interested but puzzled when the analyst drew her attention to this discrepancy. On one occasion, when the patient was pursuing her apparently "ritualistic" and "spiralling self-disparagement," which again culminated in her having "no right" to think and being "all wrong" (p. 135), Black departed from attempts at affirming and understanding her patient's experience and, instead, said to her, in a "firm but slightly amused tone—'You don't really believe that!'" (p. 135). The patient "sat quiet—momentarily stunned— although a slight smile crept across her face. Then she gamely acknowledged, 'You're right'" (p. 135). Black's challenging her patient's articulated sense of herself and her experience "broke the therapeutic stalemate and [revealed] an additional set of meanings to her self-constriction" (p. 135).

How did this happen? Clearly, it is not possible to answer this question with any conviction without a detailed description of the case and the therapeutic process, much of which is available in Black's article, but which, for lack of space I have not been able to reproduce here. (The paper was reviewed by discussants from different analytic perspectives.)

Black herself acknowledges that one could make a case for maintaining that her comment fell within the definition of "accurate empathy," since one could conclude that it "accurately addressed a newly consolidating aspect of Christine's self-experience . . . her strength" (p. 140). The patient's response does appear to indicate that the latter was a disavowed aspect of the patient's subjective sense of herself, which could justify the claim that Black's comment was empathic; yet, as Black observes, the analyst was effective in confronting the patient with a position that was different from her own. We may recall that Jeffrey Trop was similarly effective in helping his patient Alan (Chapter 7). Kenneth Newman's responses that were initially optimal for his patient (Chapter 5, Clinical Example 3) did not echo her subjective experience; rather, they invalidated her defensive/addictive requirement that every man who deserved her was beneath her consideration. My own view of what happened in Christine's case is similar to that of Black's—that, at a certain point, the analyst stopped accepting (i.e., empathically responding to) the patient's conscious view of herself and confronted her with a disconfirmation of it that reflected the analyst's belief in her, as well as her sense that the patient had actually changed—even though the patient herself was unaware of it.

How the patient's subjective experience should be addressed in any instance depends on a variety of considerations, which preeminently include an assessment of the state of the patient's organizing principles or patterns, the strength of the patient's self, and the corresponding need for defense. In the Black example, for instance, the analyst was conveying to the patient not only that her organizing principle—that her views had no value in the eyes of authority—had actually altered, but also that she was more ready than she realized to drop her defensive experience of the other as someone who legitimately devalues her. In effect, the analyst was conveying to the patient her recognition of her patient's growing self-regard and strength as a result of the work they had done together. Thus, Black's challenge, which invalidated the patient's subjectivity at that moment, did not, as Black observes, undermine the patient's sense of self; rather, it constituted an optimal response that "instead permitted strengths that [the patient] needed to keep hidden to become exposed" (p. 137). There may, of course, have been other effective ways of working with the patient's problem. One of the more obvious ways would be to attempt to understand the continuing difficulties that the patient had with authority figures as representing a split-off attitude of "pathological accommodation" (Brandchaft 1994, in press) that she unconsciously retained toward her woman analyst.

In an intervention that has become famous for its ostensibly—and startlingly—non–self psychological character as well as for its efficacy, Kohut confronted an analysand who was bragging about his reckless driving on the way to the session by telling him that he was "a complete idiot" (Kohut 1984, pp. 74–75). Kohut's reason for describing this incident was to demonstrate that "[a] self-psychological orientation will not prevent the analyst from confronting the patient with the necessity of curbing his dangerous behavior, to control his 'acting-out'" (Kohut 1984, p. 75). However, it is evident to me, from a careful reading of Kohut's account of the case, that the meaning to the patient of Kohut's confrontation was that of a sorely missed demonstration of caring and involvement on the part of Kohut-as-father, which Kohut had now provided with his confrontational, but apparently therapeutic, response to his analysand.

Mr. D., a patient whom I saw briefly in consultation, illustrates the limits to empathy as a response; it also demonstrates the limits to therapy when the analyst is unable to provide the optimal response for the patient. Mr. D.'s dynamics were somewhat similar to those of Kohut's patient, but his therapeutic experience was not so fortunate.

> Mr. D. was a brilliant, married businessman in his early fifties who had had an analysis for seven years with an eminent self psychologist in

Chicago, which terminated in disappointment and anger about six years previously. Since then, he had wandered from therapist to therapist without finding relief for his symptoms. Essentially, he had felt well prior to the analysis, which he undertook to relieve a disruptive obsessional thought that he might have cancer. As the analysis proceeded, his life became progressively disorganized and chaotic. He began an affair that went nowhere, but which had continued to that day. He became addicted to cocaine—a habit he subsequently kicked on his own—and, although he had been making a good income in a business he enjoyed, he spent his money thoughtlessly and ended up in, and remained in, serious debt. Mr. D. experienced his analyst as intelligent, lovable, and dedicated to his emergence as an individual in his own right, and he felt the analysis, as a whole, to have been enjoyable and stimulating. He also experienced the analyst's empathically inquiring attitude as frustrating and inadequate.

When he consulted me, Mr. D. was desperate about whether to leave his wife or give up his mistress, who had just given him an ultimatum that she would have nothing more to do with him unless he left his wife. During his consultations with me (which did not proceed to ongoing therapy), it became evident that the most significant bond in his life had been with his father, whom he had experienced as powerful and ambitious for him, but also as denigrating, neglectful, narcissistic, and uncaring. His major complaint, however, was about his former analyst, to whom he was still quite attached, albeit aversively (Lichtenberg 1989). He was very angry at him. "It was as if anything goes. The ordinary things in my life were falling apart and he didn't seem concerned!" It would appear that, as devoted as the analyst was to the patient, he was so committed to an empathically inquiring attitude and to the deep-going self-development of his patients—one might legitimately call this a kind of self-psychological organizing principle—that he did not hear his patient's desperate need for the guiding and regulating responsiveness of a parental figure. Mr. D. tried to elicit this responsiveness from me by attempting to involve me in his agonizing decision about the two women as well as to give him advice about his everyday real-life struggles and challenges. I have wondered, from time to time, why this patient did not choose to continue with me. While I can only speculate about this, since he disappeared after a series of consultations, some of what he said would lead me to believe that he experienced me as organized a bit too much like his former analyst. I learned, early on in the consultative process, that interpretations were useless to him; yet, I suspect that my efforts to infuse "authoritative reality" into my communications to him about the practical issues of his life fell considerably short of what he was looking for. This is not my therapeutic forte, and thus I likely failed to provide him with the responsiveness that he needed.

My failure to engage this patient has led me to wonder to what extent psychoanalysts who successfully present "reality"—*their* reality—to their patients may be offering responses that are optimal for those patients who have a therapeutic need to experience a relationship with an authoritatively regulating parental figure.

Thus, while the optimal responsiveness concept preeminently includes a progressively fine-tuning of our empathic capacities and the careful communication of this understanding to the patient, this is not the only response of the analyst that will facilitate a therapeutic experience for the patient.

OPTIMAL RESPONSIVENESS, EMPATHY, AND SPONTANEITY

While the analyst's spontaneity will sometimes land him in a disruption that will have to be analyzed, it will just as frequently turn out to constitute an optimal therapeutic response. (Susan Lazar has provided examples of this in Chapter 10.) While the analyst's spontaneity may be informed by his empathy, it may or may not constitute the provision of an attuned understanding of the patient's subjectivity. It may, for example, constitute the natural expression of the analyst's personality as a response to the selfobject need of the patient, and in so doing, provide the patient with an experience of significant selfobject relatedness. In effect, the patient will experience who the analyst is at that moment, and that will constitute the therapeutic factor. Perhaps the most common expression of the analyst's spontaneity is his smile, although there are some analysts, even today, I am told, who never smile. The analyst's smile may be a more valuable therapeutic experience, for a period of time, than all the accurate interpretations he may offer; yet, we must not overlook the possibility that, for another patient, it is an overstimulation that may constitute a significant disruption that requires careful analysis.

Analysts sometimes make "spontaneous"—that is, not carefully considered—comments that may sometimes be dramatically helpful. A psychiatry resident who was suffering from severe self-esteem vulnerability, who was improving through her experience of an idealizing selfobject relationship with her analyst, mentioned to him that she was looking for a new job. The analyst suggested, in an off-hand, friendly way, that she consider applying for a position on the staff of the local mental hospital. Many years later, the patient recalled this as one of the analyst's most valuable responses to her in a long analysis. She knew that he taught there and, therefore, for her, his spontaneous suggestion was the highest endorsement she could obtain. We may consider that the analyst's response was informed by his empathic grasp of his patient's low self-esteem, but the response itself went beyond the provision of empathic attunement; it expressed the analyst's feeling about the patient, which she empathically grasped correctly. The clearly spontaneous nature of the therapist's response was preeminently optimal* for the patient and may well have significantly undermined the patient's (very different) view of what the analyst thought about her at that moment.

There is a famous example of Kohut's allowing his suicidal patient to hold on to his fingers when he was afraid he might lose her. While he interpreted to himself that "it was the toothless gums of every young child clamping down on an empty nipple," he said nothing to the patient. And he comments, "I wouldn't say it turned the tide, but it overcame a very very difficult impasse at a given dangerous moment" (Kohut 1981, p. 535). While it was Kohut's intent to demonstrate that empathy alone could be therapeutic, that is, without offering an articulated explanation to the patient, he could respond in a way that was consonant with the patient's ability, that is, her developmental capacity, to use his empathy, I believe, now, that this stretches the meaning of "providing empathic attunement" too far. Kohut used his empathy to appreciate the patient's state; but what

---

*This vignette illustrates how the therapist's *unconscious* intent to provide a response that is optimal—i.e. specific for the patient's therapeutic experience— can be just as effective, through its spontaneous expression, as the therapist's *conscious* intent.

he did was not the provision of empathic attunement, or understanding, if you will, to the patient's state of near-deadness; rather, Kohut's response constituted a gesture—the offer of a tangible link with himself as living and believing in life—that he felt would be optimal, that is, that might help lift the patient out of her hopeless despair.

Empathic attentiveness (vicarious introspection) is the predominant way that the analyst obtains information that enables him to understand the patient. Although the analyst's provision of empathic attunement is, in effect, the response that is most consistently experienced as optimal by most of our patients, self psychologists, as well as other analysts, sometimes erroneously equate optimal responsiveness with the provision of empathic attunement. Optimal responsiveness constitutes the therapist's acts of communicating to his patient in ways that that particular patient experiences as useable for the cohesion, strengthening, and growth of his self. Goldberg (unpublished), citing Poland, refers to the former, that is, empathic attentiveness, as the "afferent branch of empathy" and to the latter— the response—as the "efferent branch of empathy." In my view, the idea of "efferent empathy" does not do justice to the nature and range of the therapist's efficacy. Thus, I prefer the concept of optimal responsiveness (see Chapters 1 and 7). It is important to remember that the patient experiences any attitude or behavior on the part of the analyst as a form of response to his psychological needs and defenses. Optimal responsiveness may *entail* empathic attentiveness, the provision of empathic attunement, interpretive intervention, quiet acceptance, or forthright confrontation, but it is not, a priori, synonymous with any of them.

References

Bacal, H. A. (1995). The essence of Kohut's work and the progress of self psychology. *Psychoanalytic Dialogues* 5(3):353–366.

——— (1997). The analyst's subjectivity: how it can illuminate the analysand's experience. *Psychoanalytic Dialogues* 7(5):669–681.

Basch, M. (1983). Empathic understanding: a review of the concept and some theoretical considerations. *Journal of the American Psychoanalytic Association* 31:101–126.

Black, M. (1987). The analyst's stance: transferential implications of technical orientation. *The Annual of Psychoanalysis* 15:127–171.

Brandchaft, B. (1994). To free the spirit from its cell. In *The Intersubjective*

Perspective, ed. R. Stolorow, G. Atwood, and B. Brandchaft, pp. 57–76. Northvale, NJ: Jason Aronson.

———— (in press). Obsessional disorders: a systems perspective. *Psychoanalytic Inquiry*.

Goldberg, A. (unpublished). The limits of empathy and the value of misunderstanding.

Kohut, H. (1959). Introspection, empathy and psychoanalysis: an examination of the relationship between mode of observation and theory. In *The Search for the Self, Selected Writings of Heinz Kohut, 1978–1981*, vol. 1, ed. P. Ornstein, pp. 205–232. Madison, CT: International Universities Press.

———— (1981). On empathy. In *The Search for the Self: Selected Writings of Heinz Kohut, 1978–1981*, vol. 4, ed. P. Ornstein, pp. 525–535. Madison, CT: International Universities Press.

———— (1984). *How Does Analysis Cure?* Chicago: University of Chicago Press.

Lachmann, F. (1986). Interpretation of psychic conflict and adversarial relationships: a self psychological perspective. *Psychoanalytic Psychology* 3(4):341–355.

Lichtenberg, J. (1989). *Psychoanalysis and Motivation*. Hillsdale, NJ: Analytic Press.

Tuch, R. (1997). Beyond empathy: confronting certain complexities in self psychological theory. *Psychoanalytic Quarterly* 66:259–282.

Winnicott, D. W. (1960). The theory of the parent–infant relationship. In *The Maturational Processes and the Facilitating Environment*, pp. 51–55. London: Hogarth.

Wolf, E. (1978). On the developmental line of selfobject relations. In *Advances in Self Psychology*, ed. A. Goldberg, pp. 117–130. New York: International Universities Press.

———— (1988). *Treating the Self: Elements of Clinical Self Psychology*. New York: Guilford.

D. Developmental Considerations

15

Optimal Responsiveness in a Systems Approach to Representational and Selfobject Transferences*

FRANK M. LACHMANN AND BEATRICE BEEBE

EDITOR'S COMMENT

The authors describe the process whereby an intervention that was intended to provide an optimal response to an evident representational transference triggered a disruption in the relatively hidden, but simultaneously operating and psychologically predominant, selfobject transference. The authors indicate that their terms *representational transference* and *representational configurations* (which are synonymous) have the same meaning as "repetitive dimension of the transference," but that they additionally imply the coexisting repetitive and transformative potential that is characteristic of these configurations. They use their case example to illustrate the challenge to the analyst's optimal responsiveness in such instances. They also demonstrate how their dyadic systems approach to the

---

*An earlier version of this chapter originally appeared in *New Therapeutic Visions: Progress in Self Psychology*, volume 8, edited by A. Goldberg.

repair of disruptions promotes the acquisition in the patient of expectations of reciprocal responsiveness, or mutual regulation, in the process of addressing future disjunctions.

There is significant similarity between Wolf's description (Chapter 11) of the therapeutic usefulness of a blameless acceptance of participation in the disruption and Lachmann and Beebe's view of the therapeutic value of expressive recognition that the tie has been interactively ruptured and that the patient has experienced the analyst's response as nonoptimal. I would only add here, which both Wolf's and Beebe and Lachmann's clinical examples demonstrate, that, as I described in Chapter 7, the responses of the therapist following the rupture must be specific to the disjunctive issues that both patient and therapist are now facing. The principle of optimal responsiveness applies equally in situations of disruption and situations in which the patient experiences the analyst's responses to be "just right."

The authors also use their case example to illustrate the difference between a linear and transformational model of development and the implications this has for the optimal responsiveness of the therapist. In contrast to a linear model, which assumes that what the patient offers derives essentially from particular experience in the patient's past and is not significantly affected by later or current context, a transformational model recognizes the continuing influence on experiences of self and other of all stages of development as well as interactions with the therapist. This particular example demonstrates the benefit of recognizing how a later organization of self and other may better capture a certain transference predicament, defenses, and resources than an earlier one.

We heartily concur with Bacal's view, elaborated in Chapter 7, that optimal responsiveness should in fact be termed "reciprocal optimal responsiveness." We view the entire psychoanalytic enterprise as defined by reciprocal interaction, on a moment-by-moment basis. Reciprocal interaction is conceptualized within a systems model that integrates mutual regulation with self regulation (Beebe 1986, Beebe and Lachmann 1988, 1994). The terms *reciprocal responsiveness*, *reciprocal interaction*, and *mutual regulation*

are used interchangeably. We thus broaden the field of this discussion from optimal responsiveness to the larger question of the system of interaction within the transference.

We conceptualize transference as co-constructed by both partners. In this chapter, we define two dimensions of the transference: the selfobject dimension and representational configurations. Within the selfobject dimension we propose that nonoptimal interactions are as significant as optimal interactions. What may seem appropriate from the dynamic standpoint of the representational configurations may turn out to be nonoptimal from the selfobject viewpoint. Thus, the definition of what is optimal and nonoptimal must be jointly defined by both dimensions of the transference. Finally, a critical additional feature of our systems model is the recognition that these two dimensions of the transference are organized at multiple levels across developmental transformations. The case we present illustrates the advantage of recognizing how a later organization may better capture a particular transference dilemma, defenses, and resources than an earlier one.

Although they are not identical with each other, three pairs of concepts cover a similar terrain: one- and two-person psychologies, self and mutual regulation, and selfobject and representational transferences. We have previously argued (Lachmann and Beebe 1992) that the integration of self and mutual regulation is one way of articulating the integration of one- and two-person psychology perspectives. Our terms, *self* and *mutual regulation*, and *selfobject* and *representational configurations*, cut across the distinction between one- and two-person psychologies, potentially provide finer clinical distinctions, and do not carry an either–or connotation.

In our "dyadic systems view of communication" (Beebe et al. 1993), the organization of behavior and experience are viewed primarily as a property of the patient–analyst system rather than as a property of the individual. However, the individuals each bring their own range of self-regulatory capacities. A psychoanalytic theory of interaction must specify how each person is affected by his own behavior—self regulation—as well as by that of the partner—interactive regulation. The nature of each partner's self regulation affects the interactive regulation and vice versa.

A dyadic systems view incorporates a transformational perspective. Development is in a constant state of active reorganization, and transactions, between the child and the environment, undergo regular restructurings (Sameroff 1983, Sameroff and Chandler 1976). At each stage of development experience is reorganized. In psychoanalytic treatment the contributions of each stage are recognized, not just the earliest. A transformational view can be seen, for example, in the concepts of epigenetic stages (Erikson 1950), narrative point of origin of pathology (Stern 1985), and model scenes (Lachmann and Lichtenberg 1992, Lichtenberg et al. 1992). According to this view, earlier is not deeper, and later layering is essential to full recognition of the transference.

In our proposal that transference is composed of a selfobject dimension and a representational configuration (Lachmann and Beebe 1992, 1995, 1996), we took the position that the selfobject concept is not flexible enough to encompass all therapeutic aspects of the transference. Instead it exists in a figure–ground relationship with representational configurations, defined as affect-laden descriptions of self and other (see also Lichtenberg 1983, Stolorow and Lachmann 1984/1985). Representational configurations are derived both from a person's expectations from earlier times as well as from aspects of the current patient–analyst interaction. The selfobject dimension addresses the experience of and the maintenance of the tie between self and other, as well as the requirements for cohesion, articulation, and vitality of the self. The representational configurations depict the qualities of self and other and the themes of their interrelationship. We hold that representational configurations provide the context for selfobject experiences and, in turn, selfobject experiences provide access to representational configurations. Self and mutual regulation are instrumental in organizing and transforming selfobject experiences and representational configurations.

We now turn to the one-person and two-person psychology distinction. The one-person view recognizes the patient's elaborations of his or her own experience. It emphasizes the uniquely organized expectations and fantasies to which the person adheres and that affect interactions with the analyst. This view fails, however, to give sufficient recognition to the mutual influences of analyst and patient on each other. Furthermore, the unique context of the analytic experience as it shapes, influences, and transforms the patient's experience must be considered. Whereas the one-person view underscores the centrality of self experience, the two-person view emphasizes the centrality of the interaction with the partner. The two-person view recognizes the continual, reciprocal impact of analyst on patient and patient on analyst. It underscores the analyst's monitoring of the effect of his or her theory, personality, and biases on the patient's transferences, and vice versa. Thus, we hold that both of these positions are essential for a comprehensive understanding of the complexity of the patient–analyst relationship.

Both analyst and patient contribute to the transferences, but their contributions are neither equal nor similar. Each brings to the analytic encounter his or her own organization, that is, self regulation. In addition, the treatment relationship is organized by mutual regulation. This perspective is derived from studies of early development and recognizes the lifelong organizing effects of self and mutual regulation, disruptions and repair of these regulations, and heightened affective moments (Beebe and Lachmann 1994).

In this chapter, we consider the effects of a nonoptimal interaction and its subsequent analysis and repair. Nonoptimal interactions have a therapeutic value of their own. Although such events are not specifically planned by an analyst, they do occur with some frequency. Disruption and nonoptimal interactions are ubiquitous and an essential constituent of all communication. They are mutually regulated both in their unfolding and in their repair. Establishing expectations that disruptions and mismatches can be repaired is an essential mode of therapeutic action. It is precisely these nonoptimal interactions that provide entry points to the therapeutic reevocation and illuminations of traumatic experience.

Through a clinical vignette, taken from the first year of an analysis conducted by Frank Lachmann, we illustrate the disruption of the selfobject tie through a nonoptimal interaction. We elaborate on the two dimensions of the transference: the selfobject dimension and the transference as organized by representational configurations. Finally, we illustrate the clinical relevance of a transformational model of development.

The patient is a 39-year-old divorced woman who was anxious and despondent to the point where, occasionally, she had been unable to function in her work as a travel agent. After several months of treatment these symptoms had abated somewhat. Then over the course of several sessions, she described the following events. She had met a man who thought she was a very emotional person and thought of himself as very blocked and distant. In his relationship with her he hoped he would learn how to be emotionally freer. She stated that she made it clear to him that she did not want to be his teacher. In the following session she reported a dream about her former therapist and depicted her as her daughter. The next session contained descriptions of numerous incidents with friends in which she accepted their preferences about planning various activities and later felt angry with herself for being so compliant. In the final session of this sequence, she reported a dream in which she and her daughter's cat were being drenched and flooded in a rain shower. Her association led her to recall that she had to take care of the cat while her daughter was spending the night at a girlfriend's house. The patient felt resentful about being burdened with this chore. In addition, she described feeling resentful about her work. While feeling depressed and anxious she still had to conduct her business and take care of her clients.

This is clearly a selective account of four consecutive sessions. However, implicit in this clinical material were descriptions by the patient of herself as burdened, resentful, angry for being overly accommodating, a caregiver or mother to "mother" figures, an authority for her boyfriend, and feeling deprived of protection and nurturance. Others were described as embodying the qualities of demandingness for her care, and the expectation that she serve as the adult, parent, mother, teacher, accompanier, and provider.

These affect-laden descriptions of self and other constitute a series of representational configurations. Experiences of self and other are organized in line with expectations derived from an earlier time and facets of the current analyst–patient interaction as well. Such configurations may be rigidly repeated and imposed on ongoing experience. Optimally, they can be expected to transform and be transformed by the ongoing therapeutic experience.

WHAT DO WE MEAN BY "TRANSFORMATION"?

Beginning in early development transformations are a consequence of the continuous interaction between the person and the environment. According to the transformational model, intrapsychic changes produce changes in the environment and vice versa, so that neither the person nor the environment remains static from one point of time to another (Piaget 1954, Sameroff and Chandler 1976). In this process, both earlier and later stages remain influential.

The envelope of optimal interaction will contain contributions from both the patient's and analyst's background as well as the here-and-now co-constructed moment. By maintaining this perspective of developmental transformation, the analyst can avoid being drawn into a simplistic linear perspective.

In a linear perspective the age from which a particular experience, memory, fantasy, or relational configuration derives is linked to a specific level of development. A linear model assumes that material offered by the patient comes directly from the patient's past and is unaffected by the therapeutic context. It is as though analytic responses, optimal or otherwise, are akin to diagnostic formulations, based exclusively on what the patient presents and the analyst has accurately perceived.

In contrast, the transformational model recognizes both the continuing influences of all aspects of the patient's development as well as the affect of the analyst–patient interaction. Stern's (1985) concept of "narrative points of origin" of pathology reflects his finding that the capacity for symbolization that develops at about 18 months opens the door to wide-ranging reorganizations of the child's developing capacities. The narrative sense of self both reorganizes the earlier senses of self and leaves room for their unique impact on subsequent experience. In adult treatment we encounter this reorganization in narrative form in the analytic situation. It is toward this narrative reorganization that we aim our therapeutic responses.

Representations of the experiences in the caregiver–infant dyad undergo transformations throughout development. Similarly, representation of experiences in the analyst–patient dyad are assumed to undergo transformations. These may evolve into expectations of mutuality, interactive responsivity, or, as in the present case, traumatic disruptions in the selfobject tie, and a resurgence of manifestations of self dissolution.

DIMENSIONS OF THE TRANSFERENCE

In the treatment dyad, representations of experience can be delineated along two dimensions: selfobject and representational configurations. Whereas in early development these two dimensions are indistinguishable, the distinction between them is crucial in the treatment of the adult because they address different functions and different qualities of experience. The selfobject dimension includes the experience of and maintenance of the tie, and the requirements for cohesion, articulation, and vitality of the self. The selfobject tie can be seen as varying along the dimension of "the search for a new beginning" and "the dread to repeat" (Ornstein 1974).

Representational configurations refer to the qualities of self and other and the themes of their interrelationships. The representational configurations are both repetitions of past experiences and to some extent contain the seeds for their potential transformations. As we indicated earlier, we believe that representational configurations provide the context for selfobject experiences, and, in turn, selfobject experiences provide access to representational configurations. Although representational configurations are shaped by the transactions of important relationships, they are also shaped by the person's effort to construe experience in such a way that vital selfobject functions may be derived.

Our use of the term *representational configurations* does not exclude the possibility that selfobject experiences are represented. We use this term to refer to those transferences that have been traditionally described within psychoanalysis as "object related" (see Bacal and Newman 1990). Stolorow and Lachmann (1984/1985) reformulated transference as the organization of experience and proposed that selfobject and other transferences occupy a figure/ground relation to each other (see also Lichtenberg 1983). These other transferences have also been referred to as the conflictual-repetitive dimension of the transference (Stolorow et al. 1987). We prefer the term *representational configurations* to *repetitive dimension of the transference* to emphasize the concurrent repetitive *and* transformative potential that characterizes these configurations. When rigid representational configurations shape the patient's treatment experience, they become foreground, requiring analytic attention.

In the treatment of adult patients, representational configurations may synopsize the subjective elaboration of important interactions from any phase of the person's life. Under optimal circumstances they continue to be reworked, as past experience is transformed at various times in life and in analysis. As past themes are reworked and relived, newly acquired resources and defensively instituted restrictions can be integrated. When these representational configurations are, for example, based on a dread of repeating character defenses (Ornstein 1974), they remain rigid and stereotypic.

THE ANALYST'S NONOPTIMAL RESPONSE

Following the four sessions described above, based on the patient's description of herself and her interactions with others, I reached for a response that might provide optimal support and understanding as well as open the patient's repeatedly dissatisfying experience to investigation. I commented that although she, the patient, might want to be taken care of, she frequently found herself in the position of the caring, self-sacrificing mother. This interpretation described a representational configuration based on the patient's narratives, associations, and dreams. No developmental origins were suggested, and no statement about the transference was directly made. I felt that this comment was in tune with the patient's expressed complaints and recognized her longing for an attachment in which she could feel cared for.

The patient immediately supplied confirmatory material with respect to her family, her parents, her brother, her ex-husband, and her daughter. Apparently she felt understood and used the interpretation to further organize past events in line with the interpretation, and in a manner that seemed to promise her a greater sense of efficacy.

However, shortly after the session the patient became increasingly depressed and confused, to the point where she felt she was unable to function in her work. She telephoned me in the evening after the session in which the interpretation was offered and asked what she could do, because she felt profoundly disorganized. In the brief phone conversation I connected her disorganized state to the session, which she had not done on her own. I told her that we would attempt to understand if something occurred in the session that disturbed her so. I realized that an intervention that I had thought captured her state and distress in a tactful and emotionally responsive manner may not have been experienced by her as optimally responsive. At that point, reestablishing the safety of the analytic setting was of paramount importance. Acknowledging the possibility that the prior session may have had a disruptive effect constituted an attempt at repair.

The patient reciprocated with optimal responsiveness of her own. She was pleased by the phone call and particularly by the acknowledgment that the disruption had been interactively organized. She had not been blamed.

Thus, connecting the patient's disruption to her experience of the prior session acknowledged the interactive organization of her disorganization and contributed to restoring a sense of safety in the analytic setting.

This ambience of safety (Lichtenberg et al. 1996) is derived both from the analyst's responsivity toward the patient and the patient's experience of the analyst's responsivity. Parallel experiences of the patient's responsivity toward the analyst and the analyst's experience of the patient's responsivity are, of course, also implicated. These aspects of the patient–analyst interaction are discussed by Bacal and Thomson in Chapter 12. With an opportunity for an analytic dialogue reestablished, a joint understanding of the patient's self-fragmentation could be addressed.

A DEVELOPMENTAL PERSPECTIVE: SYSTEMS MODEL

Stern's (1985) senses of self (emergent, core, subjective, verbal) are cumulative and are progressively reorganized. Thus, in the adult patient any sense of self may be more or less implicated, strengthened, or threatened at any point in development. In the case under discussion, the patient's core sense of self was shattered by the intervention. However, as it emerged in later explorations, it was predominantly the narrative sense of self around which her selfobject tie to the analyst had been built. That is, the predominant transference was organized by a selfobject tie derived from the idealization of the father rather than by a masochistic, self-sacrificing relationship organized in relation to the mother.

Viewed from the vantage point of linear development, the relationship to the mother refers to an earlier time in the patient's life than her idealized tie to her father. Following a model of linear developmental sequence would have led to the same nonoptimal response as was offered by the analyst in this instance. The analyst would have wrongly concluded that aspects of her relationship with her mother had not been sufficiently worked through and required immediate attention.

From the vantage point of a systems model, however, the analyst searches for the issues in the current interaction and the sense of self that are implicated. Using this approach, after the selfobject rupture, the analyst was led to an acknowledgment of the array of resources the patient acquired through her problematic but idealized tie to her father. Proceeding with treatment without sufficiently acknowledging the patient's developmental achievements would, in effect, have undermined her past developmental strides. The developmental model enables the analyst to recognize the relevant transformations that have contributed to the patient's increasing resourcefulness and to note where developmental advances have been precluded.

A linear model suggests that the analyst tailor responses to meet needs along a developmental ladder. Crucial contributions derived from other (often later) developmental steps could be ignored if earlier origins are always assumed to be more relevant. The patient's "complaints" about having to be the caregiver touched on the extent to which her sense of self was organized by a precarious narrative in which she depicted herself and others in complex, representational configurations. This depiction invited a responsive verbal intervention. Yet, other senses of the patient's self were also affected. My tone and affect (concern and anxiety) touched the patient as well. These nonverbal aspects of my nonoptimal intervention were part of my overall communication. As it emerged subsequently, my anxiety, as packaged in my intervention, contributed significantly to the patient's anxieties and her profound disruption.

THE PATIENT'S FRAGMENTED RESPONSE

How shall we understand the patient's debilitating anxiety? Is her reaction to be seen as a masochistic enactment in the transference, or is she predominantly reacting to an empathic rupture in the selfobject tie? Should the analyst consider the disorganization as emanating from a threat to her need to maintain a self-sacrificing position through which she maintained her self integrity?

Rather than viewing the patient's response as organized entirely by her own pathology, the interactive contributions from the analyst–patient dyad as well as from the patient's propensity for repetitive, stereotypic responses were recognized. That is, we illustrate here our use of a one- and a two-person psychology perspective.

When I suggested to the patient that there might be a link between her overwhelming anxiety and the preceding session, it had a multitude of meanings for her. It meant to her that the cause of her disorganized state was not being located solely within her. Not only was the interactive organization of her experience implicitly acknowledged, but she was also provided with a valuable contrast for the self-accusations that were prompted by her disorganization. However, her initial reaction to my response to what she told me on the phone was to blame herself for being too "vulnerable," and for being unable to retain a sense of me as a protective figure. She accused herself of attempting to "destroy," "undermine," and "undo" the help she received from me. These self accusations had been reinforced by her previous analyst who, she reported, took the stance of "observer" of her pathology. In discussing the impact of the telephone call, she felt particularly relieved because she feared that she would be rejected, abandoned, or blamed for her disorganization. She said that she now expected that her propensity for disorganization and disruptive anxiety states would be open to understanding. In offering an interactive basis for understanding her organization, I acknowledged the interactive basis for her disorganization and of her experience of my response as nonoptimal.

RESTORATION OF THE SELFOBJECT TIE

Although only clarified subsequently, the connection made between the patient's pervasive anxiety and the preceding session led to the restoration of a ruptured selfobject tie. The maintenance of this tie, and her feeling that I was invested in retaining it, enabled her to traverse the troubled waters of the crisis. Her dread that I would be hell-bent on severing this tie harked back to her expectation that her mother would abandon her.

From my perspective, the interpretation that although she might want to be taken care of, she so frequently found herself in the position of the caring, self-sacrificing mother, was an attempt to address her masochistic character structure. I had understood her to be longing for and feeling threatened by her desires to be taken care of. She defended herself against these desires through her excessive caregiving of others. Thus, through the analysis of the function served by her masochism (Stolorow and Lachmann 1980), I anticipated that her sense of competence would increase, her dependent longings would become tolerable, her sense of efficacy would solidify, and most important, she would feel understood by me.

The patient, however, did not share my perspective. The analysis of the rupture revealed that her sense of cohesion was derived from feeling overburdened and vitally needed though self-sacrificing. She perceived herself as a caregiver, and depicted those under her care—her cat, her daughter, and her analysts—as essentially helpless in the face of an inundating, "rain-drenching," hostile world. She felt effective in helping them. My response undermined this source of efficacy.

From the perspective of the selfobject dimension of the transference, the patient's complaints in relation to her friends and daughter were not expressions of a desire to change those relationships. The complaints conveyed that she had succeeded in establishing the necessary prerequisites to sustain and consolidate her self-organization as an overburdened caregiver.

In her early years the patient lived in dread of being abandoned by her mother. Her mother's attention was devoted to community affairs and to maintaining her tie with her own parents and sisters. Her father's political activities required frequent moves, so that the family was uprooted several times during her first eight years. The patient described constraining herself, since she felt that any demand she made would unduly burden her mother. She expected to be able to ensure her mother's attention by being undemanding and expecting little from her. Her ability to provide for her mother gave her a feeling of stability. That is, becoming her mother's caregiver, she avoided the experience of her mother's absence. Furthermore, she ensured her own cohesion and survival by fulfilling vital selfobject functions for her mother (Stolorow et al. 1987). Although initially derived from her relationship with her mother, her self-organization underwent a crucial transformation during her puberty years with respect to her need to retain her father in an idealized position.

Although the original interpretation, that she might want to be taken care of but found herself in the position of the self-sacrificing mother, did not address the transference, per se, it nevertheless had a powerful effect on it. She felt as if I said to her, "You are a victim like your mother and I do not need you to sacrifice yourself." She felt implicitly rejected, which led to her anxiety and her profound experience of disruption. In exploring the nature of this rupture, the hitherto silent selfobject dimension of the transference became clearer as it moved into the foreground. Exploration of the ties led to the understanding of its organization during her puberty years in relation to her father. At that time it was coupled with an array of newly developing resources, and provided the patient with the sense of efficacy and competence that she drew upon in much of her later and adult functioning. Thus, in the treatment situation when the ruptured selfobject tie was restored, she felt she could address those aspects of the representational configurations that had been activated.

The representational configuration of masochistic caregiver had been the "figure" from the analyst's perspective. An empathic grasp of the suffering and self-abnegation entailed by this stance led to the interpretation. The analyst was unaware of the silent idealizing selfobject tie in the background through which the patient gained strength by providing the analyst with support. The interpretation ruptured this tie and it no longer remained silently in the background. Through the rupture, the selfobject tie became "figure" and required attention and repair.

In retrospect it became clear that, prior to the interpretation, the patient had established an idealized selfobject transference. This tie was an outgrowth of a bond with her father, organized during puberty and based on the conviction that *he* needed *her*. In contrast to the self-abnegation that was part of her provision of a supportive milieu for her mother, through the bond with her father she felt needed, valuable, and capable. Subsequently, in her life this tie to the father was repeatedly ruptured through disappointments. A combination of unfortunate external circumstances and "bad choices" diminished her father's stature in the family and in his community. The patient explained, "My father was politically very active in those years and I thought of him as a rather daring man. As he began to decline, I wanted my competence to be of benefit to him. It would make him feel strong and effective. He could brag about me to his cronies and the family. He could feel proud and that made me feel really good."

A salient feature of the patient's organization of the treatment was her proclivity to experience ruptures in the selfobject tie. Her later ties to her father had been characterized by continuous disappointments and ruptures for which the patient held herself responsible. This representational configuration containing the selfobject tie organized the transference. The representational configuration depicted her as the overburdened caregiver of, ultimately, her father. It was she who could restore him to his active and daring, idealized position. Inherent in this representational configuration is the selfobject tie in which she gains strength by shoring up her father. She could make him strong, an idealized source of vitality, and thereby derive her sense of coherence and competence. The vulnerability inherent in the selfobject dimension of the transference organized the disruptions.

The representational configuration of self-sacrifice, established initially to provide stability for her mother and cohesion for herself, was later activated and transformed to restore her father's idealized position. Just as she had used self-sacrifice in relation to her mother to protect herself against her abandonment, she was now able to protect herself against being disappointed by her father. She imagined herself as part of her father's world, which sustained her, provided her with a sense of vitality, and promoted her intellectual curiosity. Her academic work flourished. Her world of skills and interests expanded. Her general masochistic pattern, first organized to retain a connection with her mother, to derive some nurturance through self-abnegation, was later refined and its function transformed. In being activated in relation to her father, she acquired a sense of pride and competence, as well as the feeling that she could be thought of as needed, interesting, and capable. Thus, through later transformations, her representational configurations expanded and became more varied.

The selfobject tie on which the representational configurations were built retained points of vulnerability. Unless the patient could experience herself as all-giving and self-sacrificing, and thereby bolster her potentially faltering father, who she felt needed her to restore him to an idealizable position, she feared that her precariously built world would collapse. The masochistic relationships that pervaded her life provided her with a sense of cohesion. Specifically, by providing support to her idealized father, or her analyst, she felt more solid and could sustain the resources that she derived through her father. After having established an idealizing, selfobject tie with her analyst, in parallel fashion, the interpretation aimed at the representational configuration ruptured this tie. It repeated her feeling of disappointment in that the "idealized" analyst also made a "wrong choice" in offering the interpretation. It indicated to her that she had failed to maintain him in an idealized state. Her depression and fragmentation, her sense of emptiness, worthlessness, and panic-like anxiety states were the results.

Are the patient's reaction to the analyst's nonoptimal response, her depression and fragmentation, her wish to be cared for, and her disorganized reaction rooted in an early pathogenic tie to the mother? Is her reaction based on "mismatches" and "malattunements" that were merely repeated and exacerbated in her later relationships including the analyst's nonoptimal responsivity? Are the disappointments in her father merely screens for the early deprivations she experienced in relation to her mother? Or, does an explanation that emphasizes later transformations and disruptions fit this patient better?

We are arguing for a model that recognizes both the continuous construction and potential reorganization of experience at various stages, as well as the repetition of ways of organizing experience shaped by early interactive patterns. Such a model recognizes the constant shifts and transformations that provide a complex texture to ongoing experience and avoids reductionism (see also Mitchell 1988). It also acknowledges that each transformation generates the possibility that new resources may be acquired as well as providing new ways of organizing past experience (Loewald 1980).

In the patient's continual construction of her experience, the transformations at puberty provided vital resources for her ongoing development. At that time, the patient had turned to her father, in part, in reaction against her mother's chronic sense of victimization, as well as for self-restoration. Thus, there was a decisive time period when the patient resourcefully attempted to restructure her experience in the context of a more responsive mutual regulatory system. Feeling supported by her father, she felt protected and valued. When the father's stature began to falter, she then needed to shore him up to retain her sense of adequacy, efficacy, pride in accomplishments, and her expectations of some responsivity and mutuality. She imagined that he needed her support and he could be strong again. She attempted not to be a victim or demanding like her mother, but to be a caregiver and ally to her father in a mutually beneficial relationship. By restoring her father to his preeminent idealized position, she maintained herself intact and well functioning. Nevertheless, she became more rigidly restricted in that she had to organize her experience to emphasize her caregiving to the point of self-sacrifice. The initial tie of self-abnegation to her victimized mother was thus transformed at this stage through her attempt to restore her father. Silently, this precarious balance had been reestablished in the treatment and then ruptured.

DISTINCTIONS BETWEEN REPRESENTATIONAL AND SELFOBJECT TRANSFERENCES

This case illustrates a distinction that became apparent when a masochistic representational configuration, the necessity to repeat the experience of burdened caregiving, simultaneously performed archaic selfobject functions. As a burdened caregiver to her analyst, feeling that he needed her to sustain him, she maintained a selfobject tie. She felt herself connected to an idealized protecting figure. Such dual "antithetical" functions challenge the analyst's ability to provide optimal responsivity in the analytic setting. What may be optimal from the analyst's empathic grasp of an aspect of the patient's experience (understanding the burden of self-sacrificing caregiving) may be nonoptimal for the patient from the vantage point of her self cohesion.

We suggest that representational configurations provide the necessary context in which disruptions of the selfobject tie can be understood. Thus, the analyses of selfobject transferences and representational configurations must go hand in hand, since they address different functions. In navigating between such rocks and hard places the analyst is bound to provide some nonoptimal responsivity, which, however, can still yield valuable further exploration.

A second treatment issue is also brought to the fore. If the analyst adheres to a model that explains the current manifestations of pathology in terms of the earliest prototypes, then the patient's masochistic stance as evolved in relation to her mother would again be addressed at this juncture of the treatment. The relationship to the mother would be seen as the deeper and more influential layer. But, the later feelings of worth and competence dearly acquired and constructed in relation to her father would then be bypassed. Although fragile and derived through a self organization that required self-sacrifice, they nevertheless provided her with intellectual and interpersonal resources. This idealized selfobject tie rescued the patient from the isolated, victimizing life that she felt her mother led and pointed her toward the more socially engaged, intellectually challenging world of her father. When these resources are bypassed, the patient is again confronted with a view of herself that emphasizes limitations, victimization, and masochistic self-abnegation, as was organized in relation to her mother.

Should the nonoptimal intervention not have been made? Ruptures in the selfobject tie are inevitable and lead to increased understanding. As Kohut has so crucially described, and as Wolf elaborates in Chapter 11, their repair is one source for the transformation and formation of new themes and expectations in treatment. The intervention jarred the patient because it conveyed to her that her analyst rejected her as his needed, self-sacrificing caregiver. Indeed, he appeared to her to be distinguishing himself as her rescuer to save her from her repetitively self-sacrificing behaviors. In the context of the exploration of the meaning and effect of the rupture, the patient wondered if the analyst were unduly anxious about her ability to survive in her hostile, flooded environment.

Did the timing of the interpretation, the breach of empathy that it conveyed to her, reflect the analyst's anxiety? Was the analyst as worried about her as she had been about her father when she felt that he was being overwhelmed and could not survive in his hostile environment? This perception of the analyst's anxiety increased her anxiety and escalated her disorganization. In appearing as a "rescuer" to the patient, he became unavailable to her as a necessary participant in the organization of her crucial theme. The analyst was needed as the helpless but benign ally who had to be rescued by the patient through her sacrifices. His enlivened presence would serve as a source for her self-consolidation. These various themes only emerged and became clarified subsequent to the rupture.

From the analyst's perspective, the intervention seemed optimally responsive to the patient's distress about her burdened state. The intervention assumed that when this vulnerable state was understood, such understanding would be strengthening to her. Or, put differently, when the necessity to protect her vulnerable self was diminished, she would feel freer to experience her competence with a sense of pride. In the interpretation, the patient's shame-filled wish to be more dependent was also touched. The analyst had also assumed that speaking to the patient's dependent longings in nonjudgmental terms would further their integration and contribute to the transformation of other rigidly retained configurations of, for example, her overaccommodation (see Brandchaft 1994). The interpretation of the representational configuration, even though it ruptured the selfobject tie, eventually furthered the transformational processes of the analysis by illuminating and engaging these dominant, organizing themes of the patient's experience.

In this case we illustrate rupture and repair of the selfobject tie in a somewhat different way than was proposed by Kohut (1984). He emphasized that through disruption and repair, psychic functions that had not been acquired could be transmuted, internalized, and structuralized. We have added an emphasis on the acquisition by the patient of *expectations of mutuality*. Through the very process of analyzing disruptions of the selfobject tie, a representation of the expectation of mutuality accrues. This is our two-dimensional, interactive view of the transference. In the case discussed, the specific way in which the tie is interactively ruptured and repaired transformed expectations of disappointment. She developed expectations of being understood and responded to, and to expect interactive restoration of disruptions.

In the course of this patient's analysis, the most frequent ruptures of the selfobject tie were instances in which the patient's need to feel the analyst's investment in retaining the tie was jarred. Later in the analysis, when a disjunction along this line again occurred, the patient was able to say, "Look, you make sure that our tie is retained and I'll take care of my own autonomy." By this time the patient's self expectations, as well as her expectations of the analyst, had been transformed. He was no longer required to be her needy, weak ally whom she had to support. He was now expected to carry his own weight. A step had been taken toward being able to derive selfobject functions from an occasionally more playful adversarial relationship with the analyst (Lachmann 1986). Through the analysis of the rupture and its repair, she could integrate the resources acquired in puberty that she had been able to use only sparingly. These resources depended on her self-sacrifice and made her vulnerable to disruptive anxiety. She became more gutsy, assertive, intellectually active, and fun-loving; people liked being with her.

We have illustrated the distinction between the selfobject and the representational dimensions of the transference. Each serves different functions. Through the selfobject tie, the patient derived a fragile but necessary vitality and security. Through the representational configuration, the patient repeated and transformed the complex, painful defense and fantasy-elaborated experiences with significant figures of her past. Each may illuminate aspects of the other. If we confine ourselves to selfobject transferences, as crucial as these are, we may neglect a level of dynamics, namely, the themes that organize the patient's presentation of past experiences. If we confine ourselves to the interpretation of representational configurations, we may lose our attunement to the vulnerabilities in the patient's sense of cohesion.

In the clinical illustration, the analyst interpreted a specific representational configuration to the patient and thereby ruptured her experience of the analyst as a sustaining selfobject. Exploration of the rupture of this selfobject tie revealed its specific function, its developmental history, its transformation, and its place in the analyst–patient relationship. In addition, the ongoing transformation of the patient's experience in the treatment was promoted through the establishment of new, interactively organized expectations of reciprocal responsiveness, specifically, interactive repair of disruptions in the selfobject tie to the analyst. Analysis of the rupture established for the patient the expectation of being understood, of retaining a valued tie through interactive efforts with the analyst and without self-sacrifice. Addressing the rupture established the expectation that ruptures can be repaired and disappointments understood. Restoring the ruptures in the selfobject dimension transformed repetitive, representational themes of burdened, self-sacrificing caregiver of her weak, needy, but idealizable father.

Although the concept of developmental transformations has long been accepted in psychology, it has not been consistently applied to psychoanalytic treatment. Rather than emphasizing the early mother–infant dyad and uncovering and reconstructing this phase of development as the focus of therapeutic action, we illustrated a transformational model whereby equal emphasis is placed on the contributions from later phases of development. Analyst and patient may then be alerted to the resources and defenses derived from various developmental transformations as well as currently activated themes. Reorganizations occur as both child and environment, patient and analyst influence each other in a mutual regulatory system at each phase of development and analysis. This perspective is crucial for conceptualizing interventions as well as for guiding the analyst toward maintaining an ambience of safety, for restoring ruptured selfobject ties, and for engaging the patient's pathological repetitions toward further transformations.

References

Bacal, H. A., and Newman, K. M. (1990). *Theories of Object Relations: Bridges to Self Psychology*. New York: Columbia University Press.

Beebe, B. (1986). Mother–infant mutual influences and precursors of self- and object representations. In *Empirical Studies of Psychoanalytic Theories*, vol. 2, ed. J. Masling, pp. 27–48. Hillsdale, NJ: Lawrence Erlbaum.

Beebe, B., Jaffe, J., and Lachmann, F. M. (1993). A dyadic systems view of communication. In *Relational Views of Psychoanalysis*, ed. N. Skolnick and S. Warshaw, pp. 61–81. Hillsdale, NJ: Analytic Press.

Beebe, B., and Lachmann, F. M. (1988). Mother–infant mutual influences and precursors of psychic structure. In *Frontiers of Self Psychology: Progress in Self Psychology*, vol. 3, ed. A. Goldberg, pp. 3–26. Hillsdale, NJ: Analytic Press.

———— (1994). Representations and internalization in infancy: three principles of salience. *Psychoanalytic Psychology* 11:127–165.

Brandchaft, B. (1994). *Structures of pathologic accommodation and change in analysis.* Presented at the Association for Psychoanalytic Self Psychology's Bernard Brandchaft Day Conference, March, New York, NY.

Erikson, E. (1950). *Childhood and Society.* New York: Norton.

Kohut, H. (1984). *How Does Analysis Cure?* Chicago: University of Chicago Press.

Lachmann, F. M. (1986). Interpretation of psychic conflict and adversarial relationships: a self psychological perspective. *Psychoanalytic Psychology* 3:341–356.

Lachmann, F. M., and Beebe, B. (1992). Representational and selfobject transferences: a developmental perspective. In *New Therapeutic Visions: Progress in Self Psychology,* vol. 8, ed. A. Goldberg, pp. 3–15. Hillsdale, NJ: Analytic Press.

———— (1995). Self psychology: today. *Psychoanalytic Dialogues* 5:375–384.

———— (1996). Three principles of salience in the organization of the patient–analyst interaction. *Psychoanalytic Psychology* 13:1–22.

Lachmann, F. M., and Lichtenberg, J. D. (1992). Model scenes: implications for psychoanalytic treatment. *Journal of the American Psychoanalytic Association* 40:163–185.

Lichtenberg, J. D. (1983). An application of the self psychological viewpoint to psychoanalytic technique. In *Reflections on Self Psychology,* ed. J. Lichtenberg and S. Kaplan, pp. 163–185. Hillsdale, NJ: Analytic Press.

Lichtenberg, J. D., Lachmann, F. M., and Fosshage, J. (1992). *Self and Motivational Systems.* Hillsdale, NJ: Analytic Press.

———— (1996). *The Clinical Exchange.* Hillsdale, NJ: Analytic Press.

Loewald, H. (1980). *Papers on Psychoanalysis.* New Haven: Yale University Press.

Mitchell, S. (1988). *Relational Concepts in Psychoanalysis.* Cambridge, MA: Harvard University Press.

Ornstein, A. (1974). The dread to repeat and the new beginning: a contribution to the psychoanalysis of the narcissistic personality disorders. *Annual of Psychoanalysis* 2:231–248.

Piaget, J. (1954). *The Construction of Reality in the Child,* trans. M. Cook. New York: Basic Books.

Sameroff, A. (1983). Developmental systems: contexts and evolution. In *Mussen's Handbook of Child Psychology,* vol. 1, ed. W. Kessen, pp. 237–294. New York: Wiley.

Sameroff, A., and Chandler, M. (1976). Reproductive risk and the continuum of caretaking casualty. In *Review of Child Development Research,* vol. 4, ed. F. D. Horowitz, pp. 285–296. Chicago: University of Chicago Press.

Stern, D. (1985). *The Interpersonal World of the Infant.* New York: Basic Books.

Stolorow, R. D., Brandchaft, B., and Atwood, G. (1987). *Psychoanalytic Treatment. An Intersubjective Approach*. Hillsdale, NJ: Analytic Press.

Stolorow, R. D., and Lachmann, F. M. (1980). *Psychoanalysis of Developmental Arrests*. New York: International Universities Press.

———— (1984/1985). Transference: the future of an illusion. *Annual of Psychoanalysis* 12/13:19–38.

Part III

Research and Training

16

Optimal Responsiveness and the Subjective and Intersubjective Experiences of Psychotherapists

CARMELY ESTRELLA

EDITOR'S COMMENT

This chapter is a synopsis of a Ph.D. dissertation that focuses on optimal responsiveness in the therapeutic process. The intent of this study was to explore the subjective conditions that the psychotherapist experiences that contribute to optimal responsiveness in the therapeutic encounter, in particular, to explore the cumulative effects of the therapist's experience that lead to optimal moments or turning points in therapy. My précis of Estrella's work will, for the most part, use her own words.

The author poses two major research questions:

1. What subjective and intersubjective experiences contribute to psychotherapists being optimally responsive?
2. How does the psychotherapist know he or she has been optimally responsive?

The author's methodology consisted of semistructured interviews with nine psychotherapists. The answers to question 1 are summarized in Figure 16–1. Several of Estrella's findings affirm and enrich my current conceptualization of optimal responsiveness (see Chapters 7 and 12). Other findings, which were unexpected, deepen our understanding of the concept.

Among the answers to the first question were the following:

1. The therapists experienced a selfobject relationship with their patients that fostered an identification and an essential mutuality; in other words, the therapists experienced a reciprocity of selfobject experience with their patients.
2. The therapist's attunement to and appreciation of the patient's subjective experience, along with the therapist's openness to her own subjective state of being, facilitated, and constituted a precondition for, an optimally responsive therapeutic experience for her patient.
3. The therapist's commitment to a disciplined, ethical approach to the treatment of the patient that at the same time did not exclude the willingness to take risks in her interventions that went beyond the confines of what the textbooks recommended contributed to her ability to be truly optimally responsive.
4. Seven of the nine respondents reported the experience of a major loss in their lives, and, while they did not share this with their patients, they interwove their personal loss into their responsiveness to their patients.
5. The therapist's own experience of the quality of the relationship with her/his analyst was very influential in contributing to the therapist's optimal responsiveness to the patient. An important aspect of this was the impact of the negative therapeutic encounter, that is, learning what it may entail to be optimally responsive in consequence of the failure of such response in her/his own analysis.

The answers to the second question are summarized in Table 16–2; they entail:

1. shifts in the patient's affect that signaled to the therapist that she had been optimally responsive;

2. an increased sense of vitality and well-being emanating from the patient due to a decrease in anxiety;
3. access to development of new material contributed by the patient as manifested in three areas:
    a. evidence of new and/or improved behavior in situations that had previously been difficult for the patient;
    b. expression of new insights, greater understanding, and the production of dreams, which resulted from the patients' experience of a selfobject relationship with their psychotherapist;
    c. the patients' ability to utilize their therapists in a manner in which they felt empathically understood and optimally responded to;
4. observation and experience by the therapist of a powerful, exceptional intimacy in the relationships with their patients.

The author suggests several implications of her study, most of which resonate directly with our own findings (Chapters 7 and 12):

1. It can serve to heighten psychotherapists' self-awareness and sensitivity to those subjective aspects of themselves that may contribute to, or limit, their being optimally responsive in specific situations.
2. Because the impact of specific kinds of subjective and intersubjective experiences may shape the capacity to respond optimally, therapists can usefully assess, compare, and contrast their personal experiences of optimal responsiveness, in particular by utilizing the author's thematic schema (see Table 16–1).
3. There are several areas of subjective life experience that contribute to therapists' ability to be optimally responsive. Overall, the therapist's personal psychotherapy/psychoanalysis, loss and mourning, and life-cycle issues are apparently crucial factors that can contribute to, or limit, the therapist's capacity to be optimally responsive to the patient.
4. Noninterpretive analytic work is valuable.
5. Optimal responsiveness is derived from the therapist's affect attunement to the mutually reciprocal selfobject relationship.
6. Therapists are able to tolerate their patients' overwhelming emo-

tional pain when they themselves have experienced being held, contained, and soothed via their clinical consultant or supervisor.

7. The theme of the emboldened psychotherapist moving beyond customary parameters in a manner that was optimally responsive has the important implication that the psychoanalytic community remain open to progressive ideas and interventions that shed new light on prevailing views and expand psychoanalytic inquiry.

8. The observations made by the therapists that confirmed for them that they had been optimally responsive with their patients suggest an initial framework by which therapists can verify whether their interventions are optimal and therapeutically usable.

———————— ❖ ————————

The stimulus for this Ph.D. study was my interest in clarifying my theoretical understanding of the occurrence of optimal responsiveness in the psychotherapeutic encounter. That is, I wished to study those aspects of the encounter that contribute to and promote psychological restoration and healing. I was interested in exploring the significant and critical factors that psychotherapists define as contributing to an optimally responsive therapeutic hour.

I was particularly interested in understanding and conceptualizing the contributions of the psychotherapist in the treatment situation. That is, I wanted to explore the subjective and intersubjective experiences of the psychotherapist, in relation to his or her patient, and how they can contribute to optimal responsiveness. *Subjectivity* is described in this context as the totality of the psychotherapist's own experiences, memories, associations, thoughts, recollections, fantasies, images, and reactions that he or she brings to the therapeutic relationship. It is not limited, however, to only those responses and reactions. *Intersubjectivity* is described as the interplay between two subjectivities: that of the patient (the observed), and that of the psychotherapist (the observer). This study explores intersubjectivity from the psychotherapist's (observer's) perspective. I am specifically interested in examining intersubjectivity from the perspective of the psychotherapist. I examine the psychotherapist's range of reactions evoked, initiated, and spontaneously drawn forth through the interplay between patient and psychotherapist.

I was also interested in identifying those categories of responses that may broaden the psychotherapist's overall range of therapeutic responsiveness. Essentially, the study is an exploration of the cumulative effects of the psychotherapist's experience that lead to optimal moments, or turning points, in the therapeutic encounter.

The range of differing perspectives regarding what are the optimal qualities of a psychotherapist is as vast and varied as the psychoanalytic literature. The literature on theory often seems to provide more questions than answers. To organize the multitudinous questions and issues this research raises, there are two major questions that I explored:

1. What subjective and intersubjective experiences contribute to psychotherapists being optimally responsive?
2. How does the psychotherapist know he or she has been optimally responsive?

Bacal (Chapter 1) describes optimal responsiveness as the responsivity of the analyst at any particular moment in the treatment that is therapeutically most relevant to the particular patient and his or her illness. Optimal responsiveness arises primarily from the psychotherapist's empathic attunement, although other data also inform it. The optimally responsive psychotherapist conveys a sense of understanding to the patient, and feels attuned to the patient's experience, which, in different ways, depends on the patient's level of self–selfobject organization and development. Optimal responsiveness may or may not include a verbal interpretation. It includes the psychotherapist's range of reactions, as well as the analytic ambience. Bacal states, "It is a way of conceptualizing the contributions of the therapist in the treatment situation. . . . Optimal responsiveness broadens the outlook for therapists as to what can be therapeutic" (personal communication, 1989).

Bacal's conception of optimal responsiveness provided the framework of my search for an organizing principle by which to understand and evaluate those conditions that lead to the psychotherapist's discovery of the most favorable responses to a given client. His conceptualization of the contributions of the psychotherapist can provide a broader perspective toward understanding what is optimal in the therapeutic encounter. In addition, by studying this theoretical construct, psychotherapists can enhance their mastery of therapeutic skills.

PURPOSE OF THE STUDY

The purpose of this exploratory study was to gather data about the subjective conditions the psychotherapist experiences that contribute to effective optimal responsiveness in the therapeutic encounter.

The data, which were gathered through the use of semistructured, in-depth interviews, were employed for the following purposes:

1. To identify which events or patterns of events are subjectively experienced by the clinician respondents as contributing to the development of their capacities for optimal responsiveness.
2. To identify whether there is a common pattern or common categories of these experiences among respondents.
3. To identify whether these events or patterns of events correlate with the speculations made in the literature concerning the development of a general capacity for optimal responsiveness.
4. To develop a method of psychotherapist self-evaluation of optimal responsiveness.

METHODOLOGY

I interviewed clinical social work psychotherapists to elicit their perspectives as to what constitutes optimal responsiveness during a therapy session.

Sampling Procedures

Participants were recruited through personal networking by the researcher. The sample was obtained from several potential sources: members of independent clinical consultation groups in the West Los Angeles, San Fernando Valley, and other areas; students, faculty, and alumni from the California Institute of Clinical Social Work; and the most recent California Society for Clinical Social Work membership directory. Members with fellowship standing—any social worker who holds a California state license for the practice of clinical social work and who has had three years of professional experience as a social worker beyond licensure—in the Los Angeles chapter of the Society for Clinical Social Work were recruited for the study. Nine advanced clinicians recruited from the above sources were viewed as expert subjects who met certain criteria:

1. At least five years of experience while actively practicing as a licensed clinical social worker utilizing a psychoanalytically oriented approach to treatment.
2. Post-master's level training through clinical consultation, supervision, and/or advanced formal training.
3. Experience of personal psychoanalytic psychotherapy or psychoanalysis from a psychotherapist or analyst who utilized a psychoanalytically oriented approach to treatment.
4. Ability (based on sufficient life experience, professional experience, and degree of personal and professional introspection) to differentiate their own countertransferential views from the patient's transferential view of therapy.

This sampling method was what is referred to as exemplar rather than random cases. Respondents were selected for their ability to function as informants who would be able to provide rich descriptions of the experience being investigated.

Recruitment was initiated by a letter of introduction inviting practitioners to participate in a research study exploring the intersubjective and subjective experience of the psychotherapist and what factors contributed to optimal responsiveness during the therapy hour. Each practitioner was asked to return a statement to the researcher indicating whether he or she was willing to participate in the study. The participants were assured of confidentiality. The sample was determined to be "not at risk" according to the guidelines of the Department of Health, Education, and Welfare Policy on Protection of Human Subjects, as adopted by the California Institute for Clinical Social Work.

Data Collection

Data for this study were collected through individual, semistructured, open-ended, in-depth interviews with clinical social workers. Prior to participation in the interview, each respondent completed an optimal responsiveness survey. An interrogatory stance was utilized to elicit descriptions of interviewees' subjective and intersubjective experience of optimal responsiveness.

Each interview was transcribed and coded for general themes, concepts, and variations. The broad themes were continuously reviewed, analyzed, collapsed, compared, contrasted, combined, and integrated. Shared themes and common forms emerged from the broad themes. The shared themes and common forms were then organized under preliminary categories. Categories were checked for discreteness of properties and condensed whenever possible.

The themes and categories listed are not intended to imply that there is a discrete order of experiences that psychotherapists believe they must have to be optimally responsive. Rather, there was an overlap of categories among the psychotherapist interviews.

The themes are reflective of the varying degrees, dimensions, properties, conditions, contexts, similarities, and differences among the psychotherapists interviewed, as to what contributed to their being optimally responsive. As per Strauss and Corbin (1990), "The discovery and specification of differences among and within categories, as well as similarities, is crucially important and at the heart of grounded theory" (p. 111). Grouping of the data according to emerging patterns, that is, according to repeated relationships between properties (attributes or characteristics pertaining to a category) and dimensions (locations of properties along a continuum) of categories, was delineated as specifically as possible. Additionally, the themes are reflective of the core issues reappearing throughout the interviews; the categories are the specific components mentioned by one or more psychotherapists that make up a portion of the major theme.

The Respondents

The nine clinical social workers who participated in this study all held masters' degrees, and five also held doctoral degrees. Among those who did not have doctoral degrees, four had advanced training, or were currently participating in advanced training. All informants had participated in psychoanalytically oriented psychotherapy or psychoanalysis as patients. All were currently engaged in private practice, employing a psychoanalytic or psychodynamic orientation. The breakdown among the nine respondents of years in clinical social work practice is as follows: 5–10 (2), 11–20 (1), 21–30 (4), 31–40 (1), and over 41 (1). Their theoretical orientation is:

self psychology (4), ego psychology (2), object relations (2), classical Freudian, ego psychology, object relations, self psychology (1). There were eight female respondents and one male. All nine respondents were Caucasian.

Table 16–1 is an overview of the results of responses to *Research question #1: What subjective and intersubjective experiences contribute to psychotherapists being optimally responsive?* The psychotherapists mentioned a variety of interventions that they felt contributed to what they believed was optimally responsive. As explained in the methodology section of this paper, I have grouped those preconditions and precursors into themes and categories as set forth in Table 16–1. This is further illustrated and expanded in Figure 16–1. A more detailed analysis of the data is available for review in the completed dissertation. For purposes of this chapter, however, only the unexpected central findings are discussed via excerpts from the interviews. For example, under theme 1 illustrative examples will be given from two of the three categories set forth in Table 16–1.

TABLE 16–1.   FINDINGS

Research question #1: What subjective and intersubjective experiences contribute to psychotherapists being optimally responsive?

THEME I: THE PSYCHOTHERAPIST'S SUBJECTIVE LIFE
                EXPERIENCES

    Category #1: Losses and mourning
    Category #2: Current life-cycle issues
    Category #3: Psychotherapist's relationship to his/her analyst or
                    psychotherapist

THEME II: HIS/HER IDENTIFICATION WITH A PARTICULAR
              PATIENT

THEME III: THE PSYCHOTHERAPIST'S AFFECT ATTUNEMENT
           WITH THIS PARTICULAR PATIENT

    Category #1: The psychotherapist's subjective state of being

        Subcategory #1a: The psychotherapist's use of images and internal
                          dialogue

Subcategory #1b: The psychotherapist's use of metaphor and internal dialogue

Category #2: The psychotherapist's view of the patient's subjective state of being

Category #3: The psychotherapist's attunement to the intersubjective state of being

THEME IV: THE INTERACTION OF HOPING, HOLDING, AND BEING HELD

Category #1: The support of consultant or supervisor
Category #2: Maintaining hope in the face of the intolerable
Category #3: Support of the holding environment
Category #4: The psychotherapist's commitment and primary responsibility to the patient

THEME V: THE MOVE BEYOND CUSTOMARY PARAMETERS IN A MANNER WHICH WAS OPTIMALLY RESPONSIVE

Category #1: A disciplined responsible fashion
Category #2: To risk, regardless of the psychotherapist's need for support and safety

---

THEME 1: THE PSYCHOTHERAPIST'S SUBJECTIVE LIFE EXPERIENCES

Category #1: Losses and Mourning

Seven of the nine respondents reported that they experienced a major loss during their lives. During the interviews, three therapists openly mourned the personal loss with tears and concomitant emotional pain. Although the psychotherapists were sensitively in touch with their losses and pain, they did not share this with their patients. These therapists, however, interwove their own personal losses—grief and mourning—into their responses to their patients.

Figure 16-1

Thematic schema of optimal responsiveness. This is not a universal schema of optimal responsiveness. This figure illustrates the series of preconditions associated with the optimal responsiveness for most of the respondents in this study.

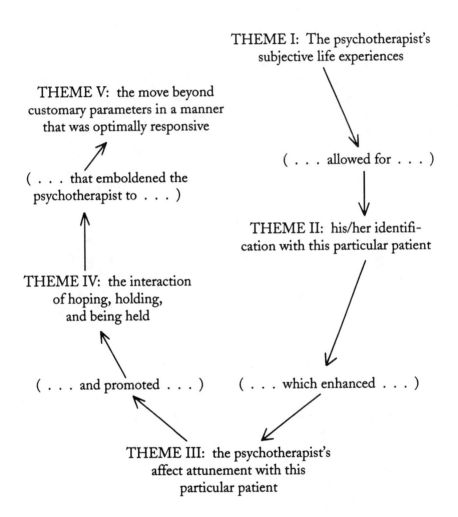

THEME I: The psychotherapist's subjective life experiences

THEME V: the move beyond customary parameters in a manner that was optimally responsive

(. . . allowed for . . .)

(. . . that emboldened the psychotherapist to . . .)

THEME II: his/her identification with this particular patient

THEME IV: the interaction of hoping, holding, and being held

(. . . and promoted . . .)   (. . . which enhanced . . .)

THEME III: the psychotherapist's affect attunement with this particular patient

Therapist 7 presented a couple who had lost their 23-year-old son in a plane crash. During the interview, she shared her own recent loss of her father, which seemed to have an impact on how she understood and was attuned to this couple's grief. The following excerpt illustrates this:

> There's pathological mourning for five years going on with this couple, so that their inability to deal with the loss of their son obviously has something to do with their interdynamics. So, that's been there all along . . . it turns out, as these strange things in life often do. I started with them two weeks after my father died. When they first came I thought about it, and I thought, Is my loss too recent for me to be able to deal with this? I thought no, and I thought it might even help me to be sensitive to what I assumed are the normal processes of mourning and dealing with the loss, and my awareness. Had I never lost anyone I still would think I could handle it, but I don't know if I would have been quite as emotionally responsive, so I . . . I don't know . . . I'm very much aware of my own mourning process, sort of how it comes in and out in waves, and that's not something I would have expected, or felt aware of, but that's what happened. . . . Then all of a sudden the missing of the person just hits you, and there is an intense reaction. But I also think it's helping me see that what they're doing is very pathological, and that it has to have other meaning. . . . I could feel the intensity of the sadness of not ever seeing the person again, and I think that related directly to the loss of my father, my recent loss.

Therapist 2 shared a portion of the interviews of a patient whom she experienced as a challenge in that she had to deal with the patient's intense anger manifested in a barrage of attacks. The psychotherapist became aware of her personal experience of loss and how it was related to the current treatment of this patient.

> I know we had a real upheaval after a month of analysis . . . because my mother died. And there were times with the patient that I just didn't want to be there, you know. I was mourning my mother and there were times when I could be very sensitive and be there, and I think there was something, you know, I was in the same feeling state.

Therapist 2 elaborated on the effects of the loss in her personal life as it interrelated with the treatment of her patient. "I think it's the whole issue of separations and how it can feel, and the struggle with attachment is one that I can resonate with in terms of my own makeup. My patient is very interrelated in the whole thing because my mother died on a Tuesday night. I had to rush to the hospital . . . and I thought in my mind it would be very traumatic for her to find this note on the door canceling that [Tuesday] evening saying I would call her the next morning . . . and that was extremely traumatic for her." Therapist 2 was sensitive to the potential effect this would have on the patient, "because we both had our traumas to go through." The patient was working on issues related to her own trauma of loss in the analysis. The fact that therapist 2's own personal loss also occurred during the patient's analysis may have contributed to her increased sensitivity and empathic resonance with the patient.

The following is illustrative of category #3: psychotherapist's relationship with her/his analyst or psychotherapist. Psychotherapists' experience as patients, and the quality of the relationship between psychotherapist and analyst, were extremely influential in contributing to the psychotherapists' optimal responsiveness to their particular patient. The respondents unanimously agreed that the quality of the responsivity of their own analyst or psychotherapist was extremely important to their ability to respond to their patient.

An important part of the theme is the impact of the negative therapeutic encounter on the psychotherapist's ability to be optimally responsive. That is, the psychotherapist learns what it might take to be optimally responsive as a consequence of the failure of such response in her/his own analysis. The following description by therapist 8 adds a different and unexpected dimension to this category.

Therapist 8 recalled an event early in her therapy, which caused her to believe that in order to be truly available and to "go to the line" for her patient, she needed to experience the same from her therapist. She recalled:

In June I had a birthday party, and I said to him you didn't come. And he gave me a cock-and-bull story as to why. I knew it was a cock-and-bull story. I said you're not even being honest with me. Which I would never do to a patient. He couldn't handle it. And I said . . . you could have helped me a lot, but I guess the rest of my growth I'm gonna have to do on my own. I said because you didn't come through for me. For me it was very concrete. Put your money where your mouth is . . . you say I'm terrific. I'm a wonderful therapist, that you love knowing me, well, I want to see it. Come to my party. You don't have to marry me, you don't have to go to bed with me. . . . And I said I'm gonna do my work on my own now.

Therapist 8 needed her analyst to be responsive to her needs at that time, and to understand the significance of his being honest about the party. What was symbolically significant was the representation of the analyst's absence from her birthday party; to her, it meant that she was not accepted by him. In her view the analyst had let her down and left her disappointed and frustrated. The interview during which therapist 8 reflected on the impact of the memory reaffirmed to her how she would incorporate this experience into treatment with her own patients. She explained that it is critical for psychotherapists to be honest, direct, and authentic, and to acknowledge limitations or mistakes with their patients. For therapist 8 the affirmation of her subjective experience was absolutely necessary. The negative experience contributed to her sensitive attunement and responsivity to her patient.

Although the subjects in this study had varied experiences with their analysts or psychotherapists, it was evident that the experience of personal psychotherapy was a significant factor in contributing to their optimal responsiveness.

THEME III: THE PSYCHOTHERAPIST'S AFFECT ATTUNEMENT WITH THE PATIENT

All the respondents utilized affect attunement as the principal mode of apprehending and understanding the patient's subjective experience. Affect attunement, in this context, is described as a way of perceiving or sharing internal states. Stern (1985) held that the experience of attunement shifts attention away from simple external behavior to "what is behind the behavior, to the quality of feelings that is being shared. . . . Attunement [is] the predominant way to commune with or indicate sharing of internal states" (p. 142). It is the psychotherapist's affect attunement that translates and renders intelligible the patient's feelings.

The subcategory #1b, the psychotherapist's use of metaphor and internal dialogue, illustrated some unexpected findings: for example therapist 1's use of a metaphorical story, combined with her introspective narrative—of thoughts and feelings—in relation to her patient. During therapist 1's account of a session, and her evolving internal dialogue, she became aware of using her own "metaphor of Dorothy's ruby slippers." It was a kind of "visual imagery." The patient whom she presented was "severely abused physically, sexually, and emotionally." Therapist 1 felt it was critical for the patient, as well as herself, "to have something to hold on to that would provide some special meaning." Ruby slippers meant to this patient a sign of "hope and home," that is, "to start building a new home, for someone who had been left out."

The significant aspect is that the psychotherapist apprehended the critical need for hope with the severely abused patient. There was an initial subjective experience that inspired the psychotherapist to acknowledge the imagery of the ruby slippers, "and somehow being so in touch with what R. had lived with, lived through, inspired me. There was more of a quality in my voice, and I communicated to her . . . that really made her feel inspired. That I really believed her, and that I really felt that she could do it, and I was right there to help her with this thing . . . that we were together." What unfolded during the interview was the patient's increasing ability to hold on to the hope that was associated with the meaning of the ruby slippers.

The significant difference in this subcategory was that therapist 1 concretized the metaphor by actually giving her patient a tiny pair of ruby slippers. The enactment was an optimal response for this particular patient. In subcategory 1a, the other psychotherapists utilized imagery themselves, but did not necessarily share these with the patient either metaphorically or literally.

Category #3: The Psychotherapist's Attunement to the Intersubjective State of Being

The theme of attunement to the intersubjective state of being of both parties, that of the patient (the observed), and of the psychotherapist (the observer), came up in all the informants. The views of Stolorow and colleagues (1987) provide a frame of reference for this category. They posit a fundamental assumption: "All that can be known psychoanalytically is subjective reality—the patient's, the analyst's, and the evolving, ever-shifting intersubjective (psychological) field created by the interplay between them" (p. 6).

The following excerpt demonstrates that therapist 5 felt she was attuned to her patient's subjective state of being as well as her own subjectivity.

> She had a mother who had abandoned her and a father [who was abusive]. . . . Her mother abandoned her and never protected her children from this brutal father . . . and I felt that that was the most important thing that I could do. Now in addition to this, with her being so fragile and so on the edge, she also had a serious eating disorder. She was bulimic and anorexic at the same time. When she went into the hospital, we had seen each other for about once a week, for about six weeks, and I decided that it was very important for me to see this young woman every day that she was there.

Therapist 5 felt she was acutely aware and sensitive to the patient's subjective experience of terror and the antecedents of that terror. Additionally, she reflected as follows on her own self-observations and experience of herself as a psychotherapist in the treatment of the patient:

> I'm very warm, outgoing, and responsive, and I'm expressive . . . and it's just, that's my personality. And I would find that I would express my pleasure and excitement in where she was going, and nonverbally to be able to lead, help her, by my facial expressions and bodily expressions, get to where she was going, with little verbal help on my part. There is something I find that I do at times . . . and especially that I had done with her . . . that mother–child interaction, in which she would say something and I would applaud [clapping in the background]. Isn't it wonderful? You know, that kind of a feeling [clap] . . . like you're wonderful . . . and I could do that, and have done that with her.

Therapist 5 shared another aspect of attunement to the intersubjective state of being. Prior to the therapist's one-week vacation, her patient was "terrified of my being away." The patient was hospitalized for psychiatric treatment at that time. The psychotherapist's attunement and empathic resonance to the patient's subjective state of being, as well as her own readiness and awareness of her complementary state of being—the inter-subjective state of being—prompted therapist 5 to promise the patient that she would telephone her. And she did. Additionally, her therapeutic enactment of attunement included bringing back for the patient something she had made while on vacation at a ranch. Therapist 5 stated, "I made it in the colors that I knew that she would so enjoy and meant something to her. So when I came back I could tangibly give her something so that she would know that I had thought about her while I was gone, and that she was very special and very precious."

On the day therapist 5 returned from vacation her patient was released from the hospital. This was a patient who "had an eating disorder, and could never eat in front of anybody. . . . Typically she would gather very little food and go hide in a corner and eat." So on the day she was discharged, the therapist told her that "this was a very special day, a new beginning for her." This psychotherapist felt it was responsive to this client to celebrate and took her out to lunch near the hospital. The patient "ordered her favorite food that she loved—Italian food," and they had lunch together. Therapist 5 added that she knew this was something that the patient's mother had never done. Additionally, the patient's mother never came to visit or telephone the patient while she was hospitalized.

The psychotherapist's affect attunement and apprehending of the patient's subjective experience, coupled with the psychotherapist's open-ness to her own subjective experience of self, not only facilitated but constituted a precondition for an optimally responsive therapeutic experience for her patient.

THEME V: THE MOVE BEYOND CUSTOMARY PARAMETERS IN A MANNER THAT WAS OPTIMALLY RESPONSIVE

The psychotherapists sometimes moved beyond customary parameters, even though such a move might have conflicted with the professional community. They valued a professional response that was deemed to be in the patient's best interest. They grappled with attending to the subjective experience and needs of the patient while discerning their own subjective experience in a disciplined manner. Moreover, they reported the necessity of risking their colleagues' support as they proceeded to treat the patient in a fashion that they believed was optimally responsive.

This was illustrated in category #1: a disciplined responsible fashion. Although the psychotherapists were convinced that their interventions were optimally responsive, all of the informants cautioned that optimal responsiveness should not involve "wild analysis." A firm belief was that one must respond in a manner that fits the subjective experience of the patient, rather than gratifying some experimental need of the psychotherapist. The psychotherapists universally believed that this required a disciplined and responsible approach to their interventions.

Therapist 6 said that utilizing an intersubjective approach that is truly optimally responsive personally meant "to be human." This included being very disciplined as a psychotherapist. He believed that there are certain guidelines such as "being ethical and maintaining a professional stance that is in the best interest of the patient." However, it also meant to therapist 6 to be able to risk with therapeutic interventions, rather than relying only on what therapy professes in terms of technique. This was illustrated in the case that he presented during the interview. He said that if he had relied only on what the textbooks recommended he would have missed an optimal opportunity with his patient. That is, he would have missed an opportunity that allowed for mutually experienced understanding and insight between patient and psychotherapist.

Therapist 6 felt that he had to risk at times with interventions, explore them, reflect upon his subjective feelings, and proceed if appropriate. He felt that he needed to distinguish

> how best to meet the patient's needs, and to make sure that if it's just a matter of meeting my own need, as some therapists do when they disclose or tell stories—then I do nothing—I just let the thought pass over me. It's called discipline. Then if I find something useful in that, that I can use, something useful that is going to help the client, I tend to listen to it and don't let it pass over me. It's hard for me to describe.

As part of the disciplined approach, therapist 1 felt that to be truly in the service of the patient, the psychotherapist must be very focused. She elaborated as follows:

You have to put everything else out of your mind. When you close the door and it is time for the session, put yourself in the place of the patient or whatever. But, regardless of, and no matter what's going on . . . there's no way you can allow intrusive thoughts coming in, unless you analyze them, and realize what's going on. I don't know if this is really spelled out enough in therapists' training.

The psychotherapists identified a sense of heightened self-awareness, openness to self-reflection, analysis of countertransference, use of clinical consultation, and personal psychotherapist/psychoanalysis as assisting them to maintain a disciplined approach. They believed that this disciplined approach contributed to their being optimally responsive to their patients.

Within category #2: to risk, regardless of the psychotherapist's need for support and safety, the psychotherapists reacted against a rigid adherence to traditional psychoanalytic views. Additionally, they reported feeling judged, criticized, and unsafe about airing their differing views among their colleagues. Regardless of this unease, they proceeded with those interventions that they felt were most beneficial, and produced positive results with their patients. They were willing to risk losing their colleagues' support in taking a stance that they were convinced was optimally responsive to their patients. This was a significant move beyond customary parameters.

Therapist 8 felt that it takes a great deal of courage to be a real therapist. That is, to be one who is willing "to be genuine, and to have the courage to allow oneself to risk being the kind of therapist that can allow the patient to experience hope." She said at times it was difficult to share her innermost beliefs and perspectives with colleagues because she feared their criticisms when they did not share her views. She believed the professional community often held opposing views on psychotherapists' interventions and responses. Traditional psychoanalytic views made it difficult for her to be genuinely open, self-disclosing, and candid in making interventions that work with patients and result in positive changes.

Therapist 8 emphasized that she "doesn't follow the rules for rules' sake. . . . If one breaks the rules, one had better be ready to take the risks involved in breaking the rules. . . . One better be ready to go the line, right to the line," where the patient needs the psychotherapist to go. This therapist felt strongly that her patients must flourish and improve and that results would confirm and validate that her interventions were optimally responsive.

Therapist 1 shared many personal responses that arose through her work with the client she presented. She found herself offering provision, and gratifying a need for the patient (i.e., offering the patient something to eat—cookies and milk, tea—giving of symbolic gifts), actions that she would not ordinarily discuss in a professional group. Although she felt certain her interventions were optimally responsive, she was also concerned about the criticism, judgment, and negative reactions she expected to receive from her colleagues. Despite differing views, however, therapist 1 did not adhere to prevailing views of standard psychoanalytically oriented practice but continued to practice in a manner that she felt was optimally responsive. Therapist 1 believed that her approach was "healing and beneficial for the client . . . and [was] in the best interest of the client." Finally, she explained, "I can share all this with you, but I wouldn't in a large professional group."

Therapist 5 shared an experience she had had in a clinical consultation group that required her to make a major decision whether to continue with the group after she had disclosed an intervention that another group member challenged. She related the following scenario:

> In this small consultation group I was presenting a case and I said it was very [appropriate] this patient had come into therapy. I was waiting for her to tell me something, which she absolutely somehow was avoiding. I finally asked her, which was the appropriate thing to do. And one of the persons in my small consultation group said to me, "You did what? You asked her a question?" So I said you mean you wouldn't have asked her? You'd let her sit like an elephant in the room and not respond to that? She answered, of course. This other therapist comes from a very traditional, classical analysis. She is very bright, mature, and very rigid, and would never be able to be responsive in the way that I and others would respond. Also, the supervising analyst heard the discussion and did not in any way intervene.

The consultation experience posed serious concerns for therapist 5. She continued:

> I no longer felt safe to be in that group. I realized that I could no longer develop or grow within that group. So I called and informed the group

leader that I would no longer be able to continue in the group. It's a matter of being safe, not judged, and not criticized.

SUMMARY

Research Question #1: What Subjective and Intersubjective Experience Contribute to Psychotherapists Being Optimally Responsive?

Five broad themes emerged in the data, which illustrates a progression, or a process of subjective and intersubjective experience among the psychotherapists studied. The thematic schema of optimal responsiveness was constructed to conceptualize this process (see Figure 17–1). This schema is useful as an illustration, but the data might be organized, conceptualized, and interpreted within a different schema for another researcher. The schema is not postulated as a model in which optimal responsiveness occurs. Moreover, it is not intended to imply that there is a distinct order of experiences psychotherapists must have to be optimally responsive. Rather, it is intended to illustrate a conceptualization of the process, and a course of themes and categories of experiences that contribute to psychotherapists' being optimally responsive. Some of the central and unexpected findings are summarized in light of this thematic schema as follows.

The psychotherapists' subjective life experiences allowed them to identify with their particular patients. For these psychotherapists, there was a sensed correctness of fit with the patient. Essentially the psychotherapists experienced a selfobject relationship with their patients that fostered an identification and an essential mutuality; they felt a reciprocity of selfobject experience. Related to this concept Bacal and Thomson assert:

> The analyst's therapeutic function is highly contingent upon reciprocal responsiveness on the part of the patient. . . . The analyst's experience of the patient's selfobject responsiveness is ordinary and ongoing and, in many respects, identical to selfobject experience that are at the heart of the patient's experience of the optimal responsiveness of the analyst. [Chapter 12, this volume, p. 251]

This finding was a precondition that enabled the patients to have a selfobject relationship with their psychotherapists. Additionally, the selfobject experience was a precursor for the psychotherapists to feel able to be optimally responsive with their patients. The psychotherapists' identification and sensed correctness of fit enhanced their affect attunement with these particular patients.

The intersubjective state of being was described as the interplay between two subjectivities, that of the patient and that of the psychotherapist. The psychotherapists resonated with their patients' subjective experience while maintaining affect attunement to the interplay of both subjectivities. The psychotherapists' stance of affect attunement—to both subjectivities—contributed to their perceived optimal timing of response, intervention, and provision of experience. This provision of experience offered a new reference point for the patient, which facilitated change. The psychotherapists' affect attunement, as a precursor, promoted the creation of an environment in which the interaction of hoping, holding, and being held could occur.

The psychotherapists emphasized a primary preoccupation stance necessary to provide interventions that would be in the best interests of their patients. They expressed their commitment and primary responsibility to their patients through their caring, loving, and unwavering inner resolve to help the patients improve. Their commitment and primary responsibility to their respective patients emboldened the psychotherapists to move beyond customary parameters in order to respond to their patients optimally.

Table 16–2 summarizes the findings relative to *research question #2: How does the psychotherapist know he or she has been optimally responsive?* The themes and related categories are the effects and results that confirmed for the psychotherapists in this study that they had been optimally responsive. The themes and categories are not intended to imply that there is a discrete order of effects or results. Rather, they are reflective of core issues reappearing throughout the interviews. The categories are the specific components mentioned by one or more psychotherapists that make up a portion of the major theme. The findings for research question #2 are summarized here. Details of specific examples with in-depth analysis are available for reference in the completed dissertation.

The psychotherapists observed apparent shifts in their patients' affect, which signaled to them that they had been optimally responsive. The first shift was an observable reduction in the patients' anxiety. The fact that the psychotherapists were attuned to their patients' subjective experience

TABLE 16–2.   FINDINGS

Research question #2: How Does the Psychotherapist Know He or She Has Been Optimally Responsive?

THEME I: APPARENT SHIFTS IN PATIENT'S AFFECT

Category #1: A reduction in anxiety
Category #2: An increased sense of vitality/well-being emanating from the
patient due to the decrease in anxiety

THEME II: EXTERNAL OBSERVABLE SIGNS

THEME III: ACCESS TO AND DEVELOPMENT OF NEW
MATERIAL

Category #1: New and/or improved behaviors
Category #2: There is increased self-disclosure of new material evoked from
within the patient
Category #3: A powerful exceptional intimacy in the relationship

---

facilitated a decrease in anxiety. They utilized affect attunement to engage their patients, and together they moved toward the achievement of affective intersubjectivity. The result was a reduction in anxiety, which was mutually felt by patient and psychotherapist.

The second type of shift in the patients' affect was an increased sense of vitality and well-being emanating from them due to the decrease in anxiety. Several of the psychotherapists reported that their optimal responses brought about a restoration of the patients' sense of cohesion and a vitality of the self. The psychotherapists maintained a stance that contributed to helping the patients create or restore selfobject experiences.

The psychotherapists listed significant external observable signs that were reflective of a shift in treatment. These signs occurred at turning points in the therapeutic encounter as well as at different phases in the treatment process. The external signs were manifested in a variety of forms such as tears, shifts in posture, and facial expressions reflective of a change in affect—smiles, reddened faces, or evident expressions in the patients' eyes. These external signs were viewed by the psychotherapists as confirmation of their own empathic understanding, which was "confirmed by the patient's expression of his own empathic grasp" (Bacal 1992) of the psychotherapist's optimal response at that moment. This process confirmed for the psychotherapists that they had been optimally responsive.

Another theme was the access to and development of new material contributed by the patients as manifested in three areas. One area was the psychotherapists' reports of observed shifts in behaviors among their patients that were either new or improved. The improved behaviors often took place in situations that had previously been difficult for the patients. The patients were observed to have greater self-awareness and less vulnerability; as they began to feel differently, they subsequently acted differently. The inference is that the psychotherapists' responses to their patients were reflective of an optimal response in that the patients began to evidence new and /or improved behaviors.

An additional manifestation of the disclosure of new material was the expression of new insights, greater understanding, and the production of dreams. The patients' production of new material resulted from the experience of a selfobject relationship with their psychotherapists. Further, the patients were able to utilize their psychotherapists in a manner in which they felt empathically understood and optimally responded to. Through this selfobject experience, the patients were able to utilize the qualities of the psychotherapist that prompted them to disclose new material.

Finally, the psychotherapists observed and experienced a powerful, exceptional intimacy in the relationships with their patients. They responded to their patients' needs by taking "cues that emanated from their patient's unconscious search for what is necessary to meet unmet needs" (Bacal 1992). The psychotherapists allowed their patients to feel a sense of entitlement in their special relationship. In this way, the patients were able to respond reciprocally to their psychotherapists, and thereby they engaged in a powerful and exceptional intimate relationship.

IMPLICATIONS FOR CLINICAL PRACTICE

There are several implications of this study. It has provided knowledge as to the kinds of subjective and intersubjective experiences psychotherapists have that contribute to their feeling that they have been optimally responsive. This study can serve to heighten psychotherapists' self-awareness and sensitivity to those subjective aspects of themselves that may contribute to, or limit, being optimally responsive.

This study suggests that there are certain precursors that contribute to psychotherapists' ability to be optimally responsive. Although certain experiences may predispose a psychotherapist to be optimally responsive with patients, it appears that the impact of specific kinds of subjective and intersubjective experiences shape the capacity to respond optimally. The thematic schema of optimal responsiveness (Figure 16–1) was developed as a way of conceptualizing these experiences. Psychotherapists can assess, compare, and contrast their personal experiences of optimal responsiveness utilizing this schematic process.

This study identified several areas of subjective life experience that contributed to the psychotherapists' ability to be optimally responsive. Overall, the psychotherapists' personal psychotherapy/psychoanalysis, loss and mourning, and life-cycle issues are seen as crucial factors that can contribute to, or limit, the psychotherapists' capacity to be optimally responsive with their patients.

Another implication of this study was the value of noninterpretive analytic work. That is, for some patients noninterpretive work allowed for the development of a selfobject relationship with their psychotherapists. This was a necessary precondition for the treatment to progress. The psychotherapists' sensitive awareness of the significance of the selfobject relationship contributed to their ability to respond to the developmental needs of the patients. (This point is corroborated by Bacal and Thomson, Chapter 12, this volume.) This is particularly applicable in the treatment of patients with early selfobject deficits. This study suggests that the range of responses should be broadened to include other noninterpretative work that is responsive to the patient's particular developmental level.

Further, this study has illustrated the significance of the selfobject relationship that is mutually and reciprocally experienced between patient and psychotherapist (see Chapters 7 and 12). It suggests that optimal responsiveness is derived from the psychotherapist's affect attunement to the mutually reciprocal selfobject relationship. This process can be referred to as *intersubjective optimal responsivity*.

The theme of hoping, holding, and being held has significant implications. The psychotherapists were able to tolerate their patients' overwhelming emotional pain when the psychotherapists themselves had experienced being held, contained, and soothed via their clinical consultant or supervisor. This allowed the psychotherapists to be able to contain, hold, and provide hope for the patients in the face of very difficult treatment situations. The interaction between psychotherapist and supervisor/consultant instilled and affirmed a powerful commitment and an intense primary responsibility to their patients.

The theme of emboldened psychotherapists moving beyond customary parameters in a manner that was optimally responsive was a finding with important implications. Also significant was the psychotherapists' need to feel safe in order to risk disclosure in psychoanalytic settings. Psychotherapists who do not feel support, safety to risk, and trust in psychoanalytic settings will tend to withdraw or withhold from colleagues valuable information that was beneficial for the treatment of their patients. Psychotherapists will risk disclosing those interventions in settings that promote, encourage, and value discussion on the intersubjective aspects of psychoanalytic work. This study suggests that the psychoanalytic community should remain open to progressive ideas and interventions that shed new light on prevailing views and expand psychoanalytic inquiry.

The findings for research question #2 had several important implications. There were a number of observations made by the psychotherapists that confirmed for them that they had been optimally responsive with their patients. The cumulative effects were reflected in three themes: (1) shifts in the patients' affect, (2) external observable signs, and (3) access to and development of new material. These findings suggest an initial framework by which psychotherapists can verify whether their psychotherapeutic interventions were optimal and therapeutically valuable.

DIRECTIONS FOR FURTHER RESEARCH

As an adjunct to the present study, it would be valuable to explore the patients' perspectives of what contributes to their feelings of being optimally responded to by their psychotherapists or psychoanalysts. It would be interesting to know whether the experiences of patients match the experiences of psychotherapists in terms of their view of what was optimally responsive. Also, it would be interesting to investigate what are the complementary selfobject needs that contribute to a good fit between patient and psychotherapist.

In addition to descriptive studies, quantitative research might be undertaken to assess the differential effects of variables such as age, gender, ethnicity, geographic location, treatment with specific patient populations, and brief psychotherapy versus long-term psychoanalytic psychotherapy on optimal responsiveness.

The thematic schema of optimal responsiveness (Figure 16–1) could be reconceptualized, and adjustments could be made for the inclusion of additional significant subjective and intersubjective experiences. Also, new insights and indicators could be generated via a study that expands on how the psychotherapist verifies whether he or she was optimally responsive.

References

Bacal, H. A. (1992). Optimal responsiveness: the patient's experience of the analyst's therapeutic function. Maurice Levine Lecture presented at the Department of Psychiatry, University of Cincinnati, May 20.

Bacal, H. A., and Newman, K. M. (1990). *Theories of Object Relations: Bridges to Self Psychology*. New York: Columbia University Press.

Stern, D. N. (1985). *The Interpersonal World of the Infant*. New York: Basic Books.

Stolorow, R. D., Brandchaft, B., and Atwood, G. E. (1987). *Psychoanalytic Treatment: An Intersubjective Approach*. Hillsdale, NJ: Analytic Press.

Strauss, A., and Corbin, J. (1990). *Basics of Qualitative Research*. Newbury Park, CA: Sage.

17

Optimal Responsiveness and Psychoanalytic Supervision

ALAN R. KINDLER

EDITOR'S COMMENT

In this chapter, Kindler demonstrates how the application of the principle of self-psychologically informed optimal responsiveness to psychoanalytic supervision can expand the supervisor's functions and enhance the supervisor's efficacy.

Thus, the supervisor need not feel constrained to limit his interventions to checking, correcting, or teaching "proper" technique, or to restrict his help with a student's countertransference reaction to a suggestion that she consult her analyst. The Weltanschauung in self psychology focuses not on the objective elucidation of psychopathology, as do the more traditional analytic approaches, but rather on the subjective experience of the participants. Thus, in-depth discussion between supervisor and supervisee is less likely to threaten the sense of safety of the supervisee or impinge upon her privacy. The supervisor's work that is guided by the principle of optimal responsiveness can now include the addressing of any of the three participants' (patient's, therapist's, and supervisor's) particular experiences in any of their relationships that may significantly affect the treatment of the patient, providing such discussion is acceptable to both supervisor and supervisee.

Kindler recognizes that such an approach does not preclude the occurrence of disruptions in the supervisor–supervisee relationship. He illustrates how disruptions in this relationship can occur and how they can affect the supervisee's treatment of the patient. Kindler's views on the determinants of disruption in the supervisory relationship parallels the views of Thomson and myself on the determinants of disruption in the therapeutic relationship—that is, the frustration of needed reciprocal responsiveness to selfobject needs (see Chapter 12). Kindler illustrates how the supervisor's attention to these determinants of disruption constitutes the optimal responsiveness that not only "rights" both participants and restores their relationship, but also significantly assists the student in restoring her relationship with her patient and enhancing the efficacy of the treatment.

As Kindler points out, this approach to supervision significantly diminishes the "teach or treat" dichotomy that is held by traditional analytic therapists. It is very much in line with a self psychological perspective in which optimal responsiveness is directed to the strengthening of the self, the facilitation of task and phase-appropriate selfobject relatedness, and the modification of meanings and representational configurations that contribute to maladaptive interpersonal relationships. It is, moreover, in my experience, highly effective.

❖

Bacal has defined optimal responsiveness as the reciprocal responsivity between the particular analyst and the particular patient that is therapeutically most relevant at that moment for the patient. That is, Bacal regards as a central aspect of optimal responsiveness both the particularity of the analyst as well as that of the patient in their interaction (see Chapter 7). With his construct, Bacal allows us to consider that all the therapist says, does, and is, contributes to the therapeutic process in one way or another. With Bacal's more pragmatic stance regarding "correct" technique in any particular clinical situation, our therapeutic influence is no longer confined to specific acts of technique and we are free to participate in treatment more flexibly and creatively. In this chapter, I propose that the freedom and flexibility in the analyst's therapeutic participation encouraged by Bacal's therapeutic ideal of optimal responsiveness may be usefully applied to the conduct of psychoanalytic and psychoanalytically oriented psychotherapy supervision.

There has been a gradual but progressive evolution in the theory and technique of supervision corresponding with, but always lagging well behind, changes in analytic practice (Levy and Kindler 1995). Several factors may have contributed to this conservatism. First and perhaps most significantly, far less attention has been given in the literature to the supervisory process than to that of clinical treatment. Second, when supervisory material has eventually been published, there has always been a significant lag between the development of new clinical approaches and their application to supervision. Third, the allegiance of analytic supervisors to the training institutes with which they are affiliated is expressed in their supervisory practices, which tend to preserve the principles and practices of that school.

Estelle and Morton Shane (1995) describe some of the inflexible and arbitrary standards set by some educational institutions and their destructive impact on the educational process, at times "lead[ing] to a caricature of how psychoanalysis is actually practiced" (p. 237). Furthermore, problematic learning associated with supervision tended to be formulated according to the principles of psychopathology that informed the analytic school of the supervisor. Distortion of reality due to unconscious conflicts or pathological object relations have typically been emphasized in material demonstrating supervisory interventions, impasses, and analytic failures. Candidates were expected to take to their personal analysis their difficulties in learning demonstrated by their blind spots or resistance to understanding their patient in the same way as their supervisor. The lack of "safety" (Doctors 1996) implicit in supervision based on such models of therapeutic intervention made such hands off rules necessary for successful supervision. It is for this reason that so much emphasis has been placed on distinguishing the supervisory experience—teaching how to analyze—from the analytic experience—treatment.

Self psychology in all its manifestations, including selfobject theory, intersubjectivity, and motivational systems theory, has yielded a very different form of psychoanalytic treatment. An increasingly complex and rich model of supervision is emerging from these theoretical advances. These include the empathic and other-centered listening perspectives (Fosshage 1995, Kohut 1959), the attention to the self states and dominant motivations (Lichtenberg et al. 1992), the selfobject needs (Kohut), and repetitive self and other configurations of all three participants (Stolorow and Lachmann 1984/1985), the intersubjective dimensions of each dyad (Fosshage 1994, 1995, Stolorow et al. 1987), the co-construction models of transference and countertransference (Fosshage 1994, 1995), the models of learning and change (Bacal this volume, Chapter 1, Fuqua 1994, Lindon 1994, Terman 1988, Wolf 1989) and the awareness of the influence of extraneous factors on the therapeutic process (Fuqua 1994, Shane and Shane 1995).

As a natural emendation to these new ideas I would like to propose that, in many supervisory situations, the specific qualities of the supervisor's responsiveness to the supervisee's experiences of supervision may contribute most significantly to the successful outcome. Such a hypothesis immediately raises two important questions. How does the supervisor decide which of the myriad of responses available to him will facilitate his supervisee's progression? How do we, as supervisors, evaluate our contribution to the supervisory process at any moment?

One of the important emphases of modern self psychology is the provision of detailed process material in order to reduce the confusing usage of theoretical constructs. When, in *Alice's Adventures in Wonderland*, Humpty Dumpty told Alice scornfully, "When I use a word it means just what I choose it to mean—neither more nor less," he could have been speaking for psychoanalysts who tend to use theoretical constructs in increasingly idiosyncratic or personal ways. Even such a recently conceived body of ideas as self psychology has already acquired this "Humpty Dumpty" quality. Empathy, selfobject, mirroring, attunement, and transference are examples of this tendency. Humpty Dumpty would have approved of the way we make our words, that is, our theoretical constructs, work so hard for us by allowing them so many meanings.

To illustrate the other theoretical and practical issues that emerge from a review of the literature, I will provide some material taken from the early stages of the supervision of Dr. Mary T., conducted along self psychological lines by the author. To anchor these theoretical constructs in clinical events, I will use the process material of the second, third, and sixth sessions of Dr. T.'s weekly supervision as she began the psychoanalytic treatment of Donna. Dr. T. was already an experienced psychiatrist practicing outpatient psychotherapy when she came for supervision. She was an analytic candidate who presented the case of Donna for consideration as a first training case.

Donna was a 26-year-old graduate student, married to a man she had known since high school. She suffered from insomnia and depression since her mid-teens when she entered a training program to prepare for national-level competition in her sport of competitive figure skating. After a meteoric rise she dropped out of competition in her early twenties just as she was preparing for world championships. Her coach forced her to progress too quickly in order to reach competitive levels. As a result she lost her "nerve" and had to withdraw from competition. In the process she was subjected to intense shame and humiliation by her outraged coach.

In addition, Donna was plagued by confusion and ambivalence about her career in particular and her life in general. She felt pressed to sort out her academic plans before school started in September. She could not decide between a Ph.D. in sport psychology, medical school, or a professional dance training program.

Donna had responded well to antidepressants but hoped to "beat the medication" and not be on it for the rest of her life. She described herself as "phobic" about a relapse of her insomnia if she were to try coming off the antidepressants. Her mother and maternal grandmother were both on antidepressants.

Her parents were constantly fighting and Donna grew up with a constant fear of violence between them. Her older sister often intervened and protected her, leading her as a child into gymnastics where she excelled. Donna felt close to her mother, relied heavily on her, and consulted her about everything. Her father was described as an absent figure who became interested in the patient as she became more prominent as a figure skater. Her older sister, who now lives in another city, is benefiting from psychotherapy, and encouraged Donna to obtain help for herself.

Dr. T. had herself been an international-level competitive diver who had had similar experiences with her coaches, and so had an immediate sensitivity to her patient's experiences. In the third session the supervisor noted Dr. T.'s enthusiastic support of Donna by vigorously criticizing her coach for his inappropriate behavior toward her, a sympathetic stance based on her own very similar experiences with coaches. The supervisor suggested that this might inhibit the exploration of her patient's own experience of her coach's humiliating behavior and its specific meanings to her. Dr. T. agreed with the suggestion, acknowledging that this tendency to sympathize in order to be supportive had been an ongoing concern for her in her psychotherapeutic work. She was eager to work further on it and to develop alternate strategies.

In addition to questioning her sympathetic intervention, the supervisor suggested that the difficulty she seemed to have with proposing more frequent sessions to her patient, whom he understood to be willing and enthusiastic, might have something to do with Dr. T.'s own doubts about her value to the patient. Picking up cues from Dr. T.'s self-effacing demeanor, he wondered if she might have a concern about being experienced as too presumptuous in suggesting the patient might benefit from more frequent sessions. She appeared to enthusiastically agree to all of his suggestions.

Dr. T. arrived for the fourth supervision session with a tape recorder and requested permission to tape the session. She explained that a very familiar problem had arisen in the previous session. She had found the supervisor's suggestions very exciting and helpful, but then began to find herself unable to concentrate on his words and to request that he repeat what she had not comprehended. Shame about appearing stupid or incompetent blocked her, and she was only able to stay present by nodding in feigned comprehension and enthusiastic acknowledgment for the rest of the session. This was a familiar experience for her in learning situations, often interfering with her grasp of new material. This time, she was determined to prevent further repetitions of this sequence by taping future sessions so that, at her own pace, and in the comfort of her own home, she could listen to the tape as slowly and as often as she needed to understand the material.

Her supervisor welcomed her innovative plan and assisted her with the setting up of her recorder and microphone. When the tape was rolling he complimented her on her initiative. He indicated that he would also like to listen to the tape for his own purposes (which ultimately included the writing of this paper) and she agreed to lend him each tape when she had finished with it. Supervisor and supervisee then spent some time talking about Dr. T.'s experience of the previous session. She described her stimulation leading to excitement about the supervisor's input. She remembered thinking, in response to the supervisor's comments about her sympathetic stance, "It's just what I need to really master this problem." This was followed quickly by a distracting "noise" in her head that prevented her from concentrating on the supervisor's comments. She felt a shameful sense of inadequacy that prevented her from asking him to repeat or explain something she had not grasped. In fact she dreaded revealing any sign of her discomfort and nonreceptiveness.

> *Dr. T.:* It's because I'm so eager to understand what you have to say that the panic about not being able to "get it" begins to take over. At the very moment I'm excited and thinking "What is that?" and "How or why did you do that?" and all sorts of questions I might want to ask about it. Then this thing will be underneath, completely— and the emotion gets too high.
>
> *Supervisor:* So that is the sequence. I say something that is inspiring . . .
>
> *Dr. T.:* (interrupts) Yes! I really want to get it. Then this other thing comes in and I'll be nodding my head saying, "Yes, yes," but I'm not really there.

The bulk of the session was spent exploring this state of buzzing confusion and shameful incompetence apparently triggered by her excitement at the prospect of mastery. The supervisory process thus became a model of the therapeutic process in which the supervisor paid close attention to the supervisee's subjectivity and helped her put into words the detailed sequence of events as she experienced them, including her experience of the supervisor's "exciting" opinions about her case. Dr. T. felt that similar things happened with her patients, in both directions. Sometimes she failed to understand them but pretended to be in touch with them, and sometimes they pretended to comprehend her.

As the session progressed, it emerged that Dr. T. was quite troubled by the supervisor's suggestions about the possible meanings of her discomfort with his sudden recommendation that she broach the idea of more frequent sessions with her psychotherapy patient.

Dr. T.: You could see so automatically that I could go ahead and talk to my client about being in psychoanalysis with me. When I raised doubts about not feeling ready for that, you said something about me not being aware of Donna's need for me. While it made sense to me, in my mind I was not oriented to such frequency of sessions. Your suggestion felt like a big leap for me.

Supervisor: (reflectively encouraging further thoughts) My suggestion felt like a big leap?

Dr. T.: Yes. You did not seem to hear my reluctance to make this move with the patient, especially with you going away now. Instead you said, "Perhaps you do not recognize her need for you," and I was immediately considering the validity of your comment. "That's true!" I thought to myself. It does make sense for me. I tend to have a difficult time understanding a patient needing me. It must be why I have trouble with the idea of her needing more frequent sessions.

It became clear to the supervisor that his insistent and interpretive responses to Dr. T.'s reluctance to start her patient in analysis had caused some difficulties for her. He had failed to appreciate Dr. T.'s prior training and her inexperience with more intensive psychotherapy as well as her concern about a long break in the supervision schedule after only three sessions. She appeared to be only too willing to disavow her own insecurity about increasing frequency of sessions and to attempt to accept his interpretation about her motives. Excitement quickly gave way to panic and disorganization in response to the supervisor's directions and his interpretation of the meaning of her hesitance to follow his directions. She did not register the injury but suffered its impact and adapted in the shame-disguising manner with which she had become familiar. She nodded her head, provided him with the acknowledgment she assumed he needed, and concealed her own inner turmoil. The supervisor also had not registered his own injury triggered by Dr. T.'s reluctance to start the analysis before he went away, as he had hoped to do. He dealt with her reluctance to push ahead by asserting his opinion and "enforcing" it with an interpretation focused on her relationship with Donna. The recognition of this disruption and the elucidation of the contributions from each side was followed by a fruitful discussion of the supervisor's clinical and theoretical rationale for more frequent sessions.

Dr. T. was able to quickly right herself by the innovation of recording the sessions. Her freedom to exercise this option might well have been influenced by her preexisting positive attachment to the supervisor. Her initiative was experienced by the supervisor as an affirming expression of her interest and confidence in him. He received it with enthusiasm and cooperated fully. Both could now go forward in a process that had become permanently modified by the enactment and the freedom it elicited for both participants to attend to subjective issues. Dr. T. became more aware of her repetitive relational pattern contributing to the disruption and the supervisor found it helpful to understand his own contribution.

I will return to the supervision of Dr. T. as I review the evolving concept of supervision in the self psychology literature and the evolving emphasis on the therapeutic participation of the analyst.

SELF PSYCHOLOGY AND SUPERVISION

Kohut made only two references to supervision in his writings. One is merely a passing reference to the value of drive theory in explaining symptoms and dream elements when teaching psychoanalysis to beginners. In the other he described the supervisor's role in the treatment of a most difficult-to-empathize-with patient. Kohut was commenting on the harrowing experience of the supervision of the psychoanalytic treatment of a man who, in fits of rage, would hurl his pet cats against the wall, often killing them. It was the supervisor who finally understood the developmental significance of his behavior toward his pets. Trials of empathy by supervisor and supervisee had failed to "hit the mark" until Kohut, the supervisor, protected from the direct impact of the patient's upsetting accounts, came up with the correct reconstruction concerning the patient's experience of his mother's sudden and unpredictable ridicule when she would suddenly belittle the very attributes he was proudly demonstrating to her. He was now repeating her bizarre behavior toward his animals, who were cruelly tossed about, just as the patient had experienced himself to be by her unpredictable shifts in mood.

His purpose for detailing the clinical material in his essay, "The Psychoanalyst in the Community of Scholars" (1973), was to demonstrate the humanizing or healing influence of empathy: "empathy that is capable— of reclaiming psychological territory that seems to have become irretrievably dehumanized, and of returning it to the domain of living, feeling man"

(p. 721). Kohut also demonstrated, I would suggest, an emerging model of supervision in which the supervisor participated, along with the supervisee, in trials of empathic immersion in a shared attempt to understand the particularly repugnant and reprehensible symptomatic enactments of the patient. Guided and strengthened by the ideal of analytic exploration as the route to change, and by their shared conviction that sustained empathic immersion was the only route to the deeper meaning of the patient's behavior, supervisor and supervisee may have supported each other. Perhaps they provided alter-ego selfobject experiences for each other through their shared repulsion of the patient's ghastly behavior (they were both partial to cats), and through their shared ideals concerning treatment. They both realized that giving way to their natural urges to castigate him for his behavior would have little therapeutic impact. He was already ashamed of his loss of control and destructive acts toward animals to which he was deeply attached. Confrontation would lead to further humiliation and would not further the therapeutic process in the direction of accessing deeper meanings.

Kohut was interested in the research implications of this special position of the supervisor, protected from the direct experience of the challenging patient. His explanation seemed to focus on the distance from the offending patient provided by the supervisory relationship. As Kohut stated:

> The relatively shielded position enjoyed by the supervisor (or consultant) deserves serious attention as a methodological factor in psychoanalytic research. The benefits resulting from the protection of the consultant's cognitive processes (including the greater relaxation with which he can extend his empathy toward the data) have to be weighed against the detrimental effect resulting from the possible distortion of the material through its passage via the analyst and through the artifacts introduced by the supervisory situation. On balance, I believe that the advantages may often be greater than the disadvantages—especially where the investigation concerns emotionally trying, regressive forms of psychopathology. And I believe, therefore, that the situation we have traditionally used as a teaching device is also a promising instrument of research. [p. 711]

In line with the author's proposition that the supervisory relationship may also be a significant element in the successful outcome of supervision, we might consider the value of that relationship as an important source of selfobject experiences for both participants. They were able to persevere successfully with their empathic inquiry and remain in the assertive/exploratory mode (Lichtenberg 1989) rather than succumb to the aversiveness so powerfully evoked by their patient.

Another view was advanced by Michael Basch (1980), who emphasized the value of supervision as a place to teach theory by linking it to clinical material. "The supervisory situation enables the teaching therapist to generalize from the particular aspects of a case to the broader implications of its analysis and management" (p. 88). Basch's emphasis on theory is reflected in his concern that difficulties in treatment were often erroneously attributed to countertransference problems in the supervisee when in fact they stemmed from faults in the theory guiding the supervisor and analyst's understanding of the patient. Basch's emphasis on the value of theory reflected his own interest in the development of improved theories of treatment. In this sense he resembles the image of Kohut the supervisor (Galatzer-Levy 1988) in his interest in extending the influence of his own theoretical position by demonstrating its usefulness to the supervisee.

Basch would have disagreed with the supervisor of Dr. T. for interpreting her motives for avoiding the increased frequency of sessions. He would have preferred him to have formulated the patient's problems theoretically and to have proposed treatment, analytic or otherwise, on the basis of such a formulation. This major dimension of supervision, repeated trials of empathy, and the construction of model scenes and theoretical explanations to understand the patient and guide the analyst's participation, is not the subject of this chapter. For many supervisors, including Kohut and Basch, this activity is the essential activity of supervision and the supervisor's knowledge and skill provides a sustaining source of idealization for the supervisee. The latter's interest, appreciation, and evolution as a competent analyst serve as an important source of affirmation for the supervisor.

Ernest Wolf (1989) may have been interested in Dr. T.'s supervision because it illustrated the principle of the close tie between teacher and learner, a tie involving the selfobject needs of both. Analogous to Winnicott's mother and baby and Kohut's self and selfobject, Wolf's teacher and learner are inseparable entities, each incapable of independent existence. A mutually responsive active relationship between them is essential for learning to take place. "Teacher and learner function as a unit sharing and creating not only information about the world around them but simulta-neously and necessarily also sharing, creating and participating in each other's inner experience of themselves and of the other" (p. 380). Dr. T.'s tie to her supervisor included, at that time early in the supervisory relationship and immediately preceding a vacation break, her partly conscious need for his acceptance of both her clinical judgment and her anxiety about in-creased frequency of sessions. The supervisor needed her to move on and start the analysis thereby affirming his role in her development as an analyst. Dr. T. preserved her tie to the supervisor by using tape recordings, which would continue to function, like an auxiliary self, if she became disorganized, and which would allow her to listen at her own rate once she had self-righted. Once she could effectively influence the rate of informa-tion input, she became organized, self cohesion was restored, and she could participate in the supervisory process.

It is interesting to note that Dr. T.'s specific difficulty comprehending her supervisor did not recur after she began recording her sessions with him. Wolf (1989) might explain this as the emergence of structure follow-ing a sequence of disruption and repair. He conceptualizes the acquisition of psychic structure, whether occurring in development, the process of therapy, or the teaching/learning situation, as the evolution of an expanding core of ordered experience through the process of disruption and reorgan-ization. In all three contexts—development, treatment, and learning—defensive strategies may emerge to protect this emerging, and therefore still vulnerable, sense of order. Dr. T. became aware of one such "order-protecting strategy," one that was familiar to her from previous supervisory and learning situations. Her distracted nonreceptive state rendered her unable to take in more information while her automatic nodding accom-modated to the supervisor's insistence that she do things his way, rendering him unaware of the "true" state of her self. Pleased and satisfied that she understood and accepted his opinions, he was unlikely to intrude any further.

In contrast to Wolf, Bacal would have emphasized different elements of the clinical interaction to explain Dr. T.'s structure formation. He might explain her acquisition of self-regulatory function on the basis of the supervisor's enthusiastic acceptance of her need to assume greater control of the interaction through the tape recording, and the affirming quality of the supervisor's responses to her need for something different in the supervi-sory relationship. These responses would convey his understanding and acceptance of her needs, make the basis for them more accessible to intro-spection, and open up the possibility of altering her expectations of her self with the other. Wolf's "expanding core of ordered experience" could also be described as an expanding core of modified self and self-with-other repre-sentations leading to more reliable and effective interpersonal expectancies based on new and different experiences of responsiveness. It seems likely that these new experiences may include, but need not be confined to, disruption and repair. Although their formulations of curative change may seem contradictory, Bacal and Wolf are explaining at different levels of abstraction. Bacal's proposition may be understood as a broader and more inclusive clinical description of how the hypothetical structural changes proposed by Wolf come about.

Jonathan Schindelheim (1995) provides one of the few contributions to the supervisory literature from the point of view of the supervisee. He eloquently describes the impasse he experienced in his learning with Evelyn Schwaber as he eagerly attempted to master her listening perspective, one in which the analyst's attention is focused completely on the patient's experience, including the patient's experience of the analyst. Schindelheim dreamed about his supervisor and brought the dream to supervision. Through the analysis of the dream, they were able to understand his need to have his supervisor appreciate his experience of her, in order for him to fully internalize, "into his bones," the ideas he had absorbed intellectually. The lesson he draws from his experience reflects Wolf's emphasis on the importance of each participant in the supervisory relationship being aware of the other's experience. For Schindelheim and Schwaber, it required a dream to make them both aware of the supervisee's deprived state evoked by the supervisor's single-minded attention to his patient's experience. When Schindelheim's intense need for her affirmation of *his* experience and *his* participation was understood from the dream, articulated, and accepted, "supervision became much more alive as I became more involved in 'supervising' my supervisor about my learning needs" (p. 160).

Many comparisons could be made between the supervisory process of Dr. Schindelheim and Dr. T., but perhaps the parallel between his dream and her tape recordings of the sessions is the most striking. In both cases, the experience of the supervisee was conveyed to the supervisor indirectly but evocatively. Both expressed the vulnerability of the supervisee, protect-ing them against further humiliation while creatively suggesting new approaches to the disrupted relationship affecting the learning process.

Hershberg and Unterman (1996) provide an example of the supervisee's experience of supervision as a source of selfobject experience, but with the interesting addition of the supervisor's perspective. The supervisee dreams that her supervisor and her patient announce that they are going shopping together without her, despite her protests. The dream expresses themes of abandonment and betrayal in the lives of both patient and supervisor, as well as the supervisee's sense of the unseen influence of her supervisor on her patient.

In their focus on the candidate's affective responses to the patient, Lester and Robertson (1995) emphasize a different aspect of the supervisory process—the supervisor's understanding of the patient. When his patient reveals her dreams and fears of impending catastrophes, the analytic candidate in supervision understands her to be avoiding her previously announced intention to discontinue her treatment because she was talking "as if analysis was continuing forever." The supervisor hears a very different theme, one involving the patient's estranged husband's possible depression and suicide, leading to the patient's fears of impending disaster. The candidate was gently made aware that he should explore this theme further with his patient as it seemed "extremely significant." The candidate ends the session by acknowledging his omission and relating it to significant events in his own past. The supervisor states, "He was unconsciously avoiding a very painful memory which surfaced only when I pointed out that he was neglecting an important part of the material" (pp. 218–219).

In the strategy depicted here, the supervisor identifies the supervisee's "blind spots" and brings them to his attention in order to encourage reflection and expanded self-awareness. The approach demonstrates a model of the analytic process applied to supervision in which the supervisor's (in treatment, the analyst's) perception of reality is contrasted to that of the supervisee (in treatment, the analysand) and given greater weight in determining the supervisee's appropriate response (in treatment, the analyst's interventions intended to make conscious the patient's internal reality-distorting mechanisms).

Perhaps because of the impact of the patient's anguish on her, the supervisor seems to minimize or ignore the patient's impact on the candidate. Instead she insists that the candidate attend to the patient's concerns as she, the supervisor, hears them. As many of us can attest from experience, even the most resilient candidate is profoundly affected by the threatened loss of a control case. Such a sword of Damocles hanging over the analyst-in-training is likely to influence all his subsequent experience of the patient. In this example, the supervisor's experience determines the correct response and the candidate's reality is amended, eventually regarded as impaired by developmental experience and in need of correction. No attempt is made, in the example provided, to explore his actual experience of the patient as avoiding the issue of termination. One could speculate that the supervisor's attention to the patient's subjectivity as she, the supervisor, understood it, to the exclusion of the candidate's subjectivity, threatened the self cohesion of the candidate. From this perspective, the candidate's parting explanation of his perception, that he was avoiding painful memories of his father, might have been a self-protective strategy analogous to that described above in the supervision of Dr. T., who automatically nodded to the supervisor while concealing her inner state of panic and disorganization. In both cases, the supervisors were more focused on their own experience of the patient, and less on the supervisee's.

Fosshage (1997) captures the "state of the art" of modern supervisory practice. He integrates the self psychological and intersubjective approaches to psychoanalytic treatment with the tasks of supervision, illustrating his thinking with a vignette from group supervision. It would be impossible to do full justice to this rich article in a brief description, but some of his points bear close attention.

As Fosshage described in earlier work (1994, 1995), the analyst has two main perspectives from which to listen to the patient: the empathic perspective, which is from within the patient's experience, and the other-centered perspective, the viewpoint of one in relationship with the patient. In the more complex supervisory process each of these perspectives can be adopted to listen to any of the three participants, providing a choice of six different sources of data. In addition, the supervisor can attend to the intersubjective field between any pair of the threesome, patient–supervisee, patient–supervisor, or supervisor–supervisee. Fuqua (1994) and the Shanes (1995) might add many other intersubjective dyads outside the supervisory situation, such as the candidate's student group or class, the institute administration, national and international professional organizations, and other social influences on the treatment process, such as insurance systems, and cultural attitudes toward treatment. While the empathic perspective provides the most important data for the analytic and supervisory work, that is, the data of the subjective experience of the participants, the other-centered listening contributes to the understanding of rational issues.

Fosshage suggests that the supervisor oscillates between these two listening perspectives in a foreground and background pattern.

The choice of listening perspective along with the choice of dyad to be attended to in supervision at any moment may determine substantially the usefulness of the supervisor's participation. Optimal responses in supervision may be precisely determined by these considerations. In the case described above, Lester and Robertson emphasize the subject-centered perspective applied to the patient, perhaps at the expense of the supervisee. The same critique could be made of Schindelheim's experience with Schwaber before his dream made him and his supervisor aware of his subjectivity and his need for her to attend to his experience of the supervision. In both cases the intersubjective field between supervisor and supervisee seemed to need attention. The same problem was identified in the supervision of Dr. T. in the early sessions. Dr. T.'s supervisor interpreted her difficulties on the basis of his understanding of the patient as willing and enthusiastic but, in so doing, ignored Dr. T.'s relationship to him and her sense of the patient. When the impact of this had been understood, the focus returned to the dyad of Dr. T. and Donna, her patient.

For Fosshage (1997), the primary task of the supervisor is to "understand as well as possible the patient and the patient–analyst interactive experience occurring in the analysis in order to facilitate the analytic process and the development of the supervisee" (p. 194). The persistent and patient use of the empathic listening stance by the supervisor contributes to all aspects of this task. Kohut's (1973), Lester and Robertson's (1995), and Schindelheim's (1995) examples of supervision demonstrate both the advantages and potential problems when the supervisor's empathic stance toward the patient is emphasized.

I wish to stress the importance of the empathic listening stance of the supervisor toward the supervisee and suggest that at times, maybe for long periods in some supervisory relationships, it may preempt the supervisor's attention to the patient. The supervisor's understanding of the supervisee, including the supervisee's experience of the patient and of the supervisor, contributes to the regulation of the supervisee's self cohesion and vitality and serves to model the analytic process itself. The supervisor's empathic immersion into these dimensions of the supervisee's experience may establish the best learning environment and the most secure base from which to expand analytic understanding and technique.

In some supervisions such sustained empathic immersion may occupy significant periods of time and facilitate important expansions of self awareness in the supervisee, who, in turn, becomes better able to center his listening on the patient's subjectivity. One experienced supervisor describes an example in which her supervisee arrived for the first supervisory session in an extremely disturbed state (Beebe, personal communication). He had waited for many months for her to be able to start the supervision and had hoped she might call him earlier with an opening. She had forgotten her promise to call him if an earlier appointment became available and she had not given him the instructions she usually gives people about how to reach her difficult-to-find office. He finally found her waiting room, feeling unwelcome, angry, and full of doubts about his ability to treat his patient adequately. The first three sessions were entirely spent exploring his experience of the supervisor and the contributions each made to his disruption. Only then did he feel able to turn to the case he had eagerly brought for supervision, knowing that his supervisor was interested in his well-being and that he was free to return to his own issues with her if required in the future. He felt that her lack of defensiveness and retaliatory responses to his anger allowed him to feel safe to return to the case after three sessions.

After she had alerted him, Dr. T.'s supervisor attended closely to her experience of him, facilitated by her tape recordings of their supervisory sessions. He heard her disrupted state as she experienced him hurrying her and ignoring her anxieties about her patient and about her soon-to-be-interrupted connection with the supervisor. This became the focus of supervision until it was more completely understood from her point of view, and she felt confident enough to recommend to her patient that they start an analysis.

Let us return to the supervision of Dr. T. some weeks later, as she describes her initiation of the analytic contract. The supervisor and Dr. T. had been exploring the theme of self-regulation in the face of overstimulating demands. On one occasion the supervisor had been excited about one of her ideas and once again she found herself panicky and unable to listen. She recognized her self-defensive strategy of withdrawal and avoidance while at the same time her excited need to be involved and affirmed for her competence. She could see the same conflict in her patient, Donna, who also enjoyed being recognized as hugely talented but felt afraid of letting people down.

Dr. T.: Well, lo and behold! I went ahead, and the door opened and I walked through it. I made the suggestion about coming more frequently and, to my surprise, she was most receptive. Not only that, she was actually most relieved because she took from my recommendation that I believed there was something deeper that we could get to. I was so surprised. It shows how distorted my sense of things really is.

Supervisor: Perhaps it's not so much a distortion as a reflection of your own expectations based on the kind of thing we've just been discussing. Until she revealed her own way of understanding your suggestion, you were confined to being concerned about her feeling pressured and rushed as if you were a coach expecting too much of her and she'll feel it is too much for her to cope with. Perhaps you assumed you would be experienced like the coach insisting she perform beyond her comfort zone.

Dr. T.: I did feel concerned that I might be experienced as pushing her. But instead she felt tremendous relief and said, "Now I don't have to rush so much." She actually felt it as empathic attunement! I'm still mystified (we both laugh). In fact, now I feel on the hot seat. Now I have to perform up to her expectations and earn all that money she has agreed to pay me. Now my performance is on the line. She has overstimulated me by her enthusiastic acceptance of me. I feel like I'll have to overperform to live up to her expectations of me. I have to work on this further so I can allow her to idealize me as she seems to need to do.

Supervisor: Now she's become your coach and expects too much. If you fail, you'll disappoint her and she'll react by humiliating you.

At this point in the session the supervisor discussed idealizing transferences and the common reactions they elicit in therapists. This led to further introspection by Dr. T. about her concerns about disappointing her patient and further appreciation of her significance to Donna.

Fuqua (1994) regards the management of the supervisee's states of disruption as one of the fundamental roles of the supervisor. She is referring to the supervisor's active contribution to the maintenance of optimal levels of self cohesion in the interests of the supervisee's learning. In this supervision, as perhaps in most, the management of Dr. T.'s states of disruption was shared by Dr. T. and the supervisor. Dr. T. contributed initially with her self-defensive head nodding to fend off the supervisor's intrusiveness and by her self-righting strategy of taping of the supervisory sessions. The supervisor contributed by his attention to Dr. T.'s experience of him and her patient, his facilitation of her articulation of her experience, and his acceptance of her need to influence the supervisory process before he understood the reason behind it.

The concept of parallel process, originally postulated by Searles (1955) has powerfully influenced supervisory thinking in recent decades. The supervisor's experience of and responses to the supervisee may at times replicate those of the supervisee toward the patient. Donna's difficulty with her coaches who hurried her made her lose her nerve, so that she was unable to function effectively, and then they shamed her for letting them down, which had its parallel form in the analytic and the supervisory relationships. Dr. T. was concerned about rushing Donna and asking too much of her by suggesting more frequent sessions. The supervisor found it necessary to hurry Dr. T. into initiating analysis before she was ready and then shamed her with an interpretation of her inability to comply. In the traditional models of supervision, this material might have been understood in terms of the patient's influence on the supervisory process via the transference and countertransference through the process of projective identification. Fosshage (1997) critically evaluates this approach and contrasts it to the model in which the transference and countertransference are understood from an intersubjective perspective in which each participant contributes to the organization of the experience. The continued focus on experience as co-organized by both participants of each dyad, rather than as induced in one participant by another, leads to a different understanding of these parallel phenomena illustrated by Donna, Dr. T., and the supervisor. All three participated in the interactions in both dyads, which were organized by the twin dreads of overstimulation and of disapproval. And each contributed to the self-righting achieved by all three participants, which, in turn, enabled the supervisory and treatment processes to unfold in a positive manner.

OPTIMAL RESPONSIVENESS AND SUPERVISION

In this model of psychoanalytic supervision modified by self psychological theory and practice, the participation of the supervisor has been expanded beyond the traditional roles of imparting technique, teaching theory, and formulating the psychodynamic meaning of the patient's communications. The supervisor now contributes in more diverse ways to the acquisition of therapeutic skills and knowledge of the supervisee, and to the effectiveness of the treatment under supervision. The supervisor recognizes that each analytic dyad is unique and that the newly established triad influences, and is influenced by, each of its members. Along with the appreciation of the "three-person psychology" which pertains in supervision (Levy and Kindler 1995), the supervisor requires a certain creative freedom in order to understand and participate effectively and creatively in the entity he or she has become a part of.

It is important, as Fosshage points out, that the supervisor has in mind some clear guidelines for both successful supervision and successful treatment in order to evaluate and monitor the usefulness of his participation. Lichtenberg (1989) has proposed three interrelated criteria for evaluating analytic progress, and therefore for evaluating the effectiveness of sequences of interventions made by the analyst. These criteria might usefully be applied to the process of supervision:

1. *Increased capacity for self-righting*, that is to take a developmental step toward normal functioning or establish (or reestablish) a normal experience or self-state. Dr. T., for example, was able to listen without panic and disorganization after she had established the procedure of tape recording her supervisory sessions.

2. *Expansion of self-awareness* through increased capacity for introspection, that is, the increased ability to be aware, through self-reflection of his or her own mental state—a reference to general (self) awareness of feelings, sensations, thoughts, fantasies, and values (Lichtenberg and Wolf 1995). "With favorable intersubjective conditions the capacity for empathy and introspection increases in range and sensitivity" (p. 4). The supervisor's comfortable acceptance of Dr. T.'s self-righting efforts allowed her to articulate more of her experience in the supervisory process and enabled her supervisor to further understand his impact on her. This, in turn, enabled him to reflect on his own need to push her to move more quickly into the analytic process, a need he realized expressed his need to be effective.

3. *Symbolic reorganization* or the modification, through insight, of

meanings and symbolic representations that contribute to maladaptive psychic structures. As a result of this experience, we might assume that Dr. T. achieved a slight modification of her symbolically elaborated self-with-other representation. Her initial representation as "stupid me in the presence of a too-brilliant-to-understand supervisor" was associated with head buzzing and paralyzing shame. After the supervisory exploration of this state, her self representation shifted away from the overidealization to a more comfortable respect. Her self shaming gave way to a self-possessed sense of agency, which allowed her to regulate the supervisory interchanges more comfortably and even reflect with humor on her prior self when she becomes aware of her importance to Donna. With her capacity to reflect reestablished, Dr. T. was now closer to her "optimally functioning" self (Doctors 1996) and able to participate effectively in both the supervisory and analytic process.

With these criteria for understanding and evaluating the impact of any intervention, supervisory or therapeutic, we might now consider various supervisory interventions. To expand the supervisee's awareness of relational patterns of self and other, the supervisor might facilitate the supervisee's reflection on the interaction with the patient, especially the supervisee's specific impact on the patient and the patient's specific impact on the supervisee. This expanded awareness may then contribute to the supervisee's ability to empathize more accurately with the patient, and from this position, respond more optimally. Dr. T.'s expanded self-awareness was demonstrated in her sensitivity to the interchange between herself and her patient after she had proposed the increased frequency of sessions. She could see that her own proneness to anxiety when rushed by another shaped her expectation that her patient would feel reluctant to accept her recommendation for more intense treatment, which subsequently contributed to her anxious response to her patient's enthusiasm about her proposal. This expanded self-awareness allowed her to self-right easily and with humor. We both laugh as she spontaneously exclaims, "She actually felt it as empathic attunement! I'm still mystified." She gently mocks herself and plays with her new understanding of Donna and herself. "Now I feel on the hot seat. Now I have to perform up to her expectations and earn all that money she has agreed to pay me. Now my performance is on the line. She has overstimulated me by her enthusiastic acceptance of me." As in the treatment relationship, these moments of intense positive affective sharing and intimacy with the supervisor may be significant in shaping the future therapist's self-image.

Perhaps more frequently the supervisor participates at a more cognitive or conceptual level by contributing his own formulations of the patient, thereby providing new meanings to all the patient's communications to the supervisee. Levy (1995) demonstrates this strategy. As he and Fuqua suggest, this model provides a theoretical framework to allow the supervisee to orient him- or herself to the material from a safe distance. When supervising a beginning therapist, I often find it useful to provide an orientation to the study of subjectivity and perhaps a "cognitive map" of basic theoretical constructs to get started. This orientation to subjectivity is especially important for medical trainees who are most comfortable with the positivist scientific tradition and its emphasis on objective data about the patient.

Because it is of particular importance when disruptions or impasses occur in supervision, I have emphasized in this chapter the supervisor's facilitation of the exploration and articulation of the supervisee's experience of the supervisor. Dr. T.'s initial experience of her supervisor's interpretation of her reluctance to increase her frequency of sessions was one of interest and excitement. When she was able to connect this event to her distracted dysfunctional state she became aware of feeling rushed and overruled by her supervisor's insistence and became more aware of her need to move more slowly before the vacation break. This expanded self-awareness contributed to her self-righting capacities and her ability to participate more effectively in both the supervision and the analysis. Schindelheim also illustrates this expanded self-awareness through his use of his dream during his own supervision to clarify his experience of his supervisor and his need for recognition of his own competence by her.

The emphasis in self psychology on the subjective experience of each participant in the treatment situation and on the understanding of organizing principles has dramatically changed the ambiance of psychoanalytic treatment (Wolf 1976). In more traditional approaches, the display of distortions, omissions (blind spots), defensive structures, and mechanisms were at the center of technique, and naturally, at the center of supervision. The "teach or treat" dichotomy was motivated by concerns for the supervisee's privacy and safety in the supervisory situation. Treatment was not compatible with a comfortable learning environment. Therapeutic work on the difficulties that arose in supervision were sequestered to the supervisee's relationship with his own training analyst. Fosshage's self-psychological emphasis on all experience as pertinent to the intersubjective field, which depathologizes the countertransference, liberates the supervisor to respond optimally to the supervisee's experiences of both patient and supervisor.

To reiterate: a different kind of analysis requires and yields a very different form of supervision. The modern emphasis is on the elucidation and articulation of subjective experience as a route to the unconscious organizing principles that contribute to the construction of subjective reality. The traditional emphasis was on unconscious distorting influences that contribute to the distortion of reality (a guiding aphorism of clinical technique informed by ego psychology was "the patient is always wrong," capturing the emphasis on transference as distortion). With this shift in emphasis from distortion to construction and organization, the atmosphere of the supervisory process has changed. The threat to the supervisee's self implicit in the supervisor's "skeptical stance" (Spence 1985) is now replaced by the self-enhancing experience of consistent attention to, genuine acceptance of, and careful elucidation of the supervisee's subjectivity. We are particularly sensitive to aversive cues and responses in the supervisee triggered in the supervision. The very act of supervision with this mode of listening in the foreground actually contributes to, rather than threatens, the supervisee's self cohesion. Since this is the same mode of listening that predominates in treatment, the dichotomy between teaching and treating diminishes. When this manner of attention to the supervisee's subjectivity is called for in the supervisory process, it will contribute positively to the self cohesion and vitality of the supervisee. Supervision can then become another opportunity, in addition to, rather than instead of, treatment, to expand self-awareness and gain insight into personal meanings that organize subjectivity and interfere with self-righting abilities (Lecomte and Richard 1996).

The challenges to supervisors who function as agents of training programs may be analogous to those that all analysts face in their conflicting roles as healers and scientists (Wolf 1992). The need to impart good technique that conforms to the accepted standards of psychoanalytic tradition and the training body to which the supervisor belongs may conflict with the need to optimally respond to the specific sensibilities, skills, and healing instincts of the trainee. As a guide to the resolution of this inevitable dilemma, I offer Wolf's rules for conducting psychoanalytic treatment, paraphrased to pertain to supervision:

1. Provide the supervisee with friendly responsiveness and understanding.
2. Be firmly on the supervisee's side, including stopping the supervisee from doing things that will be harmful to him- or herself or to the patient.
3. Be guided by the supervisee's interests and welfare rather than by your need to advance correct technique, theoretical formulations, and your own point of view.

CONCLUSION

The literature reviewed demonstrates clearly that a new kind of supervision is emerging. As more psychoanalysts and psychotherapists apply their knowledge of self psychology to the supervisory process, they will, in all likelihood, find themselves heading in the same direction. There is much more to be learned. As our models of analytic process and change become more sophisticated their application to supervision demands consistent attention. More case material needs to be reported in detail involving participants at all levels of experience. Only through the honest documentation and study of supervisory participation, be it optimal or not, will we truly expand our self-awareness as supervisors and improve our capacities to self-right when things go wrong in supervisory encounters. Let us look forward to a growing number of papers written by supervisors and supervisees together, illustrating their successes and, perhaps more importantly, their failures. It is the author's hope that this chapter contributes to this ongoing evolution.

References

Basch, M. (1980). *Doing Psychotherapy.* New York: Basic Books.
——— (1992). *Practicing Psychotherapy: A Casebook.* New York: Basic Books.
Doctors, S. (1996). Notes on the contribution of the analyst's self-awareness to optimal responsiveness. In *Basic Ideas Reconsidered: Progress in Self Psychology,* vol. 12, ed. A. Goldberg, pp. 55–63. Hillsdale, NJ: Analytic Press.

Fosshage, J. (1994). Toward reconceptualizing transference: theoretical and clinical considerations. *International Journal of Psycho-Analysis* 75(2):265–280.

—— (1995). Countertransference as the analyst's experience of the analysand: the influence of listening perspectives. *Psychoanalytic Psychology* 12(3):375–391.

—— (1997). Toward a model of psychoanalytic supervision from a self psychological/intersubjective perspective. In *Psychodynamic Supervision: Issues for the Supervisor and the Supervisee*, ed. M. Rock, pp. 189–210. Northvale, NJ: Jason Aronson.

Fuqua, P. (1994). Teaching, learning and supervision. In *A Decade of Progress: Progress in Self Psychology*, vol. 10, ed. A. Goldberg, pp. 79–97. Hillsdale, NJ: Analytic Press.

Galatzer-Levy, R. M. (1988). Heinz Kohut as teacher and supervisor: a view from the second generation. In *Learning from Kohut: Progress in Self Psychology*, vol. 4, ed. pp. 3–42. Hillsdale, NJ: Analytic Press.

Hershberg, S. G., and Unterman, D. (1996). *The influence of the selfobject experience in supervision on the therapeutic process.* Presented at the 19th Annual Self Psychology Conference, Washington, DC, October.

Kohut, H. (1959). Introspection, empathy, and psychoanalysis. *Journal of the American Psychoanalytic Association* 7:459–483.

—— (1973). The psychoanalyst in the community of scholars. In *The Search for the Self*, vol. 2, ed. P. Ornstein, pp. 685–724. New York: International Universities Press, 1978.

Lecomte, C., and Richard, A. (1996). *The process of self-supervision: from external to internal supervision.* Paper presented to the Training and Research Institute for Self Psychology, New York.

Lester, E. P., and Robertson, B. M. (1995). Multiple interactive process in psychoanalytic supervision. *Psychoanalytic Inquiry* 15(2):211–225. Hillsdale, NJ: Analytic Press.

Levy, J. (1995). Analytic stalemate and supervision. *Psychoanalytic Inquiry* 15(2):169–189. Hillsdale, NJ: Analytic Press.

Levy, J., and Kindler, A. (1995). Epilogue. *Psychoanalytic Inquiry* 15(2):268–273. Hillsdale, NJ: Analytic Press.

Lichtenberg, J. D. (1989). *Psychoanalysis and Motivation.* Hillsdale, NJ: Analytic Press.

Lichtenberg, J. D., Lachmann, F., and Fosshage, J. (1992). *Self and Motivational Systems: Toward a Theory of Psychoanalytic Technique.* Hillsdale, NJ: Analytic Press.

Lichtenberg, J. D., and Wolf, E. S. (1995). *General principles of self psychology 1995: a position statement.* Presented at the fall meeting of the American Psychoanalytic Association, New York.

Lindon, J. (1994). Gratification and provision in psychoanalysis. Should we get rid of "the rule of abstinence"? *Psychoanalytic Dialogues* 4:549–582.

Ricci, W. F. (1995). Self and intersubjectivity in tne supervisory process. *Bulletin of the Menninger Clinic* 59(1):53–68.

Schindelheim, J. (1995). Learning to learn, learning to teach. *Psychoanalytic Inquiry* 15(2):153–168. Hillsdale, NJ: Analytic Press.

Schlesinger, H. J. (1995). Supervision for fun and profit: or how to tell if the fun is profitable. *Psychoanalytic Inquiry* 15(2):190–210. Hillsdale, NJ: Analytic Press.

Searles, H. (1955). The informational value of the supervisor's emotional experiences. *Psychiatry* 18(2):135–146.

Shane, M., and Shane, E. (1995). "Un-American activities" and other dilemmas experienced in the supervision of candidates. *Psychoanalytic Inquiry* 15(2):226–239. Hillsdale, NJ: Analytic Press.

Spence, D. P. (1985). *The metaphoric unconscious*. Presented at the meeting of the Chicago Psychoanalytic Society, November.

Stolorow, R., Brandchaft, B., and Atwood, G. (1987). *Psychoanalytic Treatment: An Intersubjective Approach*. Hillsdale, NJ: Analytic Press.

Stolorow, R., and Lachmann, F. (1984/1985). Transference: the future of an illusion. *The Annual of Psychoanalysis* 12/13:19–37. New York: International Universities Press.

Terman, D. (1988). Optimum frustration: structuralization and the therapeutic process. In *Learning from Kohut: Progress in Self Psychology*, vol. 4, ed. A. Goldberg, pp. 113–125. Hillsdale, NJ: Analytic Press.

Wolf, E. S. (1976). Ambience and abstinence. In *The Annual of Psychoanalysis*, vol. 4, pp. 101–115. New York: International Universities Press.

——— (1989). The psychoanalytic self psychologist looks at learning. In *Learning and Education*, ed. K. Field, B. Cohler, and G. Wool, pp. 377–393. Madison, CT: International Universities Press.

——— (1992). On being a scientist or healer: reflections on abstinence, neutrality, and gratification. *Annual of Psychoanalysis* 20:115–129.

——— (1995). How to supervise without doing harm: comments on psychoanalytic supervision. *Psychoanalytic Inquiry* 15(2):169–189.

Credits

The editor gratefully acknowledges permission to reprint material from the following sources:

"Optimal Responsiveness and the Therapeutic Process," by Howard A. Bacal, in *Progress in Self Psychology*, volume 1, edited by A. Goldberg. Copyright © 1985 by Guilford Press.

"Optimal Responsiveness and a New View of Structuralization," originally titled "Optimum Frustration: Structuralization and the Therapeutic Process," by David M. Terman, in *Learning from Kohut: Progress in Self Psychology*, volume 4, edited by A. Goldberg. Copyright © 1988 by Analytic Press.

"Optimal Responsiveness and a Search for Guidelines," originally titled "Self Psychology in Search of the Optimal: A Consideration of Optimal Responsiveness, Optimal Provision, Optimal Gratification, and Optimal Restraint in the Clinical Situation," by Morton Shane and Estelle Shane, in *Basic Ideas Reconsidered: Progress in Self Psychology*, volume 12, edited by A. Goldberg. Copyright © 1996 by Analytic Press.

Index